The Two Americas

Stanley B. Greenberg

the

TWO AMERICAS

Our Current Political Deadlock

and How to Break It

FRANCIS W. PARKER
Charter Essential School &
Theodore R. Sizer Teachers Center
49 Antietam St. Devens, MA 01434

THOMAS DUNNE BOOKS ✿ NEW YORK

ST. MARTIN'S GRIFFIN

THOMAS DUNNE BOOKS.
An imprint of St. Martin's Press.

www.stmartins.com

Book design by Judith Stagnitto Abbate

Library of Congress Cataloging-in-Publication Data

Greenberg, Stanley B., 1945–
    The two Americas : our current political deadlock and how to break it / by Stanley B. Greenberg.
        p.   cm.
    Includes bibliographical references (p. 369) and index (p. 415).
    ISBN 0-312-31838-3 (hc)
    ISBN 0-312-31839-1 (pbk)
    EAN 978-0312-31839-0
    1. United States—Politics and government—1945–1989. 2. United States—Politics and government—1989– 3. Presidents—United States—Election—History—20th century. 4. Democratic Party (U.S.)—History—20th century. 5. Republican Party (U.S. : 1845–)—History—20th century. 6. Political culture—United States—History—20th century. I. Title.

E839.5G745   2004
324'.0973—dc22

                                                                2003058771

First St. Martin's Griffin Edition: June 2005

10 9 8 7 6 5 4 3 2 1

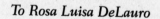

To Rosa Luisa DeLauro

Contents

Preface

Sometime after one in the morning of America's extended Election Day, about ten top campaign aids to John Kerry were huddled in a very small room, just off the war room of John Kerry's Washington headquarters. Some sat at the table that nearly filled the room and others stood against the walls, but all listened intently to the speaker phone where the top operatives from Ohio reported on the vote count. The issue was the current margin for Bush, the yet unreported votes from Franklin, Hamilton, and Cuyahoga counties, and the number of "provisional" ballots. Some in Ohio thought the margin could get down to as low as 30,000, but that estimate kept rising as the official vote count became more complete. The Bush lead was stuck at around 130,000. The big issue was the provisional ballots, real votes cast for Kerry or Bush but held up because of some problem with the list or a challenge at the polls. In recent elections in Ohio, four out of five were eventually considered valid and counted. Under the new federal election law, these would be counted over the next 10 days. But in this early hour, we could not get the exact number, as the count and the ballots were kept in each county courthouse. Some in the Ohio headquarters thought there were 250,000 or more ballots outstanding, mostly from heavily Democratic Cuyohoga county. Campaign workers were feverishly canvassing the counties. After some delay, the state director got back on the phone and reported, deadpan, only 150,000 ballots and just 25,000 from Cuyohoga. Somebody asked him to repeat the numbers, but everyone knew the meaning, as the mood became very dark. Nobody discussed the numbers. Somebody said he would call the Senator in Boston.

Had 60,000 Bush voters in Ohio come to a different conclusion and switched to support Kerry, he would be the president. Four years earlier, 300 Florida voters had that kind of power in their hands. Then, I witnessed Al Gore, his family and campaign team in a small room deep inside Nashville's War Memorial take in the reality of Bush's sinking Florida lead, triggering the vice president's call to Bush to recant the concession. Still vivid for me is Bill Daley, his campaign chairman, now alone at the podium speaking to those gathered in the plaza and to the world, "our campaign continues."

With these two historic elections behind us, there is no escaping the reality of our divided country. We are trapped in an ugly parity that drives both parties, each tantalizingly close to tasting the fruits of victory, to more intense battles that leave the country more divided and its citizens forced to choose between contending cultures and, increasingly, between Two Americas.

I am frustrated with the politics of parity, first of all, because I believe the Democrats, including myself, could have done more with their moment to win the public's confidence, with important consequences for the country.

I am also frustrated with the diminished politics that parity fosters. The Republicans hold on to office with an uncertain mandate at home and limited public support, use their power ruthlessly to entrench their incumbency, and use cultural issues equally ruthlessly to scare voters and deepen the divisions. The Democrats, short just a handful of seats or Electoral College votes, encouraged by modernizing trends, maneuver and seize tactical opportunities rather than challenge the Two Americas.

My frustration with the current divide, however, is more personal. Some years ago, I decided that cultural politics is not very good for the Democrats or the nation. I never quite understood why I pulled back and became a conscientious objector to the culture war. I grew up fully a child of the age, indeed, a poster child for the postmodernists. I started as just a little speck in America's new diversity, moving at age five to Washington, D.C., not to a "power" neighborhood, but to an inner-city black one. Three years later my family moved into a Jewish neighborhood bursting to be middle class, until we bought a house in the suburbs when I was in high school. My first immersion in politics was the civil rights movement and the March on Washington. I was an exuberant Young Democrat for Hubert Humphrey; I joined the antiwar movement and picketed the White House, and I volunteered early and labored hard for George McGovern. As a professor, my first book was about the politics of inner-city poor neighborhoods, and the second was about racial and ethnic conflict, mainly in the Deep South and South Africa, with excursions to Israel and Northern Ireland, wherever the trail of culture politics was still hot.

My head, however, was taking a different road. While I worked to break down the ethnic and racial barriers in society, my research took me face-to-face with real people struggling to advance their interests or just survive, some bigoted, some not, but through their actions raising the barriers higher. The white steelworkers in Alabama and the white mine workers in South Africa, whatever their awful role in excluding blacks, were not without social democratic impulses.

My research in 1985 on the defecting working-class Democrats of Macomb County, Michigan, was a turning point. While stunned by the scale of the anger and racial antipathy of the "Reagan Democrats," I tried to convince my party that these were real people, workers with families, living in neighborhoods and going to church, skeptical of big business and supportive of broad social insurance programs, who had to be part of the Democratic narrative. At the time, others were becoming alert to the dangers of the emerging cultural divide and the possibilities if Democrats could somehow transcend them—political leaders like Governor Bill Clinton of Arkansas; social commentators like Mary and Thomas Edsall, who wrote *Chain Reaction*; and E. J. Dionne, who wrote *Why Americans Hate Politics*. But all of us were either swept up or pushed rudely aside by the accelerating and polarized cultural politics of the 1980s and 1990s that gave us the 2000 and 2004 elections, which is itself just a symptom of a greater impasse.

I decided to write this book to figure out the new rules, the new configuration of voters, and new opportunities, so that none of us have to settle for its ugly choices. I do not believe the Two Americas is a very healthy place, even though plenty of people like myself, Democratic and Republican, will figure out how to win power in our divided world.

The Republicans learned their lessons well, but they are now invested in continuing and deepening the cultural divide. I joined the Kerry campaign in its last two months in hopes of helping tip the balance in the election, but with little hope for a new politics. This book is intended to empower the people who still hope for One America.

I got the opportunity to tackle this challenge only because much earlier some uniquely talented leaders, first Senator Chris Dodd and then Senator Joe Lieberman, put their faith in me before I deserved it.

President Bill Clinton, Vice President Al Gore, and Senator John Kerry are special leaders and a big part of this book's story. They served this country proudly, and I never forget that I am on this stage, playing whatever role, because of them.

While I have concentrated my attention for this work on America, my perspective on social democratic possibilities and leadership has been shaped by my work for President Nelson Mandela, Prime Minister Tony Blair, Chancellor Gerhard Schröeder, Prime Minister Ehud Barak, President Thabo Mbeki, and President Gonzalo Sánchez de Lozada. They have more than a passing interest in what transpires in America.

This book would not have been possible without the generosity, progressive idealism, and pragmatism of Steve Bing, who, together with other stalwarts, took a chance on Democracy Corps and stuck with it. Most of all, he accepted the core idea that quality research, widely disseminated and discussed, creates the basis for effective action.

James Carville and Bob Shrum are my colleagues in Democracy Corps and so much else, both in America and abroad. James may sound like an in-the-trenches partisan on TV, but there are few like him who can see the big picture. If not for Bob Shrum, I would not have had the chance to work for Al Gore in 2000 or be witness to such eloquent political speech. In fact, while underscoring what made this work possible, I would never have had the chance to work with Bill Clinton from the beginning if not for Frank Greer.

My entry to the 2004 election came through Wes Boyd, then Eli Pariser, and the whole MoveOn.org phenomenon that trusted me to help their millions of members join this process in a powerful way. Bill Zimmerman and Pacy Markman produced remarkable media. I was privileged that Harold Ickes of the Media Fund and Steve Rosenthal and Ellen Malcolm of America Coming Together allowed me to serve as chief strategist for their historic efforts. Mary Beth Cahill and Gerry Salemme opened up the Kerry campaign for last hand on deck to make a difference at the end.

My partners at Greenberg Quinlan Rosner Research are both voluntary and involuntary collaborators in this book. Al Quinlan, always sensitive to the nuances, knows how to win, and with Jeremy Rosner and Anna Greenberg have shaped my thinking, advanced their own innovative research and writing, and created a company where such work is normal. They unleashed a whole staff that made this book their own life's work. From the management team, Edie Nardecchia made sure we had the resources to manage and analyze the massive amount of data; Joe Goode, our chief operating officer, made sure the rest of the company did not collapse.

Philip Gould has reinvented social democracy in Europe and is my collaborator in Britain; Tal Silberstein and Gadi Katz are like collaborators at GCS and in so many countries in the world. They have all indulged the Americans who, once again, are obsessed with ourselves. They fully understand that the process of global change starts here.

Mistique Cano worked on the manuscript with the intensity of a co-author and led the support team at GQR that created and managed the research and databases at the core of this book. Mistique brought great talent, a creative spirit, and personal commitment to producing a book that I hope allows her to feel more than proud of the product. Pitching in to get the job done were analysts and programmers like Missy Egelsky and Andrew Mercer, and a succession of talented interns, including Jeff Crouch, Rebecca Horwitz, and Rachel Weiser. Chris Doray at Floodlite produced graphics that, I believe, bring the data to life. Finally, Tim Jensen, the head of programming at GQR, took on this book as a second job. He did magical work and made it look easy.

Democracy Corps has taken on a life of its own, with Jim Gerstein as executive director, Karl Agne now as an established analyst and commentator, and Matt Hogan as the driving force that makes everybody else look good, including me.

This new edition was made possible by the work of Sam Weston, my project coordinator at Greenberg Quinlan Rosner Research, Inc., and leader of the new team that oversaw the analysis of the 2004 election and the final chapter. He brings a nuanced understanding of our elections and deep professionalism to this work, despite his roots in New Zealand. He was aided by Matt Hogan and John Brach.

A number of organizations sponsored research and freely made it available for this book, believing that we all benefit from a better public understanding of the Two Americas. Behind those organizations are committed people: Bill and David Harris (Children's Research and Education Institute), Bob Borosage and Roger Hickey (Campaign for America's Future), David Hawkins (Natural Resources Defense Council), Bobby Muller (Vietnam Veterans of America Foundation), and Arch Gillies, who began supporting my work when he was head of World Policy Institute. Many of these people offered inventive policy ideas for the book, as did Janice Gruendel, Scott Lilly, Will Marshall, and Bob Boorstin.

Obviously, I take responsibility for what I have written here, but there are some colleagues and friends who went to great lengths to keep me from making egregious errors and who pushed me to get the story right. Apparently, the promise of a happy ending for the book kept them coming back for yet more chapters.

Douglas Sosnik, Samuel Popkin, and David Mayhew provided such rich commentary and shrewd guidance on the whole manuscript that the book would have been greatly diminished without their handiwork. I only hope I paid sufficient attention. David Axelrod, Nick Butler, Robert Dahl, Rahm Emanuel, Philip Gould, Anna Greenberg, John Podesta, Theda Skocpol, and Ruy Teixeira critiqued major portions of the book.

I want to thank my publisher, Thomas Dunne of St. Martin's Press, who left the Greenberg book proposal sitting for a couple of weeks on the corner of his desk before suddenly saying one day, "I want to do this." Sean Desmond, my editor, made it real, saving me from myself and getting the book focused, but also giving me the space to say what was important. I am no Hillary Clinton, but that in no way deterred Bob Barnett from working doggedly to get this in the right publisher's hands.

Freda Amar is fully in charge of my professional life, and through a very intense year, has operated with grace and kept everyone to a very high standard. She made this a better book and me a better person. My project coordinators, Annemarie Spadafore, and for the critical crunch at the end, Sam Weston, had the difficult job of making sure all our clients, as well as St. Martin's Press, were well served.

I have been able to carry on my work because our family takes so much pride in what each of us gets to do on his or her own and what we all get to do together. We cannot wait to share news with each other. I am proud of what our children, Anna, Jonathan, Kathryn, and her husband, Ari, are doing, each in his or her own world, and I never doubted their pride in this book, done at last. We all prayed or just willed, successfully, as it turned out, that Kathryn and the new baby, Rigby, would make it to the New Year and to many, many more.

Rosa DeLauro is my wife, stepmother to our kids, and my congresswoman. Rosa and I share everything—our family, our ambitions and hopes. Neither of us would embark on anything important in our lives, whether in the Congress or on a book like this one, without sharing it every step of the way. Even as she battled to get drug prices down or get low-income families tax relief, she made the time to share her views and made the space I needed to complete this book. *The Two Americas* was completed within days of our twenty-fifth anniversary, and I joyfully dedicate it to her.

PART I

The Politics of Parity

America is divided.

We live during a moment in history when the two big political parties have fought to a draw, reflecting the intense partisanship of our times. The loyalties of American voters are now almost perfectly divided between the Democrats and Republicans, a historic political deadlock that inflames the passions of politicians and citizens alike. This is a deepening divide, giving us the Two Americas, with immense consequences for our politics. The leading politicians of both parties instinctively believe that they are as likely as the others to win. The fact is, the parties are so evenly matched that the slightest shift in the political winds could blow the balance. A handful of new votes, maybe in just a single state, could bring wholesale change in which one political crowd has control of the government of the United States of America.

That the Supreme Court—itself divided 5 to 4—was forced to end the counting of votes and decide the 2000 presidential election underscores the poignancy of this new American reality. The fact is, 50,992,897 Americans voted for Al Gore and 50,458,002 of them voted for George W. Bush. On that day in November, 48.4 percent of the nation aligned with one party and 47.9 percent aligned with the other.

This produced the vivid maps of America, divided between the red Republican states and the blue Democratic ones. Colored blue was the whole stretch of states up the Pacific coast and the ones on the Atlantic, from the Chesapeake Bay up through New England, around the Great Lakes and the upper Mississippi. And even more vivid was the vast, almost uninterrupted expanse of red America—the states running across the whole of the South and lower Mississippi, but also America's immense plains and mountain West.

That red and blue map soon morphed into a constitutional exercise, when 271 electors did their duty in the electoral college and cast their ballots for George W. Bush, while 266 backed Al Gore. Had one small state changed from red to blue—indeed, had the county election supervisor of

Palm Beach County, Florida, decided one fateful day not to use a butterfly ballot—America might have had a different president. But had a few thousand voters in Iowa, New Mexico, or Wisconsin made a different choice, blue would have become red in these states and again flipped the election's outcome.

"The virtual tie in Florida was a once-every-few-centuries proposition," the political staff of *The Washington Post* wrote, "and so was a presidential election that hinged on a single deadlocked state. It was a longshot wrapped in a longer shot."[1] But for all the imagery of political operatives rushing to Florida, election officials holding ballots up to the light, and new heroines Theresa LePore and Katherine Harris on the national stage, 2000 is much more than an eccentric drama: 2000 is just the current moment in an era of political deadlock.

In the year and a half after the country was attacked on 9/11, I conducted 15 national polls and spoke with 15,045 voters. The surveys simply asked, "Do you think of yourself as a Democrat, a Republican, or what?" With the election debacle of 2000 seemingly well behind us, 46 percent of today's voters still aligned themselves with the Democrats and 46 percent with the Republicans.[2] In the intervening period, terrorists mounted an attack on America, we responded with two wars and two regime changes, and the president and Republicans had a good congressional election, yet still the parties remained at parity in the public consciousness.[3]

In the most recent off-year elections, the Republicans took control of the U.S. Senate and enlarged their majority in the House of Representatives, seeming to deny this divided moment. With the Republicans taking control of all the national institutions—the Senate and House, along with the White House and Supreme Court—there was reason for a lot of hyperbole, and a number of commentators provided it. The day after the election, *Washington Times* columnist Diana West proclaimed it "Mourning in America," crowing, "They don't color Democratic states blue for nothing." Pointing to the "no gloating" edict handed down by the White House, West wrote that there is "no time to gloat," closing her column with the line, "The Bush era, with its midterm mandate, is well under way."[4] Democrats were suitably dejected and a few no doubt burned their copies of John Judis and Ruy Teixeira's recently published book, *The Emerging Democratic Majority.*[5]

But such are the pathologies of this current era. After the 2000 election, the 100-member U.S. Senate was tied at 50–50 but was presided over by Vice President Dick Cheney, armed with the constitutional authority to break ties. However, the Senate came under Democratic control when one Republican turned independent, painfully dropping the Republicans to 49 seats. Nevertheless, the Republicans reclaimed the Senate in turn when the 2002 election gave them the princely majority of 51 seats.

In the House, the Republicans increased their majority from 50.8 percent of the seats in 2000 to 52.6 percent after the 2002 election—a meager 1.8-point gain. While intense efforts to protect incumbents make big changes much harder to achieve, a switch of only 12 seats out of 435 would shift partisan control. Such small gains and losses have big consequences in this moment of parity.

In 2000, as voters went to the polls to select their president and the Congress, they also elected state representatives and state senators. Here, too, the tally was even. In 2000, the voters elected 5,411 representatives to sit in the statehouses and gave the Democrats an edge, though barely. The main story was still partisan parity: slightly more than half of the legislators were Democrats (51.8 percent) and slightly less than half were Republicans (48.1 percent). In 2002, the Republicans gained the advantage, but by only a few seats. Despite the tilt to the Republicans, near perfect parity remained: 50.0 percent of the legislators were Republican and 49.6 percent were Democrats.[6]

After the state-by-state elections for governor in 2002, the Democrats took occupancy of the governors' mansions in 24 states, while the Republicans held on to 26. The Democratic governors represented 54 percent of the population and the Republicans 46 percent.

The dead-even race for president in 2000 that took 36 days of recounting and litigation to bring to an end was produced by an America divided at every level.

The 2000 election is the culmination of a half century of American history in which no party has managed to dominate. Because of 2000, social critics and the political class, including people like myself, are compelled to root out the social trends and currents to gain some key to the future. But if one pulls back far enough, one sees larger contours to our current situation, an era that is very different from the earlier times in our nation's history. The last fifty years is an era of no party dominance and has led us to our current parity and political turmoil.

What does it mean that no party has dominated the era?

In this half century, our presidential elections have been uniquely competitive. The Republicans have won eight of the elections and the Democrats five, but that Republican edge is readily discounted. General Eisenhower, leader of the Allied forces, courted by both political parties, produced the two Republican victories at the beginning of the era. By 1954, the country gave him a Democratic Congress to set the domestic course. And the last election of the era, 2000, produced a Republican president but without a plurality of the popular vote.[7]

In two of the elections, the major parties nominated candidates perceived as extremist at the time—Barry Goldwater in 1964 and George McGovern in 1972—which resulted in offsetting, landslide majorities.

More typical in this era of no party dominance, the public has repeatedly produced razor-thin majorities and nail-biting election nights. The elections of 1960, 1968, and 2000 were decided by less than a 1-point margin. While 1984 was Reagan's high point, it was bracketed by two competitive elections. In 1980, Ronald Reagan took the lead only in the final weekend before the election, according to most public polls,[8] and won with just 50.7 percent of the vote, with an independent taking 6.6 percent, mostly moderate voters.[9] In 1988, Michael Dukakis led George H. W. Bush by as much as 17 points in the polls, before faltering in the fall. In five of the postwar elections, including our last three, the winning candidate was unable to muster a majority of the vote. Indeed, because the era is so competitive, third-party candidates significantly impacted the outcomes in 1968, 1980, 1992, 1996, and 2000.

During only one period in this half century did one party hold the White House through three consecutive elections: Reagan in 1980 and 1984 and Bush in 1988.

And since 1952, when Dwight Eisenhower was elected the first post–World War II president, not only has no party dominated our elections, no party has dominated the ideas of the era. We live in an era without a hegemonic party that sets the fashion and common sense, whose identity and sense of purpose are aligned with the emerging challenges before a constantly changing country. This is why America in this period of political parity faces an accumulation of challenges, disconnected from our very passionate politics.

That has left us not just with political parity but with the Two Americas—the country divided politically and, increasingly, culturally, with distinct and counterpoised views about government, values, the family, and the best way of life. These Two Americas encompass coalitions of voters, virtually equal in size, leaving neither view of the world easily dominant, exacerbating the conflict and elevating cultural passions.

As we shall see, that is not the way it was and, most important, not the way it has to be.

Chapter 1

TOWARD HEGEMONY

Our country has certainly produced other very tight, inconclusive, and disputed elections—including the election of 1800 when Thomas Jefferson and Aaron Burr tied the Electoral College, which threw the election into the House of Representatives; 1824 when a four-way race allowed John Quincy Adams to become president with only 31 percent of the popular vote and fewer electoral votes than Andrew Jackson; 1876 when the Republicans had to negotiate away Reconstruction and the rights of blacks to vote in order to settle the Electoral College impasse; and the post-Reconstruction elections (1880, 1884, 1888) when all were decided by less than 1 percentage point. In the same decade, the congressional parties became locked in parity, with the Republicans finishing the decade with a two-seat majority.

But the contested elections, no matter how dramatic, do not characterize our history the way the elections of 1960 and 2000 characterize our current untamed era. For most of our history before 1952, one of the major political parties was dominant electorally and hegemonic in the area of ideas and policy, elevating some issues central to their purpose and identity and suppressing, when possible, those they cannot handle effectively. The hegemonic parties became associated with a particular direction for the country, resolving some important dispute or issue, and defined the nation in a particular way—before giving way to another party and usually a new set of issues and social cleavages.

This argument about party dominance and hegemony is minimalist in terms of the heated debates in the political science literature, though not minimalist in terms of our understanding of the current era. This analysis of party dominance does not require "realigning elections"—historic elections, like 1932, everybody's agreed realigning election—where the deck is reshuffled for some decades to come. Nor does the argument of this book require the hypothesized patterns sometimes associated with realignment, such as surges in voter turnout, pioneering third-party activity, enhanced ideological polarization, or spans of unified party control of the Congress.[1]

The country has periods of party dominance when the following is true:

1. *One party wins the overwhelming majority of elections during a period.* A party is dominant when it wins the presidency and is in control of the White House and the executive branch for extended periods, often decades. The party's capture of the presidency is usually made possible by changes evident in earlier elections, but for our purposes, it is becoming the dominant national party that creates periods for potential hegemony.

2. *The dominant party is associated with a set of ideas or beliefs, a position on a critical issue of the day, or maybe just a perspective about the proper direction for America.* The dominant parties in these periods do not necessarily win election on these issues or ideas; voters may choose them for many reasons—spoils of office, stands on wars long past, settlement of some sectional issue. But their stand on important issues and on grappling with some national challenge is associated with their entrenchment in office and hold on the presidency.

3. *The dominant party's hold on the presidency begins to give way when, among other reasons, it cannot handle rising issues or conflicts.* The dominant party has a vested interest in the dominant issues and conflicts, where it has marginalized its opponents. But its consolidation of power around the old issues makes it unsuited to deal with new, emerging issues and divisions. Its hold on power may be destabilized and soon give way.

THE PERIODS OF PARTY HEGEMONY: 1800–1950

The Jeffersonian Republicans

The Jeffersonian Republicans, forerunners of the Democrats later in the century, held the presidency through six successive terms—two each for Thomas Jefferson, James Madison, and James Monroe. It was hard to know in this new nation that the factions would soon evolve into parties, as Madison warned of them in *Federalist Paper Number 10* and Jefferson described them as the "last degradation of a free and moral agent." In some sense, the "Virginia dynasty" won dominance on the cheap; few voters actually participated in elections, about a third in the first decade of the nineteenth century, and party competition resembled more a fight among elite factions. Moreover, the Federalists, with no stronghold outside of New England and little support for their aristocratic posture, failed to compete from the beginning and fell into disrepute with New England's stern opposition to the War of 1812. Electoral competition was effectively over by 1820.[2]

Democrats in the remainder of the century would look back to the Jeffersonian Republicans as formative figures—not just because of their revolutionary role but also because of the ideas they advanced for the new nation.

But Jeffersonian "principles" soon became the stuff of Democratic Party hacks and heroes, up until William Jennings Bryan took the stage. Jefferson stood against Hamilton's statist ideas—for "good administration" and an expansive executive, for an empowered federal government, with a capacity for managing finance, taking control of debt and banking, and encouraging manufacture. Hamilton had wanted to "unite the interest and credit of rich individuals with those of the state" in order to foster economic growth. The Jeffersonians, in heated contrast, proposed to limit the intrusiveness of the federal government in the market. Instinctively, the Jeffersonians aligned themselves with the likes of the Whiskey Rebellion and thus with popular rule over federal authority. Jefferson set out his party's core principle as "equal rights for all, special privileges for none," thus ennobling the ordinary producer and landowner, and diminishing the status of the privileged, requiring deference. He heralded a "civic virtue" where "free [white] men" would make proper judgments about issues of public importance. His hope was for a nation of "freeholders."[3]

Ignoring whether Jefferson and his successors consistently governed by those principles, their unhindered dominance and the evaporation of the Federalists settled some big issues for the new nation. "Why did the first party system disintegrate?" Jacksonian historian Richard P. McCormick answers his own question, "Because the chief purpose for which it has been formed had lost its urgency." Perhaps Louis Hartz is right that politics in America was then left free to develop, but within the parameters of a Lockean consensus.[4]

Jacksonian Democrats

Andrew Jackson's election in 1828 kicks off the second period of party dominance, putting the Democrats in the White House for six of the next eight elections, but this time with genuine popular engagement and real parties rather than factions or clans. Turnout jumped from 26.9 percent in 1824 to 57.6 percent in 1828. This was a tumultuous period, with the country swept by very big crosscurrents—the rise of manufacture and mills, large-scale immigration and the nativist reaction, and the extension of slavery into the frontier and the Free-Soil reaction. Andrew Jackson won the presidency as a populist figure, war hero, and vulgar man by Washington standards who allowed the multitude to swarm the White House. On the big "questions" of the day, however, for the resurgent Democrats, one observer noted, "There was no clear-cut party stand." That Jackson himself had no discernible positions on these issues made it easier for the party leaders to construct a flexible agenda for the elections. As one political scientist observed crisply, "It was not a tidy political event."

But the Jacksonian Democrats emerged with their gut sensibilities and philosophy of government and citizens consistent in content if not style with those of their adopted Jeffersonian forebears. They gained clarity in opposition to Henry Clay's "American system"—where the government expanded credit, protected industry, and financed internal improvement—for the purpose of promoting America's modernization. But while the Whig opponents proffered a government that "should exert a beneficial, paternal, fostering influence upon the Industry and Prosperity of the People," the Democrats wanted to stop government from overreaching. The Democrats, as they put it, preferred "the voluntary system"; "they desire to drive no man." Government, they believed, is inherently corrupt and bound to fall into the hands of the "rich and powerful." Thus, President Jackson waged war and defeated the United States Bank, and President Van Buren deployed Democrats against the "privileged banking corporations," the "self-constituted, dangerous and irresponsible power." In that spirit, they opposed high tariffs that protect manufacture, arguing that this is really a "system" for "plundering the laboring classes." The Democrats assumed to themselves a "special guardianship" over the principles of the Constitution, to block those who would expand government with a "doctrine of expediency and general welfare."

The Democrats sought to center America in the "common man"—the central passion of their politics. Jackson joined the "planters and farmers" to the "mechanics and laborers" in opposition to "monopoly power," or more aptly, against the forces driving America's commercial development. In his farewell address, Jackson used the pulpit of the White House to note that the success of these laboring people "depends upon their own industry and economy" and, together, "they are the bone and sinew of the country."[5]

Their visions of the common man did not include slaves or Native Americans, who were mistreated and dispatched in this era with particular cruelty. That omission enabled the Democrats to build support in all regions of the country, establishing the patterns of support by 1836 or 1838 that would keep them in power for decades, until the Democratic-Whig system crashed against a number of issues that the major parties could not address, including the surge of immigration and unresolved issues of slavery.

The Democratic Party was constructed as a national coalition that would submerge sectional issues, that is, slavery. Every Democratic ticket from 1836 to 1860 was by design regionally balanced, one Southerner and one non-Southerner. The Democrats' rules required then, and up until 1936, that the nominee win two-thirds of the votes at the convention, ensuring a Southern veto and presidential leadership that took no extreme position on sectional issues. With the Whigs operating under their "gag" order, the United States struggled through this period of frontier expansion, operating under the terms of a series of deals—the Missouri Compromise from an earlier period and the Compromise of 1850—to divide up the new states between free and slave. The political arrangements held in 1848 even when Martin Van Buren broke with the Democrats to head the Free-Soil Party. But the system of compromises brought neither a stable economic arrangement nor political peace, as third parties rose to take advantage of the silences.

The Republicans—America's Party

"The victory of the slave issue," John Aldrich points out, ended the Democrats' dominance and, indeed, undermined both the national parties that depended on sectional compromise. With slavery the issue, the cleavage line changed and the parties became necessarily sectional. The new Republican Party won in 1860, based exclusively in the North. The pre–Civil War Democrats were perhaps our clearest case of a dominant party crashing, hamstrung before the emerging issues of the day.[6]

The Republican Party would become "America's party," winning the great majority of elections between 1860 and 1928. Its ascendancy was hardly unchallenged; the Republicans fended off the post–Civil War Democrats in very close elections in 1876, 1880, and 1888, the last without a plurality of the vote. Cleveland won the White House in nonconsecutive terms in 1884 and 1892; and the post-Bryan Democrat, Woodrow Wilson, defeated the faltering Republicans in 1912 and, with the promise to keep America out of war, won in 1916 as well. The essential voting patterns, established as early as 1856 and confirmed in 1880 when the South was reintegrated into the Union, largely held until the Depression of 1929. In the Deep South, no state voted Republican again until 1956.[7]

Lincoln established the Republicans as the party that held the nation together—in some sense, they took on the biggest challenge that had bedeviled the country since its formation. They had defended the Constitution. And in abolishing slavery and breaking the power of the Southern landed classes, they set the country irrevocably down a modernizing and industrial path. Republican leaders from Lincoln to Teddy Roosevelt to Coolidge described their party as the American Party, ready to defend America. The Civil War was a reference point where Republicans could continually remind voters that they defended America's virtues with force of arms. The great majority of the party's presidential nominees were military figures, especially in this period after the Civil War.[8]

Of course nobody knew in 1856 or 1880 that the Republicans would be ascendant for so many decades. Indeed, with the chicanery of the Hayes-Tilden election and the dead-heat finishes in 1880, 1884, and 1888, both parties were driven to other means. The states of the Old South at the outset of the 1890s began enacting statutes to disenfranchise the black voter and to end the prospect of competitive general elections in the Southern states. The Republicans, for their part, in addition to waving the bloody shirt, constructed a system of Civil War pensions available only to veterans of the Union Army—one in ten voters concentrated in the Northeast and Midwest. The payments exploded from 1880 to 1910, when the Republicans were entrenching their position and fending off the Populists. The Grand Army of the Republic, 400,000 strong, backed the Republicans through all the election battles.[9]

The Republican Party was defined by its modernizing, unifying, and nationalist vision for the nation, but that became much more ideologically developed as the parties battled through the economic transformations of the late nineteenth century and turn of the century. This was a period of tremendous economic growth and upheaval, with America emerging as a manufacturing and industrial society. Between 1880 and 1910, national wealth increased 275 percent; the urban population grew from 28 to 46 percent; massive immigration brought downward pressure on wages, as one quarter of immigrants' children aged ten to fourteen years were at work; farmers faced declining prices and monopolistic control of transportation and marketing. This was a time for the rise of corporations, holding companies, trusts, and monopolies, but also a time for deep downturns, including most of the 1890s, after the panic of 1893.[10]

The election of 1896 was the "hottest," Frederick Lewis Allen wrote, "perhaps, in the whole history of the United States." The Democrats, breaking with their tradition of running fiscally austere, antigovernment nominees, chose William Jennings Bryan—the populist, evangelical candidate who would change the identity of the Democratic Party. His politics were rooted in the civic virtue and common man themes that carried the Democrats through the nineteenth century, but it included the premise that the country should be enriched from the bottom up: "If you legislate to make the masses prosperous, their prosperity will find its way up through every class which rests upon them." Bryan also broke from the past as he sought to create a new Democratic Party organized against the emerging industrial order. He began with the farmers, some of whom had channeled their protests through the Greenback Party and antimonopolist leagues and, in the 1890s, the Farmers' Alliance. He appealed to "laboring interests, and the toilers everywhere," though his support was mostly confined to the West and rural areas, including the South. The Democrats wanted the government to break up monopolies, regulate the railways, introduce an income tax, abolish the industry-protecting tariffs, and shift the country's currency from the gold standard to free silver.[11]

For the Republicans, the battle against William Jennings Bryan through three national elections allowed them to emerge as the party indispensable to modernizing America. In their view, reminiscent of earlier Hamiltonian, Whig, and pre–Civil War Republican thinking, the government's role was to promote the country's growth and advancement, which in its crudest and most material form was a kind of mercantilism, which political scientist John Gerring defines as "a general economic philosophy mandating the subordination of economic activity to the interests of the state and nation." Within this nationalist framework and in McKinley's hands, the government was to create markets, protect American manufacturing behind high tariffs, and create a favorable climate for the surging big corporations. The tariff was the symbolic and real heart of their mercantilism, as this was the primary source of government revenue but also the principal weapon in the Republican economic nationalist arsenal. To stand with the Republicans on high tariffs was to support their route for industrializing America. McKinley imbued it with national aspirations that enlist all classes and raise the nation: "I believe in it and thus warmly advocate it because enveloped in it are my country's highest development and greatest prosperity; out of it come the greatest gains to the people, the greatest comforts to the masses, the widest encouragement for many aspirations, with the largest rewards, dignifying and elevating our citizenship, upon which the safety and purity and permanency of our political system depend."[12]

Embedded in the tariff was the idea that laboring people would benefit equally with the capitalists as the country grew. McKinley first won election to Congress after championing striking mine workers and opposing Chinese immigration. He was schooled in what would become an important theme in this period: "There are no descended titles here; there is no way in the world of getting on and up, or earning money, except by work." Thus, faced with the populist challenge, McKinley could speak against division and for a unity of interests: "We are not a nation of classes, but of sturdy, free, independent and honorable people . . ."[13]

The Republicans associated themselves, without apology, with business and with the presumption that growing industrialization would improve the general welfare. Voters knew what they were getting, and Republicans mostly won the elections in this period by healthy margins. America, faced with what seemed an antimodern challenge, opted to accept the basic contours of this procapitalist agenda. McKinley's campaign manager was Marcus Hanna, himself a wealthy businessman, who recruited virtually all of America's top industrial magnates and assessed them a percentage of their assets to finance the campaign. McKinley attacked class divisiveness as "unpatriotic" and finished the campaign with a "flag day" that underscored the Republicans' ability to associate a business-led prosperity with the American way of life.[14]

Calvin Coolidge at the end of this period of Republican dominance would make a similar case. He was the president for the 1920s, when incomes grew by 20 percent between 1921 and 1929 and the number of automobiles rose from 9.3 million to 23.1 million; by the end of the decade, there was almost one car for every family. But this was also a decade for speculative booms, with rising inequality. Coolidge, with Andrew Mellon, likely the wealthiest man in the country, as his secretary of the treasury, proceeded with an economic policy of aggressive tax slashing for the wealthy: they cut the inheritance tax in half, abolished the gift tax, and reduced the income tax to 5 percent. Like their predecessors in 1896, Coolidge and Mellon attacked those who "seek to perpetuate prejudice and class hatred" and pit "one class of taxpayers against another." The Republican bargain, Mellon declared, was straightforward: "In no other nation and at no other time in the history of the world have so many people enjoyed such a high degree of prosperity."[15]

Roosevelt's New Deal Democrats

When the stock market crashed and the country went into depression, there was no more reason to vote Republican. Once again, the change in the issue and the choices changed the party. It was time for a party that could deal with the dire economic challenges ahead.

Franklin Roosevelt won in 1932, beginning a new era of Democratic political dominance, enduring through five successive terms. While Roosevelt was vague on his economic policies and recovery and relief program, the country sent an electoral message perhaps stronger than any other election in our history. The voting patterns forged in the 1850s and 1880s were radically disrupted. The Republicans had identified themselves with the concept of business-led prosperity, which turned to ash. The problem was likely compounded by Hoover's turn to a more modern conservatism ideology that eschewed an expansive role for government. He opposed food relief and unemployment insurance, vetoed a bill for national employment exchanges, and encouraged private charity.[16]

Roosevelt made the Democrats the indispensable party for an America that would recover economically and honor the mass of laboring and working people. Although without a real policy direction, Roosevelt was hardly without basic instincts for how to align the Democratic Party for these times. Roosevelt was simply for the "forgotten man," who is the starting point for public policy: "These unhappy times call for the building of plans that rest upon the forgotten, the unorganized but the indispensable units of economic power, for plans . . . that build from the bottom up and not from the top down, that put their faith, once more in the forgotten man at the bottom of the economic pyramid."[17]

Roosevelt only reluctantly articulated a philosophy of bigger government. In his pragmatic state of mind, he was more inclined to speak of "bold, persistent experimentation." But with the experience of President Wilson's wartime expansion of government and with the growth of corporate power, Democrats, like Roosevelt, began to warm to the role: "Government must be empowered to deal adequately with any business that tries to rise above Government."[18] Accordingly, the New Deal government introduced market controls in agriculture, bank regulation, labor standards in the workplace, labor-management relations, minimum wage, unemployment insurance, Social Security, relief and public works, electrification, and expanded credit and investment.[19]

Under Roosevelt, government accepted a bottom-line responsibility for employment, and by that formal change altered the electoral equation for the parties. During the 1930s, most federal government expenditures were devoted to stimulating employment and providing jobs directly. "Provide work and economic security to the mass of the people," Roosevelt advised, "in order that they may be free to live and develop their individual lives and seek happiness and recognition."[20] With the war, America employed all of its people and sealed the contract that Roosevelt had offered.

In 1932, Roosevelt had run "for the forgotten man," but in 1936, with opposition to the New Deal growing in business circles, Roosevelt took on the "economic royalists." Before a joint session of the Congress, he pointed to the "resplendent economic autocracy" that wants control of the government and "enslavement of the public." Indeed, it was only "a people's government in Washington," Roosevelt said during the campaign, that could protect against that kind of concentrated power and greed.[21]

Roosevelt won in a landslide, and later Truman would use those themes, that philosophy of government, and the issue of employment to turn back the postwar Republican challenge. But with the war and the Depression behind America, people were moving on with their lives and the country with its issues. They did not realize then that America was entering an era, unlike the previous century and a half, when no party would succeed in dominating the times.

THREE FAILED EFFORTS TO DOMINATE THE ERA

Over the last 50 years, unlike our nation's first 150, no party has succeeded in dominating at the polls or commanding the realm of ideas, which has set us on the road to political deadlock and deepening political divisions, particularly in the last decade. In this culminating period, closed by three national elections, the division and most-important voting issues have become increasingly cultural, crowding out other important issues for the country.

This parity and lack of a dominant party has invited a series of bold efforts by the Democrats and Republicans to become the leading party of the era, but each fell short, shaking up political loyalties without creating a new majority in the country. Each created new partisan loyalists but also contested groups that could not be accommodated by the emerging political divide. Each took on important issues and tasks for the country, but because they failed to achieve political ascendancy, their ideas left people even more divided over the country's essential beliefs and direction. Each contributed to the building of the Two Americas, which reflected a country ever more polarized on cultural issues.

The first political initiative was the work of the Opportunity Democrats, John Kennedy and Lyndon Johnson. Their core principle was America's abundance and inclusiveness, creating the exceptional American task described by Kennedy: to make sure all can "share in the benefits of our abundance and natural resources."[22] That key social task kept Democrats focused on those left behind and building opportunity, including for America's large middle class. The Opportunity Democrats were optimistic about America's capacity to meet modern challenges and manage economic growth by using government expansively as an instrument of change and community. All of the world, they hoped, would look to America, not just because of our military superiority but also because of the kind of America we would create together. Though they moved reluctantly to meet the challenge on civil rights, the Opportunity Democrats nonetheless attacked traditional institutions, public and private, that held back black Americans and, ultimately, those that held back women and other emerging groups. While their vision of opportunity was very broad, the challenge of addressing America's racial history proved tumultuous and narrowed the vision and political task. Riots racked the cities and new cultural forces were set loose. White and black voters began marching en masse to new political homes.

The Democrats won a landslide majority in 1964, but this was a precarious ascendancy. The Republicans made major gains just two years later in the 1966 congressional elections, before the Vietnam War became unpopular. Hubert Humphrey could not hold the White House in 1968, and George McGovern could barely maintain the party's legitimacy in 1972.

However short-lived was the ascendancy of the Opportunity Democrats, they moved the country to a different place on the issues of race and diversity; they opened the door on individual rights, changing the position of women in the home and workplace. Those values would endure to make possible the postmodern claim on the Two Americas. The Opportunity Democrats' expansion of the regulatory state and the welfare state, particularly for the old, far outlived their short time in office. Indeed, the ascendancy of their ideas about rights and opportunity and to some extent government, but without a sustained political ascendancy, contributed mightily to political deadlock and the country's divide.

Then, the Reagan Revolutionaries made the second major effort to dominate this untamed era. It was stronger and more enduring—indeed, it even undermined the capacity and legitimacy of government action—but it also fell dramatically short, creating even more political turmoil.

This conservative political project began ignominiously with Barry Goldwater's landslide defeat, though he helped define the Republican Party as hostile to government and civil rights, a defender of the South, and champion of a well-armed and assertive America. Richard Nixon abandoned the antigovernment side of the conservative project in order to remove the barrier in the way of defecting white Northern workers and Southern Baptists. But Nixon ran an unflagging law-and-order campaign and championed states' rights, self-consciously polarizing the country, to align the "forgotten Americans" with the Republicans.

Only with the rise of Ronald Reagan, however, did the Republicans create a seemingly new national majority centered on conservative ideas and values. It would honor business, entrepreneurship, and markets, and advance a vision of their success enriching the country. Cutting taxes became the centerpiece both of conservative economic policy and for turning ordinary voters against government, bureaucrats, and liberal elites. The Reagan Revolutionaries stood against liberal permissiveness, as had the conservatives before them, but now they aligned the Republicans with religious conservatives and people of faith and against the growing force of secularism. Abortion and school prayer, along with tax cuts, were to be the subject of politics. The Reagan Revolutionaries, impatient with the moral neutrality of détente and angry with America's humiliation under Jimmy Carter, insisted on a military second to none and on an America prepared to act on its own to defeat tyranny and defend freedom. The Reagan landslide of 1984 created the Republican South and the "Reagan Democrats," the blue-collar "defectors" who were to change suburban politics in the country.

But this bold conservative attempt to dominate the times was also short-lived, though the moment lives vividly in the consciousness of today's modern conservatives. The Republicans lost heavily just two years later in the 1986 U.S. Senate elections, just as the Democrats had lost ground two decades earlier as a prelude to their crash. George Bush held on in 1988 by waging cultural war, but even Willie Horton tactics could not save him in 1992, as the Republicans lost their hold on the country. With growing anger about corporate abuses and a middle class angry about stagnant incomes and growing inequality, the Republicans lost support in the countryside, among senior citizens, and in the growing suburbs, where blue-collar and many rural voters defected to Ross Perot. Professionals and better-educated women, the most secular of the voters, began pulling back from the Republicans of the Reagan era. When the conservative majority crashed, the national Republican vote on average barely topped 40 percent in the next two national elections.

But even as the conservative political project crashed electorally, it too had advanced ideas and took on tasks that changed the country. The public no longer imagined big things from government, which in any case now lacked the resources to do serious things. Markets were now honored, and global trade and industrial transformation were presumptions in the popular mind and economy. The values of personal responsibility competed successfully with the values of individual rights. That those conservative ideas have lived beyond the conservative political moment only contributes to the character of this period, divided politically but also on values and the nature of the American community. The legacy of these two attempts to dominate the era is a cultural politics competing with the more long-standing class politics that centers on how people order their lives.[23]

The Reformed Opportunity Democrats made the third bold effort to dominate an era, and like the others, fell short and contributed to the building of the Two Americas. As Ronald Reagan had built on Barry Goldwater's failed candidacy, Bill Clinton benefited from the fiscal caution of Jimmy Carter and Michael Dukakis and the reformist, high-technology politics of Gary Hart, who sought new ways for government to address new problems. In 1992, Bill Clinton pulled together the emerging strands and wove them into a bold offer. He and Al Gore called themselves New Democrats or a "Third Way," but I label them the Reformed Opportunity Democrats, given their attempt to offset the history that had left the Democrats so narrowly based in society.

Their new insistence on responsibility enabled more traditional middle-class voters to trust Democrats again. Their focus on changing and reinventing government was aimed at restoring the legitimacy of government as an instrument of community and the country's sense of capacity to address problems and the future. With the explosive inequality of the Reagan era and the Bush recession, Bill Clinton was able, for the first time in two decades, to make a broad offer about opportunity involving the middle class as well as the poor. He attacked the irresponsibility of CEOs while championing the squeezed middle class, whose values and living standards were threatened. He promised to focus on restoring economic growth. He took up the Democrats' commitment to rights and made it a broader commitment to diversity that strengthened America in the global economy.

This combination brought the Reagan coalition crashing down in 1992 and allowed the Democrats to win a plurality of the vote in the last three presidential elections of the era. Had there been no butterfly ballots in Palm Beach County or had Ralph Nader taken on a different cause, the three successive Democratic wins would have matched the longest previous streak of the half-century era. The Reformed Opportunity Democrats built their political advantage by restoring fiscal balance, leading the economic change, and orienting the United States toward the global economy. Although inequality continued to grow, incomes began to rise broadly, at least in Clinton's second term, and poverty rates began to fall. In their entirety, the Reformed Democrats advanced postmodernist ideas about America that won them growing support in the cosmopolitan states, mostly on the coasts, in metropolitan areas across the country, and among the better-educated, women, racial minorities, and new immigrants.

But the Reformed Opportunity Democrats won only 43 percent of the vote in 1992 and 49 percent in 1996, and Al Gore consolidated their position, short of a majority. Had Perot not run in 1996, Clinton might have won 53 percent, far below that for Johnson in 1964 and Reagan in 1984, the high points of the other two efforts to dominate the times.[24] The Reformed Opportunity Democrats faltered because they were forced, for various reasons, to abandon key elements of their political project. They pulled away from the middle class as a central passion of their work and, indeed, working-class incomes were the last to rise. The issues of gays in the military, Monica Lewinsky, and impeachment broke the Democrats' link to the value of responsibility and, with it, their link to many mainstream families.

The uneven fortunes of the Reformed Opportunity Democrats have very important consequences for the character of our current era and the political deadlock. With the losses of the more traditional rural, religious, and married voters, the Democrats crashed up against an electoral ceiling barely higher than a majority. And while Clinton and Gore focused on and ran well at the top and bottom of the socioeconomic ladder, they lost ground badly in the middle. Many of them were Ross Perot voters—nearly 20 percent of the vote in 1992 and nearly 10 percent in 1996—who remained among the most alienated, antigovernment, and financially pressed. Finally, the "Clinton Wars," as Sidney Blumenthal aptly described them, reduced much of the work of the Reformed Opportunity Democrats to cultural politics. With Gore so instinctively secular and modern in his thinking and Bush so instinctively religious and traditional, the 2000 election produced an even higher cultural barrier and even greater electoral polarization, the building blocks of the Two Americas. It left the Democrats, like the Republicans, with the support of half the country.

THE POLITICS OF PARITY

So the 2000 election, as it turns out, was not simply "a once-every-few-centuries proposition," as *The Washington Post* staff writers put it. It was an all too predictable consequence of nearly a half century of political struggle, unsuccessful in the end, to achieve dominance. The election was not a fluke but a dramatization of our new politics. And the real question becomes, What has changed since 2000? When will this parity end? What party can aspire to hegemony?

Up until 2000, many observers, including myself, misread the signs. They focused on the public revolt against congressional incumbents in 1990, the crash of the Reagan coalition in 1992, the Gingrich earthquake in 1994 ending decades of Democratic control in Congress, and Ross Perot's historic third-party performance in 1992 and 1996. These events that brought to an end the Democrats' four-decade control of the House and the biggest third-party win seemed to suggest that both parties were failing the voters and saw not only volatility but a public pulling back from both of the parties. I wrote, "Either the lack of rules is now the rule or new rules yet to be revealed are proving to be determinant."[25]

But we now know, in light of a decade of elections and the 2000 impasse, that there are new rules, and they center on the parties and the parity itself. The successive efforts to create a sustainable majority produced a lot of turmoil that disrupted traditional coalitions and voting patterns and created newly contested groups, indeed, created new loyalists. With each party tantalizingly close to winning any election, the goal now is to get your coalition inflamed, engaged, and united, perhaps to bring over some of the contested, to edge past parity.

So what does the politics of the Two Americas look like? What are the new rules of this period that we cannot easily escape?

First of all, the politics of parity has seemed to lock the country into a politics of culture. Culture does not simply mean a line drawn in the sand between the religious and secular. In the cultural politics of this era, the country is also divided between the individualists who want government to get off their backs and those who want to use government's regulatory capacity to advance community goals, limiting what some individuals can do. On one side of the divide are those who think America is the best and most admired country in the world and should take care of its own business, and on the other are those who revel in the country's pluralism and diversity and openness to the world and global trends. For the most part, these are overlapping divisions, which raise the barrier between two Americas whose politics are increasingly about their way of life, not just issues. Abortion, guns, taxes—all are incendiary devices under the rules of this new game.

Second, the politics of parity has changed the partisans. With the two parties closely matched and with each party having an equal chance for victory, there are strong incentives to get as many votes as possible out of your existing partisans. Political scientist Martin Wattenberg was actually one of the first to notice this when looking at the 1988 election. Compared to previous elections, a higher proportion of self-identified Republicans were voting for the Republican presidential candidate, reaching 78 percent in that year. With the new period just evolving, he identified the logic of this dynamic, though he understated it: "With the new parity in size, both parties have come to focus more on holding on to their own base."[26] In fact, in the last decade, they have come to focus on building a winning coalition by first increasing their partisan performance among their most natural supporters.

The conservative political project did not create a sustainable majority, but it did create a sizable and sustainable bloc of partisan loyalists that helps make the party plausible in any election. Their loyalist world includes disproportionately the white Evangelicals; voters in the rural areas, the Deep South, and high-growth outer metropolitan areas in the South and Southwest; blue-collar married men; and the most privileged. Except for the last, the Republican loyalist camp is composed wholly of groups recruited during the various cultural skirmishes and runs the gamut from rural and working class to upscale suburban to superrich. In this period of parity and polarization, there is a tremendous incentive to get the most from each of these groups.

The Reformed Opportunity Democrats have also forged their own bloc of loyalists, fully able to keep the Democrats in the game with a chance to win, if engaged. Their loyalist camp draws heavily from the African-American and Hispanic communities, women with postgraduate degrees, the least religious and most cosmopolitan areas, especially on the East and West coasts, as well as union families. These loyalists too have been recruited and nurtured during the ongoing cultural battles, which have largely left workers outside the Democratic loyalist camp, except for the party's durable union supporters. However they got there, Democrats too have strong incentives to maximize their vote from these groups.

It is striking how out of place the privileged and the union families are in their respective loyalist worlds, which says a lot about the increasing dominance of cultural politics on both sides of the divide. The result is indeed the culture war where each party works to excite the passions of its loyalists, address their issues, and raise the symbols that define the election on their terms. The goal is greater engagement and unity, which gives them the best chance of winning.

The result: partisans have become more partisan. Politics has become more polarized. America has become more divided.

While the parties lost some of their hold on voters in the 1960s and 1970s, during the biggest upheavals in the country—from civil rights and riots to Vietnam and Watergate—the percentage calling themselves "strong Democrats" and "strong Republicans" began rising throughout the 1980s, paused in 1992, then rose again to a new level in 1996 and 2000, as the parties worked to engage their partisan loyalists. In fact, in the last three presidential elections—framing this period of parity—the country has witnessed a crash in ticket splitting, as partisans responded with a more unified vote.[27] Some of this is a result of the death of the Old Democratic South, which voted Republican for president and Democratic for Congress until Reagan brought them over. But if one looks outside of the South during the 1990s, the rest of the country has moved to a new plateau of increasing partisanship.[28]

The increasing polarization of the voters on either side of the cultural divide has been matched and perhaps led by the political elites. Starting in the 1970s but rising dramatically by the end of the 1980s, members of Congress were voting with increasing partisan unity, as the ideological gap grew between the parties.[29]

The growing intensity of partisanship and polarization of the political class is creating parties with increasingly distinct identities, which divide the country in this period of deadlock. Since 1988, there has been a sharp rise in the number of voters who can express "likes" and "dislikes" about the parties. And there has been a dramatic jump in the number of voters saying that there are important differences between the parties—now over 75 percent.[30]

The battle to get the most out of the partisans deepens the divide in the country. That the two parties are more distinct, polarized, and mobilized does not mean that the voters feel greater affection for the parties. Both receive thermometer scores just over 50 degrees, the midpoint, representing neither warm nor cool, on a 100-degree centigrade scale of favorability. Before 1990 and the last decade of increasing partisan acrimony, the Democratic Party with its high standing in the South always scored over 60 degrees and the Republican Party in most years just under, but well above the current parity in lost affection.[31]

But the successive battles to dominate the era and the determination to mobilize the partisans have also produced a lot of political turmoil. Some groups, like the professionals and college graduates, that were predictably Republican for many decades are now contested. Some groups have become simply volatile, politically detached from any partisan coalition, swinging wildly as the parties battle over the unresolved direction of the country. This, for instance, is now the state of Catholic voters, married women without college educations, and the young.

The resulting landscape of groups and political coalitions looks very different from even the most recent past. You need a new program to understand the players in this drama built around parity.

Much of the political landscape is composed of groups in neither camp that divide their votes evenly between the parties. The parties contest these groups, lest they begin to tilt one way or the other and threaten the parity. Many of the contested groups are attracted to both parties, usually on different issues, and their ambivalence or fickleness gets them a lot of attention. Some are not particularly interested in the current political battles and issues but have learned the benefits that can be won Chicago-style, particularly in a period of parity, seeing which has the most to offer. The parties may up the ante with farm subsidies, trade protections, or a prescription drug benefit that may tip a group without the party having to pull back a bit from mobilizing its own partisan loyalists.

Many groups are contested because they have issues of their own that the two well-established parties, battling for advantage, dare not consider, lest it change the rules of the game that keep both parties at parity. The need to feed the loyalists keeps political leaders focused on the issues and policies that produce greater partisan engagement and unity. The politics of parity leaves a lot of issues off the table, which in turn leaves a lot of voters not fully integrated into the battle and many problems unaddressed. The aging blue-collar and rural voters, for example, are frustrated with the excess influence of big corporations and the rising inequality, yet those issues are not central to our current politics. The married working-class women are very concerned about health care, but the current policy debate, centered on prescription drugs for seniors, barely touches their lives. Many college-educated men and women are looking for a more robust public discussion about how to advance our new economy, but they get mainly tax cuts from the Republicans and spending from the Democrats. Young voters fit in almost no box; they are tolerant on the cultural issues, particularly with respect to gays and lesbians, and strongly supportive of the president on the war on terrorism, yet hard-pressed to see the relevance of this polarized politics in their own lives.

The result is a large bloc of the electorate, as big as the Democrats or Republicans, who call themselves "independents." In 2000, 35 percent of the voters called themselves independents, which may represent the new level for this period of parity. The number of independents is marginally higher than in the 1970s and 1980s, and much higher than in earlier periods.[32]

The bloc also ought to include the potentially volatile groups that could disrupt the developing patterns. The 2000 Nader voters say they are "independents," for the most part, but align overwhelmingly with the Democrats. Many of the Gen Y and older blue-collar voters include a disproportionate number of "independents" and may be open to a Perot-like revolt at some point.

In any case, the political turmoil and intense partisan battle leave a lot of voters amenable to a different kind of politics, if one of the parties can break free of the current deadlock.[33]

But while they are open to different issues and political debates, that is all theoretical, as the politics of parity has consolidated the partisans on both sides of the divide and contained the issue agenda, leaving the contested still contested and conflicted. That has produced a period of remarkable electoral stability and parity, where each election looks more and more like the election before it. Looking at the state-by-state results, Larry Bartels puts the spotlight on the presidential elections of 1988, 1992, and 1996—elections with very low volatility and only minor swings from election to election, a level of stability matched only a century earlier.[34] Since 1988 at the presidential level, since 1994 at the congressional level (when the Old Democratic South was finally put to rest), and since 1998 at the state legislative level, the Democrats and Republicans have settled at virtual parity. Each year, their battles are fought with increasing intensity and ferocity, but to the same result.

This produces a political map of the United States for the future wholly reflective of this history and emerging politics around parity. The dependably Democratic "blue states" and dependably Republican "red states" each encompass exactly one-third of the likely presidential electorate; more important, they represent an almost identical number of Electoral College votes (179 to the blues and 189 to the reds). In each case, the party won the state with 53 percent or more of the vote. In the case of the Democrats, they have won all 12 of their states and the District of Columbia in the last three presidential elections and more than half in the last four. With a weaker performance in the 1990s, the Republicans carried just 16 of their 22 states in the last three presidential contests, though they carried all 22 in the 1988 presidential contest. What is most striking, however, is the battleground, contested states where the future will be decided. They comprise 170 Electoral College votes and one-third of the likely vote. When

AMERICA DIVIDED
ELECTORAL VOTES

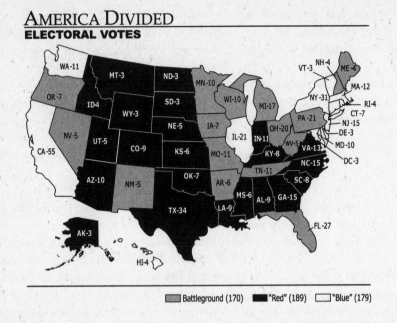

Battleground (170)   "Red" (189)   "Blue" (179)

one asks the voters in those states with which party they align, 46 percent say the Democrats and 46 percent the Republicans. What distinguishes these states are their relatively high rural populations, which will likely favor the Republicans in the future, unless contested, and the high Hispanic growth, which will likely favor the Democrats, unless contested.[35]

So when we asked earlier, almost ironically, "What has changed since 2000?" we underscored the character of this era, a divided country operating under new rules.

BREAKING THE DEADLOCK

But are we left simply to relive 2000 as our political future? Michael Barone, an astute conservative commentator, believes the social trends will shift the elections toward the Republicans. He looks across the battlefield, highlights the divide, and then concludes, "Demography is moving, slowly, toward the Bush nation." Perhaps more as an act of faith about the future, he concludes that "George W. Bush, though he won fewer votes than Al Gore, is more in line with the grain of American history."[36]

John Judis and Ruy Teixeira, progressive observers, look across the same battlefield that left the parties exhausted and at parity, but they highlight the social and cultural trends that take the country toward the Democrats:

"When the fear of terror recedes, and when Americans begin to focus again on job, home, and the pursuit of happiness, the country will once again become fertile ground for the Democrats' progressive centrism and post-industrial values."[37] They align the Democrats with an increasingly dominant "postindustrial society," centered on theoretical knowledge and science, as sociologist Daniel Bell described it—a society where education is the route to social standing and knowledge and information is the new capital. Bell has sought to capture the explosive changes in the last few decades, including the shift from manufacture to service, the rise of professionals and technicians, the explosion in higher education, and the shift from ports, highways, and railroads to the new infrastructure of communication. But there is a point where simply being "postindustrial" is insufficient to describe the emerging social forces that could tilt the political balance. "Postmodern" captures the associated diversity, tolerance of different lifestyles, individuality, social flexibility and openness to discontinuity, new roles for women, and diverse definitions—and skepticism—of absolutes, religious truths, authority, and traditions.[38]

David Brooks in his *Bobos in Paradise* describes the peculiar evolution of postmodernism in America, with the emergence of the culturally dominant "bourgeois bohemians." While Brooks avoids a demographic and electoral projection, he does view the Clinton-Gore moderate synthesis as the kind of politics most congenial to the Bobos. With the bourgeois bohemians forming a new "establishment," pervasive and powerful, that might well shift the political balance.

We shall see that the social trends favor the Democrats but not decisively, not immediately, and not without countercurrents. The country's electorate is becoming more racially diverse and better educated; it is also becoming less rural, with fewer white, married, working-class voters. These trends tend to enlarge the Democrats' America and diminish the Republicans'. On the other hand, there are some counterbalancing factors, including the growth of the Deep South and the metropolitan areas or Exurbia and the immutable overrepresentation of small rural states in the Electoral College. Some of the Republican counterbalancing is simply a shuffling of the population—the movement from one area to another—and not real national growth. But all that is beside the point if the Republicans do not simply accept their demographic fate and actually use politics to change reality. They will certainly use their hold on government to try to win more Hispanic support, reverse the trend among seniors, or make inroads with suburban women. Or they will try and fail. That uncertainty is yet one more incentive to continue to fight a decade or more of elections, perhaps increasingly intense, under the rules that parity gave us.

That leaves the country at risk, not just of another 2000 but also of not addressing the serious problems facing the country. This is certainly not 1852 or 1856 when the main parties were trapped by their old issues and powerless to address the slavery question; this may not be 1888 or 1892 when the main parties were still battling over what the Civil War left and were unable to face a rapidly industrializing America. Our country is now responding to the terrorist threat, as it must, but beyond that, the current politics strongly favors revisiting the issues that brought all these voters to their respective sides of the divide and the issues that have been used to lure contested voters. But can the parties so embattled take up in a non-symbolic way the problems of health care, growing inequality, the welfare state, the viability of retirement programs, the growing pressures of work and family, changing education and skill requirements, global environmental issues, global trade and the erosion of national sovereignty, and other international threats beyond terrorism, among others?

This book addresses how we can break America's current political deadlock. I do not leave the reader standing on the sidelines, impotent, able only to watch the parties battle one more time to an inconclusive result. I explore how the Democrats and the Republicans, thinking tactically and strategically, can win elections within the current framework or shatter it completely.

The Republicans go into the period ahead with the home field advantage. Ensconced in the White House, Congress, and Supreme Court, they are in a position, to be brutally honest, to use power to help their friends, co-opt issues, address problems, and raise lots of campaign money. With the parties at parity, the Republicans will likely want to preserve the status quo of the Two Americas, given the abundance of opportunities to build up numbers on the Republican side of the divide. The political advantages of wartime leadership may be just enough to maintain Republican rule without having to remake what is at this point a fairly predictable political map. Over the past decade, Republican loyalist groups have given their party steadily higher support as the country has become more polarized, but perhaps the support groups can be pushed to even greater unity. The Republicans—using symbolic appointments and policies, playing language games, seeking pictorial diversity, and stealing issues—can try to soften the tone and diminish the counterreaction on the Democratic side of the divide. The Republicans can work assiduously to gain support among Hispanics and suburban women, and thus offset the emerging Democratic trends in the country.

With so many tactical opportunities to win within the Two Americas framework, Republicans are very likely to opt to win by maintaining the political status quo. But the real advantage for the Republicans is how easily tactics could become strategy. Republicans believe it is possible that their incremental, tactical actions to hold on to power could cascade into a bigger victory within the Two Americas framework. That is plausible because virtually all modern Republican leaders come to this battle with the Reagan vision intact, emphasizing the individual over government, tax cutting, religious faith and the traditional family, and a strong America prepared to take on the lonely task of defending freedom in the world. Republican strategists believe, particularly in light of 9/11 and the war on terrorism ahead, that the prospect of successful governance à la Reagan could attract a growing majority to the Republicans. In short, the Republican strategy for becoming the indispensable party and breaking the deadlock is to enlarge their side of the Two Americas, allowing the other America to wither. For Karl Rove, President Bush's principal strategist, the hope is for a replay of 1896, after which the Republicans were the hegemonic party for the country.

Whether they are correct depends on whether the Reagan Revolution is really a viable model, whether the Reagan coalition is still a majority coalition, and whether its vision and policies are relevant, given the challenges ahead for America—and how correct they are also depends on what the Democrats do.

The Democrats, we shall see, have an abundance of strategic opportunities that can keep them in the game, given the parity in the country and important underlying trends. After all, this battle takes place against a backdrop in which the country grows rapidly more diverse and better educated and cosmopolitan. Most of the Republican tactics are meant to offset these demographic trends, but each change is driven by big forces and involves underlying values and beliefs not easily changed by politicians. It is very possible that a postmodern and multicultural America, abhorred by conservative thinkers, represents the future.

Many of the tactical opportunities discussed at the end of this book center on how to free voters to travel to that side of the Two Americas and build a Democratic advantage. Voters are most likely to move, in the first instance, if the Republican tactics are blunted and the public grows more doubtful—compassionate conservatism appears not so compassionate, big business interests win out over the public interest, and Bush policies become at odds with the public's agenda for the country. Second, voters are more likely to move if they regain their confidence in Democrats on values and family, defense, and patriotism—against the backdrop of the impeachment and 9/11 and Iraq. After all, even though the fires of the "Clinton Wars" were still smoldering and although Al Gore ran as a very secular candidate on the cultural issues, he won a plurality, and Gore's and Nader's votes together were a majority. Reassurance on values and patriotism, on the need for responsibility, could take Democrats to a higher level.

That does not even address the prospects of introducing an added element, the economic and corporate critique. Little contemplated in the Republican strategy is a major character of the current period, which includes visible corporate abuse, endangered pensions and 401(k)s, CEO villainy, and excessive corporate influence in Washington, on top of an extended period of stagnant incomes, rising costs for health care, job losses, and increasing inequality. Voters are not as angry in this decade, it seems, as they were at the beginning of the last, but the sense of grievance and irresponsibility creates openings with voters in the rural areas and among working-class families that could enlarge territory on the Democratic side.

While the war on terrorism has given new scope to the role of commander in chief, it has also raised new uncertainties about America's course in Iraq and approach to the world. That has inflamed sentiment within the Democratic camp and even beyond.

Bottom line: if we end up with another election that looks just like the last, the Democrats have a coalition of loyalist supporters as large as that of the Republicans that could be energized and organized to even greater unity behind the Democrats.

Without the levers of government, Democrats may have significantly fewer tactical opportunities than the Republicans, but they have many plausible routes to winning within the current framework, without overturning the Two Americas. Nonetheless, given the Republicans' determination to use government in so many ways to hold on to power, status quo strategies just may be too big a risk, and the lesser risk is to think more boldly, beyond the Two Americas and the ravages of culture war.

The Democrats' best chance of breaking the impasse is by changing the subject and putting at risk the current game. That is a difficult course for either party, since both are so invested in the current battle lines and issues, which they have used to deepen their loyalist support and to contest the rest. But there are a host of new battle lines and new issues waiting to be made relevant. In highlighting these, I confess some continuing inspiration from E. E. Schattschneider, a legendary political scientist who got some important things wrong, but not the nature of conflict and politics. "In politics as in everything else it makes a great difference whose game we play," he wrote with reference to both elections and war. "The rules of the game determine the requirements for success," which for him goes "to the heart of political strategy." The greatest threat to the current parity and issue conflicts is a "new fight"—the drawing of new conflict lines with new issues that diminish or replace ones that were previously all-important and that make politics more or less important for various groups. As Schatt-schneider warned, "Commanders who are not agile when this happens are likely to be left in possession of deserted battlefields." He concludes, *"The substitution of conflicts is the most devastating kind of political strategy."*[39]

The Democrats may choose to elevate the election and pose a big choice between the Reagan view of the future and the view best articulated by the original Opportunity Democrats, particularly John F. Kennedy. As we will see by the end of this discussion, Democrats can take to the voters a historic choice about opportunity—about how America makes sure our bounty enriches everyone—and about our capacity as a nation to use government on behalf of community. "Opportunity" has been battered and narrowed by the cultural battles of the era but may now have gained new relevance in a time of growing income inequality and growing diversity. Within such a framework, Democrats can offer a bold policy agenda that addresses the problems that could not be seriously addressed within the political deadlock of the Two Americas. In order to break open that deadlock, Democrats must bet that they are taking up the challenges that make them the indispensable party of the future.

PART II

Half Century Untamed

1952–2002

1952
marked the beginning of a half century that no party would dominate—after the Democrats' five successive terms of control of the White House and the Republicans' seven terms, interrupted only by Woodrow Wilson. What would happen next was certainly not obvious.

This era starts off quietly enough. Brewing below the surface are many of the social and political trends that will disrupt the calm in time, but in 1952—indeed, that entire decade—Americans thought the country was headed toward greater unity and shared national purpose, not polarization and division.

New Deal politics had one last burst of electoral success in 1948, but the success foretold the end, already evident in the return of Republican control in the Congress two years earlier. Harry Truman saved the Democrats from defeat by fanning resentment against a Republican Party still tainted by the Great Depression and its opposition to the New Deal. Standing before the Democratic convention, Truman described the Democrats as "the people's party" and the Republicans as a party pursuing a "rich man's" agenda that "sticks a knife into the back of the poor."[1] His whistle-stop campaign stopped in Dexter, Iowa, where he pointed to the "cunning men" who lead the Republican Party, "the gluttons of privilege" who "believe in low prices for farmers, cheap wages for labor, and high profits for big corporations."[2] Truman won against all predictions and polls and the Democrats reclaimed the Congress with big majorities, but the end of Democratic dominance was near at hand. The party fragmented to the left and to the right, losing four Deep South states to the Dixiecrats. That would presage broader defections to Eisenhower among poorer whites, people in the border states and the growing metropolitan areas of the South, and ethnic Catholics in the cities of the North that continued through the decade.[3]

Dwight Eisenhower, a commanding wartime figure, was vigorously courted by both parties to become their presidential nominee and spoke only gingerly about the interests of party. "[No] one, late in 1951, knew whether he was even a Republican, let alone a politician," observed David Halberstam, biographer for the decade.[4] To be sure, Eisenhower accepted the Republican nomination and voiced many orthodox Republican views. He saw America as unique and the embodiment of the "dreams that men have dreamed since the dawn of history." A nation united, he stated, should give no "special rights" or "peculiar privileges" to any group. Nor should "government . . . deprive the individual of his just reward, presumably by excessive regulation or taxation."[5] But Eisenhower was elected not because he would play the partisan. He was elected primarily to bring down the curtain on the Korean War and to usher in a new play, where Americans got on with their lives and families were freed from the Depression and war. The Republicans, desperate to bring an end to the Democratic era, took the lifeline from the popular Eisenhower, buried their ideological splits, and put on their buttons, "I like Ike."

He got some help from Adlai Stevenson, the Democratic nominee for president in both national elections of the fifties, who also worked to lower the curtain. Reflecting Eisenhower and the tone of the times, Stevenson lowered the heat: "We Democrats, win or lose, can campaign not as a crusade to exterminate the opposing party . . . but as a great opportunity to educate and elevate a people whose destiny is leadership."[6] Stevenson spoke elegantly about many things, but never of "economic royalists."

The seeming calm after 1952 came, in part, because some of the most contentious issues were settled at the outset of the decade and others put off until its close. In 1950, North Korean troops caused a storm when they crossed the thirty-eighth parallel, and in 1951, Truman fired Douglas Mac-Arthur, creating his own firestorm. Senator Joe McCarthy waved his list of State Department Communists in 1950, but by 1954 McCarthyism fell suddenly into disrepute and the Senate censured him. The United States decided to contain communism and, after some debate, to build "the super," the hydrogen bomb. In fact, the presidential ticket of Dwight Eisenhower, the quintessential internationalist, and Richard Nixon, the rabid anti-Communist and ally of the Republican isolationists, brought a truce on one of the most contentious issues before the country.

Put off to the next decade were other potentially contentious issues, like the introduction of the birth control pill and the feminist critique of the role of women, which would explode the idealized suburban family, but later. What could not be put off was the challenge to segregation, though national political leaders moved ahead with extreme caution. The Montgomery, Alabama, bus boycotts brought Martin Luther King to national attention, and Governor Orval Faubus's resistance to court-ordered desegregation of the Arkansas schools forced President Eisenhower to send the 101st Airborne to

Little Rock. That galvanized the Congress to take the first modest steps and pass the first civil rights legislation since Reconstruction.

But these were small steps and both parties were reluctant to polarize politics along race lines. Adlai Stevenson, to keep the party united, urged a go-slow approach on civil rights, saying, "Further government interference with free men, free markets, free ideas, is distasteful to many people of good will." Republican platforms were bolder, and Eisenhower had expanded the role of the federal government in the face of the problem. Not surprisingly, voters at the end of the decade found no differences of importance between the two parties on race—the biggest unresolved issue facing the country.[7]

Off the table in the fifties was any challenge to the whole New Deal edifice of social insurance. While Republicans might deplore creeping socialism and call for a return to "Americanism," they swore off any challenge to the expanded role of government. In Eisenhower's first term, the Republican Congress expanded eligibility for Social Security and later, working comfortably with Sam Rayburn and Lyndon Johnson, the two Texan Democratic leaders, Congress added disability insurance and regularly raised benefits. Indeed, under the umbrella of national defense, they created the Federal-Aid Highway Act, costing a daunting $33 billion, to build 42,000 miles of roads. After the Russians launched *Sputnik,* Congress passed the National Defense Education Act to expand access to college and aid universities.[8]

The two political parties that divided control for nearly the entire decade did so civilly, it seems, as both the Democratic Party and Republican Party were held in high esteem. The legacy of this era of good feeling is the voters' warm thermometer ratings for the parties—near 65 degrees on a 100-degree scale—when pollsters began asking such questions in the first part of the 1960s.[9] At the same time, people identified more strongly with their own parties, knew better what they stood for, and less often split their tickets.[10] But when you added everything up—leaving out the South, which was in its own world—the two parties divided the country fairly evenly.[11]

With the most contentious issues displaced, consensus achieved on domestic issues, and politics generally civil, the public decided to trust their leaders. Remarkably, three-quarters believed you could always or usually trust the government in Washington to do "the right thing."[12]

Meantime, the economy burst through the three downturns, barely noticeable from our vantage point at the turn of the century. For the first two decades after World War II, real median family income was rising 2.8 percent a year while, in contrast to our times, inequality was dropping.[13] The middle class was coming on strong. *Fortune* noted that the number of families earning more than $5,000 after taxes was increasing by 1.1 million a year, and if the editors were right, half the country would be middle-class by end of the decade.[14]

They were busy raising their baby-boom children and buying homes in Levittown, appliances and television sets for their new kitchens and families, and new car models in amazing numbers.

They watched the Brooklyn Dodgers through four consecutive expectant seasons, only to lose the National League pennant twice in the last inning of the last game and the World Series twice to the New York Yankees. But Jackie Robinson, an "uncompromising ebony," was the "cynosure of all eyes," Roger Kahn observed from the press box. "Amid twenty snowy mountains, the only moving thing was the eye of a blackbird." Robinson, he wrote, "had intimidating skills, and he burned with a dark fire." It was Robinson who survived and the Southerners who backed off.[15]

On television, they watched "a wonderfully antiseptic world of idealized homes in an idealized, unflawed America," Halberstam writes. "There were no economic crises, no class divisions or resentments, no ethnic tensions, few if any hyphenated Americans, few if any minority characters." You watched the untroubled lives of the Nelsons on *Ozzie and Harriet* or the humorous travails of Lucy and Desi or the Honeymooners. Things became contentious when Ed Sullivan, guardian of public tastes, decided that Elvis Presley's body gyrations were too suggestive and refused to put him on Sunday night television. But Steve Allen did, forcing Sullivan to back down. "The old order had been challenged and had not held," Halberstram observes. "New forces were at work . . ."[16]

The retirement of the wartime president brought the time-out to an end and brought the first real national election of this new era, 1960. And guess what? The parties stood at parity. John F. Kennedy won enough Electoral College votes, 303 to 219, to settle the election, but his popular margin was a scant 118,574 votes, much less than Al Gore's margin in 2000. A cloud hung over the voting in Chicago and Texas, where Mayor Richard Daley and Lyndon Johnson worked assiduously for their candidate. There were recounts in Illinois and New Jersey.[17] When the dust settled, 1960 had brought a historic high turnout of 64.5 percent, but Kennedy was a minority, 49.7-percent president. In his memoir, speechwriter Richard Goodwin wrote, "The numbers yield only one certainty: From the beginning to end the election was a tie." The whole "extravagant exercise" was meant "to keep from losing votes, to forestall the abandonment of those unmeasurable numbers whose preferences—volatile, ambivalent, liquid—might shift under the slightest pressure of . . . what?"[18] And thus 1960, the first national election of the period, gave us a taste of Florida circa 2000 and what the politics of parity can mean.

Given the presumptions of our history and the great opportunity created by the absent party hegemony, the two major parties would vie to dominate the times. How could they do otherwise? Three bold political thrusts sought to create enduring electoral majorities and to dominate the thinking of the times—the efforts of the Opportunity Democrats, the Reagan Revolutionaries, and the Reformed Opportunity Democrats. Each won power but then faltered in a few short years, contributing to the chasm running through the Two Americas.

Chapter 2

THE OPPORTUNITY DEMOCRATS:

Redefined by Race

Whan John Kennedy sought the presidency in 1960, it was not obvious that he and his running mate, Lyndon Johnson, aspired to remake fundamentally the partisan political landscape or to dominate an era. They certainly wanted to win the White House and keep Richard Nixon out. Kennedy ran under the banner of change, a message that became incendiary only in light of the tumult that was to follow. He represented a new generation that would supplant the aging Eisenhower administration and get the country moving. He offered an aspiration for a dynamic America that would be greeted with cheers, not jeers, as Nixon faced in Latin America. Kennedy decried the so-called missile gap, symbolic of America falling behind the Soviet Union in technology and education. And he promised to get the economy moving after the Republicans' three recessions. In the now historic Kennedy-Nixon debate, Kennedy zeroed in on the change theme: "This is a great country but I think it could be a greater country." Highlighting the unused capacity in the steel industry and lowest economic growth rate among industrial nations, he declared, "I'm not satisfied."[1]

The Democrats' prospects rose and fell on a number of developments that were very specific to that election: Eisenhower's prediction of "the most prosperous year in our history," followed shortly by the recession;[2] a "missile gap" that never existed; a heated debate over Quemoy and Matsu, two islands never heard of again but important for showing a sense of proportion about nuclear weapons; the Catholic vote for Kennedy and the very considerable anti-Catholic vote as well.

Whom you could trust to deal firmly with the Soviet Union but also forestall a nuclear nightmare was central to the choice in 1960. Kennedy challenged voters at the end of the campaign to imagine a president "in the thick of the fight," to be sure, "who not only prevented war but won the peace."[3] Indeed, on his watch, Kennedy is most identified with managing a nuclear crisis and achieving an agreement to end nuclear testing. He set the stage for a détente that would get the world through the Cold War. However important that was historically and to our survival, it is not clear that these positions took the party beyond what Roosevelt and Truman had already established with the public.

On the other hand, the Kennedy campaign highlighted other issues and ideas that history would take over and ultimately make powerful, defining principles in the work of what I call the Opportunity Democrats. Kennedy accepted for America an obligation to ensure that all have the opportunity to share in our way of life, from the poor to the new middle class; he expressed a faith in our capacity to use government as an instrument of change and community, to face modern challenges and manage our economic growth; he accepted that discrimination must end and that equal rights must be extended to all groups, starting with black Americans; and facing the world, he sought greater partnership based on new respect for the reality of a changing America.

The most explicit and most enduring principle for the Democrats was the theme that America's prosperity should be inclusive and not leave anyone behind. In his final speech of the campaign, Kennedy asked the citizenry to vote for someone for president who "cares deeply about the people he represents" and wants them "to share in the benefits of our abundance and natural resources."[4] In his inaugural address, that principle broke through national boundaries and became a universal idea: "If a free society cannot help the many who are poor, it cannot save the few who are rich."[5] That principle joined the Alliance for Progress abroad and the new attention given to poverty in America.

That is very different from the political project of the New Deal Democrats who sought to lift up the whole country from its Depression—one produced by the malice and greed of a few.

Influenced even before his presidency by John Kenneth Galbraith's *The Affluent Society* and during it by Michael Harrington's *The Other America* and other works on the hidden poor, Kennedy determined to attack the poignant polarities that come with rising prosperity but that underscore our shortcomings. The intense attention to poverty and the underprivileged came with the nomination of Kennedy in 1960, not Johnson in 1964.[6] Kennedy gave a high priority to raising the minimum wage, introducing government health insurance for the elderly, and attacking poverty in the cities and in Appalachia. In a conversation with Walter Heller, his chief economic adviser, Kennedy intended to take two- and three-day trips to poverty-stricken areas to "rouse the American conscience" as part of a "campaign to break the cycle of poverty in which so many elderly and minority Americans lived."[7]

While the tales of those left behind were a motivating principle for the Kennedy presidency, it was always tempered by a determination to keep the emerging middle class invested in the Democrats. Kennedy told Heller to "make clear that we're doing something for the middle-income man in the suburbs as well."[8] A White House planning meeting for the 1964 campaign that started with a discussion of the severe poverty of eastern Kentucky gave way, under prodding from Richard Scammon, then director of the census, to a focus on the new upwardly mobile families in the suburbs.[9]

In part, that is why Medicare was probably the highest public priority in Kennedy's domestic agenda. Medical insurance for seniors would have broad effect, and Kennedy referenced it in almost every campaign speech in 1960. The administration sent the bill to the Congress in 1962 and, despite Cuba, Berlin, and other international crises, organized Medicare rallies in thirty cities, with a final one at Madison Square Garden, televised by the three national networks.[10]

Kennedy championed with great eloquence a second principle: collectively, as a country and people, with government as our tool, we have the capacity to do great things. Thus was the call of his inaugural, "For man holds in his mortal hands the power to abolish all forms of human poverty and all forms of human life." But his call was to man's better nature, "to struggle against the common enemies of man: tyranny, poverty, disease and war itself."[11]

That principle translated into the federal government taking on greater responsibility for projects necessary to the welfare of the country—raising education levels, expanding the transportation system, addressing urbanization, achieving economic growth. But it also included the Apollo program to land a man on the moon.

The urgency for Kennedy was the Cold War and the importance that people and countries across the globe look to America. "I want people in Latin America and Africa and Asia to start to look to America," Kennedy told Nixon during the debate. "I think in the final analysis it depends upon what we do here. I think it's time America started moving again."[12]

That principle also translated more concretely into a confidence that government could manage the economy to avoid recession and inflation and produce high growth and employment. In retrospect, that seems like an ordinary enough idea, but at the time it conflicted with the orthodox thinking about deficits and the thinking of conservative Republicans and Southern Democrats in control of the Congress. Franklin Roosevelt had affirmed the progressive shift from antimonopoly economics to a Keynesian one even before the war, but even the success of wartime deficit spending did not break down the conventional wisdom about deficits among the politicians.[13] But Keynesian ideas underlay the four questions Kennedy posed to Walter Heller before asking him to head the president's Council of Economic Advisers—the first, "Could government action achieve a 5 percent growth rate?" and the last, "Could a tax cut be an important economic stimulus?" When Heller and other economists later pushed for tax cuts, lower interest rates, and deficit spending to avoid an impending downturn, Dwight Eisenhower came out of retirement to condemn the principle. Kennedy proposed the tax cuts, which were his highest priority in 1963, not the civil rights bill, and Johnson ultimately enacted both.[14]

The last principle of the Kennedy presidency is no doubt the most enduring for the Democratic Party and the one that produced the most electoral tumult—the right of black Americans to enjoy equal rights with white Americans and, more broadly, the universal idea that no group could be discriminated against or denied the rights that would enable them to enjoy the American way of life. Kennedy did not rush to make this the centerpiece of his campaign or presidency. Many urban Democratic machines worked very hard to win the "Negro vote" in the North, but the campaign offered no bold initiatives on addressing the building civil rights crisis. After considerable debate within the campaign, Kennedy phoned Coretta Scott King, the pregnant wife of civil rights leader Martin Luther King, then in jail in rural Georgia, just two weeks before the election, which sent a powerful signal. But even Robert Kennedy warned that he did not want any more "bomb throwers" making it more difficult to win.[15]

The president's much-quoted inaugural address does not mention civil rights, and the administration did not prioritize the issue. Indeed, before the 1962 midterm congressional elections, he delayed issuing an executive order barring discrimination in federal housing programs and told his advisers to keep him out of "this Goddamned civil rights mess."[16] After the elections, he signed the executive order, but Lou Harris, Kennedy's informal pollster, warned that 1962 had brought slippage in "pivotal industrial states" and among blue-collar Catholics, including the Irish, who were more con-servative, seeing few economic gains, and who were not sympathetic to black demands. In 1963, while the country was at a boil over race, Kennedy was trying to pass his tax cuts to avoid a slowdown but was running into growing resistance from Southern Democrats opposed to federal deficits.[17]

But as evident in the State of the Union Address in 1963, the president began stating a clearer and clearer principle. The right to vote, "the most precious and powerful right in the world," must "not be denied to any citizen on grounds of his race or color."[18] And with rising violence in Birmingham in that year and the confrontation between the federal and state govern-ments over the admission of a black student at the University of Alabama, Kennedy moved up to a moral high ground as he asked for comprehensive civil rights legislation. In a televised address to the nation, Kennedy stated, "We are confronted primarily with a moral issue. It is as old as the Scrip-tures and is as clear as the American Constitution. The heart of the ques-tion is whether all Americans are to be afforded equal rights and equal opportunities." On this night, Kennedy extended the inclusive principle to African Americans: "[This] Nation, for all its hopes and all its boasts, will not be fully free until all its citizens are free." So "now the time has come for this Nation to fulfill its promise."[19]

The civil rights bill, along with most of Kennedy's legislative priorities, remained stuck in the Congress, especially in the face of Southern resis-tance. In the queue was health insurance for seniors; poverty legislation; a redevelopment and housing bill; federal support for elementary, secondary, and higher education; an increase in the minimum wage; the tax cut and tax reform; and civil rights legislation to guarantee the right to vote, bar discrimination in public accommodations, and expand the federal govern-ment's role in enforcing court-ordered school desegregation.[20] According to Theodore Sorensen, Kennedy was already looking to a second term, with a larger majority in the Congress, when he could achieve "far-reaching break-throughs to meet the modern problems of automation, transportation, ur-banization, cultural opportunity and economic growth." The prospect of reduced international tensions and military spending "would enable him to devote a larger share of expenditure increases to domestic and particularly urban needs."[21]

While Kennedy might not have been as expansive as Johnson, after Goldwater's defeat, it is fair to say, Robert Dallek concludes, that the "most important of the Great Society measures deserves to be described as Kennedy-Johnson achievements."[22]

But when President Lyndon Johnson took up this agenda in 1963, the same issues were reinterpreted within the cauldron of America's racial upheaval. For all the aspiration to keep it inclusive and to address middle-class needs as well, opportunity soon meant racial equality. It is hard to imagine how America could have overturned its racial past without such a redefinition, but the Texan decided to embrace it with a Johnson-like hug.

At the outset of his term, Lyndon Johnson spoke for the country, backed by a majority of both parties in the Congress, declaring racial discrimination unlawful and equal rights unstoppable. Johnson broke the Southern grip on the Congress and the Constitution, enabling the president to sign the Civil Rights Act of 1964 and give the country the last word on racial discrimination: "Our Constitution, the foundation of our republic, forbids it. The principles of our freedom forbid it. Morality forbids it. And the law I will sign tonight forbids it." With the passage of the Voting Rights Act of 1965, again with bipartisan support, Johnson could deliver the last word on this new but now sacred right. So whatever else happens in the history of this tumultuous period, the Opportunity Democrats will have addressed one of America's biggest historic challenges and changed forever the presumptions about rights and opportunities.

Before the elections, President Johnson went before the graduates at the University of Michigan to expand this national commitment to civil rights into an aspiration for a "Great Society," a higher national purpose. As his speechwriter Richard Goodwin would later recall, "Johnson and I, and the rest of Washington were not just officers of government. We were citizens of the age." The aspiration grew from the moment being created by civil rights protests, but also student activism and the new feminism. But Johnson decided to make the Democrats' political project about opportunity the common sense of the times and lay the basis for a new majority.[23]

In May 1964, the graduates in Ann Arbor applauded and later cheered his call to create a Great Society. The capacity of government, rhetorically empowered by Kennedy, achieved a new scope in Johnson's hands. "The Great Society . . . demands an end to poverty and racial injustice," and it demands we take up an array of challenges that leave our country short of its aspiration for greatness. Central cities are in "decay"; "open land is vanishing"; "there is not enough housing"; "the water we drink, the food we eat, the very air we breathe, are threatened with pollution." In education, 8 million adult Americans had not finished five years of school, and 100,000 high school graduates "of proven ability" failed to enter college for lack of funds.

Johnson underscored that the social energy of the Opportunity Democrats comes from an unwillingness to settle for mere prosperity: "There are those timid souls who say . . . we are condemned to a soulless wealth. I do not agree. We have the power to shape civilization. . . . Your generation

[has] the chance . . . to help build a society where the demands of morality, and the needs of the spirit can be realized in the life of the nation." And then he asked, "Will you join in the battle to give every citizen the full equality which God enjoins and the law requires . . . ?"[24]

In the election of 1964, the country repudiated the conservative Republican nominee, Barry Goldwater, who rejected not only the emerging norms on racial discrimination and civil rights, but the whole edifice. The country seemed for a brief moment to affirm the national project on opportunity, promoted by an expansive federal government. Through the end of 1965, large majorities of the public supported his legislation on civil rights, Medicare, aid to education, and the war on poverty. Over 60 percent approved of the job he was doing as president.

But what began as an isolated riot in Watts in 1965 turned into an urban insurrection that spread to 43 cities, and then to 164 cities in 1967, and after the assassination of Martin Luther King in 1968, to every American city. Black power leaders competed now with civil rights leaders. Court-ordered school busing plans in the North supplanted the school desegregation battles in the South.[25] Busing, Thomas and Mary Edsall observed, "transformed the politics of city after city" because it made clear that "the new liberal agenda would demand some of the largest changes in habit and custom from the working-class residents of low- and moderate-income enclaves within the big city."[26] The Democrats' big opportunity project, they now understood, did not include them.

For Johnson, with his eyes focused clearly on the goal, that exclusion seemed incidental. When battling to win passage of the Voting Rights Act, he went on television, peered directly into the camera, and said, "We shall overcome"—and thus fully identified his presidency with the struggle for civil rights. Then, in a speech at Howard University, he went farther and declared that "negro poverty is not white poverty" and the gulf separating blacks from whites had formed "another nation." For America, Johnson declared, the goal of opportunity must now become a commitment to racial equality, with almost no tolerance for falling short: "We seek not just legal equity, but human equality, not just equality as a right and a theory but equality as a fact and equality as a result."[27] In practice, the social programs created by the Johnson administration focused primarily on the poor, particularly poor blacks.[28] The great majority of the new federal spending went to programs for the elderly, but in either case the Opportunity Democrats gave a powerful impetus for the idea that government will miss "the middle," defined "in both a socioeconomic and a generational sense."[29]

The national majority for the vision of the Opportunity Democrats disappeared almost before it existed. By 1966, a majority now concluded that the federal government was overreaching on civil rights, which was reflected in the midterm congressional elections. The Republicans picked up 8 governorships, including Ronald Reagan's victory in California; doubled their number of state legislators in the South; gained a net 47 seats in the House; and picked three new senators in the South.[30] By 1967, well over 60 percent of the country thought that Johnson had gone "too far" and fewer than 20 percent approved of the job being done in the "war on poverty."[31]

It was Governor George Wallace of Alabama who exposed the deep fractures and disillusionment of the Democrats' traditional blue-collar supporters with their exclusion from the mission of the government and the times. It fell to him, not Richard Nixon, to lead the attack on the liberal intellectuals who made others feel guilty because of their prosperity and who were "destroying" the ever more expansive federal government, "trifling" with children, and intent on social engineering at the expense of the working people of the country.

Wallace had sent up warning flares in 1964 in the Wisconsin, Indiana, and Maryland primaries, but in 1968, he took his case to the white Catholic suburbs in the primaries, challenged the unions, and then ran as an independent. "I think that if the politicians get in the way in 1968," Wallace declared, they "are going to get run over by the average man in the street, this man in the textile mill, this man in the steel mill, this barber, the beautician, the policeman on the beat."

Wallace battled the Democrats' traditional union supporters right on the shop floor. There were plenty of warning signs that the members were responding to Wallace's call to the common man. A quarter of the AFL-CIO members polled in Pennsylvania were for Wallace and, in Flint, Michigan, where the sit-down strikes were memorialized in labor history, the members of UAW Local 326 at GM endorsed Wallace.[32]

The Republicans' strategy was not to offer an alternative vision, but instead, in Spiro Agnew's quaint words, to contribute to "a positive polarization of the electorate." He aligned the Republican ticket with the "silent majority" and the Democrats with the "radical liberals." Richard Nixon, for his part, was to champion issues that sent the signals to the disillusioned Democrats, the "forgotten Americans." He was for "law and order" against the disorder of the times. He warned of the "violence and fear, which pervades this nation and its cities today." With the polls showing Humphrey closing fast in the final weeks, Nixon's campaign ran ads interspersing shots of Humphrey with scenes of shouting protestors, soldiers, body bags, and porches of blue-collar America. But Nixon was on message in the ads, promising "to rebuild a respect for law across this country" and "recognize the first civil right of every American"—"to be safe from domestic violence." To the end in the campaign, he opposed new civil rights laws and school busing, which he described as "a new evil . . . disrupting communities and imposing hardship on children—black and white."[33]

The goal, Nixon's strategists understood, was to "align" the Democrats with "Negro demands," which the Democrats had already taken on as a historic task, but to make it exclusionary, to make the Democrats a "Negro party." The Republicans need only qualify as understanding observers to the political turmoil.[34]

While Humphrey nearly passed Nixon on Election Day, the result was an awe-inspiring collapse, compared to Johnson's high-water mark in 1964.[35] Humphrey took less than 43 percent of the vote, a fall of 18 points. The majority of Americans voted for candidates who opposed the Great Society: 43 percent for Nixon and 14 percent for Wallace.

The Democratic collapse, according to Kevin Phillips, Nixon's chief electoral analyst and later social critic, was most pronounced among downscale, lower-middle-class voters: manual workers (down 21 points from the 1964 high), farmers (down 24 points), and high school graduates (down 20 points). In 1964, only 21 percent of Catholics had voted for Goldwater, but in 1968, 37 percent voted for Nixon. Below the Mason-Dixon Line, Phillips points out, "Hubert Humphrey was annihilated," taking less than 20 percent of the white vote, and so was the national Democratic Party. In 1972, Nixon would take 78 percent of the white Southern vote.[36]

Wallace obviously ran strong in the South, carrying five Deep South states that had been looking elsewhere for some bulwark against integration and doing particularly well among poorer whites. But nationwide Wallace took his campaign to the working-class base of the Democrats, carrying 13 percent of those without college degrees and 15 percent of manual workers. Among white union households, Nixon took 42 percent of the vote and Wallace won 15 percent (including 22 percent of white union members themselves), leaving Humphrey with an embarrassing 43 percent in the core of the organized downscale electorate. In 1972, Nixon's union vote would climb to 60 percent, leaving the Democrats' proud labor history in tatters.

African Americans knew that the polarization was about them, and 90 percent voted for the Democrats—recognition of the historic task the Democrats took on for the country. But this was a labor of love, as Democrats, despite the crash, built their identity around a racially defined opportunity agenda that won them support among African Americans but also among intellectuals and the best educated. The party's 1972 platform trumpeted rather than muted that identity, endorsing school busing and calling for "enacting new legal rights" to achieve "a more equal distribution of power, income and wealth."[37]

As we shall see in the later chapters, the racial polarization of the parties and the attempt to use the federal government to achieve equality for the least privileged set in motion an unprecedented political migration, leaving the land strewn with political refugees.

But for all that, the country did not repudiate the broad direction that Kennedy and Johnson sought for the country. Today, conservatives view the 1968 and 1972 elections as a repudiation of liberalism. But no matter how short-lived the reign of the Opportunity Democrats, their political leadership on civil rights changed social attitudes then and for the rest of the century. Support for the principle of blacks and whites attending the same schools has risen continuously since the Supreme Court decision in 1954, but support rose noticeably after 1968, when the voters surely turned against its political proponents. After 1968, the country increasingly opposed segregation in housing and laws barring interracial marriages.[38] Similarly, the public never quite drew back from a more expansive, regulatory role for the state to achieve other social goods, like a clean environment. Here, 70 to 90 percent of the public, depending on the area of environmental threat, favored increased controls, barely diminished by the deregulation initiatives of the 1970s, '80s, and '90s.[39]

The Opportunity Democrats' political project moved the country to a different place on race, rights, and diversity, which would be enlarged over the coming decades to encompass the changing role for women and immigrant minorities. It left citizens with the idea that, from time to time, they have the capacity to use government to engineer social change. But the growing force of these ideas on rights and inclusiveness and diversity and government, without a sustained Democratic political ascendancy, ultimately contributes powerfully to the unresolved cultural divide and the Two Americas.

Chapter 3

THE REAGAN REVOLUTIONARIES:

Reduced to Culture War

The conservative Republicans would make the second bold attempt to dominate the politics of this untamed era. Ultimately, it was Ronald Reagan's revolution, as only he offered an authentic claim on hegemony, but he was preceded by two leaders and a movement that changed the party and the electoral equation.

Barry Goldwater's failed run for the presidency in 1964 offered a libertarian's skepticism of government and an economic conservative's faith in free markets. He contributed a patriot's instinct to use American power, free of international constraints. He produced virtually the first Republican gains in the deepest of the Deep South states, and ultimately and perhaps most important, he delivered the ground troops that would storm the liberal fortress in the 1980s.

But in Barry Goldwater's hands, the first conservative foray before the nation scared people to death, expressed in his meager 39 percent of the vote. He carried only 16 congressional districts outside the South, and the Democrats ended up with two-to-one majorities in both the House and Senate.[1] But Goldwater's marker was a "conservative conscience" that is "pricked by anyone who would debase the dignity of the individual human being." He called for an uncompromising individualism that requires a revolution against government: "I do not undertake to promote welfare for I propose to extend freedom. My aim is not to pass laws, but to repeal them." Later, he would propose a 5 percent a year tax cut for five years, a 25 percent tax reduction. His conscience also calls on conservatives to support an uncompromised opposition to the most statist regime of all, the Soviet Union, where he challenged the United States to "not regard Mr. Khrushchev's murderous claque as the legitimate rulers of the Russian people or any other people." For Goldwater, that meant getting out from under the "balance of terror" by developing more usable nuclear weapons.[2]

On the idea front, Goldwater gave new life to the *National Review*'s attack on "humanism," "egalitarianism," and "utopianism," as Rick Perlstein described it in *Before the Storm*—the magazine's explicit repudiation of Kennedy and his attempt to empower "man" with a sense of capacity for change. At the grassroots level, Goldwater set things aflame. He created space for minutemen who called for armed vigilance against socialism. He inspired many thousands who joined John Wayne, Jimmy Stewart, and Roy Rogers for Dr. Fred Schwarz's Christian Anti-Communist Crusade in the Hollywood Bowl. But he also inspired the conservative youth who would join the Young Americans for Freedom and the Republicans' Operation Dixie, which *Time* called the "furrow-browed, button-down, college-trained amateurs who, one by one, took control of the state parties. . . ."[3] The Republicans carried five Southern states.

But at the same time, Goldwater sought to bring down Social Security, the progressive income tax, and farm subsidies, without offering people a route to progress and prosperity. He proposed to unravel bipartisan consensus on civil rights and on the use of nuclear weapons. He frightened America and marginalized the conservative ideological project.[4]

More important, the rejection of his form of conservatism gave the Opportunity Democrats a mandate to use government and expand rights. The narrow and racial form of that opportunity project was rejected in a short time, but the public continued to support the big social insurance programs, environmental and consumer regulation, and an ever-expanding application of equal rights—elaborated over the next two decades.

Richard Nixon was also predicate to the conservative revolution, but he was not a part of it. He fanned the flames, kept the country focused on disorder and race, and put forward a Republican face that was welcoming to disaffected Catholics, blue-collar workers, and white Baptists of the Southern countryside. Arguably, the only areas where Nixon was genuinely conservative were civil rights and crime, where his administration intervened to slow school busing and school desegregation plans and where Nixon himself repeatedly pressed his staff to adopt the hardest line possible on civil rights.[5] Even here, the federal government proceeded with deseg-regation plans in the South and developed the Philadelphia Plan to speed integration of the building trades in the North.[6]

In nearly every other area, Nixon affirmed the public policy instincts that he had inherited from the Democrats, going back to Johnson, Kennedy, and Roosevelt. Rather than advancing the conservative thrust in American politics, he helped legitimate the expansive, liberal state, from social spend-ing to regulation. Whether from a lack of ideological proclivity, over-learned lessons from Goldwater, or a tactical desire to put no barrier in the way of defecting blue-collar and Southern Democrats, the result was the same: expansive government, unchallenged.

On the simplest measure, government spending, Nixon remained an apostle in a different movement. He personally rejected attempts by his own administration to cut the federal budget, and indeed, with the 1972 election approaching, he presided over a massive 20 percent increase in Social Security benefits and accelerated federal spending to minimize un-employment. By 1974, Nixon administration spending for social programs was 58 percent above what Lyndon Johnson had proposed for the Great Society.[7]

Nixon's signature domestic initiatives were not tax cuts and deregula-tion, but a family-assistance plan and general revenue sharing with the states. The former was not a proposal to abolish "welfare as we know it," à la Gingrich and Clinton, but a proposal by liberals in the administration to modernize the welfare state. The latter offered a "new federalism," paid for with $30 billion of new spending, not tax cuts.[8] With the prospect that Ted Kennedy might be the Democratic presidential nominee in 1972, Nixon proposed a family health insurance plan that guaranteed every American health insurance benefits.[9]

With a lot of help from the Democratic Congress, Nixon presided over perhaps the greatest era of regulation since the early New Deal: clean air and water, consumer and workplace safety, and women's rights. Up against the pressures of growing inflation, big wage settlements in major industries, and a world monetary crisis, Richard Nixon, the Republican, opted for na-tional wage and price controls. Nixon topped every other postwar president on the number of new statutes and new agencies created to regulate busi-ness.[10]

We now know Richard Nixon better, and he was no conservative by current standards. Based on his frank comments to his inner circle of ad-visers and supporters, he was surely a racist and an anti-Semite, but those hardly qualify him as a conservative.[11]

That leaves the revolution to Ronald Reagan, whose conservative convictions and vision for America allowed Republicans to aspire to something grander for this era. Looking back through the decades, it is easy to re-create an instinctive popularity for Reagan, but it did not come so easily. Jimmy Carter had to play his part, as well as the Ayatollah Khomeini and John Anderson, the independent candidate who took Democratic votes on the Equal Rights Amendment, the draft, and gun control. With voters worried until late in the campaign that Reagan might take America to war, Reagan won with only 50.7 percent of the popular vote. In 1982, his popularity headed down with the recession and along with it Republican congressional fortunes—as 26 seats swung from Republican to Democratic in the House.

But with the same easy assurance that he displayed all his adult life, Reagan remained steadfast in his worldview. Drawing upon multiple strands of conservative thinking and his own re-created and idealized biography, he offered a positive conservative vision that made the Republicans more than a vessel for the disaffected. Indeed, it made possible both a broadened coalition and a strengthened bond with Republican voters. Reagan accepted Goldwater's starting point: honor the individual and the entrepreneur; decry big government and taxes. But to move beyond Goldwater, the Reagan Revolutionaries had to turn the conservative mantra against government, taxes, liberal elites, and communism into a vision that would advance the nation and the well-being of citizens.

The Reagan political project has four key elements that, if advanced successfully, allowed the Republicans to dream of bigger things, even dominating our times. First, it would honor business, the entrepreneur, and markets and make the case that their good fortune would apply generally to the entire country. Reagan would be the first successful conservative to speak unapologetically about the concept of "trickle down." Businessmen, after all, are the wealth and job creators. And while this ran up against the barriers of appearance and plausibility, Reagan broke down many of them by his own accessibility and common man qualities.

Second, tax cuts had to become mythic in scale—big and inescapable, year after year—and the core policy for relieving financial pressure on families and achieving a broad prosperity for the country. But taxes would also become the central focus of Reagan's morality play. He would slap the hand of the federal "tax spender" in order to free the money and get it back to the "taxpayer" where it belonged. That would allow Reagan to scorn the liberal elites and bureaucrats and to side with the working people who were uninterested in the government's crazy social engineering.

Third, Reagan and his revolutionaries would align with faith and the religious communities that were embattled before rising modernism, secularism, and social permissiveness. They would legitimate, as Goldwater and

Nixon never did, the rising evangelical call to elevate politics to advance Christ's teachings and protect their faith against the courts and government. By acknowledging the turmoil, affirming God's proper role, and siding with the embattled family, Reagan took the conservative revolution deep into the life of working-class neighborhoods and small towns and farm communities across the country.

And fourth, with Carter's foreign policy humiliations near at hand, the Reagan Revolutionaries committed themselves to "bring America back." Impatient with America's softness, the liberal establishment's conventional wisdom, and the UN's hostility to the United States, they were determined to make America militarily stronger than any other nation, able to act in our own interests and willing to confront the Soviet Union with our unshakable faith in freedom. They hearken to perhaps less-complicated times, when America could dispel despots and conquer tyranny, unconstrained by the moral compromises that seem second nature in Europe and international forums.

These elements brought the prospect of genuine hegemony. These interwoven ideas proved relevant and expansive enough to convince a growing majority of Catholic working-class voters in the North, virtually all white people in the South, but particularly the Evangelicals, small and big businessmen, and the most economically privileged that there was both advantage and hope in the Reagan Revolution. It allowed people for a short time to blur the distinction between their individual advantage and the nation's welfare.

FROM TAX CUTS TO TOP-DOWN PROSPERITY[12]

Ronald Reagan drew his inspiration more from Herbert Hoover and Calvin Coolidge than from the Republican postwar presidents and conservative candidates. John Gerring thinks the main inspiration was Hoover and the themes, "neo-liberal."[13] Based on Reagan's actions moments after he took office, there is a stronger case for Coolidge. Reagan had the White House curator remove the portraits of Jefferson and Truman from the cabinet room across from the Oval Office and put up the portrait of Calvin Coolidge. For Reagan, Coolidge offered a confident vision about business, investment, and prosperity that had been lost to the country now for some five decades:

"If you go back, I don't know if the country has ever had a higher level of prosperity than it did under Coolidge. And he actually reduced the national debt, he cut taxes several times across the board. And maybe the criticism was . . . that [he wasn't] activist enough. Well, maybe there's a lesson in that. Maybe we've had instances of government being too active, intervening, interfering." He failed to note that Coolidge's "across-the-board" tax cuts gave breaks to just 2 percent of the population, but he was confident that such policies would bring a general prosperity. Reagan also failed to take note of the crash and Depression that had followed the speculative boom of the 1920s, which left that brand of Republicanism in disrepute and barely talked about above a whisper for over two decades. Those historic realities were, for Reagan and many Americans, less important than "the faith."[14]

Reagan reached out to ordinary people: he touched them first with his essential honesty and then with his heartfelt proposal to lift their financial burden by cutting tax rates. He sought to restore faith in the market and in entrepreneurship in order to allow people once again to believe that American business could lead America to a new age of growth and prosperity. For a moment, it all seemed quite magical; it was, as the 1984 campaign ad suggested, "morning in America."

Ronald Reagan understood better than establishment Republicanism that a top-down view of the world could win broad support in society only if business was honored and valued. Businessmen had to be seen as the creators of wealth and jobs, the engines of growth. McKinley and Coolidge understood that business and industrial prestige and leadership were the best counter to populist assaults on the market and Democratic claims to represent the people, and Reagan planned to follow their lead.

From 1954 to 1962, Reagan had been the host of *General Electric Theater,* and as such he promoted not only appliances but also the notion of capitalism and progress. Reagan threw himself into the promotion, visiting all 135 GE plants and offering his vision of a nation in which business would be free to create a richer life for everybody.[15] In his post-GE period, Reagan associated himself not with the big corporations in the East and the industrial Midwest but the Sun Belt entrepreneurs. This newer brand of capitalist was more individualistic and entrepreneurial, more self-confident about his new wealth and social role.

As president, Ronald Reagan gave voice to a romanticized view of business long absent from the political debate. The president of the United States now fully identified wealth as a positive good for everyone in society. He passed on to all who would listen a kind of bible of the new ethic, George Gilder's *Wealth and Poverty.* Gilder scorned defenders of capitalism who apologized for its values and expressed ambivalence about its ends.

The starting point for Gilder (and Reagan) was the entrepreneur: "creative" and courageous, willing to face danger and "radical perils and uncertainties" and "fight." The possibilities for investment, production, and growth lie in the liberation of the entrepreneur. The entrepreneur is the "creative center of the system."[16]

The role of the entrepreneur was at the core of supply-side Reaganomics, which asserted confidently that tax cuts for the wealthy and business would bring economic growth and a general prosperity. This assertion required a lot of faith. As David Stockman explained, "It's kind of hard to sell 'trickle down,' so the supply-side formula was the only way to get a tax policy that was really 'trickle down.' " Since the "means of production" are located within the entrepreneurial world, Gilder argued, freeing business and the wealthy from taxes frees money for investment and growth. In the end, "the benefits of capitalism still depend on capitalists."[17]

But it was not ideas in the first instance but the spectacular economic recovery of 1983 to 1985 that gave reality to Reagan's economic vision: 12.3 percent real growth in the economy and a steady decline in unemployment, from the recessionary high near 10 percent to 7.5 percent in 1984 and below 7 percent in 1986.[18] That Reagan's prospects rose and fell so directly with the economy's fortunes suggests a little caution when concluding that Reagan's conservative ideas account for his high standing with the public.

But Reagan's sunny economics also gained force against the gloomy backdrop of Jimmy Carter. Peggy Noonan underscored the power of the contrast: "There was no Reagan without Carter."[19]

Still, at the heart of his vision was apparent contradiction: the interests of ordinary people would be advanced by a policy that begins by helping the most privileged. He overcame the tension, at least in the short term, by associating himself with ordinary Americans on a number of fronts: his "everyman" style, his low regard for big government and welfare, his hostility to taxes, and his expressions of faith.

Reagan had a special window on Middle America because he represented so many of its idealized remembrances. As a young man, he had cleaned up at his mother's church and had worked as a lifeguard in Dixon, Illinois; his father was fired on Christmas Eve during the Depression, only to be saved by Roosevelt's New Deal; Reagan joined a dry fraternity at Eureka College, hitchhiked to Chicago to look for a job in radio, and became a sportscaster, making up all the action off a ticker; he went to Hollywood and put his happy innocence on-screen.

"He was the wholesome citizen-hero," biographer Lou Cannon writes, "an Everyman who was slow to anger but willing to fight for the right and correct wrongdoing when aroused." He played the role of citizen with innocence and honesty, without a touch of meanness, challenging the bullies above all, the Establishment and bureaucrats who make life miserable for ordinary people.[20]

He told people from his days with GE to his time in the White House that "government does not solve problems, it subsidizes them."[21] But in his campaign for reelection in 1984, he underscored the dysfunctions of government that stood against the progress he was trying to achieve for the country. "The power of the federal government," he would point out in his reelection stump speech, "had, over the decades, created great chaos—economic chaos, social chaos." He could not resist, whether on the campaign trail or meeting with foreign leaders, telling the story of a Chicago "welfare queen" with multiple identities, Social Security cards, and non-existent deceased husbands.[22]

His instrument to bring government down to size was tax cutting, which could get Reagan an audience among Catholics and suburban Southern whites who were financially pressed but resentful of government. Indeed, the tax revolt caught up to Ronald Reagan, who had for years warned of the evils of the federal income tax and preached the simple gospel of lower taxes and a smaller, less obtrusive federal government. Whether it was a talk to a clutch of GE factory workers, a nomination speech for Goldwater's presidential bid, a debate with Walter Mondale, or inaugurations in Sacramento and Washington, Reagan found his voice on taxes: this money belonged properly to the people. You could feel his personal indignation. Lower taxes along with reduced federal spending, reduced regulation, and more military defense formed his center as president. That was Reaganism and Reagonomics.[23]

Part of the allure of the Reagan vision was that, in the end, it did not require any sacrifice or hard choices. Reagan did not rein in domestic social spending and never touched Social Security. When David Stockman, the too-outspoken head of the Office of Management and Budget, proposed raising the retirement age, a unanimous Senate and, ultimately, the president repudiated the idea. For the country, the alternative was spiraling budget deficits and the firing of Stockman, who described the budget as "economic Dunkirk," but that was the price they were apparently willing to pay for their vision.[24]

FROM REAGAN'S FAITH TO THE TWO AMERICAS

Ronald Reagan's expressions of faith were long-standing and simple enough, usually just affirming that we are subject to "a higher law" or, after being shot in an unsuccessful assassination attempt, "God must have been on my side." They did not stop him from signing into law California's liberal abortion legislation, putting him on the sidelines for at least one of the first big battles of the emerging cultural war. As president, he did not speak often about the issue, and his administration committed few resources to enacting an antiabortion constitutional amendment.[25] But his election came at the end of a decade of building cultural conflict and anger, and there could be no Reagan Revolution without the cultural warriors who would join his revolutionaries in 1980 and then in much bigger numbers in 1984.

For both the more traditional and more secular, the decade before was defined by Congress passing in 1972 the Equal Rights Amendment (ERA) to embed equal rights for women in the Constitution. It passed its final hurdle in the Senate, 84 to 8, and seemed to be headed for sure ratification by the states, but the ERA got into increasing difficulty and fell three states short when time ran out in 1982. Almost simultaneously in 1973, the Supreme Court in *Roe* vs. *Wade,* "like a bolt out of the blue" for many in traditional America, overturned state laws that had barred legal abortions in most areas of the country. These explosive actions came at a time that also brought rising female participation in the labor force, reaching over 50 percent in 1980. At the outset of the decade, just 42 percent favored all this activity to change the status of women, but by the end, it was 64 percent.[26]

Little wonder that many Evangelicals and many traditionalists, defenders of the traditional family and its role for women, felt under siege. Their way of life was now threatened by distant, liberal institutions that took unto themselves the power to decide issues that previously were settled privately or locally. "For many conservative Americans," Jane Mansbridge wrote, "the personal became political for the first time when questions of family, children, sexual behavior, and women's roles became subject to political debate."[27] Over the course of the decade, more and more of the Christian conservatives, including a lot of homemakers and noncollege-educated women, stepped forward to defend marriage, their views of motherhood, and the special world of the family.[28]

Ronald Reagan instinctively aligned himself with the traditional reaction against the liberal challenge to the family on school prayer and abortion and thus touched the more traditional communities under siege—Northern Catholics, Orthodox Jews, Western Mormons, and white Southern Fundamentalists, to take Kevin Phillips's list. Reagan may not have got himself up on Sunday morning to go to church, but he so closely identified with the traditional family and traditional America that people took his faith and commitment as given.

The platform in 1980 staked out cultural ground for the Republicans that was new territory for the party. It placed the party against the ERA. It committed the party to appoint federal judges who "respect traditional family values and the sanctity of innocent life." And Reagan reminded voters that he recognized the "great hunger in America for spiritual revival."[29]

With the turmoil of the preceding decade, the political deck was being shuffled. The fundamentalist clergy got the message. Southern Baptist ministers, who had supported the Democrats over the Republicans by 41 to 29 percent in 1980, shifted loyalties four years later, choosing Republicans by 66 to 26 percent.[30] The ERA, which a decade earlier had broad bipartisan support, was now divvied up by the party activists: 92 percent of Democratic National Committee members supported it but only 29 percent of those on the Republican National Committee did.[31]

President Reagan did not often elaborate his views of the deepening divide, as his advisers at least were willing to bank the political gains from the more simple expressions of faith and his support for popular policies, like prayer in school and opposition to court-ordered school busing. But when addressing the National Association of Evangelicals in Orlando in 1983, he told the ground troops for his revolution that their mutual support for "institutions" like the family and the church that foster "respect for the rule of law under God . . . puts us in opposition to, or at least out of step with a prevailing attitude of many who have turned to a modern-day secularism, discarding the tried and time-tested values upon which our very civilization is based. No matter how well intentioned, their value system is radically different from that of most Americans."[32]

By 1984, the Republicans would pick the fruit of this division with a simple contrast, the work of both parties: Walter Mondale warned that "politicians should keep their nose out of religion," while Reagan expressed his "faith in God" and underscored, "We're going forward with values that have never failed us when we lived up to them."[33]

THE MILITARY IS BACK; AMERICA IS BACK

An enhanced military defense, a credo of the conservative isolationists, including Goldwater in the postwar period, along with reduced government spending and cutting taxes, was always central to the Reagan creed. And just as his tax cutting gained force in his opposition to big government liberalism, his commitment to military defense gained force from his opposition to communism and the Soviet Union—the ultimate enemy of freedom and America. With no fondness for Nixon's détente policies, Reagan never stopped reminding people of the Soviet Union's uncompromised Marxist-Leninist objectives and its essential evil. Such statements almost cost him the presidency in 1980 and were banished from his 1984 campaign. But in between, he laid out clearly the triumph of America's freedom. At Westminster, he proclaimed, "The march of freedom and democracy . . . will leave Marxism-Leninism on the ash-heap of history as it has left other tyrannies." Speaking to the National Association of Evangelicals, he went on to describe the Soviet Union as "the focus of evil in the modern world" and "an evil empire."[34]

He backed up his commitment to winning this war and protecting America by nearly doubling defense spending (from $158 billion in 1981 to $304 billion by 1989), launching the Strategic Defense Initiative or "Star Wars," and supporting "freedom fighters" around the world from Angola to Nicaragua.

Whether or not this was a successful foreign policy, it created a change in patriotic spirits and expressions of manhood at the level of popular culture. The *Rambo* movies gave us a "new tough-guy American style, Sylvester Stallone," wrote David Ignatius at that time. "Here was the raw imagery of American power, a nation seemingly free at last from the pain and self-doubt of Vietnam, personified by a muscular hero with an oversize machine gun." It described what Reagan promised: "America is back."[35]

Reagan elevated his association with the American experience when he went to Normandy and Omaha Beach, where so many American soldiers lost their lives in World War II. By all accounts, he spoke movingly of the sacrifice, declaring, "We will always remember. We will always be proud. We will always be prepared, so we may always be free." He spoke, Lou Cannon tells us, as a man whose portrayal of wartime America allowed him to speak from the experience of his own mind but also of America's own remembrance via film.[36]

During Reagan's first term, the public esteem for the military grew accordingly, with 68 percent saying they had "a great deal" or "quite a lot" of confidence in the institution in 1985, up from 52 percent in 1981.[37] Harris polls taken at the beginning and end of Reagan's first term showed that the number of Americans with "a great deal of confidence" in military leadership had climbed from 28 percent in 1980 to 45 percent in 1984.[38]

Right before the 1984 landslide, President Reagan hosted the Olympics in Los Angeles and shamelessly co-opted this international event, absent the Soviet bloc, for his American purpose. On opening night of the Olympics, he declared, "The American ideal is not just winning; it's going as far as you can go." The Games became immense pageantry, the crowds waving American flags, chanting "We're number one!" And Reagan's campaign events relived the spirit, this time with chants of "U.S.A.! U.S.A.!"[39]

UNEVEN REAGANISM

Reagan's offer drew on different strands of modern conservatism, but he brought them all together, bonded by his own optimism, his common touch, and the rising prosperity in the country. With the economy in recession in 1982, the Republicans lost heavily in the off-year congressional elections, but the president held to his faith, and when the economy took off, a large majority of the country seemed to affirm the conservative revolution. Optimism about the future soared: a striking 39 percent concluded that the government is now run for the "benefit of all"—up 10 points from 1982 and 18 points from 1980.[40] Reagan had brought the country, it seemed, to a new way of thinking about government and markets, values and family, indeed, about America.

At the end of the campaign in 1984, Reagan traveled to Waterbury, Connecticut, an older factory town where every inhabitant, it seemed, had turned out to hear John Kennedy close his campaign. This time Ronald Reagan looked out on the crowd and said, "I see our country today and I think it is springtime for America once again." He reminded them, "You know, I was a Democrat once," and expressed regret on their behalf that "the Democratic leadership" abandoned "the good and decent Democrats of the JFK, and FDR, and Harry Truman tradition."[41] Reagan was foretelling of a political shake-up that would make a new Republican majority possible.

In the 1984 election, Reagan took 59 percent of the vote and won all but the District of Columbia and Mondale's home state of Minnesota— except for Roosevelt in 1936, the biggest Electoral College landslide ever.

This election, unlike 1980, produced real and enduring shifts in how people align with the parties. Republican identification, barely a third of the population when Nixon was president, jumped to 43 percent. In the South, Republican identification rose from 21 to 31 percent; among Catholics, it rose from 17 to 26 percent. Born-again Christians shifted sharply to the Republicans, and they have never looked back. Among union households, the core of the organized working class, the Democratic advantage declined in 1984 and continued down in 1988. The political work of the Reagan Revolutionaries was producing not just Reagan Democrats but also new Reagan Republicans.[42]

But for all the celebration of the new era, the Reagan majority was very fragile, dependent in the first instance on the economic growth that was finite in years and uneven in impact. To be sure, median income rose between 1983 and 1988, but the decade also brought unprecedented rises in inequality and new wage pressures on the middle and bottom, followed by an anger-producing recession.[43] For that period, median family income overall rose about a half percent a year, up $2,911 per family—unimpressive by postwar standards (2.8 percent a year during 1947–67) and even by the standards of the 1990s (up 0.9 percent a year).[44] But it was impressive, maybe even breathtaking, for those at the top, which is why they probably did not notice the income stagnation for those in the middle and at the bottom. In 1979 the family income of the top 5 percent was 15.7 times the income for those families in the bottom 20 percent; after the Reagan decade, the multiple jumped to 19.1. There is a good reason for that. The income of the bottom fifth had not risen at all over the decade, while those for the top 5 percent rose at a pace of 1.8 percent a year.[45]

The education a person brought to the Reagan years had a lot to do with what he or she took out. Wages went down for men without four-year college degrees, and those without high school diplomas really lost ground— down 1.7 percent a year. Those with college degrees gained, particularly if they had advanced degrees—up 1.2 percent a year. A similar pattern held for women, though those with less education saw a smaller drop in wages. In fact, women with some college won a modest increase, and if they had college degrees, they did very well, up 1.5 percent a year.[46]

Managerial, professional, and technical workers, whether men or women, made wage gains during the period of "prosperity." For the rest, good increases were hard to come by, particularly for men. In sales and clerical positions, service and blue-collar jobs, wages for men went down over the decade, indeed, by more than a half percent a year (remember that even in 2001, about 40 percent of men in the labor force still worked in blue-collar jobs). Women in sales and clerical positions gained about a half percent a year, but those in service and blue-collar positions lost ground too.[47]

People in the middle or at the bottom were working harder to earn less, which may account for the developing popular frustration. The middle fifth of married couples with children worked 11.2 percent more hours a year to support their families, about nine weeks of additional work, and a similar pattern held for all those below the median income; the top fifth, on the other hand, actually worked somewhat fewer hours at the end of the Reagan decade, and for a much higher return.[48] Good work if you could get it.

To compound the potential grievance, the Reagan promise on tax cuts turned out to be a promise only for top-rate taxpayers, whose taxes were slashed dramatically. The middle class got no relief: the effective rate for the mid-income group, 16.5 percent in 1980 (including Social Security), remained unchanged in 1988, though it was no doubt pushed upward by increased state and local taxes. No wonder voters after the 1988 election said their highest priority for the next president was getting the wealthy to pay their fair share of taxes.[49]

The image of the entrepreneur—investor and wealth creator—gave way to images of Michael Milken and junk bonds. By 1988, confidence in bankers had plummeted to 26 percent from 38 percent in 1985; in business executives, to 16 percent from 23 percent. Indeed, voters wanted to check the power of those who had risen to new levels of prosperity in Reagan's good times.[50]

In the end, the public was not won over to the assumptions about profits and the resulting broad social benefits—"that profits of large companies help make things better for everyone." At Reagan's best moment, only 43 percent believed that "the profits of large corporations help make things better for everyone." Throughout the Reagan era, more than 70 percent believed that the concentration of power "in the hands of a few large companies" was too great "for the good of the nation."[51]

THE FALL OF REAGANISM[52]

As with the Opportunity Democrats, the voters began quickly to punch holes in this aspiration for political greatness. In the 1986 midterm elections, just two years after Reagan's triumph, Democratic attacks on the "Swiss-cheese" economy and the specter of possible Social Security cuts led to big Democratic gains (in the South and West), with the Democrats recapturing control of the Senate.

George H. W. Bush defeated Michael Dukakis in 1988, taking 53 percent of the popular vote and maintaining the Republican hold on the South and West, but only after Dukakis had gone ahead in the race after the Democratic convention. To win in the face of growing anger about the corporate consolidation and the excesses of the wealthy and weak income growth, Bush reduced the Reagan vision to no tax increases and, reminiscent of Nixon and Agnew, to an attack on elitist liberalism, an extreme form of culture war.

Bush dramatically pledged, "Read my lips: no new taxes." That was sufficiently antigovernment to satisfy some conservatives and sufficiently generous to satisfy some of those with moderate incomes, but apparently not enough to put Bush substantially in the lead. Republicans held on to the White House by waving their variant of the bloody shirt, with Willie Horton and flag burning as new forms of the old law-and-order and antibusing campaigns. These were still combustible materials in 1988, and George Bush used them to hold on to power. In Lee Atwater's terms, Bush worked to show that the Democrats "are the party of the liberal elites who're not in touch with the mainstream of the country."[53]

To smash the Dukakis challenge, Bush set aside Reagan's vision and took up, with relentless repetition, a litany of issue contrasts that, perhaps better than any other statement of the period, captures the Republican attempt to reduce all politics to the cultural choice:

> Should public school teachers be required to lead our children in the pledge of allegiance? My opponent says no, and I say yes. Should society be allowed to impose the death penalty on those who commit crimes of extraordinary cruelty and violence? My opponent says no, but I say yes. And should our children have the right to say a voluntary prayer, or even observing a moment of silence in the schools? My opponent says no, but I say yes. And should free men and women have the right to own a gun to protect their home? My opponent says no, and I say yes. And is it right to believe in the sanctity of life and protect the lives of innocent children? My opponent says no, and I say yes.[54]

With Dukakis playing his part, ACLU membership card in hand, Bush overtook Dukakis and ultimately won handily.

While the election of 1984 had raised the public's spirits, this one depressed them. It was an alienated electorate, with a lower voter turnout than any election since 1924.

The Bush presidency was itself disfigured by the cynicism it fostered and the load it was carrying. George Bush was heir to the Reagan Revolution, but he held on to power by abandoning many of its core ideas and instincts. The material state of the country, itself a product of Reagan's policies, would only worsen the Republicans' position. Under those policies, the top 1 percent of the population reaped extraordinary income gains— 62.9 percent between 1980 and 1989—while the average family saw its income stagnate—up just 2.8 percent—during the twelve years of the Reagan and Bush presidencies. The country fell into recession between 1990 and 1991, and the federal deficit rose to what then were unimagined levels. George Bush lived in the world of his father, banker and Senator Prescott Bush, while job and income growth and the trajectory of the country completely stalled.[55] His economic plan, more reminiscent of Goldwater than Reagan, offered no tax cuts and a parody on "let them eat cake": the "people will do great things if only you set them free." And full of Persian Gulf bravado, he declared, "This will not stand."[56]

The combination was incendiary for George Bush and the Reagan Revolutionaries. Only a third of the population thought they would be prosperous in the years ahead; confidence in corporations dropped to just 11 percent; and the number thinking the government could be trusted to do what is right headed sharply downward to just 28 percent.[57]

The 1992 election brought historic collapse for the Republicans. The Republican presidential vote sank 16 percentage points from George Bush's performance in 1988 and 21 points from Ronald Reagan's in 1984, the high point of the Republican ascendancy. Bush's 16-point collapse, as political scientist Walter Dean Burnham points out, has been exceeded only three times in American history; Hubert Humphrey's 1968 collapse of 18 points was one of them. For Bush and the Republicans, their winning of just 37.4 percent of the vote ranked as the second worst performance by an incumbent over two centuries and marked the end of the Reagan Revolutionaries' political project.[58]

The crash in 1992 swept away a lot of history. The Republicans' new standing with working-class and lower-middle-class Americans, many of whom had earlier walked away from the Democrats, was squandered over the decade. Among voters with incomes between $15,000 and $30,000, Bush lost to Clinton 45 to 35 percent, a 15-percentage-point swing away from the Republican performance of 1988. Republicans lost ground as well with many well-educated voters, particularly women, and lost every state in the East and on the West Coast.[59]

Ross Perot's historic third-party performance, gaining 19 percent of the vote, was a major part of the Reagan crack-up, and these Perot voters have been a very big part of the political landscape over the subsequent decade. The Perot voters of 1992 were predominantly, but not exclusively, alienated

Republicans.[60] Except for the young, most had a Republican voting history, but they were contemptuous of George Bush and also hostile to Reagan and his idea of how to make the country prosperous, and indeed, half said they would vote for Clinton absent the Perot protest option.[61] Perot gave these angry voters an antiestablishment option, which was taken up in particular by younger voters, noncollege-educated younger men, the more secular Republicans, and independents. He ran very well in the Northeast and the West (reaching 30 percent in Maine and 27 percent in Nevada) but did poorly in the Deep South, where the Republican coalition largely weathered the storm.

The crash of Reaganism gave the country a dislodged bloc of voters who were antipolitician. They liked Perot's honesty and straightforwardness; they said he "speaks his mind." They were antigovernment, which they saw as too intrusive in people's lives and too ready to overspend. They thought Perot "knows how to handle the money" and would "cut out the frills." The national debt, Perot's preoccupation, was a symbol of something very wrong in the country, the politicians' lack of responsibility, a straitjacket that kept government from working for the people. Perot voters were libertarian and secular, resentful of government and the orthodox telling them what to do. They were antiestablishment, particularly against corporations that enriched themselves at the expense of the workers. Perot at least "cared about people," unlike leaders who have been "so high up for so long that their heads [are] in the clouds." They were financially pressed, with a very well-developed sense of grievance about the middle class working hard but getting "a raw deal." And finally, they were pro-America. They liked Perot, who opposed NAFTA more than any of them, who "puts America first," was "totally for the country," and "wants to help people in the U.S.A."[62]

In 1992, almost a fifth of the voters expressed these angry feelings and wished to have no part of the established political parties and their attempts to dominate the era, and certainly not the Republicans, who for the moment seemed to have abandoned them.

LEGACY

The 1992 election was a repudiation of the Reagan era; voters were very conscious of the "boom and bust" that damaged the country and believed that "greed kind of became king."[63] But even though the Reagan political coalition faltered, it too, like the New Opportunity Democratic project, advanced positions that changed the public consciousness in enduring ways.

The Reagan experience, atop Carter, Nixon, and Johnson, left people even less confident in the government's capacity to act for society, which is an important conservative triumph. While corporations were badly tarnished by this period, markets survived intact. Both parties were now talking about expanded choice and change in public provision. And even with the rush of major airlines into bankruptcy after 9/11 and the Iraq war, does one hear anyone talking about the reregulation of the airlines? The value of personal responsibility that had figured centrally in Reagan's thinking remained as strong as, or stronger than, the value of individual rights that Democrats have long championed. Whatever the changing reality of the American family, a large majority wants the government to promote traditional two-parent families and to bring religion and prayer back to the public schools.

But Ronald Reagan and George Bush, building on some of the handiwork of Johnson, McGovern, and Mondale, also left the country with a strengthening legacy of cultural politics and conflict. Rather than seeing politics gravitating toward conventional economic issues and classes, David Leege and his collaborators underscore a deepening cultural politics, which is becoming an "argument about how we as a people should structure our lives." Politics now "involves disagreements about what the society and government prescribe and proscribe as the appropriate way of life."

Politics is about the "scope of the political community" and what is permissible. Cultural politics is "symbolic, not technical"; its politicians "take positions," for or against rather than looking for areas of agreement; the subject of politics is social change to "the moral order," not just the political economy.[64]

The content of cultural politics has come to include abortion and the role of women and the family, as well as race, equal rights, and the role of the federal government. Even in 1992, it was encompassing guns, rights and the role of the regulatory state, and gays and lesbians and the traditional family.

The attempt by the Reagan conservatives to win the country and create an enduring majority fell badly short, but they won and used power and left a mark. That both the Opportunity Democrats and Reagan Revolutionaries fell short made an even deeper mark that contributed to our divisions. But at least for now, that creates a moment of a possibility for the Reformed Opportunity Democrats.

Chapter 4

THE REFORMED OPPORTUNITY DEMOCRATS:

The Lost Middle

One of President Clinton's most durable speechwriters, Michael Waldman, concluded that his boss was not just successful but was also an "important president." Without that assessment, it is hard to put the efforts of the Democrats to pick up the pieces of the collapsed Reagan coalition and create a national majority on the same historic level as the other bold efforts to dominate this era. Clinton certainly thought that he was offering voters a "Third Way," explicitly an alternative to the failed politics and solutions of the Opportunity Democrats and the Reagan Revolutionaries who demonstrably came up short. But was the work of the Reformed Opportunity Democrats—the "New Democrats," as Clinton would prefer—any more than an opportunistic reaction to the political upheaval? Were their ideas or vision at the heart of the Reformed Opportunity project that allowed Democrats to aspire to dominate the times? Did they take on serious issues and great challenges to the country? And at the end of the day, having failed to produce an electoral majority for any Democratic presidential candidate, can we judge the Reformed Opportunity Democrats as politically important?

To begin with, these reform Democrats made a serious and historic effort to dominate the period. But for the butterfly ballots in Florida or Ralph Nader or Clinton's moral lapses or Al Gore's conceit, few observers doubt that the Democrats would have won the presidency three times in succession, a feat equaled only by Reagan and Bush in this half century. While the Democrats have not elected a majority president, Clinton won by healthy margins, and the Democrats were denied an outright majority in 2000 by Nader's narcissistic challenge. Had there been no third-party candidates, Clinton would have likely won with 52.0 percent of the vote in 1992, rising to 53.4 percent in 1996. Al Gore would have moved into the White House, with 50.1 percent of the vote and carried both New Hampshire and Florida in 2000.[1] From this vantage point, we would be taking very seriously the historic political changes—the Republicans' lost majority in the rural areas and among seniors, the better-educated and professionals, and older noncollege and working-class voters, and the Democrats' new standing with well-educated women, cosmopolitan states and metropolitan areas, and the increasingly diverse and immigrant electorate. We would be taking seriously the postindustrial social currents that are changing lifestyles and values concordant with this new Democratic majority and its ideas and contemplating the prospect that Democrats could end this era with a serious prospect of dominating it.

But Al Gore is not president and Democrats do not now have a majority in the country. Like the Republicans, they have only 46 percent who align with them. Thus, we need to understand how the Reformed Opportunity Democrats nearly created a majority and why they fell short.

THE DEMOCRATIC REFORM MOVEMENT

The Liberal Reform project was crystallized by Clinton and taken to a new level, but it had been building in the Democratic Party over a number of decades ever since the most inglorious defeat of George McGovern in 1972. Today, it is hard to look back on Jimmy Carter and Michael Dukakis as part of the Democratic renewal, but each contributed to the creation of the modern, more successful Democratic Party. Carter offered economically cramped policies and spoke of the country's "malaise" that formed the backdrop for Reagan's sunny policies, but Carter was a Southern fiscal conservative who ran an austere government that cut deficits. While tightfisted with money, Carter elevated energy and the environment as issues and expanded regulation to improve quality of life. As governor, Michael Dukakis trumpeted the "Massachusetts miracle" and premised his candidacy for president on promoting technology and economic competence. Although Gary Hart ran unsuccessfully for president in 1984 and 1988—barely denied on his first try and cut short by *Monkey Business* on his second—he surged ahead by attacking the special interests and old policies of the Democratic Party and presenting himself as a young "Atari Democrat," promoting new technology and new ways for government to do things. And with the Republicans increasingly hostile to big government and America's moral decline, each Democrat in turn had deepened the association of Democrats with a regulatory state that would promote a clean environment and public safety and that would defend the rights of women, starting with the right to choose.

Well before Bill Clinton's "Third Way," Democratic candidates for president were getting the attention of women and college-educated voters whose trek away from the Republicans began, in some cases, with Carter and gained speed with Dukakis.

But as Clinton began to contemplate his run for the presidency, there were still many issues left unaddressed by the Democrats. Dukakis used a Truman-like whistle-stop tour through the Central Valley of California to come clean and confess that he was a "liberal," but he articulated no vision for America and stood defenseless before Lee Atwater's assault on Democrats: pathetic on defense, soft on crime, indulgent of black murderers, for racial quotas and raising taxes, and indifferent to the values so important to America's families. No wonder Dukakis was seen as more liberal than Ted Kennedy. Despite the public's strong discontent with the Reagan Revolution, Dukakis lost every income group earning above $20,000 a year.[2]

In March 1990, Bill Clinton took up the chairmanship of the Democratic Leadership Council (DLC) and over that year articulated the core ideas that would become the infrastructure for the reformist Democratic project. Clinton was one of the prospective Democratic candidates to take the stage at the 1991 DLC convention auditioning for the role of fall guy, most thought, to challenge George Bush fresh from his victory in the Persian Gulf. Clinton spoke first and sang the hymn that would get people listening and soon catapult him above the field of Democratic aspirants for the presidency. He declared, "Our burden is to give people a new choice, rooted in old values, a new choice that is simple, that offers opportunity, demands responsibility, gives citizens more say, provides them with responsive government—all because we recognize that we are a community."[3]

His speech began with the great task before the Democrats: to address the economic decline and growing inequality produced by an era of misguided Republican governance, one that "glorified the pursuit of greed and self-interest" and was out of touch with the values of mainstream America. "In the 1980s our competitive position eroded," Clinton declared, "but the CEO's of this country gave themselves pay raises that were four times as much as they gave their employees and three times as much as their corporate profits increased." Meanwhile, "middle income families' earnings declined for the first time in our memory, and not because we are a lazy people. Working class families put in more hours at work and less time with their children in 1989 than they did in 1979."[4] In the fall, through the "New Covenant" speeches at Georgetown University that would most clearly define the purpose of his candidacy, Clinton underscored the values and critique of the era: "The 1980s ushered in a gilded age of greed, selfishness, irresponsibility, excess and neglect. . . . For twelve years, the forgotten middle class watched their economic interests ignored and their values run into the ground."[5]

In all of his speeches, starting with the Cleveland address, Clinton stressed the lack of responsibility in this era, reflected in the expanding welfare rolls, fathers abandoning their sons and daughters, and the "the number of poor women with their little children." But that said, Democrats should insist, as Clinton declared in Sioux City, Iowa, a month before his official declaration, "that those at the top of the totem pole be responsible, too." He asked, "How can you tell the farmers who till the soil to be responsible while the people whose hands are in the till do well by behaving irresponsibly?"[6] And by the time he spoke at Georgetown, Clinton offered a simple warning: "I want the jetsetters and the feather bedders of corporate America to know that if you sell your companies and your workers and your country down the river, you'll get called on the carpet. That's what the President's bully pulpit is for."[7]

Yet for all the pain of the era, Clinton told the Cleveland DLC delegates, these middle-class voters had not turned to Democrats to champion their interests at this moment, because Democrats had failed to represent them: "Too many of the people that used to vote for us, the very burdened middle class we are talking about, have not trusted us in national elections to defend our national interests abroad, to put their values into our social policy at home, or to take their tax money and spend it with discipline." A reformed Democratic Party begins with making sure the forgotten middle class is no longer forgotten.

Even at this early point, Clinton told the audience that Democrats would commit themselves to achieving economic growth in a new, competitive global economy by investing in "emerging technologies," creating incentives for U.S. companies to expand "in their own country," and investing in education and training to give "world class skills for people who live here while money and management may fly away." He would have the Democrats advance a broad opportunity agenda to help the "middle class as well as the poor" that would eventually include education and health insurance and the DLC's own tax proposal: "higher taxes for wealthy persons" and "reducing the tax burden on moderate-income and middle class families."

Clinton's goal was to return to the idea, lost since Kennedy's presidency, that "we're all in this together," that we are a community able to act together to tackle the big challenges before the country. The economic gains of the

1980s were squandered by an individualistic ethic and pervasive irresponsibility. But he now proposed to reclaim the government as an instrument of community by reforming and legitimating it. Given the citizenry's enduring skepticism about government and most recent experience with the Democrats, this required no less than cleaning the stables. Democrats must show renewed respect for the taxpayers and offer accountable government that respected people's values. Reflecting on his own experience as governor of Arkansas, Clinton put the spotlight on welfare reform to create work, higher education standards and testing, national service, and tough child-support enforcement.[8] In his announcement speech in Little Rock, he would commit "to end welfare as we know it."[9]

This reflected a preoccupation first expressed a year earlier in New Orleans, where Clinton took up the leadership of the DLC. To be a Democrat, he explained, first "you have to believe there's a role for government in solving common problems." But then you must "empower" people by giving them choices, and "whenever government does something with or for individuals who are irresponsible, it must require responsibility of them."[10] This means continually reinventing government to make it more innovative, effective, and accountable, not bigger, because our times need legitimate government. Later, he would challenge Washington to "revolutionize government and fundamentally change the relationship to people. People don't want some top-down bureaucracy telling them what to do anymore."[11]

Ultimately, the crystallized message unveiled at the Democratic convention and in the remainder of the campaign began with the preamble that "government had failed the average person" and only then affirmed, "We need a government that puts people first again."[12]

As he was closing his speech to the delegates in Cleveland, Clinton recalled that his great-grandparents, living in a "two-room shack up on stilts," believed in "personal responsibility," but "they also believed that the government had an obligation to help people who were doing the best they can." Today, there are people out there who care little for the "rhetoric of left and right" or "who is up and who is down," but "they are real people, they have real problems, and they are crying desperately for someone who believes the purpose of government is to solve their problems and make progress."[13] And so what Clinton offered in the end to his Georgetown audience was a "New Covenant, a solemn agreement between the people and their government, to provide opportunity for everyone, inspire responsibility throughout our society and restore a sense of community to this great nation."[14]

In the end, Clinton believed, this would all be tested on the anvil of race—as it has been in every election since 1960, dramatically so with George Bush's "Willie Horton" campaign in 1988. In September, appearing before the Democratic National Committee, he warned that the Republicans would soon be using the "quota" card and trying to scare the "most eco-nomically insecure white Americans." But he reminded the delegates, as if he needed to do so, "I am a fifth generation Arkansan. A Southerner born and bred. . . . Those of us who come from the South, whatever our race, know that they've been running this old scam on us for decades now." And he vowed not to "permit the Republicans to keep people staring at each other across racial divides."[15] In fact, at a key point in the primaries, he went one af-ternoon to a community college in suburban Macomb County outside of De-troit, home of Reagan Democrats who gave many of their votes to George Wallace, and the next morning to a black church in inner-city Detroit. With the spotlight turned up bright, he delivered the same message to both audi-ences. He told them of the crushing impact of Republican economic policies on these two communities (while GM executives pocketed the workers' con-cessions), of the need for more responsibility and opportunity, and finally he urged them to declare a truce on America's racial divide: "Let's forget about race and be one nation again"; "we have been divided for too long."[16]

For Bill Clinton, continuing the opportunity agenda for African Amer-icans and helping America come to terms with its racial divisions and di-versity was his life's work and a consuming theme in his politics, regardless of the message of the moment.

When he stood victorious on the stage in front of the Arkansas State House, with the opportunity to tell the world what this odyssey was all about, he spoke briefly, presented the New Democratic message in a paragraph, and then said, "And perhaps most important of all, to bring our people together as never before so that our diversity can be a source of strength in a world that is ever smaller, where everyone counts and everyone is a part of a family." This principle was reflected in a presidential transition period consumed not just with the economy but also with a very public quest to make sure the new Clinton cabinet "looked like America," balanced on gender, race, and ethnic-ity. This was all brought together for the country in the inauguration celebra-tions, under the banner and theme of an "American re-union." The racial project had supplanted the middle-class project as he crossed the finish line.

Bill Clinton's reforms were summarized by "opportunity," "responsibil-ity," and "community"—not just a mantra or a disconnected list, but some-thing more integrative. Clinton allowed Americans to imagine again that it had in its hands the capacity to bring down the old with all its inequality, elitism, and struggling middle falling behind, and create something new, built on the revolutionary idea that we are "all in this together." But, "this time, with a government finally accountable and reflecting our values, we can build opportunity broadly, insure together against misfortune, and help create a new economy, which enriches us all."[17]

UNEVEN VICTORY FOR REFORM

In 1992, that vision, along with revulsion for the Reagan-Bush era and the Perot rebellion, brought an electoral earthquake. It radically disrupted the voting patterns of the Reagan Revolution, creating the possibility of a new transforming project. Among those that pulled back were rural and older blue-collar voters, but also college graduates, Catholics, and seniors.

But in the 1996 election for president, Clinton received 49 percent of the votes, not only short of a majority but also short of a large majority characteristic of a bold effort to dominate this untamed era. If one statistically removes Perot from the race and allocates the Perot voters according to their second preference, as indicated in exit polls at the time, Clinton would have received 53.4 percent.[18] That is respectable but well short of the 61 percent achieved by Johnson in 1964 and the 59 percent for Reagan in 1984—the highest points in the two prior efforts to gain a mandate for changing the political landscape.

With the dramatic loss of the Democratic Congress and seeming repudiation of the president in 1994, achieving yet another Bill Clinton comeback in 1996 seemed like victory enough. It certainly felt like that at the time. Elizabeth Drew, a prominent observer of the Washington scene, noted that Clinton "faced potentially paralyzing party losses in November" and would have to "revive his presidency."[19] *Newsweek*'s book-length account of the 1996 election was appropriately titled *Back from the Dead: How Clinton Survived the Republican Revolution*. Political scientist Gerald M. Pomper noted that Clinton "overcame the 1994 landslide," survived the defeat of health care, outlasted "a cascade of investigations and allegations about his personal conduct, foreign policy embarrassments, and an often maladroit administration"—and "he made it look easy, even inevitable."[20]

The failings of the early Clinton administration contributed mightily to the 1994 crash. Despite this, voters in 1994 had a lot more on their minds than Clinton, and this was far from a final judgment on his presidency and did not automatically foretell the future. Many historical forces made themselves felt in 1994, including the Reagan-led Republican realignment in the South that could only be expressed after the 1990 reapportionment and only electorally starting in 1992. To be fully realized, it required the partisan polarization and culture war that diminished ticket splitting and wiped out "moderate" Democrats across the South and Southwest. Also building over a decade and leading to the 1994 crash was anger with the Democratically controlled Congress, tarnished by bank scandals, perks, midnight pay raises, and the like that fueled the term-limits movement. The final straw was a Democratic Congress and Democratic president divided and fighting on health care and crime.

But by 1996, Bill Clinton was running for reelection with the country at peace, a strong, growing economy, and the budget deficits heading downward. He was running against Newt Gingrich's assault on Medicare, education, and the whole federal government and against a fully Gingrichified Bob Dole, as Peter Goldman described him, "unplugged, an artifact from another era."[21] Nonetheless, Clinton only brought up his allocated national Democratic vote from 52.0 percent to 53.4 percent in 1996, just a 1.4-point gain.

For history's sake, 53 percent is not sufficient tribute to the seriousness of Bill Clinton's win in 1996, his high approval ratings through the second term despite the impeachment, and the political changes that left him poised to hand off the ball to a third successive Democratic president. There were good reasons to believe that Clinton's vision for the country could alter in major ways the existing political equation and produce shifts to the Democrats across many groups. But, unfortunately, the Reformed Opportunity Democrats were able to advance only a portion of their political project and agenda and had to abandon the rest. The result was victories in 1996 and 2000 that fell short of what was possible and necessary to achieve a sustainable majority. For reasons that I discuss below, the Democrats left a lot of votes on the table in 1996 and 2000 as well.

DEMOCRATS AND THE CHANGING AMERICA: FROM OPPORTUNITY TO DIVERSITY

In the early 1990s, the Reformed Opportunity Democrats advanced important parts of their mission, explaining why Clinton won a second term and Democrats now compete effectively in our period of party parity. Before elaborating where the project fell short of its goals, we should recognize the historic gains of the Clinton presidency and the Reformed Opportunity project, for both the Democrats and the country.

The most enduring and defining accomplishment of the Clinton presidency is the change in the U.S. economy—the sustained and rapid economic growth over the decade that brought job gains and full employment and, in the second half of the decade, higher incomes across the board and less poverty. In the period 1995 to 2000 leading into the two national elections, real median family income in the country rose 2.2 percent a year, an average increase of $5,304 per family. This was not quite as rapid an advance as in the fifties and sixties, but it was substantially above that for the Reagan era. More important, the Clinton economy brought gains to the bottom and middle as well as to the top. In the second half of the decade, black income rose 2.9 percent a year and Hispanic income was up 4.6 percent. Minority income rose at a rate higher than for the country as a whole. For more than 15 years since 1979, through the whole Reagan presidency and nearly the first half of Clinton's, poverty rates for African Americans remained stubbornly stuck at a high level and rose dramatically for Hispanics, ultimately to a comparable level. But from 1995 to 2000, black poverty rates fell from 29.3 to 22.5 percent and the Hispanic rate plummeted from 30.3 to 21.5 percent.[22]

The growing economy, fueled by the high-tech and stock market boom, continued to produce a more unequal economy. In 1989, the top 5 percent of families were earning 15.7 times as much as the lowest 20 percent; by 2000, that had grown to 19.1 times. The top did very well in the Clinton economy, with the top 5 percent gaining 2.9 percent a year between 1995 and 2000, compared to 2.3 percent for the lowest 20 percent. Similarly, those with a college education gained more than those without.

But at least now, starting in 1995, the rising tide was lifting all boats. People with only a high school diploma saw real gains of 1.2 percent a year in hourly wages and those with some college gained 1.6 percent, compared to 2.4 percent for those with a four-year degree. Male blue-collar workers were finally making gains, up 1.1 percent in the second half of the decade. Salaries of women in sales jobs were up a striking 2.8 percent a year, while the very large number of women in office clerical positions gained a modest 0.9 percent a year but were up nonetheless. Female service workers were up 1.3 percent and the relatively small group of women in blue-collar jobs gained 1.2 percent.[23]

From the outset of the presidential transition in 1992, before taking the oath of office, Clinton stacked his economic team with deficit hawks and pursued deficit reduction, year after year, even after his confrontations with the Congress and often over the objection of many of his political advisers.[24] Indeed, he made this his first budget priority even though his campaign had not strongly emphasized deficit reduction. On the other hand, Ross Perot had made it the symbolic center of his race—as had Paul Tsongas, the first front-runner in the 1991 Democratic primaries—which Bill Clinton remembered well.

Informed by the thinking of Robert Rubin and Alan Greenspan—and aided by many crossed fingers—the plan projected lower interest rates, more business investment, and rising productivity. Deficit reduction was the centerpiece of a robust economic policy that also included large tax increases for high-income earners and tax cuts for the lowest, reduced trade barriers under NAFTA and GATT as well as expanded exports, and significantly increased investment in education at all levels. In this, Joe Klein is right that the coherence of the Clinton project is perhaps better understood as part of a larger mission "to manage the nation's transition from the Industrial Age to the Information Age."[25]

The focus on education—the logical center of the Reformed Opportunity project—was intermittent in Clinton's first term and was as likely to be a rhetorical device, part of a list, or a place to stop Gingrich from doing harm as a priority for his administration and mission. Clinton polished his education credentials by sharply contrasting his views with Dole's cavalier attitude in the presidential debates toward the Department of Education and hostility to teachers' unions. But in his second term, education quickly rose to the top of the agenda, as unveiled in each State of the Union, and, more important, received substantial funding for a broad range of changes. The most important provision in the 1997 Balanced Budget Agreement was a $30 billion tax credit plan to cover two years of college tuition, which ten million students had used by 1999. As Klein points out, "the college tax credit plan passed in 1997 was *larger* than the GI Bill of Rights."[26] Because many of the education gains were buried in omnibus budget bills and part of broad budget negotiations with the Congress, the public may not have fully appreciated the scope of the initiatives. Nonetheless, during Clinton's presidency, overall college enrollment increased more than 10 percent, including a rise of nearly 40 percent for African Americans and 75 percent for Hispanics.[27]

The strong economy, buttressed by education, was the biggest reason for the president's high job approval. Before and indeed after the bubble burst in 2001, people proved optimistic about this high-tech, information, Internet economy, and because of the Democrats' role in promoting it, they were identified with the future. The "bridge to the twenty-first century"—the metaphor first used in Clinton and Gore's 1996 convention speeches—created an imagery for Democratic governance that was self-consciously optimistic and forward looking for the growing numbers of college-educated and cosmopolitan voters, particularly college-educated suburban women, reinforcing trends that had begun in 1988 and gained force through the nineties.

Yet before the 2000 election, it was already evident that the sustained period of growth was coming to an end, almost immediately reflected in slowed income growth. This took the country back abruptly to the mid-1990s, when the economy was only unevenly producing real income gains for families of moderate means, blue-collar and service workers and non–college graduates. Academic postelection studies underscored the declining rate of increase in disposable income, falling in the four quarters prior to the 2000 election, dropping to only 1.4 percent in the third quarter, and to −.7 percent during the election period, suppressing Gore's vote.[28]

This represented a kind of turning point for the Reformed Opportunity project, much as uneven growth threatened the Reagan project in 1986 and 1988. Would the Clinton vision of the Information Age economy also fall victim to the economy's overall fortunes?

Al Gore's campaign, starting in 1999, suffered through numerous identities, messages, and campaign teams, sometimes embracing economic progress and sometimes not. The need for Gore to establish his independent identity was normal enough for any vice president seeking to succeed a strong two-term president. But the need to establish independence was even greater in light of the Lewinsky controversy and impeachment, much as Hubert Humphrey needed to establish his own independence from Lyndon Johnson in light of the Vietnam War. The "Clinton Wars" limited Clinton's own ability to speak publicly about his presidency and the economy in this period, but it also complicated the task of his successor.

Exactly half the voters wanted the country to continue in the direction set by the Democrats in the White House, and for them the economy was the biggest factor. Gore was also seen as having the best plan for continuing prosperity (51 to 37 percent). In a Democratic Leadership Council postelection survey conducted by President Clinton's last pollster, Mark Penn, voters most concerned about the economy supported Gore over Bush by nearly 60 points (73 to 16 percent).[29]

With all these difficulties, Gore did offer a perspective on the economy reminiscent of Clinton in 1992, who had said, "We can build opportunity broadly, ensure together against misfortune, and help create a new economy, which enriches us all." This statement was itself reminiscent of John Kennedy, who, after the boom of the fifties and the slight downturn at the end of the decade, declared, "I'm not satisfied," as he challenged a prosperous and growing nation to do better.[30]

From the time of his announcement in 1999, Gore articulated the essential Clinton economic idea and commitment—"keeping our prosperity going" with fiscal discipline, global growth, and education investment, "not by letting people fend for themselves or hoping for crumbs of compassion, but by giving people the skills and knowledge to succeed in their own right in the next century."[31] But Gore added another element appropriate for these new, less heady times: "I want to extend our prosperity to the unskilled and underprivileged, to Appalachia and the Mississippi Delta, to our farms and inner cities, to our new immigrants." Later, he got the attention of the Democratic delegates at the Los Angeles convention, declaring as Kennedy had, "I'm not satisfied." Then he challenged them: "Together, let's make sure that our prosperity enriches not just the few, but all working families."[32]

That economic formulation, with its expansive view of opportunity and consciousness of the middle-income families, competed with many other themes for center stage in the Gore campaign. The primary battle with Bill Bradley centered on everything but the economy; the subject barely came up during the presidential debates. Gore himself gave frequent voice to the much narrower formulation, "people versus the powerful." In retrospect, Gore himself said that, "standing up for 'the people, not the powerful' was the right choice in 2000," adding, "and, in fact, it is the Democratic Party's meaning and mission."[33] Whether it is was the broader formulation that Gore articulated at the convention or the narrower one that he preferred on the stump, the theme demonstrably moved voters. A 15-point Bush lead before the Democratic convention in early August was eliminated and Gore moved ahead by 2 points at Labor Day and to a 4-point lead by the end of September, before the debates.[34] In fact, according to the campaign's polls, without Nader, he had moved into an 8-point lead over that 7-week period.[35]

The campaign's plan in the final month provided explicitly for an expansive focus on the economy: "how to extend our prosperity and make sure it works for all." Nearly all the non–Social Security TV advertising in the swing states underscored the economic theme, usually with Gore addressing the voters: "You know, for the last eight years, we've had the strongest economy in all of American history. And the credit goes to the American people—it's been their hard work. I want to keep that going and build on that foundation. . . . America's prosperity, working for all."[36] Carrying that banner, Gore closed the race in the final weeks and moved ahead, only to be stopped short in Florida.

Even though Al Gore did not become president, he and the Opportunity Democrats at least planted the idea that Democrats had the ability and obligation to create a broadly enriching prosperity, reflective of John Kennedy's best days.

The Clinton presidency also went a long way toward rebuilding the legitimacy of government, even though the need for reinvention never ends. This was not the state of affairs in 1994, when congressional gridlock and perks, the failure of Clinton's health-care plan, and the nagging mini-scandals produced an even more distrustful electorate. But the rising economy and declining deficits over the course of the Clinton presidency and the passage of welfare reform and declining welfare rolls drained "the most poisonous anti-government venom," as Michael Waldman described it, and reduced the anger with government and increased confidence in Democrats on fiscal issues and capacity to address problems.[37] In fact, the belief that the federal government does the right thing "just about always or most" of the time rose from 30 percent in 1992 to 32 percent in 1996 to 45 percent in 2000.[38]

The vice president pressed ahead with his reinventing initiative, spotlighting the reduction of "100,000 federal bureaucrats." Despite the many shortcomings of the Republican welfare bill signed by the president, its passage took a gigantic middle-class grievance off the table. In 1992, it was routine for voters to center their frustration on welfare recipients who get "free programs" without "worrying about working for it," picturing a hypothetical dishonest welfare recipient who is able to buy "a house and a car . . . just getting all of his money sent to him." As for the Democrats, they are simply "for the giveaways, and we are the ones that pay all the taxes." Such frustrations have nearly disappeared from the public consciousness.[39] In 1996, when Dole described Clinton as "liberal, liberal, liberal" and proposed his big tax cuts, the voters were nonplussed. After the 2000 election, whatever his penchant for programs, Gore was still more trusted than George Bush to be fiscally responsible.[40]

Voters came away from the decade with a sense that Democratic governance is characterized by a balance, which allows them to trust Democrats more on both the economy and big spending decisions.

The Clinton administration also advanced, successfully, an opportunity agenda, though it was more narrowly framed, focused on the poor and those with low incomes. Over the course of two terms, full employment and a rising prosperity broadened its meaning and seemed to dampen potential resentment. But the policy focus from the first budget and economic team was on helping those with low incomes, particularly the working poor, who were demonstrably taking personal responsibility. The Earned Income Tax Credit provided the only tax cut in the Clinton economic plan and contributed to the remarkable drop in the effective tax rate for low-income families and the corresponding drop in their overall tax burden.[41] When the president joined the battle with Republicans in backroom budget negotiations, he was much more focused on Medicaid, the federal health insurance program for low-income families, than on Medicare, the program for seniors.[42] Similarly, he pressed, again successfully, in subsequent budget negotiations to fix the most punitive and anti-immigrant provisions in the welfare law. And he found a way to fix, not abolish, affirmative action so the government could continue to target its education and employment efforts on behalf of racial minorities and women. So while working- and middle-class incomes began slowly to rise after 1996, poverty rates collapsed, particularly for blacks and Hispanics. The Reformed Opportunity Democrats, it turns out, were serious about opportunity for those at the bottom, which, we shall see, has electoral consequences.

Clinton did not place a great priority on environmental initiatives in his first term, and while committed in principle to international action on global warming, he moved ahead cautiously. But the Gingrich revolution planted explosives under the federal regulatory structure, and above all under those involving land use and environmental protection, as well as consumer and workplace safety. While the administration tried to get ahead of the Congress on regulatory reform, it clearly opposed the environmental rollbacks in the Contract with America.[43] This allowed Democrats to align even more tightly with the norm of a clean environment and the idea that this community could act together, using government regulation, to protect the public safety and foster a better quality of life. The vice president was well-known for championing global environmental issues, and the president spoke with increasing frequency about them in his last years in office. With the late executive orders on protecting wilderness and national parks, the Democrats ended the century with high marks on this central value. This will prove critical to the rising Democratic standing in growing cosmopolitan communities.

Finally, in one of his most foresighted acts, Bill Clinton turned the meaning of group rights into "diversity," not just given constitutionally but now also required by America's involvement in the global economy. In making that change, the Reformed Opportunity Democrats moved out of the era of civil rights and into the era of global change. They forged a special place for the Democrats, comfortable with the burgeoning immigration, the renewed focus on minority opportunity, and the evolving roles for women and the family. As always for Bill Clinton, the starting point and touchstone was his special relationship with the African-American community. He used it almost as a lifeline, to affirm the importance of rights but also as a part of a universal discourse rooted in rights and responsibility. With special poignancy, he told black parishioners in Memphis, at the church where Martin Luther King spoke the night before his death, if he were here today, "he would say, 'I did not live and die to see the American family destroyed. . . . I fought for freedom, but not for the freedom of people to kill each other with reckless abandon, not for the freedom of children to have children, and the fathers of the children to walk away and abandon them as if they don't amount to anything. . . . I did not fight for the right of black people to murder other black people with reckless abandon.' "[44] This gave Clinton the credibility to stand up to the conservative assault on affirmative action with his formula "mend but don't end" it, affirming the challenge that Democrats accepted more than three decades earlier for the nation: "America's rocky but fundamentally righteous journey to close the gap between the ideals enshrined in these treasures here"—the Declaration of Independence and Constitution—"and the reality of our daily lives."[45] After his reelection, he would write into his first State of the Union the nation's "greatest responsibility" and challenge: "For any one of us to succeed we must succeed as one America."[46] And as he closed his presidency and looked forward to the next century for Democrats, he stressed the continuing need "to build one America at home" but then called on the country "to make a strength of our diversity so that other nations can be inspired to overcome their own ethnic and religious tensions."[47]

But this was an administration that from beginning to end, from group to group, sent a signal about the core commitment of the Opportunity Democrats to diversity. By opposing the conservative attack on illegal immigrants, including Proposition 187 that would limit access to public education, Clinton generalized the principles. The role of the first lady, Hillary Clinton, sent a powerful message to women that this was an administration that was unfailingly pro-choice on abortion. At the launch of his presidency, the president advanced his proposal for gays to serve in the military, thus dramatically illustrating the breadth of the principle for America's ever-expanding rights.

Over the course of his government, Clinton deepened the consensus in civil society that barred discrimination and welcomed affirmative steps to expand diversity. But more than that, he helped create an America that was diverse, open, and tolerant, as part of its modernity and role in the world. This vision of America brought an increasing receptivity to Democrats among minority groups, the lowest-income voters, and college-educated women who are all intrinsic to the Democratic world.

This all adds up to serious work for the country. The Clinton presidency helped create a growing high-tech economy, rising incomes, expanded opportunity for the working poor and minorities, a greater national commitment to education and the environment, a fiscally stable and more legitimate government, and an America more confident in its diversity. The Reformed Opportunity Democrats reclaimed the idea that America is blessed and that our obligation is to enable everyone to share in the bounty. They did not get to these results linearly or easily, but Clinton's presidency placed its stamp on America, which made possible the renewal of the Democrats as a more than competitive national party.[48]

SHORTCHANGING THE MISSION

While the advances on the economy, opportunity, legitimate government, and diversity are important, what ultimately got left out of the work of their political project changes its meaning and diminishes its impact. The

Reformed Opportunity Democrats in their first term in government dropped the middle class as a central passion, which narrows the meaning of opportunity and the political possibilities. In the second, scandal and impeachment diminished the central value, responsibility, which distanced their political work and the government from people and mainstream families and left the project vulnerable before the raging cultural battles. And walking away from political reform robs the project of its reformist, change-oriented, outsider, antielitist character.

The Clinton administration abandoned the middle class. This was partly symbolic, as middle-class grievances and wants were no longer the central passion of the project; this was partly real and material, as low-income populations took priority and as middle-class incomes were slow to rise; and it was partly about values, both real and symbolic. Elite and editorial opinion never noticed, as they were always skeptical of Clinton's "pandering" to the middle class. But Middle America heard Clinton's powerful critique of the Reagan era, the assault on their values and hard work, the financial burden they carried. Clinton promised not just to make sure the CEOs acted more responsibly and paid their fair share of taxes, he also promised a middle-class tax cut. He promised a government that would respect their values and faith. The middle class as actual voters and as a symbol was the central audience in the 1992 campaign for the presidency.

The middle-class tax cut was abandoned at virtually the first meeting of the Clinton economic team in Little Rock well before Clinton took office, which, for very good reason, prioritized deficit reduction.[49] But not only did the economic plan not deliver on the promised tax cuts for the middle class, it turned around and proposed raising their taxes on energy use, in the end, resulting in a tax on gasoline. Clinton won grudging support for "A Fair and Balanced Plan" when he used an Oval Office TV address to make his case: for every $10 in deficit reduction, the middle class would be asked to cover only $1 in new taxes, with the rest covered by $5 in spending cuts and $4 in taxes on the wealthy.

The Clinton budget in fact raised taxes on the wealthy, as promised in the campaign, and in its final form raised the gas tax by only 4.3¢ a gallon and asked upper-income seniors to pay a tax on their Social Security income. But if the middle-class voters were to know that, the president would have to articulate who carried the burden of this policy within the American community and then explain the minimal rise in middle-class taxes. The proportionality of the policy had a rough correlation to the excesses and decline of the eighties, but the president, under the urging of his economic team, chose to remain silent about this central element of his budget and his vision, which had located virtue in the hardworking middle class. The economic advisers may have been right that corporate investors would have felt the chill, jeopardizing the nascent economic recovery.[50] The president chose not to be articulate about universalizing responsibility, not to create a context for the tax rise or the slight bump in middle-class taxes. When the postelection analysis was completed after the 1994 crash, support for the Clinton agenda, above all his budget, and the "biggest tax increase in history" were among the biggest factors in the defeat of incumbent Democrats.[51] That choice contributed to the middle-class flight from the Reformed Opportunity Democrats starting in 1994.

The reality of the middle class working harder for longer hours without getting anywhere continued for at least four years into the Clinton administration, despite the macroeconomic progress. Those married families in the middle of the income range—the middle fifth—worked 8.1 hours longer at the end of the decade of the 1990s atop the 11.2 percent more at the end of the Reagan era, putting these middle-income husbands and wives at work for an additional 16.5 weeks a year. The same pattern of increased work by the family holds for the lower-income groups, though the middle has faced the greatest pull on the family, barely abated under the Reformed Opportunity Democrats. By contrast, the top fifth did not work longer hours for their income.

At the same time, hourly compensation for production and nonsupervisory employees did not rise until 1997. Those in sales and service positions made considerable gains, though concentrated in the latter part of the decade; those in blue-collar positions, the largest grouping for men, and those in office clerical positions, the largest grouping for women, made similarly late gains but only a half percent a year since 1989. Those with college degrees made bigger gains and earlier, but all the noncollege groups saw rising gains mainly after 1995.[52]

This contributed to the angry reaction of noncollege voters in 1994, who felt discarded early, believing that their taxes had been jacked up while their incomes lagged and they received no help on health care. They had to be won back to the Clinton presidency by later tax cuts for the family, as well as education and later income gains.

The task was made doubly difficult by the effort to allow gays to serve openly in the military, launched in the first week of the new administration, underscoring its importance to the president. It ran into powerful opposition from Senator Sam Nunn, chairman of the Senate Armed Services Committee, and Colin Powell, chairman of the Joint Chiefs of Staff, and was quickly put on a slower track, emerging as "don't ask, don't tell." Still, this was a brave course for the president and, as with the economic plan, likely the right course for the country and for the Reformed Opportunity Democrats, testing the limits of tolerance as a social principle. But for the middle-class voters who expected Clinton to focus on the economy "like a laser" and who had been promised respect for their values, the policy looked like an assault on their views of marriage and sexuality and their respect for the military. One could not have found a more powerful symbol for more traditional blue-collar and religious voters. In fact, Clinton's first months, starting with gays in the military and the stimulus defeat and ending with the White House travel office debacle, brought an immediate and drastic drop in Clinton's approval ratings, to be built back only nine months later with the passage of his economic plan and the launch of health-care reform. But as a measure of the cultural consequences of walking away from the middle class, voters after the 1994 election cited gays in the military as the biggest reason for their disappointment with Bill Clinton, a couple points above health care.[53]

The middle-class voters were driven from the project in 1994 by the deafening silence, taxes, stagnant incomes, no welfare reform, and the assault weapons ban. But even after all of this, when Clinton climbed back to win in 1996, his second-term State of the Union addresses made almost no mention of the "missing middle."[54] Without the middle class as a central element of the vision, the Democratic commitment to opportunity gets more narrowly defined, and the political equation is changed as well. With the middle carved out, it is very difficult to build a larger majority, particularly when those voters, aggrieved, are courted by the Republicans.

What made it possible to bring the middle class into the mission of the Reformed Opportunity Democrats, to expand the meaning of opportunity and reinvent government as an instrument of community, was the value, responsibility. That the government would reward responsibility allowed people to believe that their own work would be rewarded, that their families would be respected, that opportunity would be broad, and that diversity would be more than a parade of new groups demanding their rights. Indeed, it was the integrative aspects of responsibility that allowed these reformers to imagine that they could diminish or transcend the cultural divide that had stopped Democrats short.

The long assault on Clinton's integrity and sense of personal responsibility eroded trust and diminished the strength of this thematic thread. Perhaps Clinton's right-wing opponents understood the central importance of responsibility to the whole project, thus the battle for trust that continued through the Clinton administration and the Gore election campaign.

With Monica Lewinsky and the impeachment, Clinton and the Democrats had to let go of responsibility, with powerful consequences for the unity and meaning of the mission, with powerful implications for the Democrats' prospects of overcoming the political divide and gaining a sustainable national majority.

The cost of the loss has been offset and obscured by the public's determination to protect his presidency and distorted because of the resulting counterreaction by more secular voters. The president, remarkably, maintained high job approval ratings throughout the scandal and to the end of his term.[55] Voters would not easily give in to the scandalmongers and the conservatives' attempted putsch; they understood that Clinton had brought a better America and that they had a stake in his success. They ultimately would be prepared to elect his vice president as president. But the president's personal and moral standing crashed with the public and worsened with the House impeachment process; the Democrats in general fell sharply on sharing people's values. In the two months leading up to the 1998 election, Democrats trailed Republicans by 20 points when it came down to which party does a better job with "family values."[56] While Bill Clinton was not on the ballot in these midterm elections, Democrats were, and they lost major ground in areas where the Clinton vision was expected to change the political landscape.

To all appearances, the 1998 congressional election was a setback for the Republicans, as Democrats, against the predictions of history, the odds-makers, and the specter of impeachment, picked up 4 seats. The Speaker of the House, Newt Gingrich, was forced to resign. Bill Clinton, one more time, had miraculously come back from the dead. Many of the elites and journalists were struck by the public's "laissez-faire attitudes" toward the president's private behavior, in fact, by the "almost Continental reaction."[57]

But as we will soon appreciate, the Democrats "won" in 1998 because of the intense polarization on the Democratic side that would deepen the cultural divide in the country and, at the same time, limit the possibilities of a larger majority. Angry black and union voters turned out in big numbers, while the best-educated and more secular voters refused to give in to the moral politics that were being used to bring Clinton down. White college-educated women cast 48 percent of their votes for Democratic congressional candidates, down only 1 point from 1996; Democratic support went up by 2 points among white college-educated men and, most intriguing, surged 6 points among whites earning over $75,000. The Lewinsky scandal seemed only to deepen the cultural divide, produced in part by the rising association of better-educated and more secular voters with the Democrats.

But the gains among the secular came with a very big price tag for the Reformed Opportunity project, as Democratic congressional support dropped across Middle America—two years before the loss would be affirmed in the presidential contest. Among middle-income white families earning between $30,000 and $75,000 a year, Democratic support dropped 2 points in 1998. And among the presumed guardians of family values, the white noncollege-educated women, Democratic support fell sharply, down 6 points, from 50 to 44 percent.[58]

In earlier times, as in the period leading up to 1996, President Clinton worked hard to make gains with married women with children and rural voters, and many of his initiatives, like school uniforms and V-chips to screen out unwanted TV shows, got noticed. Mark Penn, Clinton's pollster for that election, would repeat, "Public values trumps private character."[59]

But with the Lewinsky-Starr-impeachment phase, Democrats got slaughtered with the voters for whom responsibility mattered most. This reverberated across the rural areas and blue-collar suburbs where Democrats lost ground, just one indicator of what was to come in the even more polarized election of 2000. Democrats would run strongly and indeed make gains among the most and least fortunate, but lose serious ground among those in the middle.

Clinton was demonized throughout his presidency, though now with new richness, the details provided by the special prosecutor and the press. Gore the successor was exposed, as well, by his own stands on the cultural issues, which seemed to suggest an indifference to the traditional family, but more important, by press-driven doubts about veracity and trust. But without the shield of responsibility, the organized moral forces were able to attack as never before.

After a decade of ever more intense cultural war, the Democratic loyalist primary world, where Al Gore had to win the nomination, had become a secular minefield. Gore emerged from the primary battle with Bradley even more secular than his personal instincts. He had affirmed his support for legal abortion without nuance, denying the significance of his wavering fourteen years earlier on requiring parental notification; he was for registering guns, not gun owners; he favored recognition of gay civil unions, not marriage. But what was taken for normality in the Democratic loyalist world was incendiary in large parts of America outside of it, particularly against the backdrop of the cultural and "Clinton Wars." After the 2000 election, voters said their biggest doubts about Al Gore centered, first, on his untruthfulness and exaggerations, and then on his positions regarding the cultural issues, particularly gay unions and guns.[60] This was a caricature of Al Gore, but it locked him into one side of the Two Americas. The election of 2000 completely consolidated the Democrats' association with cosmopolitan America, but also their cultural and moral estrangement from large parts of Middle America.

The failure of the Clinton health-care plan—the bold attempt to achieve affordable, universal health insurance in America—nearly crashed the idea that Democrats could use government as an instrument to foster community. In this case, the Reformed Opportunity Democrats sought to use government to mitigate the consequences of the market by creating a structure in which all could be insured, thus allowing the Democrats to rally for economic growth and change as well. This was the second biggest promise of the Clinton campaign, after getting the economy moving, and no doubt its biggest failure at the midterm elections. As sociologist Theda Skocpol wrote, looking back on the experience, the attempt "to extend the New Deal's security guarantees" threatened to "trigger the outright unraveling of such prior programs as Medicare, Medicaid, and Social Security itself."[61] With major reform of health care seemingly off the table for the next six years, the Reformed Opportunity Democrats lost a principal policy tool for aiding working families and those without a college degree in the transformation to the Information Age economy.

In any case, the consequences of the defeat were breathtaking. Together with other failings, the loss in the health-care battle left the Republicans with control of Congress and a seeming mandate for their own conservative agenda to dismantle government regulations and cut social spending, particularly for Medicare and Medicaid. The Republicans this time were strengthened in government by the vast network of groups outside of government, which mobilized around the idea of government, in Grover Norquist's quaint phrase, "leaving us alone." The Brady Law and assault weapons ban were powerful symbols of intrusive government, central motivators in the NRA's assault on the crime bill and the Democratic Congress. As Dan Balz and Ronald Brownstein point out in their analysis of the midterm elections, 69 percent of gun owners voted Republican and Republican congressional candidates got one-third of their votes from gun owners.[62] But more than guns, "big government" health care was the focal point of the antigovernment coalition.

The conservative agenda and the Contract with America, Balz and Brownstein write, allowed Gingrich to fuse "the populist and ideological critiques of government into a single battering ram aimed at Washington," with deadly consequences for the Democrats.[63]

The loss of the Congress left the Clinton presidency struggling to adapt, fighting to stop the Gingrich Revolutionaries from inflicting too much damage and working to achieve incremental change where possible. With the defeat of health-care reform, the hopes of many voters were deflated—over 40 percent of whom still supported the Clinton health plan even at its lowest point—even though they never heard a word from the president on why health-care reform had failed. Instead, the Clinton administration took on the multiyear task of restoring the credibility of government for social action.

But the public was not done with the idea, central to the Reformed Opportunity project, that government had an important role to play on behalf of community, particularly during periods of downturn or change. The Republicans decided to challenge environmental regulations and the federal role in health care and its part in providing health insurance. After the 1994 congressional defeat, Clinton's job approval remained stuck under 50 percent through all the efforts to rehabilitate his presidency, including half apologies for the top bracket tax increase, talk of bipartisanship and triangulation, and even a national TV advertising campaign—except for the brief moment when he spoke for the nation after the Oklahoma City bombing. Only when he challenged the Gingrich budget and battled through two government closures did Clinton regain public confidence and an audience with the voters, with his approval heading up toward 60 percent by the middle of 1996.[64]

The battle with the Congress over the Gingrich budgets and the election of 1996 were a referendum on the role of government and the Republicans' determination to dismantle it. In fighting back, the Clinton administration did not hesitate to deploy the country's historic attachment to social insurance programs, like Social Security and Medicare. In a gesture full of symbolism, President Clinton took up the fountain pen that Lyndon Johnson had used to sign Medicare into law to veto Gingrich's proposed Medicare cuts.[65] With that engagement fresh in mind, the Democrats centered the election on Medicare, Medicaid, education, and the environment—"m2e2" in the shorthand of the time. They dogged Bob Dole with the charge that he would cut Medicare but, more important, ran TV ads that indicted Dole and his Republican allies for their assault on government: "The 1960s. Bob Dole in Congress. Against student loans [stamped on his forehead, and as the decades roll by]. Against Medicare. Against a higher minimum wage. Against the Brady Bill to fight crime, even against vaccines for children [photos of Dolegingrich float over the Capitol]."[66] The election of 1996 was a referendum on the two parties' approaches to government, and voters cast Dole aside and told the poll takers that the main reason was the Democrats' support for Medicare, education, and the environment—and much less because of other initiatives, like welfare reform, deficits, or bipartisanship.[67] When the president then proposed before Congress and the country the concrete choice between tax cuts and Social Security, he insisted, "Save Social Security First," and "in an instant," as Waldman aptly described it, "a trillion dollars silently shifted on the budget ledger from the column marked 'tax cuts' to the column marked 'Social Security.' "[68]

The Democrats clearly had a mandate to revisit the question of social insurance and the role of government in the reform project. But this was not Britain, where Tony Blair had a majority of more than 165 seats in his first and second terms, and where they could decide to double health-care spending over a decade. The Clinton administration devoted itself to incremental progress on a range of areas, making some headway on financing college and some progress on children's health insurance. But at least on health issues, incrementalism was mainly a holding action, as about a million more people found themselves without health insurance each year after the defeat of the Clinton plan.[69] With Republicans in control of the Congress, the aspiration to use government always faced limits, which placed a ceiling on both the role of the Reformed Opportunity project and the political gains that could be achieved.

Finally, the Reformed Opportunity Democrats face the question, "Who lost the Perot voters?" Or more accurately, "Why were the Perot voters never won over by the Democrats?" The Perot voters were the most angry and aggrieved of the dislodged voters in the 1992 election that brought the Democrats back to the presidency. But half of them remained out of the party fold in 1996, and they remained antiestablishment and hostile to the president. They would have split two to one for the Republicans had Perot not run. By 2000, the Perot voters had almost entirely shifted to the Republicans, making possible the dead-heat election. But why did the Perot voters not warm to the Reformed Opportunity Democrats during their period of Democratic governance? Without them or a significant portion of them, it is very hard for Democrats to aspire to a larger, sustainable majority.

The White House was continually attentive to the challenge. In the back-and-forth White House debates about supporting a balanced budget, Perot's signature issue, Dick Morris would chant to the president, "Remember the theory." He'd insist, "We have the Perot voters out there, lying in wait. This is the moment to strike—and watch the poll numbers go-o UP!" According to George Stephanopoulos, this would take him to his feet, on the tips of his toes, hands high above his head.[70]

But balancing the budget, symbolic for Perot in 1992, had different meaning in the hands of the Republicans in Congress, who included a balanced-budget constitutional amendment, than for Democrats, for whom deficit reduction meant getting our house in order, showing restraint, and helping the economy. President Clinton's lowering of the deficit year after year and announcement that an eleven-zero deficit could be reduced to only one produced few Perot converts in 1996 or afterward.

As it turned out, both the successes and failings of the Reformed Opportunity Democrats drove away Perot voters whose alienation from the Democrats is almost overexplained. The Perot voters were independent, younger, mostly blue collar and noncollege-educated, financially squeezed in the 1980s and for most of the 1990s as well, who felt a deep sense of middle-class grievance. Their sensibilities were among the first to be shunned by the Clinton administration, punctuated by an increase in taxes. They had a strong libertarian streak and were distrustful of meddling government but also of big corporations. Their don't-mess-with-me spirit explains why they were pro-choice but also pro-guns, and thus fit in neither partisan camp. They became suspicious of government programs—ranging from disinterest in retirement issues to an acquired hostility to "big-government" health-care plans. They were inveterate outsiders, antielitist and antiestablishment, which explains their turn away from the top-down Republicans but maybe also from the culturally privileged Democrats. They were cynical about the perks of corporate America but also of political America, where Democrats were involved in bank scandals, corrupt fund-raising, and the like. Thus they were looking for radical steps to change the role of big money in politics, but not only did reform never come, the parties seemed up to their elbows in corrupt or, worse, foreign money. They were pro-America, suspicious of global forces, and pro-military, and thus likely thrown overboard by gays in the military, not to mention NAFTA. Finally, they liked Ross Perot because he was straightforward, honest, and trustworthy, traits less and less associated with the president and Democrats, as "troopergate" turned to "Koreagate," then Lewinsky and impeachment.

Bill Clinton's approval rating with Perot voters fell to 41 percent by the end of his presidency, 17 points below that for the nation.[71]

To turn their big election wins into a real majority, Democrats had to win over a large portion of the Perot voters, which they did not do. While Al Gore had led the effort to reinvent government and reduce the bureaucracy by 100,000, he hardly seemed like an outsider or radical reformer to these independent voters. He seemed political, steeped in government programs, untrustworthy, and fully part of the world in Washington. His strong support for gun control, global trade agreements, and gay unions sealed the deal. The result was that two of every three 1996 Perot voters, more than 5 million people, moved quietly from the Perot side of the ledger to the Republican side in 2000, though without any guarantee against future revolts and movements.[72]

The lost middle, including the Perot voters, leaves the Democrats with the prospects of a very modest national majority at best or, more likely, just at parity with the Republicans, deadlocked at the end of this fifty-year era. The tumultuous politics of this last period has shaped the character of the Democratic support—increasingly minority, well educated, cosmopolitan—as well as the character of the Republican—increasingly religious, Southern, white working class, exurban, and rural. The Reformed Opportunity Democrats, like the Opportunity Democrats and Reagan Revolutionaries before them, aspired to dominate the times but failed—further fashioning the Two Americas.

PART III

The Loyalists

As we have seen, we look out today on a political landscape that is defined by these three failed political missions. Each shattered political conventions. Each set groups in motion. Each in turn helped deepen the divide that leaves many voters polarized. But each in its own way helped produce the unwieldy bloc of contested voters, ambivalent about the choices offered by our current politics.

The two parties are joined today in a destructive struggle—both trapped, neither really able to vanquish the other, but each with a realistic chance of winning any time the battle is rejoined. There are few incentives in this world to pull back from the intense battle, lest the other side gain the upper hand. The result is parties ever more clearly defined, more polarized, the country more deeply and culturally divided.

While such a party battle is the safest way to win on Election Day without risking one's near-majority coalition, it is all a bit surreal. In principle, either party could disengage and say, "We've had enough. This promises just more of the same." Its leaders could look out and decide to play by different rules, address different issues, wage different battles, draw different lines, and perhaps engage the big bloc of groups not currently accommodated by today's politics. However, this is possible only if you can imagine a different set of battle lines and issues.

But few have dared to think outside the rules of the game. There is too much at risk, if you step back or lose your concentration.[1] They both go into elections, as Michael Jordan went into the fourth quarter, looking in the other players' eyes for signs of weakness or a lack of will to battle through to the buzzer.

The starting point for both the Democrats and Republicans is to make sure they take into battle the core of loyalists that this era has bequeathed them. But since neither party's core support or base is big enough to assure victory, each struggles valiantly to make more of it—in the first instance, by growing the groups that are the most loyal, by fanning the passions on each party's lead issues to achieve even greater unity in their voting and more energy and a greater turnout at the polls. Each tries to get the most on "its issues" among the nonloyalists, even if these voters would prefer to change the subject. And each searches for some other groups to isolate and target for gains, particularly if the issue or the cost does not jeopardize the enthusiasm of the loyalists.

That is politics in our current era of party parity.

Our primary window into this world is the fifteen national voter surveys conducted for Democracy Corps over an eighteen-month period after the September 11 attack, with the first survey conducted in November 2001 and the last in May 2003. The surveys were conducted almost every month, each with 1,000 likely voters who agreed to respond to twenty-five minutes of questions about social and political issues. Only because of these interviews with 15,045 people are we able to get this unique picture window looking out on the Two Americas. Conventional surveys have too few respondents to look in detail at the diverse set of groupings that make up the loyalist coalitions or that are contested and dislodged. Here we can look with considerable confidence at the rich texture across the whole landscape.[2]

Our first measure of party orientation centers on party identification, which we now know is a form of social identity, not unlike ethnicity or race, with considerable durability over time. For each group, the first measure that assigns voters to the loyalist or contested world is party alignment. Respondents were asked which party they identify with and, if unsure or independent, which party they lean toward. Over the period, an equal number aligned with the Democrats and Republicans, reflecting America's current deadlock—a parity of the parties that remained stable despite tumultuous events.[3] (The results for each group can be seen in the tables in Appendixes B and C.)

To get a reading on the beliefs and sentiment within each group, we asked these presidential-year voters to give a thermometer rating to a range of groups and individuals. The thermometer is exactly what it seems, with 0 degrees meaning a very cold and unfavorable reaction and 100 degrees representing a very warm, favorable one; 50 degrees is the midpoint and means neither warm nor cold. With these thermometer scores, it is possible to see how groups react to many of the symbols of this period of growing partisan polarization: Bill Clinton, the NRA, pro-life groups, big corporations, immigrants, NAFTA, the NAACP, and the Internet. Each, as we shall see, tells us something about how the various groups related to the culture war, racial conflict, immigration-fueled diversity, the market and inequality, and technology and globalization.[4]

In this part and the next on the contested voters, I tell the story of each group—such as the white Evangelicals (the Faithful) among the Republican loyalists and the women with postgraduate degrees (the Super-Educated Women) among the Democratic loyalists—and how they experienced the party battles of this half-century era and this last decade of deepening polarization. To complete the history, I used the National Election Studies surveys, conducted after each presidential election, starting in 1952, and the exit polls conducted for various news organizations from 1980.[5]

To allow people to speak much more fully about their feelings and to help us understand how they are being drawn into the party battles of this era, I held intensive focus group discussions with people in three contested communities. These were located in Tampa Blue, the blue-collar suburban communities outside Tampa, Florida, home of Centcom, command center for American forces in Iraq; Heartland Iowa, the rural counties in central Iowa; and Eastside Tech, the well-educated and upper-middle-class suburbs mostly to the east of Seattle, an area that includes Microsoft. While these were mostly independent voters, some, like the rural voters, are drawn into the Republican loyalist camp, and others, like the well-educated women, are drawn into the Democratic camp. These discussions help us understand why.[6]

Chapter 5

THE WORLD
OF REPUBLICAN
PARTISANS

The world of Republican loyalists was forged by the three failed efforts to dominate this era, as well as by the last decade of growing partisan polarization. Nearly all Republican loyalists are children of the Reagan Revolution—not literally and not necessarily activists, but believers in the core ideas. In the most recent period, they have responded to the rising political passions and joined the reaction against moral laxity, overbearing government, and disrespect for America's military might.

The Republican world includes white rural America, the Deep South, and growing Exurbia, where religious faith and traditional family life are respected. It includes the workingmen who want the government to stop messing with them and the world to stop messing with America. And it is a world for the most privileged. These are all groups that vote overwhelmingly and with increasing unity for the Republicans.

The passions of political battle in our evenly divided country have produced a large bloc of conservative partisans, bound together culturally and arrayed against the malevolent modernizing forces of the era. Overall, 46 percent of the presidential electorate is aligned with the Republicans, including in that 37 percent who identify themselves as Republicans, two-thirds of whom also think of themselves as political conservatives.[1] But the

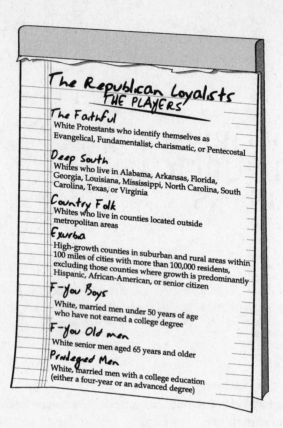

The Republican Loyalists
THE PLAYERS

The Faithful
White Protestants who identify themselves as
Evangelical, Fundamentalist, charismatic, or Pentecostal

Deep South
Whites who live in Alabama, Arkansas, Florida,
Georgia, Louisiana, Mississippi, North Carolina, South
Carolina, Texas, or Virginia

Country Folk
Whites who live in counties located outside
metropolitan areas

Exurbia
High-growth counties in suburban and rural areas within
100 miles of cities with more than 100,000 residents,
excluding those counties where growth is predominantly
Hispanic, African-American, or senior citizen

F-You Boys
White, married men under 50 years of age
who have not earned a college degree

F-You Old men
White senior men aged 65 years and older

Privileged Men
White, married men with a college education
(either a four-year or an advanced degree)

culture war is never one-sided, as we shall see in the countercultural dynamics of the Democratic world, where an identically sized bloc of 46 percent align with the Democrats and 37 percent self-identify as Democrats and stand ready to do battle. The need to build and engage the loyalist bloc has an added urgency on the Republican side because these groups may not represent the future. Many segments are losing ground demographically and are a declining share of the voting electorate. At the same time, some, like the white rural voters, hold views considered heretical in the loyalist world. But this only increases the need to highlight the issues and grievances that produce greater unity and political engagement. As a consequence, the last decade of party parity has produced increasing unity among Republican partisans (and conversely, among Democratic partisans as well).

But this too has its costs for the Republicans, both in the increased engagement and unity on the Democratic side and in the possible alienation of voters in the contested electorate. All in all, things are not so peaceful in the Republican world.

THE REPUBLICAN WORLD

PARTY ALIGNMENT

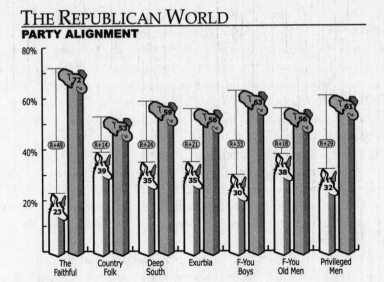

Democracy Corps database, November 2001–May 2003.

The loyalist world is comprised disproportionately of seven groups that frequently overlap, although each is distinctive and plays an important role in the politics of the Republican Party.

THE FAITHFUL At the center of the Republican world are the white Evangelicals whose faith gives meaning to the modern Republican Party and whose moral system defines what has become known as "red America." In conservative social commentator David Brooks's description, the people here are "traditional, religious, self-disciplined and patriotic."[2] The white Evangelicals comprise a range of religious identities, including Fundamentalists, born-again Christians, even some charismatics. And while there is considerable diversity of thought on religious questions and a reluctance to condemn or impose one's religion, they share a sense that America is decaying morally—a result of morality becoming relative and contingent, and not based on the Gospel.[3] America is losing ground because people do not practice their faith in their own lives, and the family is under great pressure, but also because Christian values are under serious attack. The problem is not Christians trying to impose their views on society, but society keeping religion, its teachings and prayer, out of the public domain, from schools to Christmas celebrations.[4]

These views lose their nuance and tolerance when the religious, political entrepreneurs take them public. Pat Robertson alerted the faithful to an impending choice: "Either we will return to the moral integrity and original dreams of the founders of this nation . . . or we will give ourselves over more and more to hedonism, to all forms of destructive social behavior. . . ." That is the "mandate from our Heavenly Father," says *The Christian Voice*, "to make sure government is faithfully meting out justice and punishing what is wrong and rewarding what is right."[5] For them the most destructive social behavior is homosexuality, which Jerry Falwell declared a sin "so grievous, so abominable in the sight of God that He destroyed the cities of Sodom and Gomorrah because of it."[6] And on this issue, the political ministry has a lot of followers among the Evangelical faithful who, much more than other Americans, do not want homosexuals living in their neighborhoods or gay rights groups involved in politics.[7]

Falwell and Robertson may oversimplify and overdramatize the choice, but there is no question that, as sociologist Jerome L. Himmelstein wrote, from the vantage point of the building storm in the Reagan period, "Religious persons are more likely to oppose the ERA and abortion because they possess a culture that sanctions traditional family relationships and women's roles." But the religiously observant also take conservative political stances and become politically engaged because they "are integrated into religious networks" that make them accessible to such politicized clergy.[8]

The Faithful comprise nearly one in five Americans, 17 percent, and their faith is what animates the modern Republican Party.[9] They give the party life, not just in the countryside but also in the small towns and small cities and suburbs of America.

White Evangelicals vote for the Republicans, as if it were an article of their faith. More than 70 percent of the Faithful align with the Republican Party, giving the Republicans nearly a 50-point margin (72 percent, compared to the few "lost souls," the 23 percent who align with the Democrats). In the dead-heat presidential election of 2000, four in every five (80 percent) of the Faithful voted for George W. Bush. They carried the same unified passion into the hotly contested 2002 congressional elections with nearly 75 percent casting ballots for Republicans.[10]

These are not voters who question the choice they have made in politics. They are the most committed of the loyalists: only one in five says they would consider switching and voting Democratic.

Their deep bond with the Republican Party was forged through decades of culture war. The first shots were actually fired in the 1960s, which began for the Evangelicals with the Democrats nominating a Catholic, John Kennedy, for president, and ended with the racially divisive campaign of 1968 and the Democrats choosing a full-throated cultural liberal, George

McGovern, in 1972. Mostly rooted in the South, these voters did not easily abandon their Democratic identity, but they surely abandoned the party's nominees in large numbers. Only 39 percent voted for Kennedy, even less, 24 percent, for Humphrey (26 percent voted for the white segregationist George Wallace), and just 19 percent for McGovern.[11]

Despite the next decade of battles over abortion, affirmative action, private religious academies, and school prayer, these voters remained marginally more Democratic.[12] Indeed, Jimmy Carter won 46 percent of their votes in 1976 and 33 percent in 1980.[13]

Ronald Reagan and his defining 1984 election brought these voters of faith into the heart of the Republican Party. They voted for him in overwhelming numbers, 74 to 26 percent, and for the first time, a significant number began to call themselves Republicans: 54 percent, compared to only 36 percent for the Democrats. This is where political life has remained ever since for the white Evangelicals.[14]

Nearly two-thirds of the Faithful think of themselves as ideologically conservative, and given the history, they have no doubt defined the term in cultural, rather than material, terms. But their faith, as much as that of any group in the Republican world, is absolute and encompasses conservative postures on small government, markets, and personal responsibility.

George W. Bush's simple expressions of faith go a long way here. He is speaking to the Faithful when he says, as he did in the 2000 presidential campaign, that the Bible is his favorite book and that "on the issue of evolution, the verdict is still out on how God created the earth." He elaborated, "I mean, after all, religion has been around a lot longer than Darwinism."[15]

Politically, the white Evangelicals are faithful to a fault, and if the Republicans get nothing else right, they will not neglect the care and feeding of this, their strongest loyalist group. Today, the Faithful stand as united against abortion as they are against the Democrats. They give pro-life advocates an intensely hot 66.8-degree rating.[16] These same voters give Bill Clinton a frosty 24.6-degree rating—a full 19 degrees lower than he receives from the general electorate, contributing to Christian conservative Paul Weyrich's argument that the moral majority has become the moral minority.[17] Indeed, nearly three in four white Evangelicals give Clinton a negative or cool response.

Not surprisingly, much of Clinton's harshest criticism has come from the leadership of the white Evangelical community. In a newsletter that began, "Dear Friends," radio evangelist James Dobson wrote of Clinton: "It is my belief that no man has ever done more to debase the presidency." The newsletter, mailed to more than 2.5 million Christian households, blamed Clinton's "homosexual agenda" for "undermining the institution of marriage," and on Clinton's abortion position, Dobson wrote, "Clinton's hands are stained with the blood of countless innocent babies."[18]

So the Republican agenda for this period of parity and deadlock always includes some new red meat for the most loyal: late-term abortion, cloning, stem cell research, Hillary Clinton, or the posting of the Ten Commandments in courtrooms and classrooms. These are a curiosity to the secular world, but they are fundamental to reaffirming the unity of faith-based politics.

While the whole Republican edifice depends on this near universal enthusiasm among the Faithful, their agenda comes with a big price tag—an array of groups that do not want to inhabit the same party. The divide in America is about competing moral systems, and the visible expressions of faith by "red America" produce an even greater emphasis in "blue America" on being modern, secular, self-expressive, and cautiously patriotic. Many of the postmodernists are in the Democratic camp, but there are also many in the contested world who are deeply uncomfortable in the Republican house of faith.

In addition, the secular modernizing forces to which Christian fundamentalism is partially a reaction may be catching up with the devout. The number of regular churchgoers, those who attend every week, fell off between 1972 and 1988. However, during the most recent decade and a half, the share of regular churchgoers has stabilized at around 25 percent of the adult population. But in the same period, the truly secular, those who never attend church services or attend less than once a year, have risen from 18 percent in 1972 to 29 percent in the 2000 presidential electorate, with the secular now in a dead heat with the devout, perhaps inching ahead.[19]

But in a world of political parity, this is but a signal to the Faithful to affirm their political faith with even greater fervor.

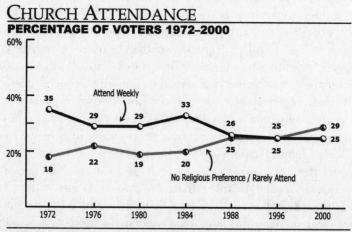

CHURCH ATTENDANCE
PERCENTAGE OF VOTERS 1972–2000

National Opinion Research Center, 1972–2000.

DEEP SOUTH   The Deep South is home to one of every five voters in the country and is at the heart of the Republican loyalist world. The Deep South states provide the Republicans with one of every two electoral votes they need to win nationally.

And more important for the Republicans, these voters are part of the growing and modernizing South, not just the world of faith and countryside. To be sure, the white South is religious: they are much more likely to go to church every week. But only a quarter live in rural counties outside metropolitan areas, with a majority living in small towns and the suburbs. A growing number, 16 percent, live in high-growth rural, suburban, and exurban counties. Republican values are now deeply implanted in the growing suburban and exurban middle-class areas of metropolitan centers, which have given the Republicans their most prominent national leaders—Newt Gingrich, Dick Armey, and Tom DeLay, for example.[20]

In some sense, they are the modern face of the Republican Party, providing the leaders and accents that dominate the imagery for the national party. Hailing from Crawford, Texas, President George W. Bush is now, more than any other leader, the face of the party and the personification of its Deep South character. In this modern age, the loyalist world is much more associated with the new suburban South (and Sun Belt) than its plantation past.[21]

These white voters are more ensconced in the Republican loyalist world than their rural counterparts across the country. While rural America has wavered in this battle, white Southerners have been there consistently since everything blew up in 1968. For them, the best days were during the Reagan era, when their president spoke a new common sense for the South: "I don't think we should have expelled God from the classroom"; "I believe in states' rights." And the Republican platform repudiated busing and abortion, called for prayer in the schools, and remained silent on the ERA for women.[22] The vote for Reagan reached an astonishing 74 percent in the white Deep South, and held for his successor, George Bush.[23] The year 1984 marked the first time that more white Southerners called themselves Republican than Democrat, a symbolic turning point for the "Solid South," though it took another decade before there was something resembling a Republican takeover of people's hearts and minds. Dan Balz and Ronald Brownstein write, "The Republican Party captured the South and the South captured the Republican Party."[24]

In this last decade, whoever the Democrat standing, whether Bill Clinton or Al Gore, his vote barely reached over 30 percent of white voters here.[25] Meanwhile, Republicans were successfully winning over virtually all of the Southern Perot voters, allowing Bush to take two-thirds of the Deep South in 2000.[26]

DEEP SOUTH THERMOMETERS
COMPARED TO ALL VOTERS

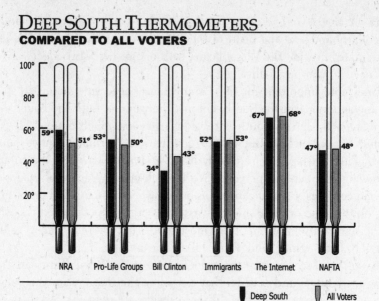

NRA	Pro-Life Groups	Bill Clinton	Immigrants	The Internet	NAFTA

■ Deep South   ▮ All Voters

Democracy Corps database, November 2001–May 2003.

Today, these white voters of the Deep South are fully and comfortably aligned with the Republicans, 59 percent to 35 percent, a 24-point margin. The political culture of the Deep South is now comfortably Republican, with new generations of voters increasingly Republican.[27]

Across a broad range of issues, white Southerners, along with the Faithful, embody the modern Republican Party. They align themselves with a party that they think is much more devoted than the Democrats to the military and keeping America strong (64 to 15 percent) and that knows how to handle their taxes in the right way (57 to 27 percent). These voters like the NRA (a thermometer of 58.6 degrees) almost as much as they dislike Bill Clinton (a cold thermometer of 33.5 degrees). These white Deep South voters are pro–big business and also cautious about government regulation, but with growing suburbanization, not quite as hostile to regulation as are other loyalists.

These white Southerners represent the mainstream of the loyalist camp. But on both the "cosmopolitan" East and West coasts and among minority voters and a growing number of suburban women, the mainstream looks very different.

COUNTRY FOLK The white voters that make up rural America are serious about their faith and way of life, and are also supposed to be serious about their loyalties to the Republican Party. In the last presidential election, they certainly added to the expanse of "red America," with its sprawling farmlands, vast plains, and mountains, peppered with small towns—all colored in red. They cover a lot of territory, as one in five presidential-year voters lives in the white countryside, split evenly between rural farm areas and small towns.[28]

But for all that, there is trouble and ambiguity in this corner of the Republican world, which will get these voters a lot of attention. The Country Folk are conflicted on the issues of the day, and only a couple of years of ago they were dividing their votes between the parties. Although they align now with the Republicans, the margins do suggest the potential for a more closely contested political future.

Across all of America, a sizable majority of Country Folk, 53 percent, now aligns with the Republican Party, while 39 percent say they stand with the Democrats. And in the last few years, when these voters got to their rural polling places, they cast Republican ballots in even larger numbers: about 62 percent chose Bush over Gore, as well as the Republican congressional candidates in 2002.[29] Those white rural voters help account for why George W. Bush was able to stay competitive in the presidential election and why Republicans took back the Senate. Indeed, they help explain why the Republicans took back the Congress in 1994. Before the election, 62 percent of the Congressional Rural Caucus were Democrats; afterward, in the next Congress, 59 percent were Republicans.[30]

This was not always so, or even recently so, which is why Republicans will work hard to hold their rural patches across the closely contested states of Oregon, Nevada, New Mexico, Minnesota, Wisconsin, Iowa, Missouri, Arkansas, Tennessee, West Virginia, New Hampshire, and Maine. In the Reagan era, white rural voters began to vote for the Republican presidential candidates in large and consistent numbers: 59 percent in 1980, 69 percent in 1984, and 60 percent in 1988.[31] But then the bottom fell out as these voters faced an uneven rural economy and came to doubt the socially distant Bush administration. Falling farmland values ate away $40 billion from Iowa's tax base during the first half of the eighties; 15 percent of Iowa farms disappeared, while land worth $2,539 in 1981 fell to $1,275 by 1985.[32] As a result, in both presidential elections of the nineties, white rural voters gave the Republicans only a small edge, while giving Perot above average support both times. Outside the Deep South, they were in fact splitting their votes evenly between the parties.[33] But the 2000 election, against the backdrop of the Clinton impeachment and Al Gore's apparent secularism, brought these voters back. The Country Folk voted almost two to one for George W. Bush: 63 to 34 percent.[34] This produced the sprawling red map and the impulse to see these voters as Republican loyalists.

These voters are the reason why George Bush spends so much time clearing brush on his 1,600-acre ranch in Crawford, Texas, the "Western White House." There, his faded jeans and work shirt are testimony to his "common man roots." In a kind of Reagan redux, a tanned Bush appears regularly before the traveling press corps, swinging an ax or chainsawing cedar. Don't let his degree from Yale fool you—Bush's fence mending is time well spent.

These voters are also the reason why the farm bill is packed with subsidies that anger and hurt the rest of the world. Farm politics can be a tricky and dangerous game, as Ronald Reagan found when he cut farm subsidies and lost control of the Senate in 1986. Bush backed the new farm bill that reversed the planned reductions and increased farm subsidies by 80 percent. The new bill raises spending in states like Iowa and Wisconsin that Bush lost by only a few thousand votes in 2000.[35]

These are voters who will keep their flags displayed, even after the war news fades, and who will protect their right to bear arms. Here, the Republicans are unsurpassed as the party that will keep America strong (56 percent, with a bare 20 percent willing to depend on the Democrats) and will defend the Second Amendment.[36] White rural voters give the NRA a very warm thermometer rating of 61.3 degrees, which helps plant them firmly on the red side of the current cultural divide. With a good majority of white voters in the countryside owning guns, positive feelings toward the NRA here have risen steadily over the last four years of culture war.[37] On these issues, they know which side they are on.

Over a two-year period, my colleagues and I have listened carefully to the Country Folk of Heartland Iowa, who talk about their values and families as if under siege.[38] Very often, they fret about the influence of Hollywood and the bad examples set by some national political leaders. On these topics, they reflect the dominant discourse of the Republican loyalist world. But they also worry about the behavior of big business and show a lack of faith in markets. In that, they are part of a discourse from a different planet, which is why the Country Folk are disconcerting loyalists, to say the least.

The rural women in our group discussions are almost wistful about the immediate problems facing families like their own. In defiance of societal trends, many of these women are "trying to get back where you have higher standards"; they're trying to "get back to the family atmosphere, where families do things together."[39] Yet they realize that this is no small feat; as one woman observed, "We're so busy with our daily lives, [we] have a hard time trying to instill these values in our kids as they grow up. . . ."[40]

The job of parenting is made more difficult by crumbling marriages. Census figures show that less than one-fourth of American households are made up of the nuclear families once deemed the ideal. As one rural woman exclaimed, "I mean, you get married," but "it doesn't mean anything, nothing."[41]

But what really drives these parents crazy are the bad influences on their children over which they have precious little control. In their own family, supported by the community and church, they make sure their children are exposed to the proper lessons. But they see dramatic forces overwhelming their best efforts. The entertainment industry, the men observed, provides their children with "videotapes that teach your kids to shoot and kill police and sell drugs." Their kids are drawn to performers, like Eminem; "that's leading all the kids into dressing that way, talking that way, rapping that way, so what comes out of his mouth, comes out of theirs. And what's coming out of his, we can live without."[42]

Ten years ago, Super Mario Brothers and Sonic the Hedgehog were all the rage. Kids honed their hand-eye coordination in "platform" video games with trapdoors and secret passages while avoiding poisonous mushrooms and man-eating plants—all in a valiant effort to save the beautiful princess. But Super Mario Brothers gave way to games like Mortal Kombat, Grand Theft Auto, and "first person shooter" games like Doom and Quake. In one of our discussions, a few mothers discussed the state of "virtual reality" gaming: "There's one game where a person could go out and rob and kill, and it's a game!" "And steal." "And you get points." "Yes, you get points." " 'But Mom, it's fun,' " one of the mothers noted in parody of her son. "No, it's not fun."[43]

Television is, if anything, worse. Children watch sensational TV shows that teach them to lie so they can get a girlfriend or win millions. To many of these parents, the Joe Millionaires, the Real Worlds, and the WWF SmackDowns hinder their ability to raise their children. "The country is closing out all of our values," one father lamented, "all of our family values." Leading to, in his words, "moral bankruptcy."[44]

The examples set by some of our most prominent national politicians, above all Bill Clinton, though some even recall Gary Hart's *Monkey Business*, compound the parenting problem. These rural voters, not surprisingly, give the former president a thermometer of only 36.0 degrees, pushed down by the nearly 60 percent of rural voters who respond coolly to his name. "Personally," one man flatly stated, "I think Bill Clinton was a disgrace to the presidency."[45]

Discussion of Clinton in these groups is rife with laughter and off-color jokes, but locker room banter is soon grounded by more serious talk, as demonstrated by one man who thought Clinton's antics dragged the presidency "through the gutter." He emphatically stated, "He lied to me, and I'm not happy about it. I never was happy about it."[46]

Here in rural America, a man's word means something and the presidency is an honor. "[In] a president, you need somebody that you can trust, you put up on a ladder," one voter observed. And while he believed "Clinton was a good president in a lot of ways," he felt that Clinton's philandering created a shameful double standard: "I mean, if we did that in our jobs, we'd be gone, you know?"[47] Another man concluded, "That's really destroyed a lot of our kids, that they think they can do what they want."[48]

But for all the worry about their families and lessons for their children, these white rural voters will require a lot of attention if they are to remain in the Republican world. The cultural and character issues have driven them deep into the Republican camp in recent years, but the culture war is not so consuming for them that all other issues are blocked out. They are less enthusiastic about Republicans when it comes to the economy and market, giving them only a 13-point edge, well below that of other loyalists.[49] The white rural voters, it seems, stand a bit apart.

Populist sensibilities are still very much alive here, as people are instinctively skeptical about those with market power. This is the only group of voters in the Republican world that is decidedly anticorporate, giving big corporations only a 44.6-degree thermometer rating and predominantly cold responses. These rural voters certainly think America has a "values problem"—and that includes the corporate boardrooms.

When asked what comes to mind when hearing the phrase "big corporations," they spit out, "money," "greed," and "Enron." They "try and run the little guy out" and have "too much control over the little people."[50] They speak of greed at the top, unchecked by values, indifferent to the consequences for others: "A lot of greed. Greed is taking over a lot of people," one rural voter told us. "They want to make more and more and more."[51]

These voters chalk many of our current economic woes up to "corporate arrogance and greed,"[52] approaching the topic with revulsion formerly reserved for Hollywood:

It really makes me really question and just lose faith in everything that we were supposed to believe in. This shows the total lack of respect. It seems like there used to be a value system where there was a respect for the people who worked for you.[53]

[You] have the superrich and the rest. There is no thought for any of the people; they will steal from the companies, they will steal from us, they'll destroy our pensions and everything else to live lifestyles beyond what they could ever enjoy. Yet they are willing to let the worker take the fall.[54]

They find themselves defenseless before the power at the top, which certainly dominates the two parties. "I think the people with money control basically everything," one woman explained. "They control other people. They control votes on everything," they "run the country." Another woman told us, "I think both the Democrats and Republicans are out for themselves." She added, "None of them understand really, like you, what paycheck-to-paycheck life is like."[55] One man summarized an alienated politics: "We have legislators who are there forever and are so in bed with all these companies that they have no objectivity and they don't want to represent us."[56]

And because they believe government is in bed with big business, these voters assume that companies are allowed to operate with a "lack of control" and "lack of regulation." As one woman said, the government is "allowing the big companies to do what they want."[57]

Not exactly stalwarts for the market, these white rural voters would give the government a lot of latitude in checking market and private behavior for the benefit of society. Remarkable and exceptional in this Republican world, 55 percent say that government regulation of business and corporations is necessary to protect the public, while just a third (36 percent) say government regulation does more harm than good.

This is the reason why the Republicans will want to keep the cultural issues aflame, lest these voters dwell too long on corporate excesses and the lack of values operative at the top and the need for government to check that market power on behalf of the public. But if the cultural issues prove insufficient, do not underestimate the temptation to open up the budget spigot. Further ethanol and sugar subsidies are but a small price to pay.

Unfortunately, no amount of money or working of the cultural levers can offset powerful historical trends, which have diminished the role of the countryside in our lives. Today, one in five white voters (21 percent) lives in the rural counties that constitute America's countryside. This once dominant landscape has fallen inexorably from just under 50 percent of the voting population in 1956 and 1960, to around 40 percent in the period 1964–72, to around 30 percent in 1976–84, dropping to a quarter through 1988–96, and finally, dropping to just under 20 percent in 2000.[58]

Fortunately for the Republicans, white countryside voters still constitute about 20 percent of America and most of them are concentrated in states that have a big say in who becomes president. So declining numbers, po-

COUNTRY FOLK
PERCENTAGE OF VOTERS 1956–2000

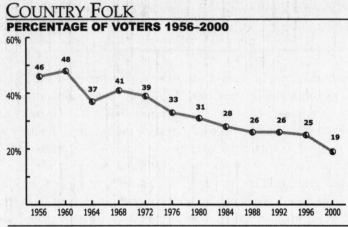

National Election Studies, 1956–2000.

tential issue ambivalence, and geographic importance all underscore the urgency of keeping these voters focused on values and off those thoughts that brought them into the world of parity just a few years ago.

THE LURE OF EXURBIA Soon after the 2000 presidential election and, indeed, after the Republican gains in 2002, strategists, demographers, and the press paid increasing attention to the fast-growing counties, both rural and suburban, forming a "metropolitan fringe" or Exurbia, predominantly in the Sun Belt of the South and Southwest.[59] This is new "red territory," it seems, and may partially offset the rural decline.

Exurbia is proving to be a popular alternative to the older, more congested, and more racially diverse suburbs of the metropolitan areas, especially those of the Northeast, Midwest, and West Coast, which are attracting so many new immigrant minorities. The move to Exurbia is a latter-day form of white flight, which includes many younger families, but also some baby-boomer empty nesters, as well as recent retirees who are looking for a change in lifestyle.[60]

For Michael Barone, this is new territory, full of "family-sized subdivisions, outlet shopping malls and booming mega-churches," and gives sufficient new life to conservative values and the Republican identity to offset the black and cultural liberal majorities in the city center. He points to Forsyth County in Georgia, which grew by 123 percent in the decade and voted 78 percent for Bush in 2000 and 77 percent for the Republican who upset Senator Max Cleland in 2002.[61] Barone might also have focused on Scott County, Minnesota, which increased rapidly in population, by more than 50 percent during the 1990s. In 1996, Dole lost the county by 6 points, yet four years later Bush tripled that margin but for the Republicans (55 to 40 percent), and just two years later, Norm Coleman doubled this figure again, defeating former Vice President Walter Mondale by 30 points in the county.

Exurbia, no matter how "red," could not offset rural decline if the focus were solely on the superfast-growing counties, which are symbolically important to conservative hopes. The top fifty fastest-growing counties in America, which include nearly all of the showcase exurban counties, all together encompass only 1.5 percent of the presidential-year voters. Even if we look at the top seventy-five fastest-growing counties, we are reaching only 2.3 percent of the voters.[62]

But Exurbia is real and important to the Republican partisan world, comprising 8 percent of the electorate. A broader definition, encompassing suburban and rural counties growing at a modest rate (26 percent or greater over the past decade, double the national average) and within reach (100 miles) of a modest-size city (100,000 or larger population), seems to capture the growth in the metropolitan fringe areas.[63]

As it turns out, Exurbia is Republican loyalist territory, aligning with the Republicans by 21 points (56 to 35 percent).

Exurban voters are completely comfortable on the conservative side of the cultural divide. Like other Republican loyalists, they are very cool to Bill Clinton (35.1 degrees) and, consistent with the polarities of the right, quite warm to the NRA (57.0 degrees) and favorable to pro-life groups (53.0 degrees). They instinctively trust the Republicans to keep America strong (66 to 17 percent), but they also give the Republicans much higher marks on handling the economy and education, reflecting the kind of conservative suburban areas Exurbia encompasses.

The strong conservative views in this growing area likely offset some of the rural decline in the last decade, but it is hard to know the aggregate effect of this growth. Exurbia is composed for the most part not of new voters but of displaced ones from the older cities of the East and Midwest, from the older inner suburbs, and from the rural areas. These socially and economically conservative voters are concentrating in Exurbia, where the way of life, values, and politics are much more congenial, but this growth does not necessarily represent a shift in the national balance.

More important, exurban areas are almost wholly a Sun Belt phenomenon: 49 percent of these voters are in the Deep South, including Texas; 9 percent more are in the border South; and 15 percent are in the mountain states—comprising three-quarters of the total. This means that the growing exurban areas tell us a lot about the character of these mostly red states. They probably also help us understand why growth in more cosmopolitan centers, like Atlanta, Birmingham, Dallas, and Austin, has not succeeded in moving these states toward the Democrats.

At this point, Exurbia is a small but important part of the Republican loyalist world and obviously a growth area that may contribute powerfully, as the Faithful and Deep South voters do now, to the identity of the Republican world.

THE F-YOU BOYS   They think President George W. Bush is their guy, speaking to them man to man. They probably wish they were from Texas, where today's leading conservative politician is unembarrassed in his support of freewheeling markets and capitalism, letting consumers and producers get on with it, disdainful of Washington elites, intellectual talk, and big government, and supportive of military values and determined to see America take care of itself.[64]

Everything about the Bush presidency seems to resonate with these voters. These white men, without college degrees, many blue collar, married, under fifty years of age, mainly with young families, like the style, values, substance, and prejudices of today's Republican politics. These men want the government to leave them alone. It has been a long time since government has done anything with them in mind. Take all the regulations and do-good policies and go somewhere else, they suggest. By more than two to one, they think government should stop telling them what to do with their lives, off-road vehicles, and SUVs and guns, rejecting the idea that government can advance a better environment and help consumers (64 to 29 percent). This is the most pro-NRA group in the conservative Republican base: a 73.5-degree thermometer. Not surprisingly, these men of very moderate incomes think the Republicans, by an overwhelming 62 percent, are better on handling taxes.

And just as they do not want the government to mess with them, they do not want anybody messing with America. While a small majority of the country thinks we should depend on allies in these times to help protect America, these Boys, by a very wide margin, say, "Bottom line, America's security depends on its own military strength" (54 to 37 percent). And to get a government with that kind of strength for America, one turns to the Republicans, not the Democrats (67 to 17 percent). They want an America strong enough to advance its interests, unfettered.

Little wonder that the F-You Boys have been consolidated as one of the strongest elements in the Republican loyalist camp. Indeed, they align with the Republicans over Democrats by better than two to one (63 to 30 percent). This makes them the most Republican of the loyalists after the Faithful.

There is one problem. They are an endangered species. They comprise only 6 percent of the electorate.

F-YOU BOYS
PERCENTAGE OF VOTERS 1952–2000

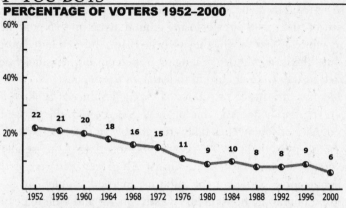

National Election Studies, 1952–2000.

They are being squeezed on sheer scale by the growing number of college-educated voters, by increasing minorities and immigrants, and by the decline of marriage for both men and women. They are being squeezed at home by the radical changes in gender roles. They are being squeezed by their wives, who do not instinctively stand with the Boys. They are being squeezed in the job market by stagnant, indeed declining, wages for men without college degrees and the narrowing wage gap with women.

It wasn't always this way. There was a time when the hardworking men of industrial America were king—as heads of household, as consumers, and as citizens and soldiers. In the post–World War II era, government and corporate America rewarded these men with houses and low mortgages, with cars and highways. After all, they represented the GIs that Ernie Pyle wrote about who, motivated by duty and patriotism, had won the war. These men were useful to the country and for that, Pyle wrote, "Goddamn all big shots." At the same time, they were part of a time when to be a man also meant to be on the rise and mastering things. *Time* and *Life* magazines wanted them to build a nation that would "exert upon the world the full impact of our influence."[65]

And indeed, in the 1950s and 1960s, they were at the heart of American politics. Most were union members and most were Democrats, though they liked Ike, who said, "All in that gigantic fighting machine agree in the selection of the one truly heroic figure in that war. He is GI Joe."[66] They had a role in the electorate commensurate with their social standing: they formed about 20 percent of the voters in the 1950s and even the early sixties, when John Kennedy called upon them to seek a "new frontier" and send American astronauts to the moon.

But over the course of this half-century postwar period, these white family men were battered by demographic, economic, social, and political trends. By the late sixties, they were already losing ground, to around 15 percent of the electorate, which is part of why they were so mad. They remained around 15 percent until the midseventies, falling to 10 percent in the mideighties, and then eroded further to their current sad state of 6 percent.[67]

The decline of the F-You Boys is being produced by fundamental changes in the family and the role of men. Since 1970, the percentage of married-couple households has fallen remarkably from 71 percent to a bare majority of 53 percent in 2000; the number of married households with children dropped from 40 percent to just 24 percent.[68] Even in the formative demographic battle for the suburbs, married couples are now outnumbered by nonfamily households, mostly singles and elderly people.[69]

The political passage for these men was even more troubled, which also poses problems for the Republicans as they try to tame their anger and frustration with everything around them. Battered by the struggles over civil rights, women's rights, and gay rights, and by the decline of their economic fortunes, to name a few, these downscale white men traveled the path from presumed Democrats, to angry protest voters, to entrenched but volatile Republicans. They were actually swing voters at the start of the era—giving Eisenhower a small majority both times but giving Kennedy and particularly Johnson big majorities. But 1968 changed everything politically, and they never really entertained backing the Democrats again.

When Wallace and Nixon took to the campaign trail in 1968, the F-You Boys of their age were surely their first audience. Wallace told them "the intellectual morons" were "trifling with children" and had "destroyed the federal government." And Nixon and his vice presidential running mate, Spiro Agnew, spoke of the "radical liberals" who had taken over the Democratic Party and federal government, and the need for "the silent majority" to be heard.[70]

They listened to the politicians who said they would not forget them: a mere 34 percent stayed with Humphrey and a tidal wave of these white, noncollege, married men broke away from the Democrats, 46 percent for Nixon and 20 percent for Wallace.[71]

It was Ronald Reagan, perhaps more than any other politician of this era, who heard their expressions of frustration and anger. I learned this in the mid-1980s in Macomb County, a working-class Detroit suburb where these mostly union voters had abandoned Democrats en masse to support Reagan. Then, these white married men looked back on the economic stagnation of the past decade and talked about themselves as the "middle-class poor," cramped financially, "supporting both ends, the upper end [that] got all the tax breaks" and "the people on welfare" who got all their money but didn't "have to worry about working for it." The middle class was virtuous, carrying the burden of the government on its back by virtue of their being responsible, hardworking, and taxpaying. They viewed the government in racial terms—rigging the game for blacks and doing nothing for them. Asked who gets a raw deal, they responded, "It's the white people"—"white, American, middle-class male."[72]

Ronald Reagan sided with hardworking, responsible, average folk and shared their disdain for "big government." In 1984, he received an impressive 73 percent of their votes, which he passed on to his immediate heir, George H. W. Bush, who got 67 percent in 1988.[73]

When the recession hit under George Bush, the F-You Boys were particularly hard hit and uniquely disillusioned. They led the charge in support of Perot: 28 percent in 1992 and 15 percent in 1996. President Bush won a plurality of the F-You Boys, but he got only 42 percent, with Bill Clinton at 30 percent.

The F-You Boys are hardly shy about telling researchers why. Sociologist Michele Lamont spoke to the white working-class men in northern New Jersey in the early 1990s. They were doubly hit by the consolidation of large manufacturers and the economic downturn, and they were pressed to provide for their families in a period of rising unemployment. But this only reaffirmed their sense of obligation as husbands and fathers—to make sure their families were protected from the disorder and uncertainty outside. They were consumed with the role of being "a provider" who put food on the table and a roof over their family's heads. They had to protect their families from the rising crime rates and neighborhood decline.

This required discipline, managing one's impulses, and is why they preferred "decent people," like themselves, who took responsibility. They trusted people who were direct. They were themselves straightforward about religion, as reflected in the comments of one man, who believed in God, "all the rights and wrongs, no grays. I don't believe in gray. Truth, honesty, responsibility, that's what I believe in."[74]

And as for the workingmen of Macomb County in the Reagan years, blacks are central to the boundaries and the walls that they were trying to build. Blacks, they thought, too often violated their norms and acted without responsibility and restraint. Part of the social task of the F-You Boys was to protect their private lives from the blacks outside.[75] On the other coast, Susan Faludi was describing a similar process among the men who were losing out in the downsizing and modernization of California's defense and aerospace industries. When the big industries fell in the Los Angeles area, also lost were the 40,000 to 80,000 heavy-industrial workers, mostly men, whose work with heavy machinery, Faludi writes, "had hoisted them into the ranks of the unionized middle class." The jobs came with high pay and benefits and relevance for the nation and family. It also made the housewife an "integral part of the aerospace formula." But now, these men, thrown out of their traditional skilled positions, struggled to be useful. Here, the unemployed men talked about a new social truth: "The male gender has taken a backseat—across the board."[76]

This loss of usefulness and ability to provide has shaped the consciousness of the working-class men right through the decade, Faludi argues. In its most extreme, cadets of the Citadel slung what they considered their most base insult at a fellow cadet: "You are not a man, you are a woman." But that bravado was more than matched by other responses, such as the sense of powerlessness and betrayal—and pathetic protests—when the Cleveland Browns abandoned Cleveland and its male fans. The Promise Keepers filled stadiums across the country with millions of noncollege and college-educated men, making their own kind of accommodation to the position of men. They sought not to undo what America's economy had wrought but to meet the desperate need of men for "significance."[77]

The struggle of the F-You Boys to be useful and provide left them with issues, to be sure.

Bill Clinton was hardly the answer to their preoccupations, and he barely got a third of their votes, and Gore barely a quarter, although they warmed to Bush in 2000. But these younger angry white men have jumped at the chance to join political revolts, despite the decades-long Republican embrace.[78] Minnesota's Jesse Ventura attracted a significant number of these supporters, "some so disaffected that they voted only because he was on the ballot."[79] This history of joining the political revolts of the day is why Bush dares not lose sight of them.[80]

THE F-YOU OLD MEN The F-You Boys find soul mates among the white retired men, the F-You Old Men, so to speak. These men are over sixty-five, but they share a lot with the younger married men. These older men lived through the tumult of the 1960s and 1970s that shaped the consciousness of white family men at the time. Like the F-You Boys, the F-You Old Men think the Republicans are the go-to party when it comes to the military and assuring that America is strong (61 to 19 percent). They too, for the most part, would rather see America depend on its own military than allies (47 to 42 percent). But unlike their younger counterparts, three in four F-You Old Men served in the military.

These senior males are not quite the cultural and conservative warriors that the younger downscale men are, as they are not as antigovernment and pro-gun; they are not quite as angry about the Democrats' attitude toward taxes. Social Security does matter here, though, which favors the Democrats. Accordingly, they are not quite as wedded to the Republicans, though still aligned with them, 56 to 38 percent.[81]

But forming only 7 percent of the electorate, the F-You Old Men do not undermine the main story of declining social and political influence. As young married men, they were once the heart and soul of America, but hardly anymore. The new generation of F-You Boys is barely large enough to be heard, but with the added voice of George W. Bush, their strong feelings and views gain renewed importance. They appreciate the attention.

PRIVILEGED MEN The Republican loyalist bloc is large enough to compete in this period of parity only because it continues to win the support of the Privileged Men—white, married, and educated—who make up 13 percent of the electorate. Their advantages in each area earn them a very high family income, well above the norm for the country and especially the other loyalists: more than two-thirds have family incomes over $50,000, about a half over $75,000, and over a quarter more than $100,000. It is hard not to overestimate how out of place these men are in a loyalist Republican camp dominated by the Faithful, Country Folk, and F-You Boys.

"Show me the money" is apparently their catchphrase. They like the Republicans, above all, because of their tax cuts and pro-business economic policies. They distrust the government's ability to correct the market and respect the Republicans' hands-off approach to the economy. As one man explained, "I get nervous when they say we're going to create more jobs. What kind of jobs? Business does better at creating jobs than government."[82]

For these men, the Republicans' tax-friendly and pro-business policies are the red meat that keeps them in this loyalist camp. Republican presidents, from Reagan to George W. Bush, have understood this need, which is why these men prefer the Republicans on taxes (65 to 25 percent) and the economy (59 to 28 percent). One man identified the disparity between the two parties on taxes as a philosophical difference. For the Democratic Party, he said, tax hikes are part of "their whole philosophy," and they think they can "just add a program, add a program, add a program. . . ." In a similar vein, one Seattle native offered the Democrats this advice: "You can't have your cake and eat it too," adding, "there is no such thing as a hot fudge sundae diet."[83]

These are voters who give big corporations a comparatively warm thermometer rating of 51.7 degrees, the highest in the Republican world. On the material issues of the economy and taxes, the Privileged Men are nearly as passionate as the white Evangelicals are about abortion.

In that spirit, barely 30 percent considered the apostasy of voting for a Democrat for president during the Reagan era of the eighties, an era when their privilege was well rewarded.[84] In the nineties, despite an even more extended period of growth and the increased attention to cultural issues, only a third voted for the Democrat; Al Gore got 31 percent.[85]

By the numbers alone, they are obviously loyalists: 61 percent align with the Republicans and only 32 percent with the Democrats.

But for all the material privilege and political support, the Republicans have good reason to keep the agenda pro-business and with plenty of top-bracket tax cuts. These well-educated men, it seems, care little about the cultural war. They share hostility toward Bill Clinton, but their grievances may be more material than moral. Strangely, they are not very hostile to a regulatory state that seeks to protect consumers and the environment and promote safety. And interestingly, they are less obsessed than other loyalists with seeing an assertive America that depends on American military power for its security. On these and other issues that divide the country along cultural lines, Privileged Men are drawn to the politics of their wives and to the politics of their more secular neighbors.

Indeed, just 45 percent of these Privileged Men call themselves "political conservatives," the lowest for any of the loyalist groups, a term whose meaning may have been hijacked by the cultural conservatives.

Their wavering on these issues may be related to the rising proportion of men with postgraduate educations, which seems to offset income patterns and align the men with a whole different set of social forces. With a large number of the Republicans intent on waging the cultural war and building an identity around faith, these Privileged Men may become less comfortable loyalists and face growing cross-pressures in the long term.

Still, not many of these privileged voters are willing to give up the money and vote on other grounds, so there is good reason for George W. Bush to be a relentless tax cutter.

The Republicans have learned over the last decade that they can break the Democrats' hold on the Congress and the White House by stoking the fires of loyalist politics. They use other tricks and maneuvers, but those are subplots to the main narrative—getting as much unity and engagement from their loyalists, making their issues palatable for the contested voters, and adding on some contested groups, without jeopardizing loyalist enthusiasm. Thus, they want the agenda of politics that centers on tax, faith, freedom, and the military.

But the problem in this era of party parity is so do the Democrats, or at least those wedded to winning under the current rules. These issues, turned on their head, inflame the Democratic world, creating very different political possibilities.

Chapter 6

THE WORLD
OF DEMOCRATIC
PARTISANS

The worlds of Democratic and Republican loyalists are directly and increasingly counterpoised, as the parties battle again and again to an inconclusive draw. Secularism has begotten faith, and faith secularism; increasingly rural has given us increasingly cosmopolitan; a party of the South has given us a party of New England and the Pacific coast; the Super-Educated women cannot bear the F-You Boys, and the feeling is mutual; the politics of today's privileged gives us the politics of the vulnerable.

The Democratic world centers on rights and government, on modern gender roles and secularism, on vulnerability before markets. This produces a range of loyalist groups each with a counterpart on the Republican side. The difference is that many of the Democratic groups seem more durable, or at least may be growing in size or trending Democratic, a specter that haunts many conservative observers. Over the long term, it is possible that such trends could give Democrats an electoral edge, but the battle of party parity is fought election after election and hardly waits on history. Each election requires that Democrats make ever greater efforts to maximize their loyalists' profile among the electorate.

Over the eighteen-month research period, 46 percent of the electorate aligned with the Democrats, but that includes the 37 percent who actually

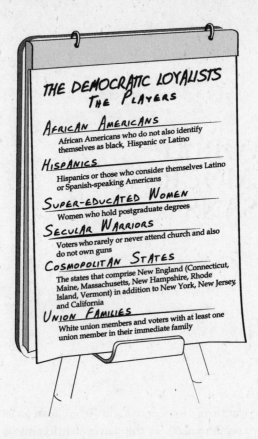

THE DEMOCRATIC LOYALISTS
The Players

AFRICAN AMERICANS
African Americans who do not also identify
themselves as black, Hispanic or Latino

HISPANICS
Hispanics or those who consider themselves Latino
or Spanish-speaking Americans

SUPER-EDUCATED WOMEN
Women who hold postgraduate degrees

SECULAR WARRIORS
Voters who rarely or never attend church and also
do not own guns

COSMOPOLITAN STATES
The states that comprise New England (Connecticut,
Maine, Massachusetts, New Hampshire, Rhode
Island, Vermont) in addition to New York, New Jersey,
and California

UNION FAMILIES
White union members and voters with at least one
union member in their immediate family

identify with the party and, true to the political deadlock, equal to the number of self-identified Republicans. The voters most strongly aligned with the Democrats, and their loyalist world, are recruited disproportionately from the African-American and Hispanic communities, from the most secular and cosmopolitan metropolitan regions, and from union households.

As with the Republicans, many of these groups overlap, but each gives us a distinct window into the Democratic world.

The battle for parity over the last decade has produced greater unity and deepening political engagement in the Democratic world. Over the last three presidential elections, African Americans voted in rising numbers, and 2000 produced their highest vote yet for Democrats. The Hispanic proportion of the electorate rose in the same period. Union Families, remarkably against the trend of declining union membership, emerged as a stable and perhaps growing share of the presidential electorate. And postgraduate women and those living in the Cosmopolitan States voted increasingly Democratic in each election of the last decade.

THE DEMOCRATIC WORLD
PARTY ALIGNMENT

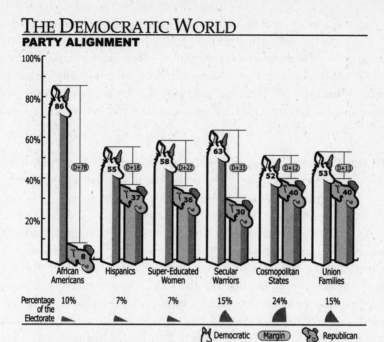

Democracy Corps database, November 2001–May 2003.

It is such rising energy in the loyalist world that allowed Democrats to battle to a dead heat over the last decade and continue the parity. But the polarization around the culture war and the battles of the last decade have made the Democratic partisan world increasingly postmodern—that is, more racially diverse but also more educated and globally engaged. With the exception of Union Families, the Democratic loyalists are more favorably inclined to immigration, the NAACP, the Internet and international trade, as indicated by views of NAFTA.

While the bloc of 2000 Nader voters is small in numbers, it is drawn disproportionately from the Secular Warriors, Cosmopolitan States, Union Families, and even Super-Educated Women, though the Nader voters are disproportionately male. They are a kind of anti-global postmodernists, committed to racial diversity, new gender roles, and the environment, but hostile to markets and international trade.

This underscores the degree to which these white Union Families are not quite at the center of the Democratic loyalist world, in some ways similar to the position of the Privileged Men in the Republican. The white Union Families are 15 percent of the electorate and very important to Democratic prospects, and except for the minority groups, they are the only group in the Democratic partisan world coming out of working-class life. This also puts the union households under pressure, as they respond to some of the working-class issues that draw voters to the Republicans and hear less and less about their red-meat issues, including big corporations and trade. But their position also highlights the degree to which the size of the Democratic loyalist world is constrained by the loss of groups in the middle.

BLACK POWER The starting point in the world of Democratic loyalists is the African-American voter. It was the battle for civil rights that transformed the parties, setting off the exodus that moved so many blue-collar and Southern whites into the Republican Party and moved successive racial minorities into the Democratic world. It started the transformation that associated the Democrats with fighting discrimination and inequality, with individual rights, and with tolerance and diversity. Indeed, in the highly charged politics of the last decade, the impeachment of Bill Clinton was for the African-American community a momentous symbolic event, an attempted coup by white conservative America to topple the African-American community's president, only to be followed by the attempted theft of the 2000 election by leaving all those black votes uncounted in Florida.

The result is an African-American community that votes, and one that votes with a nearly singular voice. Fully 86 percent of African Americans align with the Democrats, and barely 8 percent think of themselves as Republicans. This trend has realized itself with increasing force during the ferocious political battles of the last decade: 83 percent voted for Bill Clinton in 1992 and 84 percent in 1996, 90 percent in 2000 voted for Al Gore.[1]

The passion of the African-American loyalists has produced relatively high black turnout. While turnout among whites and Hispanics remained stagnant, up around 1 point between 1996 and 2000, black turnout grew by 4 points.[2] And if their interest were to lag, a wide range of groups are mobilized to remind black voters of President Clinton's impeachment and of the Florida undercount, Republican plans on affirmative action or, indeed, education or Social Security. As a result, African Americans have come regularly to form 9 to 10 percent of the presidential electorate in election after election, and they are a big factor in the competitiveness of the Democratic Party.[3]

Republicans muse from time to time about loosening the Democrats' claim on black votes. Conservative commentator George Will predicted, for example, that "the successes of African American Republicans in statewide elections will begin to produce modest—and tremendously consequential—Republican gains among African Americans in presidential elections."[4]

Thus, Republicans moved quickly to sack the Republican Senate leader Trent Lott when he spoke too fondly of the Confederacy. However, despite such thinking and actions, Republicans dare not put down the weapons that have produced so much support in their own loyalist camp. If they were to let up, Democrats would surely step up to fight Supreme Court nominees who are indifferent to protecting civil rights or a Justice Department that seeks to overturn affirmative action programs at universities across the country.

The race issue is poignant because so many African Americans are economically vulnerable, which strengthens their bond with the Democrats. For all the economic gains of the 1990s, black median income is still more than $20,000 below that of whites.[5] The unemployment rate of African Americans is still double that of whites. Blacks are still employed primarily in less skilled occupations, and 19 percent lack health insurance.[6] Two-thirds of African Americans depend on Social Security for more than two-thirds of their retirement income.[7]

African Americans have good reason to be cautious about the market and even more reason to turn to government, which has shaped their consciousness as Democrats. Blacks have a faith in government to make the country better, to bar harmful behavior, to promote opportunity, and to limit the excesses of the market and of human behavior. Little surprise, given America's tumultuous history regarding race, that African Americans are so likely to believe that government regulation of corporations is necessary to protect the public (60 to 32 percent). This point of view carries over to environmental and consumer affairs where the need to promote the public welfare easily trumps the need to let individuals act as they choose with respect to the environment and with their cars and guns (58 to 36 percent).

Indeed, faith in the capacity of government, rather than in the will of many individuals, is a principle that animates nearly all of the groups that form the loyalist base of the Democrats. African Americans carry the torch out of the most sustained battle for their rights and a place in America, but as we shall see, there are other minorities, women, and union members, who share these sentiments.

Thus, Democrats will certainly do all they can to strengthen this bond, as there is always a presidential primary candidate—from Jesse Jackson to Al Sharpton—to remind them that African Americans cannot be taken for granted. Given the battle for party parity, they cannot be.

LATIN EXPLOSION The biggest question hanging over the Democratic world is, how loyal is the growing Hispanic community? The stakes here are very high, as the Hispanic population has increased by more than 50 percent in a decade and now exceeds that of African Americans, while Hispanic registration and voting grow year after year. In the 2000 presidential election, Hispanic voters comprised 7 percent of the electorate, up from 5 in 1996 and 2 in 1992.[8]

More important than size is the strategic distribution and growth of this Latin influence. Powered by legal and illegal immigration, Hispanics are a growing minority all across the Southern rim of the United States, from Florida to Texas, New Mexico, Arizona, Colorado, Nevada, and across to California. Each of these states now has family and migration and networks that reach south to Puerto Rico and Cuba, Mexico, Nicaragua and Guatemala, Colombia, and beyond.

While Cuban migration has slowed and is concentrated in Florida, there has been an explosion of migration from Latin America and Central America, particularly Mexico, as well as continued high birth rates. There are as many Dominicans and Salvadorans as Cubans. Today, Mexicans are two-thirds of the Hispanic population and growing.[9] Except for the Cubans, all these groups begin with an instinctive Democratic identity and aversion to the Republicans, most marked for Puerto Ricans and those from Central and South America.[10]

If current population trends continue, many states with heavy Hispanic populations could tip over into the Democratic world. California is already there, with a Hispanic population that has swelled to 28 percent of the voting-age population and 16 percent of the voters. They exercise an immense amount of political muscle.[11]

Indeed, the stakes are high and both parties are playing for keeps. Karl Rove has called the Hispanic vote "our mission and our goal" and a bloc that the Republicans must pursue "in every way and every day."[12]

This is more than wishful thinking for Democrats. The great majority of Hispanics arrived in America in this half century and they are clearly in the process of forming party attachments. They are four times as likely as whites—or, more accurately, Anglos—to give a "don't know" response when asked which party they support. Mexicans, at least, are as likely as Anglos to say they are independents (33 percent) and to shift marginally their party allegiance toward Republicans with rising income and education.[13] And while Puerto Ricans have formed traditional civil rights organizations and respond strongly on civil rights issues, like bilingual education, the Mexican community has less of a history of forming advocacy groups.

But for the moment, there is little question about overall Hispanic loyalties: they are very much part of the Democratic world, with 55 percent aligning as Democrats and only 37 percent as Republicans. By that measure, they are more Democratic than are white Union Families, who are seen as longtime, old-school Democrats.

Hispanics have all the trappings of a loyalist group. They consistently support the Democratic presidential candidate, including 61 percent for Bill Clinton in 1992, rising to 72 percent in 1996 and falling back to 62 percent for Gore in 2000, reflecting George W. Bush's popularity among Texas Hispanics and his tactical retreat from anti-immigration issues. At the same time, all but five of the twenty-five Hispanic members of Congress are Democrats; indeed, nine out of every ten of the nation's 5,000 Hispanic elected officials are Democrats.[14]

Hispanics are Democrats for reasons that are going to be hard to erase. It is the national and state Democrats who have welcomed Hispanics into American party politics and who fought for civil rights protections, even as Republicans promoted English as the official language, supported severe immigration restrictions, and barred legal immigrants from getting welfare benefits while preventing illegal ones from attending public schools. California Governor Pete Wilson's Proposition 187, the statewide referendum that denied public education and other government services to the children of illegal immigrants, stands as a powerful symbol in the consciousness of the Hispanic community as it contemplates the underlying values and character of America's political parties.

To be sure, the Bush Republicans have tried to play down the anti-immigrant agenda. They are trying valiantly to put more Hispanics up front in the Republican Party. From ponying Hispanic heavyweights out at their conventions to picking fights with Democrats over judicial nominations, Republicans are propositioning the Hispanic vote.

But as with African Americans, Hispanics are, for some pretty hard-headed reasons apart from civil rights, closely aligned with the Democrats. For one thing, Hispanics are among the most economically vulnerable in the country. They are three times less likely than non-Hispanics to graduate from high school and they continue to fill the lowest-paid jobs in the lowest-wage sections of the service sector. For every one Hispanic doctor, there are approximately five Hispanic household servants, fourteen Hispanic janitors, and eight Hispanic construction workers.[15] What's more, only 10 percent of Hispanics make more than $50,000 a year, less than half the proportion among Anglos.[16] And a third of Hispanics lack even rudimentary health benefits.[17] While they represent 12 percent of the population, they make up 23 percent of families living in poverty.[18] Barely captured by these statistics is the tremendous downward pressure on wages from illegal immigration, which increases Hispanic economic vulnerability, particularly in the Southwest.

HISPANIC VOTERS
GOVERNMENT REGULATION

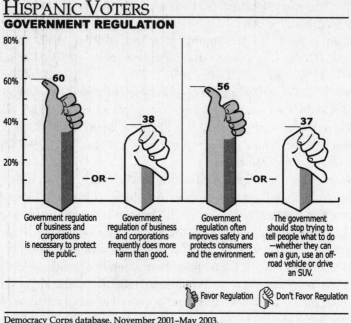

Democracy Corps database, November 2001–May 2003.

While the rise of the Hispanic middle class is real enough, this picture misses the more likely narrative: a growing Hispanic community, living on the edge financially, very concerned about jobs, education, health care, and retirement.

Hispanics, it seems, share a large part of the Democratic worldview about government and markets. Sizable majorities believe that government regulation of business is beneficial, rather than harmful (60 to 38 percent), with a nearly identical majority in favor of promoting public safety and the environment, rather than worrying about government spending too much time telling people what to do about guns and SUVs (56 to 37 percent). When a national survey asked registered Hispanic voters to make a stark choice—higher taxes and larger government with more services or lower taxes and small government with fewer services—they came down strongly for big government (55 percent compared to 38 percent for a small one). They are much more likely than whites (32 percent) and more likely than African Americans (39 percent) to opt for big government.[19]

If there are a lot of Hispanic heads to turn, it is not so evident in the gut leanings of Hispanic voters: by a margin of 21 points, they see the Democrats as more "on their side" (51 to 30 percent); on social insurance issues like health care, Hispanic voters turn almost exclusively to the Democrats (59 to 22 percent, a 37 point margin).

For all the evidence of Democratic loyalties, Hispanics seem a little less enthusiastic than other groups in the Democratic world when it comes to a broader set of domestic issues, including education, the economy, and taxes. On the latter issue, Hispanic voters are evenly divided on which party would do a better job.

More important, Hispanics are not party to the cultural battles that have helped shape the Democratic world. Two-thirds of Hispanics find both abortion and homosexuality unacceptable.[20] With 48 percent Catholic, they express a social conservatism more reflective of Mexico and Latin America than the United States.

Hispanics have modestly warm feelings about the NRA (53.0 degrees) and pro-life groups (52.0 degrees), though they lack the intense views that motivate the battle among many of the partisans on these issues.

They are a patriotic community, and indeed, like the white trade unionists, they are much more likely to turn to the Republicans than Democrats when it comes to making America strong (50 to 25 percent). Hispanics account for almost 10 percent of all active duty personnel, the product of a 30 percent growth in Hispanic military service between 1992 and 2001.[21] With Hispanics playing such a visible role in the Iraq war—including more than their proportionate share of the combat deaths—one should expect these sentiments to be reinforced, unless the war's aftermath proves less glorious."[22]

Among the Mexican population, attitudes toward the military do impact attachments to the parties, which should encourage Republicans. But Hispanics overall do not easily fit the clear battle lines of the cultural war raging among whites. Hispanics are reluctant to politicize their views on many values and lifestyle issues, particularly abortion, which is disappointing for Republicans. While abortion is strongly correlated with party attachments among whites and has some impact among Cubans, there is almost no association among Mexicans and Puerto Ricans.[23] In that, Hispanics and African Americans respond similarly conservatively on many cultural issues but do not seem to bring these views with them into the voting booth.[24]

The lack of Hispanic engagement on some of the issues that motivate other Democrats may produce a somewhat diminished enthusiasm for politics. They are one of the least likely groups in the electorate to vote.

It is certainly possible to imagine a diminished Hispanic vote for Democrats if values, patriotism, and taxes are the only issues and if the Republicans are able to fashion themselves into a more open and diverse party—even though the pressure of their loyalist camp often takes them in the opposite direction. But we should not underestimate the strength of the forces keeping Hispanics firmly in the Democratic world. Despite 9/11 and

America's war on terrorism and the Republican campaign to vilify Bill Clinton on values and the military, Hispanic voters continue to hold favorable views of the former president (54.7 degrees). They are much more inclined than Anglos and African Americans to allow more people from Latin America to come work legally in the United States and, even more, to think that illegal immigrants help our economy.[25] Hispanic voters are instinctively and philosophically Democratic, reinforced by their material needs and their concern with rights and discrimination.

Indeed, Republican urgency about dislodging Hispanics—and parading for reporters and their party faithful any evidence of Hispanic Republicanism—only intensifies the Democratic effort to highlight the symbolic and material issues that can consolidate Hispanic support.

SUPER-EDUCATED WOMEN That women with postgraduate degrees are now deeply ensconced in the Democratic world is one of the most dramatic changes of our current era. The successive party battles, and particularly the bitter contests of the last decade, have deepened the cultural divide running through the country. The Super-Educated Women know on which side they stand. In planting their feet on Democratic soil, they have confounded the politics of the Privileged Men, to whom many are married.

This reflects an extraordinary political journey. There were barely enough of these women postgraduates to survey until recently, but now they comprise 7 percent of the voting electorate (9 percent according to the exit polls)—comparable in size to the Hispanic vote and rising. And they may be bringing along, in their thinking, a broader set of educated women, as well as many of their husbands.

Today, women with postgraduate degrees align strongly with the Democrats (58 to 36 percent), a 22-point margin over those who align with Republicans. For comparison, that makes them considerably more Democratic than white union members, as well as Union Families and Hispanics. In the elections of the last decade, they have voted overwhelmingly and increasingly Democratic. Barely a third have voted Republican in the last three presidential elections, while the Democratic vote has risen from 55 percent in 1992 to 60 percent in 1996 to 63 percent in 2000.[26]

The revolt against established family and gender norms, nearly as dramatic as the revolt against established racial norms, allowed the emergence of modern, educated women. That has produced a full-fledged political realignment among the growing group of college-educated women. The Super-Educated Women are strongly pro-choice, but more than that, they hate symbols of faith and extreme (perhaps, read, male) individualism, such as the pro-life groups (38.7 degrees) and the NRA (31.9 degrees). They

SUPER-EDUCATED WOMEN THERMOMETERS
COMPARED TO ALL VOTERS

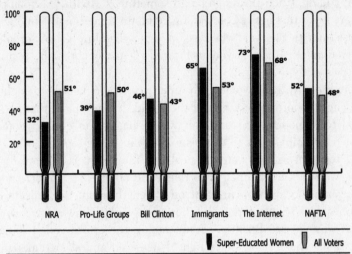

Democracy Corps database, November 2001–May 2003.

look outward when it comes to economics and technology, giving the Internet a very hot 73.0-degree rating, also responding more warmly than any other group except Hispanics to NAFTA (51.5 degrees).

They trust the Democrats instinctively and nearly unanimously on energy and the environment, health care, Social Security, and especially education.

More than any other group in the Democratic world, these women strongly believe that government has the capacity to promote the public good and public safety, and would, with gusto, put limits on the boys' toys, like guns and SUVs (68 percent). These are the voters most committed to the regulatory state. They bring the same spirit and intensity of view to America's security, where they want to see the United States build relationships in order to protect the country and citizens, rather than depend primarily on building military might (60 to 26 percent). More than any other group in the loyalist camp, the Super-Educated Women reject aggressive individualism, whether in personal behavior or for the country.

In the Seattle focus groups, conducted more broadly with suburban college-educated women, they have repeatedly questioned the patriotic fervor and male bravado and militarism that welled up in the post-9/11 America. One woman mused, in an almost boys-will-be-boys tone, "I think they just like to play more war."[27]

These women are critical of the Republicans and George W. Bush. "Every time they get in office, they always beef up the military," said one woman, adding, "they always go bomb something." Another woman chimed in, "Every Bush that gets elected wants to bomb something!"[28] In one group, held just prior to the war, when asked if they had any doubts or concerns about George W. Bush, a woman blurted: "I just fear that he might do it for his own glory."[29]

More broadly, these women see America as "being a little high powered" and "trying to control every part of the world."[30] They agree that patriotism is "good to a moderate extent" but worry that it can easily "go too far," "that's what I think leads to terrorism and war, being too patriotic."[31]

The reaction against patriotic zeal and militarism is visceral for these women, who talk about men who relish the chance for an aggressive national response. One woman went on at length about the president after September 11: "Right after 9/11, there was a clip showed, over and over again. It was George Bush. . . . Somebody in the crowd yelled something, and he said, 'That's right, that's right. I hear you and all of America hears you, and those bastards over there, they'll be hearing too.' The man must have said something, like, 'We are going to kick their ass' or something, and it struck me as being scary. It's a typical male. You slap me and I'll slap you back."[32] One woman said, "Well, it's good to be strong. It's like you go to the gym to work out, but it doesn't mean you walk down alleys and punch people either."[33]

With the parties always battling to a near draw, and the cultural guns almost certainly drawn by one or, more likely, both of the parties, the Super-Educated Women will be drawn more deeply into the Democratic world. Indeed, they will be leading the way, as they hold strong views on the role of women and changing family dynamics, religion in politics, and government regulation to ensure public safety. They prefer a nation where relationships are more important than individualism and that helps shape the Democratic worldview.

SECULAR WARRIORS Nowhere else in the developed Christian world are there so many people who are devoutly religious and who regularly attend religious services. And nowhere else do so many private citizens own guns. In that, America is exceptional but, as we now know, also divided.

Today, 25 percent of American adults attend church or synagogue every week and 30 percent every week or nearly every week.[34] That has not diminished over the last 12 years, despite the great acceleration of secularizing trends, like the dissolution of traditional marriages. Despite it all, 25 percent of voters are in church every Sunday.

And today, 34 percent of voters own guns, indeed, 19 percent have three or more in their homes. For much of blue-collar and rural America, gun ownership is considered a right central to preserving their way of life and autonomy. "Gun ownership is a simple fact of life," writes Michael Korda in an article originally penned for *Brill's Content* yet later disseminated by the NRA. It's as normal as "raking leaves, mowing the lawn, and buying Girl Scout Cookies."[35]

But our era has brought not only politicization but also polarization around faith and guns. In the loyalist Democratic camp there is a growing group of voters, profane and secular and determined to protect their emerging way of life.

Currently, 29 percent never go to church or show up less than once a year, with 42 percent going to church once a year or less.[36] This really is a divided America. Only thirty years ago in 1972, merely 18 percent never or rarely went to church, but the secular trends accelerated greatly in the 1990s, creating equivalent numbers of the most devout and nondevout with some evidence of secular gains.

The Secular Warriors, those who never go to church and who own no guns, are the true loyalists in this modern Democratic world. They are 15 percent of the electorate, equal in size to the white Union Families and minority communities, and fully align with the Democrats (63 to 30 percent) by more than two to one. These are voters who hold President Bill Clinton in high esteem (54.0 degrees). While a symbol of moral decline for the Faithful, the former president represents for the Secular Warriors an aggressive modernism—a commitment to self-expression, autonomy, and freedom, expressed most simply as "individual or minority self-determination," in James Davison Hunter's description. Rather than truth being absolute, it "tends to be viewed as a process, as a reality that is ever unfolding." And like the Faithful, Secular Warriors think that powerful groups, in this case ones calling upon a moral or religious authority, threaten their autonomy and privacy.[37]

Among the loyalists, the Secular Warriors are far and away the most hostile to pro-life groups (31.0 degrees) and rival the Super-Educated Women in their disdain for the NRA (35.0 degrees). Legal abortion and gun control are the real and symbolic means to protect their way of life against the demands of the Faithful, Country Folk, and F-You Boys.

Among the Secular Warriors, there is a tolerance for lifestyle choices, including homosexuality and gay unions, which, as we know, for the Faithful challenge the moral order and the Christian family and all the traditionally prescribed roles.[38]

At 15 percent of the electorate, the Secular Warriors are nearly identical in size to the Faithful and nearly as partisan and passionate in their views. And just as the white Evangelicals contribute mightily to the politics of the rural heartland and Deep South, the Secular Warriors are a big part of the "cosmopolitan" politics of the two coasts and larger metropolitan areas.

The Secular Warriors are ready for battle, because they know that in this day and age of party parity, they will be called.

COSMOPOLITAN STATES All of the trends that have produced a new loyalist landscape for Democrats have come together in metropolitan areas and states, much as the Republican trends have come together in white rural areas, the Deep South, and Exurbia. Growing racial diversity, new immigration, increasing education—particularly postgraduate education—modern roles for women, and secularism and declining church involvement have combined to paint large blue areas on the presidential map. In effect, New England, New York, New Jersey, and Connecticut, as well as California, together constitute the Cosmopolitan States, which are now dependably Democratic.

These Cosmopolitan States include 24 percent of the electorate and cast more than half of the 270 electoral votes needed to win the presidency.[39]

The Cosmopolitan States align solidly with the Democrats, by 12 points (52 to 40 percent), though not quite the margins of other loyalists. But when they march to the polls during the increasingly heated battles of party parity, they break more strongly for the Democrats. At the height of the Reagan era, they voted heavily Republican: 56 percent for Reagan and 43 percent for Mondale in 1984. But change was in the wind. In 1988, the New England secular-liberal Dukakis ran even in these states, including California (50 to 49 percent).[40] That was the beginning of a Democratic ascent, with Clinton winning by 13 points in the Cosmopolitan States in 1992 (47 to 34 percent) and by 19 points in 1996 (54 to 35 percent), and Gore winning by 17 points in 2000 (56 to 39 percent), despite the 4 points for Ralph Nader.[41]

What has been concentrated in these Cosmopolitan States are the trends, underscored by John Judis and Ruy Teixeira, that have made the Democrats "the party of the transition from urban industrialism to a new postindustrial metropolitan order in which men and women play equal roles and in which white America is supplanted by multiracial, multiethnic America." These trends are most evident in the rise of education and professional roles (discussed in Chapter 7), gender equality, as well as increasing racial diversity and large immigration from Latin America and Asia.[42] They come together here to create a political climate in which the Democrats are the dominant force, winning by 17 to 19 points. In these Cosmopolitan States, almost half (47 percent) of the voters have at least four-year college degrees,

COSMOPOLITAN STATES THERMOMETERS
COMPARED TO ALL VOTERS

	NRA	Pro-Life Groups	Bill Clinton	Immigrants	The Internet	NAFTA
Cosmopolitan States	42°	43°	48°	58°	70°	49°
All Voters	51°	50°	43°	53°	68°	48°

Cosmopolitan States   All Voters

Democracy Corps database, November 2001–May 2003.

including nearly one-fifth with postgraduate degrees. They are less likely to attend church than any other group in the Democratic loyalist world, except the Secular Warriors, of course. Guns mean little to their culture; just 23 percent own firearms. Almost two-thirds of the voters in these states think of themselves as moderate or liberal, which likely has taken on a cultural meaning for them, given the battles that have divided the country over the last decade.

These mostly metropolitan voters want a government that regulates for the public safety and a quality environment and that also checks the excesses of the private realm. In that, their sensibilities about government are not focused heavily on a protectiveness about individualism and private prerogatives. They fully support the Democrats on social welfare issues, including health care and retirement.

But the melding of racial and ethnic diversity and education and a secular independence from traditional institutions creates a cosmopolitan culture that is more tolerant and open, more receptive to technology, and more global. These are voters who give very positive ratings to immigrants (57.8 degrees) and to the Internet (70.0 degrees) and a slightly warmer than average rating to NAFTA (48.5 degrees).

The cosmopolitan thinking and political culture identified here may make themselves felt well beyond the Cosmopolitan States where Democrats have built up strong majorities. Judis and Teixeira describe the emergence of postindustrial metropolises, what they call "ideopolises," where there is a similar transformation and similar growth in Democratic support. These include the obvious areas, like Silicon Valley and Boston's Route 128, as well as Austin, Raleigh-Durham, and Boulder, but also whole metropolitan and large suburban areas, like Chicago, Mercer County in New Jersey, Denver and Boulder, and Seattle's King County. These are all post-industrial regions, with information technology, entertainment and media, major universities or research centers, concentrations of professionals and technicians, immigrant and ethnic diversity, and frequently thriving artistic and gay communities. These metropolitan regions—defined by concentration of technology and top universities—include around 40 percent of America's population and are growing at more than twice the rate of the rest of the country.[43]

Using the Democracy Corps database of national surveys, we identified the voters who lived in "ideopolis" metropolitan areas.[44] And indeed, these voters look very much like Cosmopolitan State voters, underscoring the degree to which this is a national phenomenon, with consequences for all fifty states.

Ideopolis voters, according to this analysis, comprise 43 percent of the presidential-year voters across the country and align strongly with the Democrats (50 to 42 percent). They look very much like the voters in Cosmopolitan States: half have at least four years of college. They are very cool to the NRA and pro-life groups and warm toward Bill Clinton, immigrants, and the Internet. They support a strong governmental role to check the corporations and ensure the public safety and a clean environment. In all of these, they are not quite as distinct as the cosmopolitan voters, but they are close.

The Cosmopolitan States and the associated postindustrial metropolitan regions across the country are a growing reality, counterposed in many respects to the rural areas, blue-collar suburbs, and Exurbia where different values and a different way of life are defended. Political entrepreneurs have waged their increasingly intense cultural battle, knowing that it would deepen the political loyalties on both sides. Which party gains the edge nationally depends on which side mobilizes more successfully and which social trends win out in the future.

UNION MADE   For this past half century, union members and their families have thought of themselves as fully part of the Democratic family. Their union leaders certainly presumed they are as closely bound to the Democratic Party as many of their union counterparts to social democratic parties in Europe.

And the voters in Union Families, even the white ones, have almost always accepted this identity, regardless of the ups and downs and political fortunes of the parties. In fact, white union members and their families are the only section of white working-class America, since the upheavals of the sixties, that still thinks of itself as part of the Democratic family.

Through the 1950s, 1960s, and 1970s, about 60 percent of those in white union households identified with the Democrats. In the Reagan era, Democratic identification slipped to an average of 53 percent but went back up to nearly 60 percent in the nineties and for the 2000 election. And throughout this whole half century, only about a third of those in white Union Families aligned themselves with the Republicans.[45]

But membership in the Democratic world has apparently never included an obligation for white Union Families to vote consistently for Democratic presidential candidates. This is the rub, and the reason the last decade has proved to be one of such intense partisan engagement. Democrats worked to build more unified support and much greater turnout from a group that is supposed to be a member of the club. The Republicans sow division, usually along cultural lines, in hopes of winning defectors, as they have in the past.

At the outset of this era, in the fifties, Eisenhower fought the white union household vote to a draw. And while the Kennedy and Johnson offers to complete the New Deal won nearly landslide support among Union Families, it quickly collapsed in 1968. White Union Families divided down the middle again and broke heavily for the Republicans in the Nixon landslide of 1972. But these were now voters in full swing, giving Carter 60 percent of the vote in 1976, shifting to Reagan at his zenith (53 percent, compared to 46 percent for Mondale) and, despite the focus on crime and other cultural issues in 1988, moved back toward the Democrats, though dividing evenly (50 percent for Dukakis, and 48 percent for Bush).[46]

But disillusionment with Reagan's corporate modernization and economic upheaval and George Bush's recession turned union members away from the Republicans. Bill Clinton won white union households with landslide margins—by 27 points in 1992 (52 to 25 percent) and 21 points in 1996 (54 to 33 percent). Al Gore won a good majority in 2000, 52 to 44 percent, but not as impressively, which is why both parties have invested so heavily in winning labor's vote.[47]

For now, white Union Families are part of the Democratic world: 53 percent align with the Democrats, and 40 percent with the Republicans, though they are among the weakest of the Democratic loyalists; the white union members themselves, however, are quite strongly aligned with the Democrats, 56 to 37 percent.

The white unionists stand with the Democrats for material and ideological reasons. After the two-decade conservative assault, they are strongly anticorporate, the most anticorporate in the Democratic loyalist camp. They hunger for a government that will finally balance the concentrated power of corporate elites. Few groups in the loyalist Democratic world are more supportive of government regulation of corporations, rejecting the risk that regulation may kill the goose that creates jobs and wealth (61 to 33 percent). They favor Democratic approaches to the economy and are open to public spending, though many are unenthusiastic about Democrats on taxes. On the vast array of social insurance issues, particularly health care and retirement, they are looking to the Democrats to provide for greater sustenance and security.

But these white households are also part of the blue-collar culture that resists government bossiness trying to tell them how they can live. Guns are an issue with meaning here. A lot of F-You Boys are among the white Union Families. Unionists like the NRA (52.3 degrees) and are so unenthusiastic about government regulation for public safety when it focuses on guns and SUVs that the landslide majority for regulation completely evaporates. They also strongly favor the Republicans on keeping America strong at a time of global threats and terrorism.

The Republicans have hardly been loath to play that hand—a strong military to defend America and fight terrorist targets; tax cuts for working families, like the elimination of the marriage penalty; and the ability to keep your guns and drive your SUVs. When the Bush administration imposed tariffs to protect the steel industry and energy policies to promote coal rather than the environment, they no doubt had these union members in mind. These Union Families are extremely cool to NAFTA (42.2 degrees), and on this issue they do not have a lot of company on the Democratic side.

Democrats, however, seem to be playing a stronger hand for white Union Families, full of health care, pension protection and Social Security, full-employment economic policies, business regulation, and middle-class tax cuts. The Democrats are more trusted than the Republicans on all of these issues. Nonetheless, the somewhat weaker Democratic showing in 2000 is a signal, particularly to Democrats, that they will have to work doubly hard to achieve greater support and unity here.

That battle has come to center on whether white Union Families will be a declining or rising part of the electorate that can tilt the party balance. These union households were 28 percent of the presidential electorate in the 1950s, which largely held at around 26 percent until Ronald Reagan became president in 1980.[48] But with strong support from the White House, employers began a process of industrial restructuring that

UNION FAMILIES THERMOMETERS
COMPARED TO ALL VOTERS

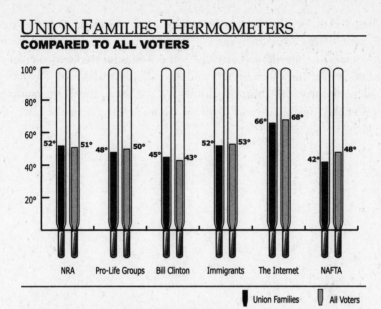

NRA   Pro-Life Groups   Bill Clinton   Immigrants   The Internet   NAFTA

■ Union Families   ▮ All Voters

Democracy Corps database, November 2001–May 2003.

drove down union membership to 23 percent in 1984 and 21 percent in 1988.[49]

While union membership in the country continued its seemingly inexorable decline in the last decade, the intense partisan battles have stabilized and possibly reversed the historic trend in the realm of politics. Union members began voting in higher numbers. Vigorous organizing efforts by the unions at the very least stabilized the percentage of white Union Families at around 18 percent of the electorate over the last three presidential elections. According to the exit polls, using a different and probably less dependable methodology, the union proportion rose from 18 percent in 1992 to 24 percent in 1996 to 26 percent in 2000.[50]

That turnout for Union Families has stabilized or risen, despite an actual decline in membership, is a symbol of what strange things can happen when two parties fight for such small margins. That the Union Families might respond to cultural and trade issues, while Democrats speak with muted voices on noncultural ones, gets the Republicans a small hearing but only heightens the need for yet more intensive organizing and political appeals.

The white Union Families are one of the few groups in the Democratic world to slip a little in their Democratic voting in 2000 and 2002, which is related to the character of the loyalist camp. It falls on the postmodernist and pluralistic side of the two Americas, which leaves the white Union

Families a little on the periphery despite close organizational ties to the Democratic Party. That pattern will carry over into the contested world, where Democrats are doing better with the well educated and secular (the "winners" in the new economy), and less well with the blue-collar and noncollege groups (the "blues"). But as we shall see, there are many here who resist the polarized world of the partisans.

PART IV

Contested America

T he contested world is pretty distant from the loyalist world. The two parties are focused, relentlessly on preserving and enlarging their bloc of loyalist supporters and making the most of their issues among the remainder of the voters. But we will see in the contested communities of Tampa Blue, Heartland Iowa, and Eastside Tech that real people are complicated and not easily allocated to a partisan place. They represent the large expanses of political landscape where no party is the presumed favorite. Here, voters are conflicted on the parties' issues and symbols and, as a result, not won over by either. For the politicians, these are the groups that can be moved just enough to make the difference.[1]

This contested world is as big and as complicated as the world of party loyalists. Fully 36 percent identify themselves as independents—equal to the number who identify with either party. These are not just fringe elements, incidental to the main political battles of our age. They are contested for a reason. These voters, forced to choose from a cultural menu, could well respond to a new one that offers the right questions, issues, and bold policies.[2]

Chapter 7

THREE CONTESTED COMMUNITIES

Within contested communities across America, real life blurs the clear lines of the partisan world. Political leaders want to win majorities here as well, but without raising concerns and issues that dampen the passions that have been stoked among the loyalists. In these contested communities, people are affected by a diverse set of social and cultural developments and many think, against the partisan orthodoxy, that both parties have something to offer. But they also include a lot, maybe even more, who view party politics as a distant farce, who eschew partisan games, and who raise issues not on the official partisan agenda.

I conducted extensive discussions with actual voters in three communities in the contested world: Tampa Blue, mainly blue-collar, suburban Hillsborough County in Florida and home of U.S. Central Command (Centcom); Heartland Iowa, the farms and small-town communities of central Iowa, which form both the geographic and cultural midpoint for the country; and Eastside Tech, the upscale suburban towns east of Seattle, home for many of the employees of both Boeing and Microsoft. These areas are ground zero in the battles for contested voters.[1]

When the counting stopped in 2000, Florida was decided by just 537 votes. A lot of counties in Florida, including Hillsborough, created that slim margin, giving Bush the edge by 3 points, though Clinton had won earlier. Iowa went to Gore by only 4,144 votes (49 to 48 percent for Bush) and was key to the Democrats' electoral hopes. Within this narrow victory are some critical heartland counties: Jasper was dead even (49 to 49 percent); Boone went to the Democrats (51 to 46 percent); and the other counties went to the Republicans by moderate margins—Polk absent Des Moines (54 to 44 percent), Dallas (53 to 44 percent), and Guthrie (52 to 46 percent). The state of Washington has been steadier for the Democrats, but the margin narrowed in 2000 to only 5.6 points, although the high-tech suburbs broke for Gore by around 7 points.

These are also the principal battlefields in the decade-long war for control of Congress. Because of partisan polarization and reapportionment, fewer than forty seats across the nation were considered competitive by the country's leading election analysts, but a large portion of them touched these communities.[2] At the outset of the last decade, in 1992, three of the congressional seats that stretched across Tampa Blue were battlegrounds and targets for both parties. By the end, the advantages of office and an aggressive, incumbent-oriented reapportionment masterminded by the Republicans had created one safe Democratic seat and two safe Republican ones. In Iowa, a decade of bloody, competitive congressional elections and an independent reapportionment commission constructed two competitive seats that encompassed the counties of Heartland Iowa. In the end, after campaigns costing roughly $1.5 million dollars each, the Democrats and Republicans each got one seat.[3] Suburban Seattle has been the site of three battleground seats. In each, the parties swapped control (and in one seat, twice), and two were closely contested over the whole decade. The incumbents have settled in, finally secure, though now a Republican congresswoman serves in a district where the same voters gave Al Gore a good majority in 2000.

The contested world, in the end, is composed of communities across America where the battles of the day are unsettled or remote. Contested voters live everywhere but they are concentrated in communities like Tampa Blue, Heartland Iowa, and Eastside Tech. These communities are away from the white rural and suburban areas of the Deep South and removed from the rich ethnic diversity of the big cities or of Southern California, where loyalist politics hangs heavy in the air. Simply said, these are communities where America is less sure of its politics and choices.

TAMPA BLUE

Tampa Blue includes the small towns of Hillsborough County, where families earn what Middle America earns, just over $40,000.[4] These towns, which flow from one to the other without any physical barrier or much physical distinction, form a semicircle around Tampa, starting within sight of MacDill Air Force Base to the south, and encompassing the areas to the east and north, until the spread is stopped short by the Gulf of Mexico. While they are not joined together by any ring road or beltway, they are, nonetheless, joined together by a way of life, one where people do not have a lot of money to spare, where conversion of farmland to small plots allows people to build affordable, decent homes in safe communities with good schools, where taxes and government are not too big a burden and church life is pervasive, and where your boat is as important as your job, though neither is as important as your country.

Each town outside Tampa is cut up by the large commercial roads that typify south and central Florida and good portions of suburban America, and is lined on both sides with strip malls, one after the other. They are nearly all one-story buildings, with storefronts and parking, interrupted by large supermarkets and sprawling used-car lots. Fast-food chains repeat themselves, almost like the chorus of a musical score—a Frostie for every freezer, a McDonald's value meal for every appetite from Happy Meal to Super Size. There are more Outback Steakhouses and Hooters than elsewhere, as they are homegrown chains. The commercial areas are resplendent with businesses that provide the same services to the people here that they would have anywhere else, from hair salons to tanning parlors, and others that advertise their importance to a cash-and-carry way of life—EZ Pawn, Pawn King, and all variety of pawnshops, with signs like "Need Cash Now?" and "Fastest Refund." There are discount gun shops, bowling alleys, and nightclubs. You can get a six-pack of Bud for $3.09 at the Kash-N-Karry. Huggies jumbo diapers, however, cost $9.99 here, like everywhere else. The same is true for a Remington 240, $389 at Wal-Mart, the same in all three communities.

In Tampa Blue, there is no Starbucks, although one opened in Tampa proper last year, complete with a drive-through window. But that is a different market and a different world.

Tampa Blue is fitted with small churches, never more than a football field away, one after the other in every direction. The ever-present strip mall, in addition to pawn and gun shops, offers all variety of storefront ministries, like God's Refuge Ministry in Seffner. Their signs lead people to "The Bible Tabernacle," "Impact Ministries," and "Gospel Meetings." Some of the bigger churches, like the First Church of Mango, stand on their own, right on the highway, but with a sign that says, under a large white cross, "Support and pray for our President and military troops." In some of the bigger towns, like Brandon, the churches are larger, like the King Avenue Baptist Church, and are set out on their own, more sheltered from the commercial world. There you find the academies and family life centers.

In the newspapers and Yellow Pages, the churches advertise almost as aggressively as the lawyers, trying to win congregants and children for their church academies while encouraging others to come to Easter Sunday or Gospel services or Bible studies. They seek congregants in the same Yellow Pages that Tampa's women's health centers seek patients. "Abortions. Early or Late—Awake or Asleep," one full-page ad read, ". . . when someone you love needs a choice."

All of this reflects the importance of the church in the lives of these families, in an environment where cultural pollution is near at hand. When queried about their community involvement, a large majority, almost half of the men and almost three-quarters of the women, mention being part of church groups, or involved in school activities, youth sports, and scouting.[5]

These are communities without big distinctive industries to employ many of the people here. In discussions, nobody mentions the Port of Tampa or even Busch Gardens, which is located here in Temple Terrace. The days when Tampa was the "cigar capital of America," with the largest concentration of Cubans outside of Havana, and the home of many immigrant workers in that industry, particularly Italians, ended with the Castro revolution and the imposition of the embargo by the United States in 1958. This was never a union town, as the cigar companies came to Tampa to escape the unionized shops of Key West. Ybor City, which was home to the factories, workshops, and warehouses, is now newly renovated and important to Tampa's nightlife. Still, this is light-years away from Tampa Blue.

The people in Tampa Blue do not bring a lot of new-economy skills to the labor market, and more than three-quarters of them do not have college degrees. Lake Magdalene has the highest proportion of college-educated people, but only a third; Brandon has 26 percent. But most of the towns are under 20 percent, and in Mango only 8 percent of residents have college degrees. If education is still a gateway to the Internet, a low proportion of the people here use it, but when they do, both the men and women go to eBay, where they can gain some market advantage.

A bulk of Tampa Blue works in modest occupations for small businesses. Some of these companies are part of national chains, but most are part of the service economy and social support system of this working-class community.

The women of Tampa Blue work as cashiers, secretaries, waitresses, and bank tellers. They sell furniture for Office Max, greet customers at Kmart, and substitute-teach. One of the women we interviewed runs the church nursery while another manages a day care center; still others work for catering services and in doctors' offices. Some are full-time mothers, yet they are a fortunate minority and appreciate this. As one stay-at-home mom told us, "I have a beautiful fourteen-month-old baby girl and I'm blessed to be able to stay home with her."

The women of Tampa Blue, like mothers throughout America, have children who are "fourteen going on twenty-five" and seek ways to be involved parents while still contributing to the family's cash flow. As such, many of the mothers we talked to have part-time jobs or operate part-time businesses rather than commit to full-time careers. One mother of four told us, "I work from home . . . do research on the computer." Another runs a paralegal business "out of her house" and another does landscaping "on the side."

The men of Tampa Blue perform similar functions in Tampa's service and support sectors. They are mechanics, foremen, sales reps, and middle managers. They work for places like Tampa Steel, Harvey's Furniture, and Verizon.

Tampa's coastal location permeates the regional economy and accounts for one of Tampa Blue's largest employers, the fisheries. The Florida Tropical Fish Farms Association supplies fish food to fish farmers in the area and across the United States. Tampa Bay Fisheries, located just outside Brandon, boasts that it provides health insurance for its employees. Nearly 70 percent of military families living off MacDill Air Force Base live in Brandon, which runs a resource center. Prominently sign-posted off the highways that traverse the area is Legends Field, the Tampa-based spring training home of the New York Yankees. While there is little evidence that the locals cheer on the millionaire ballplayers and the billionaire team owner, they think the Yankees are good enough for the local economy to put up with the stadium's address: 1 Steinbrenner Drive.

The wide multilane commercial streets and the regular two-lane ones intersect this area of Florida, creating a vast checkerboard, with more and more of the squares being filled up with housing. This is much more the center of people's lives, rather than the storefronts and businesses that service people here. More than 70 percent of the families in the Tampa Bay area own their homes, just above the average for Florida and the nation.[6] But "home" means very different things within the towns and across the different areas of Tampa Blue.

In Seffner, where the median income is the midpoint for the county and America ($43,000), trailer parks and rental homes are a dominant feature, but trailer parks are important even in the higher-income towns, like Brandon ($52,000). There, well-groomed plots with trailers extend over many acres but are divided up into distinct sections and neighborhoods. In some of the many towns, frequently within close proximity, one finds areas with trailers in rows, but more often, trailers rest on fenced-in-plots, flanked by lots of trees and well-manicured gardens.

Manufactured or prefabricated homes, fully sided in aluminum and raised on foundations, provide new developments with greater permanence and make up an ever-growing section of the housing picture. Many of the manufactured homes are in relatively new developments, which are sometimes gated and surrounded by high white fences to secure their suburban character. Some areas, which may have been all farms a decade ago, have been given over almost wholly to such communities.

The older neighborhoods in the closer-in towns have a lot of small ranch-style houses, usually clapboard but sometimes shingle, surrounded by spacious lawns that accommodate cars, swing sets, gardens, and the like. But as one moves upscale, these give way to newer, more expensive developments, where the houses are usually brick. The houses are stylish but fairly standard and close together, and laid out along streets that emulate the grid of the whole area. These are distinct developments, fenced in and protected, surrounded by some of Florida's rich greenery. They have names like Fawn Ridge and Palm Bay.

Moving east and deeper into the rural areas, there is more open farmland, particularly strawberry farms, though even these are giving way to construction of new, even bigger homes. The businesses here still provide services and goods like tractor parts and feed, which have faded elsewhere.

No matter how diverse the homes, these neighborhoods share three things that establish the common character of Tampa Blue: cars, driveway basketball hoops, and flags.

It is not unusual to see four or five cars parked in front of these homes, sometimes two or three deep. In the areas with below-median income, the cars are of an older vintage and are frequently resting on blocks or a jack, serving as a makeshift parts store. In the new areas, comfortably above the median income, the cars are newer and often kept out of sight in two-car garages, which are standard here. Regardless of area, this is a world of cars, but even more a world of SUVs and pickup trucks. And in many driveways, there are small boats or very large RVs, poised and ready to go, come the weekend.

One would be hard-pressed to find a house in all of Tampa Blue that does not have a basketball hoop and backboard at the top of the driveway. They vary in height and quality: wood and dented metal backboards and bent, tilted hoops in the older, more working-class neighborhoods, and transparent fiberglass backboards with adjustable poles in the newer developments. But pickup games with three or four kids are the norm during the afternoons.

With the Iraq war fresh in their minds, the people of Tampa Blue proudly fly the American flag from their homes and affix flag decals on their cars and pickups. In some of the newest, most expensive developments, flags are scarcer, suggesting that the cultural divide could emerge even within this blue-collar suburb. But more typical are displays of support for the troops and America, with American flags on perhaps half the homes. In some cases, the pewter and red flag of the Super Bowl champion Tampa Bay Buccaneers shares that proud place on the flagpole.

It was appropriate that President Bush came here a week after the Iraq war's start to speak at MacDill Air Force Base, headquarters for Centcom. After acknowledging the two members of Congress from this area, among others, the president spoke directly to the citizens of Tampa Blue, reflecting both their religious and patriotic sensibilities: "There will be a day of reckoning for the Iraqi regime, and that day is drawing near." He thanked the personnel at Centcom for "disarming a dangerous enemy" but also reminded them of their place in the larger mission: "The liberty we prize is not America's gift to the world; it is God's gift to humanity."[7]

This would seal Tampa Blue's place on one side of the cultural divide, except for all the contradictions that pop up in nearly every sphere of their lives.

The first clue was Martin Luther King Highway, one of the main arteries and commercial streets in Mango. There is no reason to think Tampa Blue is any more or less tolerant than any other part of the country when it comes to race relations. African Americans represent less than 10 percent of the population in nearly all of these towns, while Hispanics are a somewhat larger presence—20 percent in Citrus Park, but more often near 12 percent. Cubans used to be the largest group here, but they are now outnumbered by Puerto Ricans and Mexicans. But what is most striking is the normality of race and diversity in Tampa Blue. Neighborhood pickup games are racially diverse. The teams playing at the Brandon YMCA were too, and so were the Little League teams playing organized ball on two fields in the city park. In fact, girls were playing too.

The *Christian Voice*, the newspaper serving the towns of East Hillsborough, heralded the historic winning record of the Grace Christian Lady Patriots, which won both the Florida Christian and State Championships in 2003, along with a photo of the racially mixed team. Indeed, one Baptist church took out a full-page ad, featuring prominently both black families and white families, under the banner, "Find your place for family, friends and faith."

The civic and political education of people here includes instruction on pledge and prayer. The Brandon Y posts the Pledge of Allegiance on the front door. The religious newspapers have front-page stories on the Department of Education's new prayer guidelines. They highlight the now official right of students to read their Bibles, say grace before meals, and organize prayer groups in the schools. But their political education also includes the work of UA Local Union 123, with 1,200 active members, mostly plumbers, pipe fitters, and other skilled construction workers. Its building and social hall sit in the middle of Tampa Blue, and as the women staffing the office said, "We don't let Republicans in the door."

Community News serves Brandon, the largest of the area towns, and writes about the activities of Alafia River Chapter of the Daughters of the American Revolution. On the opposite page, it lists the upcoming outings of the Sierra Club.[8]

Then there is the huge contradiction regarding the family. While the image of the traditional nuclear family is no doubt at the heart of this world, residents' own families can be a mess. At the outset of the focus group discussions, the men and women, in separate groups, introduce themselves and talk about their lives, but that discourse is often a litany of family upheaval and change. Many of the men and women of Tampa Blue are divorced. While some are remarried, others struggle to be good single parents by throwing themselves into their children's activities, like a father who introduced himself to us by saying; "I'm divorced and I'm a Little League baseball coach for my boy's team."[9]

The Christian academies are also part of the contradictions of life here. They were created to provide young people with a Christian education and upbringing and protect them from some of the intrusive secularizing influences. Yet the academies compete for students based on their modernity and their ability to help working mothers. The Seffner Christian Academy, for example, calls itself "distinctly Christian" and promises a "Christian-centered" environment. At the same time, it features computers and a full program of athletics and fine arts, straying it seems, from the basics. More than that, Seffner and the other Christian academies highlight their ability to help working mothers with "enhanced after care," "extended care," and "before and after school care." The academies have actively made themselves part of the intersection of work and family, but with the goal of helping women work full-time.[10]

The last contradiction is television, perhaps the final ignominy for those determined to caricature these people and draw the usual lines. The men watch a lot of TV shows that seem true to type. Near the top of their most-watched list of programs is a lot of smart and physical crime fighting (*CSI*, *NYPD Blue*, and *Law and Order*) but also a lot of military and terrorism (*JAG*, *24*, and *M*A*S*H*). Top billing of course also includes sports. But their most-watched show is *The West Wing*—offering a mix of White House drama, earnest and strong presidential leadership, and ACLU politics. Which part the men take away is unknown.[11]

On Thursday nights, women turn on their TV sets and, in a single gesture, wipe away all cultural lines. Indeed, on any given Thursday these women are very likely watching NBC's *Friends,* dubbed a "yuppie sitcom" by *The Wall Street Journal* because it "consistently attracts the upscale viewers advertisers and networks covet."[12] And while hardly a "yuppie" demographic, these noncollege women who earn modest incomes tune in each week for their Aniston fix, following the trials and tribulations of New York City's six favorite friends. Whatever the draw, at least once a week one of the cultural walls between the women of Tampa Blue and Eastside Tech falls away, as yuppie meets rank and file for "Must See TV."

Their kids may also be watching, yet they are likely to bring a different perspective to the show because while the mothers and fathers of Tampa Blue did not attend college, many of their children do. This makes these parents in Tampa Blue a part of the modern social world and social currents far away from these communities.

The nuances of the family, basketball hoops, work, diversity, gender roles, and culture create a contested political world. In the 1980s, Hillsborough County was part of the Reagan Revolution in the South; Reagan won 65 percent of the vote here. But that majority evaporated in 1992, when Ross Perot took almost a quarter of the vote across these towns. In the decade since, the parties have been evenly matched. In the towns that make up Tampa Blue, support for the Democratic presidential candidate rose through three presidential elections, with Al Gore getting around 47 percent, producing the current parity.

HEARTLAND IOWA

Heartland Iowa consists of Boone, Guthrie, Dallas, Jasper, and Polk counties, heavily farm counties in the center of the state that ring Des Moines. It encompasses the rail junctions that are at the center of all the small towns, some no more than 300 people but others reaching 2,000. Mitchellville, for example, has 2,037 souls, according to the librarian checking on the Internet, but Mingo, she pointed out, with 269 people, is a "rinky-dink town." The county seats are much larger, with 16,000 residents in Jasper County's Newton and 8,000 in Boone County's Perry. The whole area is intersected east-west by I-80 and north-south by I-35 and, judging by the truck traffic, provides important links to markets far and wide.

This area really does capture the small-town and rural life, grounded in agriculture in the center of Iowa and center of the country. Iowa ranks second in the country, after South Dakota, in proportion of the state economy resulting from agriculture. These counties are roughly an hour's drive from Newton, the point farthest to the east to the Mississippi River and an hour from Ames, the geographic midpoint of the state. Mamie Eisenhower, Harriet Nelson, and Cloris Leachman were all born in Boone County. The area has been serviced from the beginning of our modern era, since 1951, by the Heartland Co-Op, which uses all those railway junctions to service and integrate these areas into the U.S. and global economy. The Heartland MX Association links them into Iowa's motor raceways, satisfying all of their motorcross needs.

Silos and grain elevators soar above the landscape and the towns, as the skyscrapers stand above New York, telling us a great deal about life below. Here, life is dominated by vast farms, with large fields of soy and corn at various stages of planting and harvest. Up the road from these farms is a small oasis, greener, usually some trees, very often a white house, replete with a full porch and swing, a whitewashed barn nearby. Just as often, the home is a manufactured house with more modest trappings. The silos, too, are a sign of the harvest that enables life to carry on here.

The silos and grain elevators next to the tracks announce why people have congregated at these points. In this part of Iowa, many of the original settlers came as homesteaders to farm, sometimes to survey and work to build the rail beds. The towns were incorporated around 1860 to 1870, which was usually accompanied by the first hotels and boardinghouses, lumber yard, millers, brick school, bank and newspapers, the first church and first elevator. In Dallas Center, for example, this all happened between 1869 and 1875.[13]

The towns today invariably have a main street or intersection of main streets, with a library, a storefront city hall, a few small banks, a hardware store, a tavern or bar, a post office, a VFW, a brick regional school, and a senior center. The general store has given way to a chain of general stores that are located not in town but as part of a gas station at the edge of town or at the highway exit. There are no movie theaters here, but the occasional bowling alley can be found. There are usually ball fields, but these look like sandlots, with no infield grass.

The commercial area is surrounded by neighborhoods with tree-lined streets and houses of great variety. These are usually clapboard. Some are small and boxlike, but many are very grand, three-story late-nineteenth-century homes, signaling the commercial vitality of these areas then and now. The flags are present and on poles that may have always been there. The "Support our Troops" and "God Bless America" signs are new. Some of the towns have small trailer parks, but these have lawns and porches and are owned by their residents.

The county seats are very different from the rest of the towns, though still very small places compared to our other contested communities. Here, there are modern schools, libraries, and hospitals. Each has a magnificent county courthouse in the middle of a central square, originally built around 1860; in Newton, it was rebuilt in 1911. Each town has a railway station. And each square has a cluster of established churches.

Indeed, competing with the silos of Heartland Iowa for skyline attention are the church steeples. At the entrance to each town and in the main square are large, long-established churches. These are not storefronts or ministries. The congregations frequently date back to the 1870s, while the church buildings were often relocated and rebuilt a number of times. But the churches are formidable structures, frequently brick, and well attended on Sundays. The center of Newton is dominated by five good-sized established churches, all within sight of each other.

On many levels, life in Heartland is fairly simple. The basics do cost a lot less here. A gallon of milk is a dollar less than in Tampa Blue and two dollars less than in Eastside Tech. It is much less for ground beef, a dozen eggs, a loaf of bread, even toilet paper. You have to pay national prices only for Huggies and Bud.

These are communities where the newspaper congratulates the family in Newton whose granddaughter in Woodbury, Tennessee, has been deployed to the Persian Gulf on the USS *Theodore Roosevelt*. In a column-long story, they track her career right up to the opportunity to be a petty officer first class and win the Anti-Terrorism Medal at the end of this deployment. Another paper, under the banner "Santiago News," tells of the comings and goings around Easter Sunday: "Easter found many families in Santiago gathering to share love and blessings. Among them were Carroll and Joyce Rose who had dinner and their three children and families were all there." Others were active: "Virginia Sigmund took her parents Bill and Ruth for a nice long ride around Altoona and to Colfax before returning home last Wednesday." And even on Easter Sunday, it is worth noting hard work: "Kathy Bishop has a commercial license that permits her to drive a semi-truck. The late Joe George would be very proud of her accomplishment." The regional paper devoted four full pages of photographs to the 2003 Southeast Polk Prom.[14]

Despite the farm setting and distances, more than half of the men and women in the focus groups said they volunteered and joined groups. The church is very important to civil society in the Heartland: 40 percent of the volunteering was in church groups, though almost a third were involved in youth sports, school activities, the Boy Scouts, and Brownies. But with nearly everyone traveling to the small towns to attend services on Sunday, the church is where people come together to help each other and their families.[15]

The Heartland is no backwater, however. Median income levels in the five counties are very close to the national median, which is also true of the small towns. While population growth lags behind that of the rest of the country, these are not declining areas. Dallas grew by 37 percent in the last decade, though that is misleading, as a growing number of people from Des Moines buy up land to build homes here and make the long commute. But even the farther-out counties, like Boone and Jasper, have grown 5 to 7 percent and Warren and Polk by 13 to 15 percent.[16] Meanwhile, the farming population continues to age. In all the counties, the proportion of seniors has risen from around 10 percent in 1978 to around 25 percent two decades later in 1997. That is probably why senior centers are prominent, frequently one of the cornerstones of the two crossroads at the center of each town. Almost inexorably, in each county over the last three decades, the number of farms has declined, and the number of farmers selling hogs, cattle, or poultry or using dairy cows has also declined. But total sales in dollars have risen steadily over the last decade, and net cash return per farm has doubled in most counties. In Jasper County, for example, the return jumped from $22,000 in 1987 to $38,000 in 1997; in Dallas, it increased even more, from $19,000 to $45,000.[17]

Heartland residents know they are part of a global economy. Poultry prices are down because of the tariff imposed by the United States to protect the steel industry. Retaliations by the Russians meant they lost their largest market, and broiler prices are down 20 percent.[18] With farmers in these counties planting half their land with soy, they are alert to what is happening with "GMOs" in Europe. At the Heartland Co-Op, they considered separating out the non–genetically modified soy a couple of years ago, but now they just throw it all together in their silos in Mitchellville and elsewhere, because the market is open and global.

In the small towns, like Colfax, median family income is $48,300 and even higher in Newton ($49,977) and Mitchellville ($52,113). The focus group participants in this round of research came disproportionately from small towns, yet only a few were actual farmers. The men of Heartland are much more likely to work in farm-related industries than they are to farm; yet some have negotiated a compromise, like one father of two who told us that he "owns a small construction company" and farms "part-time."[19] Many of these men work for tractor giant John Deere or Hy-Line, a poultry production plant in Dallas Center. Still others are carpenters, toolmakers, and land surveyors. Some work in construction and others drive rigs. And many work in the manufacturing companies that put down roots here nearly a century ago, like Maytag in Newton and Bridgestone-Firestone in Des Moines.

The women of Heartland work in factories, churches, and beauty parlors. They work the register at Wal-Mart, drive school buses, and wait tables at Applebee's. Some work for the airlines while others are stringers at *The Des Moines Register*. They have children and hobbies, although for one busy mother who serves as a high school secretary these were one and the same. Unlike other women in her group who claimed quilt making and volunteer work, she simply stated, "My kids are my hobby."

The men and women of Heartland talk with a familiarity that comes from living in a small, tight-knit community. Time and again, these men and women told us things like, "I work at Casey's one night a week," or offered statements coupled with head nods like, "I manage that peg store" or, with a slight gesture, "I work for Barney's over there."[20]

The people here have stabilized their incomes, it seems, in a period of uncertainty, by piecing together many elements of the farm and service economy. They have done so without college degrees, for the most part, which otherwise might have put them in a different market position and perhaps in a different part of the country. In Boone County, fewer than 20 percent of the people are four-year college graduates; in Guthrie and Jasper, only about 15 percent. The percentages are a little higher in Dallas and Polk, but not in the small towns, where only about 20 percent have college degrees.

A lot of their learning about the world takes place in the churches of these communities. These are established churches, not particularly caught up in the Evangelical currents that are so important to Tampa Blue. The church buildings themselves, often brick, sometimes dating back to the 1860s, show a solidity that seems enduring, even against the cold winters in central Iowa.

Unlike Tampa Blue with its pervasive Evangelical ministries, the churches of Heartland are predominantly mainline Protestant, mostly Methodist or Lutheran, but also some Catholic. Baptist ministries are only half as likely here. Thus, on Sunday, the parishioners are much less likely to hear of a mission to "witness, share, invite, go and teach in order that all may come into a living relationship" with Jesus. They are also less likely to hear about religion and politics. In the mainline teachings of Heartland, sermons are more Heartland homily than fundamentalist fervor.[21]

In a 1999 presidential primary debate in Des Moines, George W. Bush said that Jesus Christ was his favorite philosopher because "he changed my heart." In this, he no doubt thought he would touch the voters who sympathize with his Evangelical view that betterment can result by bringing people to Jesus. After the election, he pointed to his visit to Teen Challenge International in Colfax, in the Heartland of Iowa, as one of the highlights of the 2000 campaign. Here, people are saved from drugs, "people with no hope, labeled as incorrigible, have been dramatically changed through the power of the gospel and now are delivered and serving God."[22]

But people in Heartland are clearly getting a different form of Christ's message when they go to church on Sunday. The liturgy is different. But there also may be less of a sense of cultural division and threat. One Lutheran minister in Dallas County introduced his column in the worship directory of the local paper by referencing *The Blues Brothers,* with Dan Aykroyd and John Belushi as the leads. They brought their band back together, with the refrain, "We're on a mission from God," just as Jesus brought his disciples together to do their work. The world of faith here seems to lack the intensity and division that characterize the culture war.[23]

People in Heartland watch TV thanks to satellite dishes, but they are seldom engaged in the main cultural currents that get picked up there, beyond sports and news. The men are ESPN enthusiasts and devotees of the NFL. They seem intrigued by the high-tech gadgets used in *CSI* crime lab and the gritty innards of Chicago's *ER.* Yet the Heartland is as attracted to national news magazine shows like *60 Minutes* and *Dateline* as to these national TV dramas. They seem to be looking for a bigger window to the unfolding news stories of the day or for realism in their entertainment like that provided by sports.

What is most striking is what Heartland does not watch with their fellow contested voters on the two coasts. Few of the men and none of the women report *The West Wing* as their favorite show, betraying, possibly, a lack of interest in Beltway power. Many of them mention *Friends,* but clearly they are not as invested in Monica's neuroses and Joey's exploits as is the rest of America.

These are voters whose values are important to their lives but who are only reluctantly drawn into America's culture war.

When the countryside and farm economy were much more central to America, Heartland Iowa was dependably Republican. Remember that Mamie Eisenhower came from Boone County and Ronald Reagan developed his sports broadcasting chops in Des Moines. Between 1956 and 1980, these counties, like Iowa, gave Republicans double-digit victories in presidential elections—with two exceptions: 1964, when Goldwater seemed a particular threat to the way of life here, and 1976, when the Nixon scandal and Carter's agrarian virtues momentarily evened the parties. But the economic downturn of the 1980s had a greater impact here than on the country as a whole. The recession was longer, but even more significant than that, the uneven recovery was part of a larger process of consolidation and modernization, with uncertain consequences for the countryside. Total farm income in Iowa fell sharply in the mid-1980s, recovered somewhat by 1987, only to head down again in the early nineties.[24] The farm crisis of the 1980s cost Iowa its very identity: it "changed everything, from how farm families made money to how much time they had for their neighbors."[25] One in ten Iowa farms went under between 1979 and 1988. This loss translated into a dearth of confidence in the Republican leadership: while Ronald Reagan was winning in 49 states in 1984, in Iowa the Republican margin dropped to only 7 points. Walter Mondale won his home state of Minnesota and carried Boone, Dallas, and Polk counties. While Michael Dukakis, a liberal from Massachusetts, faltered in 1988, he cleaned up in Iowa and swept all five of the Heartland counties, with 60 percent of the vote. Democrats have not lost Iowa since Reagan carried it in 1984, but 2000 was settled by a slim 4,144 votes and opens up a new, contested chapter for our politics.

Bill Clinton carried the Heartland voters in 1992 and 1996, very much a result of the long-standing economic uncertainty and change that have turned these voters to the Democrats. With the president trusted on the economy and running against an economic conservative, Bob Dole, Clinton won by 10 points and received just over 50 percent of the vote in the Heartland counties. These voters were very comfortable with a president who "put people first" and did not forget the economy. But the national trauma surrounding Monica Lewinsky and the impeachment proved to be a storm cloud over Iowa. These voters are pretty muted—we have seen hesitation about bringing religion too overtly into the political world—but this upset conventions here. Freshman Democratic Congressman Leonard Boswell, who represents the eastern part of Heartland, refused Clinton's campaign help and was one of 31 Democrats to vote in favor of impeachment in the House. In the 2000 presidential election, the Democratic vote dropped about 5 points in each of the counties, the only of the three contested communities where 2000 took such a toll. In the end Al Gore won narrowly in Boone and Polk, George W. Bush squeaked out victories in Dallas and Guthrie, and they split the remaining one, Jasper, 49 to 49 percent.

EASTSIDE TECH

Eastside Tech is bounded on the west by Lake Washington and looks east to the Cascade Mountains and to Mt. Rainier farther south, which is a nearly religious icon for area residents and an ever-present backdrop for life here. No matter where one lives, there are lakes, like Lake Sammamish, and state parks, like the Cougar Mountain Regional Park, which bump up against all the rapidly growing cities of Eastside Tech. The bounty in the economy and nature has been brought together here to create a distinctive part of contested America.

The highways are truly arteries in this area. Interstate 405 is a monumental north-south highway, built at the outset of this modern era, fifty years ago, making the vast investment in this area possible. Interstate 90 runs east-west, stretching Eastside Tech out to what were once distant towns, like Issaquah, and brings tens of thousands of commuters each day west across the floating bridge, over Lake Washington and into Seattle.

The people of Eastside Tech live mostly in medium-sized cities.[26] Bellevue is the largest, with 110,000 residents, followed by Kirkland, Redmond, and Renton, each with 40,000 to 50,000. In the last decade, the population of Eastside grew by 31 percent, atop a 25 percent increase a decade earlier. Most of the towns look like suburbs, with commercial streets and strip malls, and with mushrooming housing developments from earlier eras and now. But Bellevue has a real downtown, with offices and apartment buildings. And there are major global industries based here. Boeing's engineering center and plants cover more than five million square feet here, even after the post-9/11 cutbacks. Microsoft's campus of 23,000 employees is in Redmond, as is the home of Eddie Bauer and AT&T Wireless.[27]

Every city in the area is full of new housing developments, but here the prices and the number of choices get your attention. In Renton, where people have more modest incomes than the area as a whole, the houses in Liberty Ridge begin with 1,400 square feet and a two-car garage at a cost of $233,900, but end with 4,000 square feet and a three-car garage, with an asking price of $365,900. Buyers can choose from ten different models. In a new development in Redmond, on somewhat larger lots, the houses, multilevel with skylights and three-car garages, were selling for a pricey

$700,000. The basketball backboards here are not dented, as they are fiberglass, and the hoops do not droop.

In all the cities, there are areas where single-family houses are built on the hills or around a lake and areas that look like older neighborhoods. There are also some new, often luxury apartments and condominiums. But this is all dwarfed by the planned developments. Almost all are designed with regular cul-de-sacs that impart a greater sense of privacy and community.

In the aftermath of Iraq, about one in every ten houses had an American flag hanging from it, a sign of a patriotic spirit, but hardly at the level of Tampa Blue. Like Tampa Blue, there are a lot of Chevy Bonanzas and Suburbans, Jeeps, and Ford F-250s in Eastside Tech, but also a lot of Toyota Corollas and Isuzu Troopers. A gateway to the Pacific, Japanese cars are in high demand, with many Hondas and Toyotas on the roads. The foreign-made influence extends to Europe as well with BMWs and Volkswagens at every traffic light.

People pay a bit more for this quality of life and for being part of a cosmopolitan and global setting. In Bellevue, the basics—a gallon of milk and a dozen eggs—will cost double their price in Des Moines and 50 percent more than in Brandon in Tampa Blue. You pay $4 more for a 100-ounce box of Tide. It costs $1 more to bowl after 6 P.M. and $1 more for an adult to go to the movies at night. Unleaded gasoline is about 30¢ more per gallon. And sportsmen pay twice as much for a hunting license than do those in Heartland Iowa and Tampa Blue.

But it seems these folks can afford it, which is why they live here. The residents of the principal towns of Eastside have family incomes well above the median for the country. Some, like Redmond, have a median income of $66,735, almost $25,000 above it. This is why the heart of Redmond is filled by the Town Center, block after block of new two-story brick buildings, with a mix of office and commercial uses, catering not so much to the superrich but to a large upper-middle class. But Redmond is not isolated in Eastside Tech: five other cities have incomes over $60,000, including Bellevue, the largest community ($62,000). Farther out, beyond the lake, is Sammamish, with a median income over $100,000.[28]

From the Acuras to the frappuccinos, it does not take long to realize that Eastside Tech is a world away from Heartland Iowa. Both communities are a product of their environment, and while agriculture permeates Heartland, technology drives Eastside. As one might expect from communities nestled in the shade of Microsoft's long shadow, Eastside is home to a glut of software engineers, Web developers, and IT managers. But it also hosts a slew of other brainy tenants—from engineers to brokers and self-identified nerds, like a father of two who professed, "I'm a geek by profession. I play with geeky stuff all day."[29] Indeed, the men and women of Eastside work in white-collar jobs with profit-sharing plans and flextime—a far cry from the contested blue-collars outside Tampa and Des Moines.[30]

The people of Eastside Tech are well educated, giving them market power and an opening to the cosmopolitan culture of the area and beyond. A majority of the population of Bellevue has at least a four-year college degree, twice the national average. Nearly the same is true for all the major cities of the area, including Redmond (52.9 percent), Sammamish (61.5 percent), Mercer Island (69.1 percent), Kirkland (47.4 percent), and Issaquah (48.3 percent).

There are not a lot of African Americans here. There are a few more Hispanics, though not many.[31] But Eastside is diverse in its own way, related to its position in the global economy. The biggest minority is Asian, with Chinese the largest group, but also many Japanese, Koreans, and Indians. In Redmond, 13 percent of the population is Asian, rising to 17 percent in Bellevue, the largest city. In times past, when these were bare villages, the Chinese minority in the area faced intense hostility: in 1886, President Cleveland declared martial law in Seattle to protect the community against the mobs; in 1924, more than 10,000 attended a Ku Klux Klan rally in Issaquah. By World War II, Japanese were the largest minority, but in Bellevue during 1942, three hundred Japanese Americans, one-quarter of the town's population at the time, were shipped to internment camps. Today, however, things are very different in Bellevue. One in four residents of this city was born outside the United States and sixty languages are spoken in the public schools. Bellevue's diversity is part of its role in a now more global economy.[32]

Starbucks and espresso bars are the most visible symbols of the cosmopolitan culture. There appear to be as many Starbucks in Eastside Tech as churches and storefront ministries in Tampa Blue. In Renton, which anchors the area in the south and where cosmopolitan and working-class character compete or blend, there are the conventional strip malls, some with pawnshops, as well as used-car lots, though not festooned with American flags. All the conventional chains—Pizza Hut, Walgreens, Wendy's, Denny's, and McDonald's—are in evidence. One row of shops has "CheckCashing and PayDay Loans" at one end, and the Doppio Expresso Bar at the other, reflecting the character of the city.

As one moves to the conventional higher-income cities, there is a gigantic Starbucks in a brick-and-near-colonial-style building, along with gigantic PETCO, Blockbuster, and, indeed, Charles Schwab stores. Here the strip malls are tree lined, and the occasional Burger King sits almost completely concealed behind tall, deep hedges. Across most of Eastside, espresso stands can be found in front of gas stations and supermarkets. In addition to *The Seattle Times,* the Safeway in Bellevue sells *The New York Times, The Wall Street Journal,* and *Barron's.*

It is reassuring to residents here, no doubt, that a "grande" coffee at Starbucks costs $1.64, exactly the same as in Des Moines and only 7¢ more than in Tampa.

The people of Eastside Tech, not surprisingly, are connected. Over 86 percent of the focus group participants can name a favorite Web site, double the number who say that in Tampa Blue or Heartland Iowa. For the men, their favorites were portals, news, and sports sites. For the women, eBay was the top, followed by news, portals, and travel.

The busy people here, compared to the other communities, are much less likely to volunteer or be active in a group, only about 20 percent. This is the only community where school activities, youth sports, and scouts edge out church volunteering. The churches here advertise in "worship directories," and more than half have a Web site.

The community newspapers devote a considerable portion of their advertising to women's fitness centers. The Valley Medical Center runs full-page ads depicting groups of women talking about "Valley Fitness." And American Women Fitness markets a shapely, well-tanned, glistening woman pumping weights to entice women to its Bellevue and Renton centers, while the Pelage Center advertises as the first full-service medical spa in the Northwest.

It hardly seems surprising that the women's favorite shows are *Friends* (25 percent), *ER* (22 percent), and *The West Wing* (17 percent).[33] The women of Eastside Tech are familiar with the way of life hawked in these metropolitan melodramas. They identify with both the challenges and benefits of city living and appreciate the subtle cultural references that pervade these series. Indeed, they are as comfortable with *Will and Grace* as *Law and Order.* The men, like the men in Tampa Blue, give the *The West Wing* high ratings (22 percent favorite show), along with sports programming (23 percent) but also *Friends* (15 percent), which is well received but scores lower here than in the other communities. The men of Eastside Tech also like the smart crime fighters of *CSI* and *Law and Order.*[34]

The people here seem pretty relaxed and tolerant about different lifestyles and points of view. In Issaquah, a city at the westernmost part of Eastside, the public library, rather than posting the Pledge of Allegiance as in Tampa Blue, sets out a diverse selection of community newspapers. Among them is the *Seattle Gay News* with these front-page stories: "Over 1500 Women Participate in Mexico's First Lesbian March" and "Gay Ma-

rine Surrenders to Authorities as Conscientious Objector." Also there was
the *Voice of Choice,* offering angelic assistance and discussing astrological
influences.

The residents of all three contested communities believe they have a
distinct and special quality of life. Being able to shove off in one's own boat
in Tampa Bay or look out on Big Creek in Iowa is as valued as taking a
hike in the Cougar Mountain Park. Here in Eastside, the quality of life
includes not just the mountain backdrop but also the immediacy and pervasiveness of the natural environment—the lakeside homes and cities,
housing developments that abut state parks, indeed, the cities with both
natural and manmade preserves and ponds. From your own cul-de-sac in
Bellevue, you can access the "lake-to-lake" trail that leads you to Lake
Washington to the west and Lake Sammamish to the east.

The picture postcard milieu of Seattle is not lost on its residents. People
here seem to take better advantage of their natural surroundings than those
who live in similarly beautiful parts of the country. They are avid joggers
and skiers, they like to hike and fish—the sky is the limit for outdoor leisure,
almost quite literally for one of our respondents who moonlights as a flight
instructor. Indeed, one man summed up the Eastside sentiment in one
blanket statement: "I love any kind of outdoor activities."[35] The people of
Eastside are fierce defenders and keen observers of their environment,
keeping close tabs on how varying environmental legislation and regulation
will likely impact the area and thus their quality of life.

In these cities, nature gets a lot of help, integrating social and natural,
which is part of the character of this community. In Redmond, a massive
public park, decorated with windmills and totems, includes a nature preserve and an "interpretive trail"; it also has a seemingly infinite number of
soccer fields. A survey of Redmond residents found that more than 85
percent used the trails in the city for walking or bicycling, and three-
quarters said they were willing to pay higher taxes for park improvements.[36]
In Issaquah, the local teams, clad in full uniform, from baseball caps and
jerseys to sock garters and cleats, played in a small ballpark, with well-
manicured, major league–quality infield grass. A couple of blocks away is a
relatively new community center, occupying nearly a full block, featuring
massive indoor soccer courts and, of course, an espresso bar.

These are communities that take their local public services seriously,
evident in their city halls, fire departments, and police stations. Renton has
an eight-story office building to house City Hall. Issaquah has built a $12.8
million brick complex for the police and fire departments, stretching down
a whole block, for this town of only 11,000 residents.

These are also cities and communities that take seriously government regulation to control how these areas grow and what kind of life is created here. In Bellevue, the City Council's first act in 1951, as *The Seattle Times* points out, was to create a Planning Commission, not a police department. They wanted growth then but were determined that it be "neat, orderly, efficient, spacious."[37] The city now has a population of more than 100,000, yet managed to create a "tightly controlled downtown core," with high-rises and the second largest mall in the state, while still preserving the suburban neighborhoods.[38] Today, the Eastside's own promotional material says, "Many communities are supporting master-planned housing developments and 'urban villages,' where all the amenities of living (shopping, working, schooling) are included in the development plan."[39] The mayor of Redmond, in the opening paragraph of her letter to residents, emphasizes "the need to balance the growth we have seen in recent times with the other things that make our community so special."[40]

The high-tech boom of the nineties brought another, almost equally amazing transformation. Eastside Tech became increasingly Democratic and culturally aligned with the party. At the outset of the period in 1992, Bill Clinton carried virtually every city of Eastside and tied in the rest, but his vote rarely went above 41 percent. Economic downturn and alienation from Washington, D.C., left this area in a rebellious mood and ready for Ross Perot. He got around 25 percent of the vote in most of the cities. In 1994, Washington State joined the Gingrich revolution, defeating a pro-choice Democratic woman in part of Eastside and ousting the Democratic Speaker of the House, Tom Foley, in eastern Washington. These were heated races, not just because they were close but also because they were fought along cultural lines. Randy Tate and Rick White won seats with these weapons. Tate went on to head the Christian Coalition after one term, while White would lose his seat in 1998 under attack for pursuing President Clinton's impeachment.

But in almost every city of Eastside Tech, support for the Democratic presidential candidate rose in each successive election, including in 2000 for Al Gore. From 1992 to 2000, Democratic support jumped from 41 to 52 percent in Bellevue, 43 to 53 percent in Issaquah, 40 to 54 percent in Kent, 42 to 55 percent in Kirkland, and 41 to 52 percent in Redmond. This means Al Gore won every city with more than 20,000 residents, except for the very richest. But this was still closely contested territory, with the Democrats winning just over half the vote.

Since 1992, Republican Jennifer Dunn has held the congressional seat representing most of the cities of the Eastside. She was born and grew up in Bellevue, the center of the district, went to Stanford, and worked for IBM. Her views are conservative on economic issues, and she was a "vocal deficit hawk" through the nineties, according to the *Almanac of American Politics*. She has a reputation as a "cultural moderate," but that is hardly evident by her A+ rating from the Christian Coalition and 7 out of 100 rating from the League of Conservation Voters. One of her children is named Reagan, but perhaps that is part of the split personality of Eastside Tech. With Democrats and Republicans each taking a congressional seat and with the Democrats' small presidential majority in 2000, this high-tech suburb sits in the middle of contested America.

Indeed, all three of these communities draw together the contested parts of the electorate that fall mostly outside the world of the loyalists. They are influenced by what happens in that world, and their politics has clearly evolved over the last decade of intensifying partisan battle. But they have their own issues and own reasons for failing to fall into line. The next chapter explores and defines further the contested landscape.

Chapter 8

THE CONTESTED POLITICAL WORLD

Virtually all of the significant groups discussed in this chapter are contested by the main parties and, by definition, are not part of the loyalist partisan world. Remarkably, a number of the groups—when they did vote in 2000—ended up as divided and deadlocked as the rest of the country.

For some of these groups, we have witnessed the evaporation of a four-decade-long Republican majority, giving way to a new dead-heat politics. This is the history of the white professionals, college graduates, and senior women. Other groups, such as the aging noncollege and blue-collar women—long a bellwether for the country's political swings, including the Reagan ascendancy—are now divided down the middle but continue to act as crucial indicators for the politics of the last decade. Some of the groups are volatile, swinging back and forth over more than a decade of elections, obviously not grounded by loyalist bonds. This category includes white noncollege married women and Catholics. The latter are so fragmented by gender and age that they are now hard to recognize as a group in either party camp. Many of these groups, like white youth and nonmarried women, are increasingly disengaged from politics. And some are open to third-party protest politics, reflecting a disgruntlement with the choices offered by the

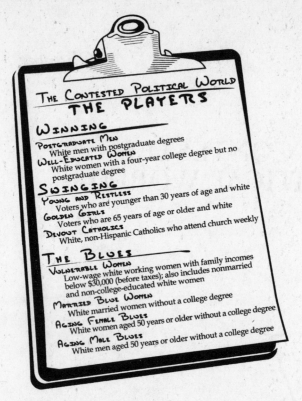

The Contested Political World
THE PLAYERS

WINNING

POSTGRADUATE MEN
White men with postgraduate degrees
WELL-EDUCATED WOMEN
White women with a four-year college degree but no postgraduate degree

SWINGING

YOUNG AND RESTLESS
Voters who are younger than 30 years of age and white
GOLDEN GIRLS
Voters who are 65 years of age or older and white
DEVOUT CATHOLICS
White, non-Hispanic Catholics who attend church weekly

THE BLUES

VULNERABLE WOMEN
Low-wage white working women with family incomes below $30,000 (before taxes); also includes nonmarried and non-college-educated white women
MARRIED BLUE WOMEN
White married women without a college degree
AGING FEMALE BLUES
White women aged 50 years or older without a college degree
AGING MALE BLUES
White men aged 50 years or older without a college degree

two dominant parties. This is the path of the aging blue-collar men, as well as that of the white youth.[1]

These contested voters, it turns out, are either winning or losing in a rapidly changing America altered by two decades of corporate consolidation, privatization, and marketization, technological innovation, rising inequality, and just sheer economic growth. For them, change raises many issues, but not all are central to the culture war that has dominated the period. Change often creates a need for political adjustment, but not necessarily the one contested in the ongoing debates of the Two Americas.

Large portions of upscale America, composed of people who are winning in our information economy, particularly the new professionals and well educated, are looking for new approaches to the economy and the world, to education, and to the environment and other quality-of-life issues. They are attracted to the Democrats on cultural issues to be sure, but they cannot figure out which party to turn to on so many others. For them, the current divisions are like a straitjacket.

In contrast, large portions of noncollege and blue-collar America are mostly falling behind in our changing, increasingly unequal economy and society. They are attracted to the Republicans on cultural issues as well as

THE CONTESTED POLITICAL WORLD

PARTY ALIGNMENT

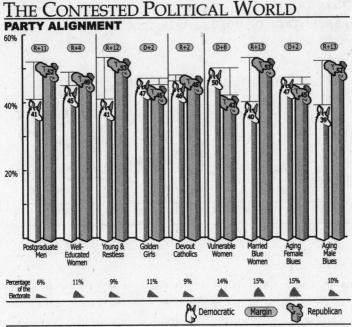

Democracy Corps database, November 2001–May 2003.

taxes, yet they are also looking for new ways to raise their incomes, gain greater security, and obtain better schools, health care, and general care for their children and families. They want to shift the balance away from the current elites and big corporate influence. Their issues too remain largely unaddressed.[2]

While these too are often overlapping groups, the Contested World clearly includes a well-educated sector, distinct age segments of young and old, Catholics and the non-college "Blues." Altogether, 36 percent of the total voting electorate belongs to at least one of the Blue groups—double the size of the contested college voters, underscoring where the battle will take place.

THE SPECIAL ORDER LINE AT STARBUCKS

WELL-EDUCATED MEN AND WOMEN This half century has brought a remarkable transformation from an industrial to an information

THE WELL-EDUCATED
PERCENTAGE OF VOTERS 1952–2000

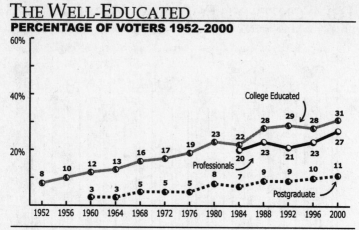

National Election Studies, 1952–2000.

economy, a change that has created whole new sets of winners—people in new professions and with more education who see their futures in this more cosmopolitan and high-tech order. It has brought about a political transformation no less remarkable. People with such privileges were conventionally Republican, but the Reagan Revolution did not stir these voters, and they soon turned against it. For the last decade, these well-educated voters have lacked a political home. Some Democratic observers have watched breathlessly, thinking these better-educated voters are on a trek from the Republican to the Democratic camp, but this is a misreading. Rather, they have pulled away from the Republicans but still appear to feel stuck with their political choices.

These new winners were produced by changes in the nature of work, impacting the nature of the skills that people need in order to succeed. Thus in the 1980s, 20 percent of the electorate was composed of professionals, where it remained for a decade. This alone represented a major change in the way people worked and learned, but the high-tech boom of the 1990s brought a surge of new recruits and new professions, with professionals rising to 27 percent by 2000.[3]

The recent growth in professionals has been produced by rapid changes across a wide range of occupations. Between 1992 and 1997, there was a 103 percent increase in the number of employees in software publishing, a 99 percent increase in home health-care services, a 61 percent increase in mortgage banking, and a 59 percent increase in management-consulting services.

Parallel to the change in the nature of work is the change in how people prepare and develop the skills they will need. Before 1960, less than 10 percent of the electorate had college degrees, rising slowly to just over 20 percent in 1980. In the mid-1980s, the first surge occurred; by 1988 and for the rest of the current period, it reached 30 percent of the presidential electorate.[4] The exit polls of the last decade, using a different survey methodology, put the college proportion too high at 43 percent in 1996 and 42 percent in 2000.[5]

The explosive expansion of higher-level education attainment in America shattered the limits at the top end, producing a growing, distinctive group of voters with postgraduate degrees. Before 1980, barely 5 percent of the electorate had reached that level, and most of those were in the traditional professions, like medicine and law. But the number of Americans holding postgraduate degrees has risen steadily since 1980, topping 10 percent in the last two presidential elections.[6]

Radical changes in gender roles and opportunities for women are reflected in the education surge, with important implications for the contested landscape. Since 1980, the number of women with at least four-year degrees has nearly tripled (from 8.2 percent to 23.6 percent in 2000); the number of men with a similar attainment has virtually doubled (from 14.1 percent to 27.8 percent).[7] At the younger ages, that almost certainly means that women have closed the gap and are becoming college educated at a greater rate than men.

Being able to win in the new economy naturally produces higher incomes and social status, and when our economy was more traditionally industrial, that translated into Republican voting. Yet the growth of professional occupations and the rising demand for advanced education have obscured the traditional political demarcations centered on income and class, at least at the upper end and certainly among the women and the postgraduate men. With increasing rapidity since the early 1980s, profession and education have been translating into changes in lifestyle, family, and gender roles; mastery of technology and information; growing social diversity and tolerance; and engagement with an ever-growing world.

The growing well-educated bloc included a rising number of David Brooks's "Bobos" who defy convention by combining bohemian self-expression with bourgeois ambition. This new elite, Brooks writes, "define our age," but they also defy it. They have delegitimated old authority while insisting on freedom and pluralism, even as they seek limits. Their doubts that anybody knows the full truth leaves them puzzled about the passions of culture war.

And as the new winners in America were pulling away from the traditional ways of doing things, Ronald Reagan was stepping up to restore faith in traditional values and traditional ways of doing things. But that produced a dramatic move away from the Republicans by the new winners, though they were without an obvious new home.

The small groups of professionals were presumptive Republicans in the America of the 1950s. The American Medical Association had fought off Roosevelt's and Truman's universal health-care proposals and opposed Kennedy's and Johnson's efforts to have universal health care at least for seniors. For nearly the entire era, the professionals gave the Republicans dependable majorities, at least until the late 1980s. The world of college graduates told the same political story. In the 1950s, 70 percent of them voted Republican, the legacy from a time long past when a college education was a privilege and for the privileged. Then, Republicans settled in at around 60 percent of the vote for two full decades, 1968 to 1988, undisturbed by Wallace or Reagan.[8] The tumult that shook the Democrats in the 1960s and 1970s, and even the Reagan presidency that shuffled political loyalties elsewhere, did not impress them. This tumult turned the world upside down for African Americans and nearly did the same for the white Catholics in the North and white Baptists in the South. But the tumult was a political nonevent for the college educated.

However, in 1992—and in the succeeding presidential elections—the Republicans' four-decade-long majority among the well-educated evaporated. Bill Clinton won the college-educated by 5 points in 1992 (44 to 39 percent) and by 3 points in 1996 (47 to 44 percent). Then Al Gore and George W. Bush battled to a dead heat: 48 percent for each.[9] The professionals first tipped to the Democrats in 1988 and then went decisively Democratic thereafter.

This parity is a little deceptive, however. The white, married, college-educated men are the most materially privileged part of the Republican loyalist camp, drawn to Republican pro-business and low-tax policies. The white women with postgraduate degrees are fully part of the Democratic camp, bound by the cultural issues of the era.

But this leaves a large portion of the college educated and professionals without a home. The Well-Educated Women are 11 percent of the electorate, and the Postgraduate Men are another 6 percent—together, one of every six presidential-year voters. Most of the college-educated women have four-year degrees, and they are genuinely contested. In Clinton's first election, the Well-Educated Women edged toward the Democratic camp: he lost them by 4 points in 1992 (39 to 43 percent) and 4 points in 1996 (43 to 47 percent). But the national dead heat in 2000 was replicated among these white four-year college graduates: Gore 48, Bush 49.[10] Today, when asked which party they align with, they are divided down the middle, with the edge to the Republicans (49 to 45 percent).[11]

The Postgraduate Men give the Republicans a somewhat greater edge, 11 points (52 to 41 percent). But they are not in any camp, as is evident in the wide vote swings of the last decade. They broke with their Republican history and supported Bill Clinton in 1992 (46 to 41 percent), but then swung back to give Dole a small majority in 1996 (50 to 40 percent) and George W. Bush a large one in 2000 (56 to 38 percent).[12] As members of highly educated families and frequently part of the growing cosmopolitan culture, they are very different from the Privileged Men who are firmly in the Republican camp.

Now that they have ventured away from the world of Republican loyalists, it is hard to imagine these voters backtracking. Almost every aspect of the current conservative response to our contested politics reminds them of why they left. The professionals and college-educated voters have stepped across the cultural divide and are deeply opposed to the religion-centered and cultural politics that so many Republican loyalists view as the reason to be loyalists. They dislike the easy antigovernment attacks, intense individualism, and overheated patriotism.

These voters dislike the NRA in particular, which seems to represent the kind of individualism and rural and working-class values now foreign to their world. Both the white male postgraduates and four-year college women give the NRA a very cool thermometer rating of around 42 degrees. The white postgraduates are almost as hostile toward pro-life groups (43.4 degrees), indeed, even more hostile than the white college women, who are ambivalent (47.1 degrees).

During the in-depth discussions held with the college-educated voters from Seattle's Eastside upscale suburbs, both the men and women responded fiercely to these issues and values. Among the words and phrases the women used to describe the NRA are: "radical," "militant," "scary," and "horrible." To many of these women, the NRA is synonymous with a gun-wielding Charlton Heston, angry bumper stickers, and Washington lobbyists.[13] College-educated men offered similar suggestions: "outdated," "extreme," "potentially scary" yet "powerful" and "effective."[14] The discussion of pro-life groups carried on in the same vein: "radical," "militant," "fanatical," "controversial," "I would have to say disgusting," "When you say pro-life, you think of extreme."[15] Some of these voters, conscious of their Republican history, are stopped in their tracks by the party's cultural focus: "I mean, I'm very divided as a Republican," one man told us. He recounted a situation where he was asked, "What are you?" and remembered "gagging" because he had a tough time admitting he was a Republican, his reluctance stemming from "a lot of this social stuff that's coming out that I absolutely don't agree with."[16]

Modern professionals and college-educated voters believe in the capacity of government to regulate—not spend, necessarily—to advance the public welfare and foster community without encroaching on individual liberties. This puts them well outside the Reagan view of the world. The postgraduate men, for example, fully accept the need for regulation of the market and checking corporate abuses and are not much worried, as modern conservatives are, that regulation ends up making things worse (65 to 31 percent). Beyond curbing market abuses, they are open to government regulation to achieve public safety and a cleaner environment and, unlike conservatives, are prepared to encroach on the freedom of individuals who want their SUVs and guns unhindered (60 to 36 percent).[17] In the Eastside Tech discussions among the college educated, there was a confidence that government could set "restrictions and guidelines and checks and balances," particularly when so many companies now seem unchecked. This was true even for the men, whom one might expect to be more cautious about government:

> We generally have safe products, but we still have a lot of companies, like Firestone, that cover up major mistakes. . . .

> I think it would be just a super mess to not have the environmental regulations. If you look at Love Canal and all these other things that have happened in the past, if there weren't regulations then, there would be all kinds of air, water, land pollution that would impact virtually millions of people. To me, that's really important. Somebody is looking for something. . . .

> If you look back to the golden age, when there wasn't any regulation at all, business and corporations just manhandled little people. And I think if there was no government regulation, then I think the public would be in trouble. . . . We always can't protect ourselves.[18]

Many of the men, in particular, worry that the government will go too far. They are drawn back again and again to the conclusion that now is a time for some government regulation, but not too much:

> [speaking of an earlier period] Government kind of harmed us more than it helped. I think now it's gotten the opposite way in terms of the pendulum.

> That's a very good point. . . . We are certainly at the point where we are not concerned about child labor like it was years ago. And we are at the

point where the government is really hurting our businesses and their ability to grow. But, most recently, . . . there's a lot of people that are now in dire straits because businesses went out of control. I'm very pro-business. . . .

. . . We frequently try to describe a personality or some kind of moral code for a big business, and they have none. And so they have to be regulated. That's the way it is.[19]

Another man said flatly, "In general, I think the government should be a lot smaller than it is, but [Enron], there's an example [where] government should have been policing that situation."[20]

When the discussion moves to the environment, the college-educated women elaborate on the values and principles that are central to their identity and that more and more distance them from the Republican world. Like most voters, they think the Democrats are better on the environment, while the Republicans and George W. Bush may be "destroying it" and are being "shortsighted," "relying on big business," and are "really antienvironment."[21]

For the educated—who are by no means antibusiness or antimarket—this is a question of community and stewardship over market thinking:

I'm not necessarily a tree hugger, but . . . just having kids, you wanna pass down something that is healthy.

[Bush is] actually trying to bring drilling to protected areas, and logging, . . . stripping natural resources . . . You know, there's a balance there.[22]

These voters are conscious that "energy is a limited resource," and that one needs to be thinking about alternatives, including "solar power."[23]

But that is crystallized as a powerful values choice, which defines Republicans as more shortsighted: "I like the the long-range view of protecting the interests of children and the environment and education. [Democrats] look a little more towards protecting the things you can't put a price tag on, whereas the Republicans look to protect things that do have a price tag. That's what I like about the Democrats. They do seem to have an interest in things that you can't put a price tag on."[24]

These feelings about mutuality and community also seem to carry over to the way America deals with the world. No other group in the contested world is so estranged from the conservative view of how to advance America's interests and security. A majority of the well-educated men and women

(52 percent) say we live in a complex world, full of alliances and relationships that can make the country more secure. Just over a third of both would depend mainly on military strength—a central tenet of the Reagan-Bush view of the world. Some of the women articulated their competing ideas and conflicted feelings: "We need to start viewing the world as a community and looking at what is good for everyone, rather than just being the bully"; "you need to discuss it until it can't be discussed anymore . . . with the people around you on what the best movement is, and if you don't, you . . . are going to ostracize yourself, and if you do that, you're cutting your own throat."[25]

This suggests that these voters will have trouble going back, as the Republicans turn up the heat on their antigovernment politics and policies. It also suggests that these voters may be open to new issues and ways of doing things, where government plays a decided role. These are future-oriented voters, expressing uniquely positive feelings about the Internet—over 70 degrees on the thermometer; over 74.4 degrees for the men. They are the most open to immigrants and presumably open to the new diversity that characterizes their world.

These voters, however, are not simply at the midpoint of a trek across the political spectrum from the Republican to the Democratic world. The intense cultural politics of this period has moved them away from the Republicans, and when it comes to the environment they seem more comfortable with the Democrats on values like stewardship and social responsibility. But these voters are not particularly attracted overall to the Democrats, and indeed may be stuck politically, given the choices. Their discomfort with the Republicans is evident enough, but they are not rushing to embrace what the Democrats have to offer.

In the Eastside Tech discussions, when asked about the Democrats, these independent-minded college voters express a lot of cynicism. One voter bluntly stated, "I think the politicians are gutless." Another complained of the control money has over politics, saying that "everybody is worried about their . . . next contribution." But perhaps most disheartening is the tired tone people adopt when talking about the Democrats. It's an "old party" lamented one voter; another agreed: "There's no new ideas."

On the big policy issues that bear on their lives—education and the economy—these voters can barely choose between the parties. On education, the white male postgraduates favor the Democrats by 13 points, but the college-educated white women give the Democrats only an 8-point advantage on what is conventionally a strong Democratic issue. They give the edge to the Democrats on education only because they are convinced the Democrats will spend more money and make education a higher priority when they think there is a need for more investment and better teachers.

"Our most valuable resource is the investment in our children," one of the men stated, while noting that the Republicans would rather "buy some guns" and "they've really dropped the ball on education."[26]

They lament the elimination of art programs and the failure to fund good teachers, worrying that they'll go become engineers or accountants. One woman said funding for the arts is "the first thing that gets axed all the time."[27] A woman who was majoring in special education in college changed her career plans when she saw how little money was going to that field. For her, the lack of funding was "astounding" and "heartbreaking."

But none of the Seattle participants described a Democratic approach to education other than a commitment to devote more resources and fund "programs." Said one man, "It seems to be talked about a lot—we're going to fix education. But I have seen nothing."[28]

In fact, in the Seattle group discussions, the college-educated voters seemed at least as animated by the issue of accountability, where the Republicans did have a clearer point of view. One woman observed, "I think there is a lot of money going into the public education, and I want to know where it is going. The money is going up, up, up, but the education level is going down."[29] They also want to see greater accountability on student performance, but some are perplexed on how to reach it: "I believe the idea of accountability . . . but you don't fatten the calf by weighing it. . . . [You] don't improve learning by testing, yet that seems to be the emphasis of the Bush administration."[30] A woman agreed that test scores may not necessarily measure success: "The new education plan stresses accountability and results. Never in there does it stress helping children achieve."[31]

This leaves these education-oriented voters disillusioned about current political discussion or education: "I don't think it's a Democratic or Republican thing. I think it's just money and effort." "I vote both sides from time to time, but I'd love to see somebody come up with a plan."[32]

When it comes to the economy, white college-educated groups give the advantage to the Republicans—by a very substantial 12 points. This may reflect their higher incomes, and many of the women are married to more economically conservative men. The Postgraduate Men give the Republicans a 30-point advantage on taxes. But in the Eastside Tech discussions, these voters are mostly drawn to the Republicans on economic matters because they see no distinct Democratic perspective on the economy other than spending on programs. These doubts are held in check by a feeling that Clinton brought good economic times and that Democrats reduce deficits. This suggests that the Democrats will at least do no harm. But none of these voters was able to discern a distinct Democratic perspective on the economy that would give them confidence about the future.

One man recalled the Clinton years fondly: "You look at the recent history, Bush and Reagan administration . . . Eight years later at the end of the Clinton administration, they had vastly improved. Interest rates were way down for a house. The jobless rate was the lowest in history. . . . All the economic indicators were favorable after eight years of the economy with Clinton."[33] At least a decade of persistently attacking deficits produced some returns under Clinton: "I have to say that I was impressed that the debt went so far down when Clinton was in office"; another man said simply, the Democrats "are antideficit."[34] Some of these college-educated voters now see the Democrats as more balanced than in the past: "After the last administration with Clinton, I think they are more economically balanced. They are more out to give the appropriate tax cuts when they are appropriate, but not necessarily going into deficit spending mode when they don't have it."[35]

What is so surprising is that the sustained economic boom did not add up to more, even in the Seattle area.

When asked to identify the good and bad things about the Democrats and the economy, these college-educated voters point to the same things: spending and programs. On the good side, people think the Democrats' economic approach is to fund the government and programs with honorable intentions, many of which they support. Their first associations are "public services," "feeding homeless people," "humanitarian things," and references to "arts programs." Simply stated: "They give money to help [communities], and they are not very tightfisted."

When asked about the bad things, the tone changes but the content is the same: "spending," "let's get some programs," "let's sign 200 different programs into service."[36] For some of these voters, by "going too far into handouts and different programs" and by "pandering to every interest, creating a new program for every problem," "you create the greatest of unintended consequences," indeed, the possibility that such spending will "destroy our economy."[37] One of the men read the Democrats' program orientation as a bigger statement about government and the individual: "I think they want to take care of the American public, rather than letting us take care of ourselves."[38]

The problem with the Democratic instinct to respond to problems with programs is that it is often viewed as a reactive, short-term approach, which leaves the Democrats outside the larger debate about where to take the American economy. One woman, though overall expressing positive feelings about the Democrats' philosophy, questioned them on their foresight: "I think of programs and Democrats doing things for the community, the negative part that I think of is that you provide all these services, but most of them are fixing things that are wrong rather than preventing things from happening."[39] And when asked about reasons that could persuade her to vote for the Republicans, one woman declared she would support Republicans for their emphasis on "long-term economic growth."[40]

These upscale voters, winners in the new economy, wonder whether Democrats have as complete an understanding of economics as Republicans:

> I don't think that the Democrats to me give as good appearance at having in-depth knowledge of the economic issues and business and capitalism.[41]

> They don't have any practical, I probably won't verbalize this right, but it seems like there's some lack of practical business sense or experience.[42]

> I think that—pains me to say it—Republicans have a kind of tighter grasp of fiscal policies and running the country more like a corporation than a free lunch.[43]

Many of the college-educated find themselves aligned with the Democrats because of the cultural war around them but stalled by Democrats' silence on the economy. One woman summarized the dilemma: "I think of issues like pro-life and things like that. I feel closer in line with the Democrats there. The economy? I'm not sure that's their strength. They get too caught up in the social issues."[44]

And so white educated America remains contested.

SWINGING

THE YOUNG AND THE RESTLESS   They are restless because they are young but also because they are impatient with the politics of the Two Americas. The parties will not easily force them to accept the current choices, and even though they tried, they will likely drive them out of politics or to third parties. That has already happened for many young voters through the polarizing politics since 1992.[45]

All young voters under thirty—Gen Y, born in 1975 or afterward—are the most Democratic generation, above all because they reflect the country's rapidly growing racial diversity. Fully one-third are minorities, compared to just 19 percent for the baby boomers and only 11 percent for the oldest,

GI generation.[46] In 2000, they supported Gore or Nader over Bush, 53 to 46 percent, and in 2002, they favored Democrats in the congressional elections, 50 to 47 percent.[47] However, because of the growing racial diversity, this tells us more about the future of the country than about young people per se.

White voters under thirty, the Young and the Restless, in fact belong to nobody. In 1992, Bill Clinton and George Bush divided up their vote evenly (38 to 38 percent each); in 1996, these white young voters moved to Clinton (45 to 41 percent) but flipped in 2000 to support Bush against Gore (55 to 39 percent).[48] Today, they align marginally more with the Republicans (53 to 41 percent).[49]

But these voters are not only contested, they are coming apart. As it turns out, young white men and young white women are headed in different political directions. The women align with the Republicans by a small margin (50 to 45 percent) and the men with the Republicans by a big one (56 to 38 percent).

Politics over the last decade has been lost on the Young and the Restless, who are progressively disengaged. In 1992, the mood was different. With the young Clinton challenging the old Bush and Ross Perot mounting his reformist campaign, young voters turned out in large numbers—the largest youth turnout since 1972 when the Twenty-sixth Amendment lowered the voting age to eighteen.[50] Indeed, they comprised fully 17.4 percent of the electorate. But then they lost interest in the heated partisan battles of the period. In the next two presidential elections, they pulled back and comprised only around 13 percent of the voters.[51] Only 62 percent say they are certain voters (10 on a 1-to-10 scale), fully 10 to 25 points below that for the other groups in the contested world.

The young are in a rebellious mood. In 1992, they gave almost a quarter of their votes to the Reform Party candidate, Ross Perot, and in 2000, they gave Ralph Nader 6 percent, double his national vote. Nearly 30 percent describe themselves as independents—again, larger than for any other group in the contested world.

They are disconcerting for politicians because they are only with great difficulty jammed into the established boxes. Looking at the whole Gen Y, whatever their political preferences, they break strongly against the conservative cultural tide. Above all, they are culturally tolerant. While a majority of all the other generations opposes gay marriages, Gen Y voters favor making it a legal right, 55 to 42 percent. They are also much less cynical about government or worried about its intrusions on the individual. Given the bold choice of "smaller government providing less services, or a bigger government providing more services," a stunning 69 percent opt for bigger

YOUNG & RESTLESS THERMOMETERS
COMPARED TO ALL VOTERS

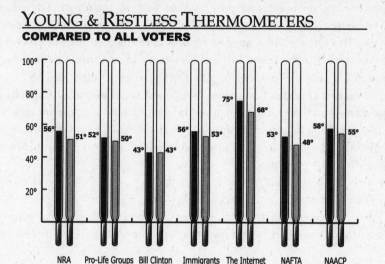

Democracy Corps database, November 2001–May 2003.

government. But at the same time, which will be some solace to conservatives and reformers, they are very supportive of initiatives providing more choice and market options, including private investment accounts in Social Security and private sector involvement in prescription drug coverage.[52]

The Young and the Restless share the values and beliefs of the racially diverse Gen Y and seem to go their own way. They are strong supporters of the regulatory state and not motivated by a defensive individualism. They are tolerant and globally open, reflected in their uniquely warm responses to immigrants, the NAACP, NAFTA, and the Internet. At the same time, they are strongly internationalist (57 percent), proving very skeptical of national security strategies that depend too much on the military (35 percent).

But the Young and the Restless are nonplussed before the symbols that send most other voters rushing to either side of the cultural divide. They are ambivalent about big corporations (50.1 degrees), though more positive than most voters; similarly, with pro-life groups (51.5 degrees); and they are pretty favorable toward the NRA (56.4 degrees).

The Young and the Restless are so dislodged from partisanship that, for the moment, the two parties have little to say to them. The 2000 and 2002 campaigns heavily concentrated on retirement issues, but just 8 percent of these young white voters choose that as either their first or second concern. On the other hand in the post-9/11 period, 37 percent choose education,

33 percent the economy and jobs, and 23 percent terrorism. They do not give either party big advantages on the official issues of the day. Indeed, they give the Democrats a modest 8-point advantage on education and the Republicans a 10-point one on the economy. They throw up their hands on Social Security (39 percent say the Democrats are better and 38 percent the Republicans). On a few issues, the young seem pulled in radically opposite partisan directions. They give the Democrats overwhelming advantages on handling the environment (60 to 21 percent), but then turn around and give the Republicans similarly titanic advantages on keeping America strong (58 to 18 percent).

So when the Republicans whip up religious passions and the Democrats stir up the retirement issue, they ask, "What is in it for me?"

These are voters apart from the established battles and are unconstrained by the partisan boundaries that are important elsewhere.

GOLDEN GIRLS In this past decade of party parity and building animus, retirement issues dominated all others. Seniors, after a near half century of Republican voting, can now swing either way in any presidential or off-year election. From 1996 through the 2002 congressional elections, the parties have vied desperately over Medicare, Social Security, pensions, and prescription drugs, with hopes of tipping the electoral balance. Both parties throw money at their prescription drug plans and challenge seniors to discern the differences. With so much at stake, money has trumped ideology, at least in this part of the contested electorate.

Seniors take up more space in the contested and dislodged world than any other group. Seniors comprise 21 percent of the electorate, and they split their votes down the middle (47 percent for the Democrats and 46 for the Republicans). When one peels away the minority seniors who are securely in the Democratic world and the white retired men who are securely in the Republican, the swing senior bloc of white senior women, the Golden Girls, is still fully 11 percent of the electorate. And they too divide right down the middle: 47 percent aligned with the Democrats and 45 percent with the Republicans.

This Golden Girls split is quite uncharacteristic of the whole of this postwar era. In every election between 1952 and 1988, the Golden Girls cast a majority of their vote for the Republicans, averaging nearly 60 percent. Right through the Reagan years, they went about their assured, almost timeless ways: down slightly to 55 percent in 1980 but back to 60 percent in 1984.[53] Each generation of retirees has found a reason to spend its golden years voting Republican, until now.

In 1988, the Republican majority fell to 52 percent, despite the fact that George H. W. Bush promised lower taxes and law and order, which likely presaged the politics of the next decade.

But then, suddenly, the Golden Girls flipped. The Republican majorities disappeared, in favor of a small but consistent edge to the Democrats. Bill Clinton narrowly beat George Bush in 1992 (47 to 44 percent) and widened the Democratic advantage in 1996 (52 to 42 percent). Al Gore held the Democrats' new modest majority with the Golden Girls in 2000 (52 to 46 percent).[54] This has created a frenzy of attention to seniors, where the incentives are very great to throw a lot of promises and money into the battle for these votes.

While we are not entirely sure why the Republican majority suddenly evaporated, it may have something to do with the Reagan challenge to government spending. Prior Republican presidents, from Eisenhower to Nixon, lavished higher Social Security benefits on seniors. While Reagan did not actually touch Social Security, many in his administration speculated about cuts and his young apostles in the Gingrich revolution sought major reductions in Medicare, the health program for seniors, which figured centrally in the government closure and the elections of 1996. In the political battles at the turn of the century, government spending on seniors had taken center stage, with Democrats and Republicans touting their competing prescription drug plans. Indeed, in 2003, competing plans passed in the House and Senate—the former supported almost solely by Republicans, and the latter with Democratic support. At a time of explosive deficits, both parties supported over $350 billion in new spending for seniors.

For future elections, Democrats go into the battle well ahead with the Golden Girls on retirement issues and health care and on their skepticism about big business and markets. They are very wary of big corporations. They presume a large government role in providing income support and health care for retirees, which has taken on the quality of a norm. The Golden Girls are little troubled that a larger governmental role intrudes on the individual. They will leave such worries to other generations. And they are not so sure America should hang its security on military might when there are allies who could be helping us out.

But the Golden Girls remain, even now, very hostile to Bill Clinton (40.7 degrees), and their overall support for the Democrats over the past decade has risen and fallen with each "scandal" of the "Clinton Wars." The Republicans now have presumptive advantages on values, like responsibility and knowing right from wrong, which gets the door open for Republicans, as long as they are not undermining Social Security. The Golden Girls are also very cautious about diversity and immigrants, who get a chilly thermometer rating of 47.6 degrees, reflective of their discomfort with the Democrats' postmodern path. That likely explains why so many of the Golden Girls, 46 percent, describe themselves as politically conservative. Even though they are not animated by the most heated issues, like abortion and guns, values and America matter here.

With the Golden Girls conflicted about these two worlds and now divided evenly after years in the Republican camp, they are likely to remain front and center of the political battles of the day.

DEVOUT CATHOLICS   In 1928, the Democrats, to the amazement of the country, chose Al Smith, the Catholic and very Irish governor of New York, as their presidential nominee. From that historic point on, Catholics were poised to become the heart of the New Deal coalition. They became the troops for the unions and urban machines. And as David Leege points out, "Through depression and war, this was the party of Catholic aspirations, incorporating group respect, economic justice and security as rewards for hard work, and firm challenges to totalitarian states who threatened the homeland, Catholicism, and American interests."[55]

Catholic support for John Kennedy topped 80 percent, the highest point in a Catholic coming of age in America.

Then, after the riots and busing and affirmative action, Catholics wondered whether their values and aspirations were reflected in the Democratic Party. The Democratic vote faltered in 1968 and collapsed in 1972. The social-liberal Democrat McGovern lost to the law-and-order conservative Nixon, 63 to 37 percent. The defection was driven, above all, by white Catholic resentment of black civil rights tactics and attitudes toward welfare and social programs intended to help them.[56] Carter momentarily won them back before Reagan set off a decade-long run of Republican victories among white Catholics. At his height, Reagan won 57 to 42 percent over Mondale and Bush also won strongly over Dukakis, 56 to 43 percent.[57]

The three-decade battle for the hearts and minds proved inconclusive in the end, as white Catholics never really realigned like the white Evangelicals did in the same period. The result is that Catholics are very much up for grabs. For some parts of the Catholic community, Reagan settled the issue of aspirations and values, but in fact, a majority of the New Deal–generation Catholics remained Democratic into the nineties. The Catholic male baby boomers became Republicans with Reagan, but the women did not. And the youngest generation of Catholics are dividing along gender lines, deepening the parity, with the men strongly Republican and the women strongly Democratic as both have come of age.[58] By the end of the century and this era, Democrats and Republicans had reached parity in party identification in this very fragmented community.[59]

White Catholics comprise one-quarter of the electorate and are closely

WHITE CATHOLICS – PARTY ALIGNMENT
PERCENTAGE SUPPORTING PARTY 1952–2000

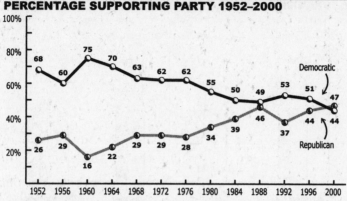

National Election Studies, 1952–2000.

contested and volatile.[60] Clinton won them with small margins and without an outright majority in 1992 (42 to 37 percent) and in 1996 (48 to 41 percent), but Bush came back and defeated Gore by a slightly better margin (51 to 46 percent).[61]

The scope of the Catholic battleground has been reduced by secularizing tendencies and by rising education and social mobility, leading many to abandon the old city neighborhoods and parishes for the suburbs. In 1972, 50 percent of white Catholics attended church weekly, but this figure dropped inexorably and dramatically to 35 percent over the three subsequent decades. Thus, the number of Devout Catholics—white, non-Hispanic Catholics who attend church weekly—has fallen from 12 to 9 percent of presidential-year voters.[62]

The Devout Catholics—almost one of every ten voters—are those most committed to and identified with the church and most likely to bring their Catholic identity into politics. They trace their families back to Europe, dominated by Ireland (21 percent), Germany (19 percent), Italy (15 percent), and Poland (9 percent).[63] With more political focus on values and moral questions in the last decade, these are voters most likely to be impacted by the battle. After a half century of political tumult, much of it centered on them, the Devout Catholics divide their party loyalties almost evenly: 46 percent for the Democrats and 48 percent for the Republicans.[64] These Catholics were already dividing their vote evenly in 1992, but the values battle line of the 2000 election drove them into the hands of the Republicans. Bush overwhelmed Gore in this devout world, 58 to 40 percent, suggesting how volatile their values-driven politics has become.[65]

The Republicans have gotten their attention on abortion. The Devout

DEVOUT CATHOLICS
GOVERNMENT REGULATION

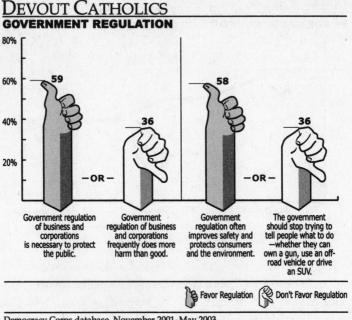

Government regulation of business and corporations is necessary to protect the public.	Government regulation of business and corporations frequently does more harm than good.	Government regulation often improves safety and protects consumers and the environment.	The government should stop trying to tell people what to do —whether they can own a gun, use an off-road vehicle or drive an SUV.

👍 Favor Regulation 👎 Don't Favor Regulation

Democracy Corps database, November 2001–May 2003.

Catholics give pro-life groups a remarkably warm thermometer score of 65.4 degrees, including almost 60 percent expressing warm or positive feelings.[66] Indeed, by the mid-1990s, as the cultural war has become total, Catholic views on moral questions like abortion, women's roles, and homosexuality are starting, for the first time, to produce Catholic defection from the Democrats.[67] And now, 45 percent of the Devout Catholics say they are politically conservative.

But these Catholics remain aloof from the white Evangelicals because a more complex set of views keeps them contested. With deep urban roots and in light of Catholic social teachings, the Devout have shown little interest in the other parts of social conservatism. They have joined the discussion of values, but not in the prescribed cultural terms. The Devout Catholics have no special regard for the NRA. They do not rush to the Republicans on taxes. And they fully reject the conservative position on markets, government, and individualism. They are skeptical about big corporations. Fully 58 percent believe that government should act to protect consumers and the public safety and environment, while only 36 percent say government should get off people's backs and leave them free to drive and bear arms as they wish.

Their history and their values leave the Devout Catholics in their own place, clearly in the contested and dislodged world but ill fitted to the established cultural lines of the Two Americas. They are not loyalists because they respond, sometimes strongly, to the symbols of both warring parties. They might well prove attentive to political leaders who draw lines and approach America's challenges in new ways.

THE BLUES

The greatest bloc of contested voters watching politics from a distinct perspective is noncollege and blue-collar America, where voters lack college degrees for market advantage and work in service or lower-wage positions, where income and benefits are under pressure. These are voters for whom church and faith are important and who think values and family are under pressure too. They watch the cultural and corporate winners set the tone for the times, including politics, and wonder about their lives. They know they are not winning now and may not be in the future. However, the two parties have set traps for them: the Republicans baiting with abortion, guns, and taxes; the Democrats using Social Security, Medicare, and a little class warfare. But they are at the center of most of the problems that are now off the agenda in this era of party parity and unaddressed problems for the middle. These problems include the rising cost of health insurance and the rising number with no insurance, slow to stagnant incomes and growing inequality, weakened family structure, and difficulties guiding and nurturing children.[68]

The two parties appeal to these contested voters, but they center on the party's key issues rather than the key concerns of noncollege and blue-collar voters. This is why these voters feel that politicians are not talking to them.

VULNERABLE WOMEN The most vulnerable in this downscale world are the single white women without college educations. They lose on two counts in a world where marriage helps women achieve greater security and stability and where college skills increase their choices and incomes. Single noncollege women comprise fully 10 percent of the electorate. They are joined by the low-wage white women workers, forming 6 percent of the voters. Their consciousness is shaped by the simple fact that they work, yet their families do not make very much money—less than $30,000 a year. That puts them largely in the lower-paid service sector jobs, short on money as well as benefits: one in four do not have health insurance (28.2 percent).

Together, these Vulnerable Women comprise 14 percent of the electorate and form an important part of the contested blue-collar bloc.

Their vulnerability and their hopes have led them to turn to Democrats who ought to be more relevant to their lives. Indeed, in 1992 and 1996 they voted for Bill Clinton. The single noncollege white women gave him a 9-point margin in 1992 (46 to 37 percent), growing to 22 points in 1996 (55 to 33 percent). The same was true for the white low-wage women workers: 10 points (45 to 35 percent), rising to 15 points (52 to 37 percent).[69] Faced with the Gingrich Revolutionaries in the Congress ready to slash Medicare and a Republican presidential candidate ready to abolish the Department of Education, these Vulnerable Women decided to go with the Democrats, who were in fact cutting taxes for low-wage workers and at least discussing health care.

But the ambition of the Democratic agenda waned and values issues reemerged. These voters, who think they should be comfortable in the Democratic world, now give Bill Clinton a quite cool thermometer rating of 42.3 degrees. In the heated 2000 election, these women still voted Democratic, but with a somewhat reduced margin. The single and vulnerable women gave Gore a 15-point margin (56 to 41 percent) and the low-wage women about half that, 7 points (51 to 44 percent), with 5 percent going for Nader.[70]

So currently, these women nod Democratic, but not with much confidence, which suggests that something is missing for them. The Vulnerable Women give the Democrats an 8-point advantage, with 50 percent aligning with the Democrats and 42 percent with the Republicans.

Their high expectations for the Democrats produced a good turnout in 1992, when the single noncollege white women, for example, comprised 18 percent of the presidential-year voters. According to one estimate, they were nearly one out of every five people voting in the 1992 election that brought Bill Clinton to the White House. But then as the heated battles over party parity stamped out their hopes for progress on many fronts, including health care, they pulled back, forming 15 percent of the electorate in 1996 and dropping to just 10 percent in 2000.[71]

Except for the young voters, these Vulnerable Women are among the least likely to say they will vote in upcoming elections.

The Vulnerable Women, then, are in this contested world because they are put off by the Democrats, who have not offered real help or solutions for their lives, and they do not have much time for games.

The culture war is not this group's fight, as important as it might be for the Republican faithful on one side and the Secular Warriors on the other. As it turns out, the Vulnerable Women rate the NRA right at the midpoint on the thermometer scale (49.6 degrees) and hold back on regulation when it is telling people what kinds of cars or guns they can have. Interestingly, they divide evenly on pro-life groups as well (51.2 degrees). They apparently do not have a horse in this culture race. But these women also hold back because Democrats have not done much to address the insecurities and pressures in their lives. The Vulnerable Women are intensely anticorporate, indeed, as anticorporate as any group in the electorate, including Union Families. They give corporations about a 41.8-degree thermometer rating, with negative reactions exceeding positive ones by nearly two to one.

They are very open to an expanded role for government that would act as a check on the powerful and lend a hand to the vulnerable. Very large majorities see a government that can act to make things better (56 percent), while barely a third see government causing more harm than good. In general they are looking for a government capable of changing the fortunes of those living with the consequences of an uncertain market and world.

On health care above all, they would turn to the Democrats rather than the Republicans (49 to 25 percent). This is their great uncertainty, particularly as employers cut back on benefits and as government seeks to place more of the responsibility on the individual.

The party preference on education is revealing. Among these Vulnerable Women, the Democrats have a mere 5-point advantage. While it is in part testimony to President Bush's focus on education since his winning the Republican nomination in 2000, it is also about Democratic silences on a broad range of issues that impact the lives of Vulnerable Women who might otherwise turn to the Democrats.

MARRIED BLUE WOMEN   The married counterparts of the Vulnerable Women are under pressure from all sides, much like the F-You Boys, to whom many are married. That they are apparently in a different political world no doubt reinforces the frustration of the men, who are forced to travel alone, at least politically. Only one in five of these married women are homemakers. The great majority work predominantly in blue-collar and service jobs. They live in both suburban and rural areas, and are more likely than others to go to church every week. From this vantage point, they watch the political world from an uncertain and pressured position.

In an increasingly diverse America, with rising education requirements and professional jobs and fewer people getting or staying married, these women are self-conscious about their declining presence and role. In the 1950s, they were 35 percent of the presidential-year voters and remained near a third until 1964, but then dropped to about a quarter through 1980, continuing to drop to 18 percent in the 2000 presidential electorate.[72]

MARRIED BLUE WOMEN
PERCENTAGE OF VOTERS 1952–2000

National Election Studies, 1952–2000.

Throughout the era, the white noncollege married women have reflected historical currents almost exactly. They seem almost a bellwether on the balance of forces. They voted solidly for Eisenhower in the 1950s, divided evenly with the country in 1960, supported Johnson in landslide numbers in 1964, and did the same for Nixon in 1972. In the 1980s, they voted around 60 percent for Reagan.[73]

These women were also fully part of the reaction against the Reagan Revolution and no doubt felt the recession deeply. Non-college-educated women as a whole were earning less in 1992 than they had under Reagan.[74] So while the Married Blue Women gave the edge to Bush in 1992, the Republican margin was reduced to 7 points (42 to 35 percent), while a large bloc of 22 percent supported Ross Perot. Bill Clinton battled them to a draw in 1996 (44 to 45 percent), putting them at the heart of the battle of party parity. But they clearly responded when Bill Clinton's campaigns championed the forgotten middle class, promoted welfare reform and middle-class tax cuts for children and college, and promised investment in education, while restoring fiscal balance.

Perhaps no other group of voters has been so hotly contested. These women would like America to offer a politics that affirms their values as well as honors them and helps them achieve a better life for their families. The Republicans appeal to them through their values and way of life, which took on great force during the Monica Lewinsky scandal and subsequent Republican impeachment campaign. Bill Clinton weighs on their consciousness and is viewed badly here: an icy 35.0 degrees, with 58 percent offering cold negative responses. Echoing the feelings of many in their group, one

Heartland woman wondered, "When you get into ethics . . . how much worse can you get?"[75] As a result, in the midst of that scandal, these women turned sharply away from the Democrats in the 1998 congressional elections.[76] And when George W. Bush gave expression to his faith and in God's word and vowed to restore dignity to the White House and when Al Gore spoke of tolerance for alternative families but little of his faith, the consequences were evident enough.

The Democrats, nonetheless, appeal to these married women to remember their blue-collar and New Deal inheritance and to think about a broader set of family needs, like health care, education, and retirement. At the same time, Democrats are highlighting other issues that seem, from this vantage point, to threaten the family and their guns.

For now, the culture war is winning out over class warfare. George Bush vanquished Al Gore among the Married Blue Women: 56 to 41 percent.[77]

Today, they are 15 percent of presidential-year voters and appear to be looking to the Republicans, much as the Vulnerable Women seem to be looking to the Democrats. They give the Republicans a 13-point edge, with 53 percent aligned with them and 40 percent with the Democrats.

If we look only to the younger of these women, they have virtually joined the Republican world. They broke heavily against Al Gore in 2000 (63 to 33 percent), after giving Bob Dole only a small plurality in 1996 (45 to 40 percent).[78] They are balanced by the older women—married with grown children, who find themselves facing increasing health-care and retirement concerns—who are contested and only lean Republican (49 to 44 percent).

More important, these voters are losing out, and they know it. They want a politics that will champion their interests as well as their values. The market for them holds little romance. They are skeptical too about corporations, giving them a thermometer score of only 44.2 degrees. They are also leery of markets and support the idea of government doing more to regulate business (54 to 35 percent). They pull back when the regulatory agenda seeks to tell blue-collar America what they can drive and shoot.

These women in Tampa Blue and Heartland Iowa use words like "greedy," "untrustworthy," and "impersonal" to describe corporate America.[79] "I worked for a big corporation for thirteen years," one woman explained, "and you're just a number, that's all."[80] "True, you never know when you're gonna go," said another woman. "I mean, it's not like where twenty years ago or whatever, if you were in a job, if you were in that job for years and years, you knew you had a place to retire. Now you can get two years from retiring, and, *See ya!*"[81] And it is not just the instability of today's corporate world that troubles these voters—corporate scandal has inspired profound distrust. "Big corporations are only out for one person and that is the CEO," huffed one disgusted Tampa woman.[82] Another declared that they're "killing the little people."[83]

For now, these married women still peer out on these political battles from behind cultural walls. The wall have gotten higher because of government's cultural agenda intruding on their lives and because the Republicans have made Bill Clinton their "poster child" for America's moral decline.

All of that brings these women to the edge of the Republican world, but they are held back by the hope for a more expansive politics that addresses their needs.

THE AGING FEMALE BLUES—ON THEIR OWN? The older, white, noncollege women, whether married or not, with grown children, have a different view on the world—rooted in aging, financial marginality, and the prospect of being alone. This produces another large space in the electorate—15 percent of the voters—where the parties are at parity.

These women are less consumed with sheltering their children from the intrusive influences of pop culture than their younger counterparts. These aging women are troubled by rising health-care costs, as their own health becomes a greater worry. They are consumed with their inability to pay the bills and still manage to save, and they live with the specter of some unforeseen event. As one woman explained, "You're just one paycheck away from having something taken away from you."[84] These women want assurance that the government retirement system will be there for them, and that employers will not play fast and loose with their (or their husband's) pension. And they no doubt worry about their own families and the prospect of growing old on their own. Indeed, over 40 percent of them are separated, widowed, or divorced, and this weighs on their minds.

These older women, who are mostly blue collar, certainly want a restoration of values in the country. These are God-fearing women, over half of whom go to church every week. Like most of the other noncollege women, they loathe Bill Clinton and what he came to stand for morally (39.4-degree thermometer). They also want a restoration of control over the country's borders, as reflected in their feelings about immigrants (48.1 degrees). One woman speculated, "I think there's this big push to bring in people from other countries to keep our wages down."[85] A distressed Tampa Blue woman expressed a similar sentiment: "We're losing our jobs. People are out of work. I think they're shipping too much work out of this country to other countries."[86] The looming pressures of aging compound these anxieties and create competing preoccupations, particularly health care and retirement.

These aging women resent the health-care industry and take issue with drug companies that "manufacture a pill for a dollar and then charge you ten."[87] They are outraged by the cost of health insurance and moved by the experiences of family members and friends. As one Heartland woman explained, "My mom is seventy-three and she's still working so that she can have her health care." Exasperated, she added, "She can't retire!"[88] These women describe the burdens exacted on Americans by the health-care industry as "ungodly," "pathetic," "outrageous," and above all, "unfair."[89]

And when it comes to these quality-of-life issues, aging women look to the Democrats. They are much more likely to trust them on health care (45 to 28 percent) and on retirement and Social Security (13 percent).

These voters reflect historical swings, very much like all the white non-college women. Their counterparts came out of World War II, solidly Republican, like most older voters, and gave the Republican Party over 60 percent of their votes since the 1950s, including 1960, when 64 percent voted against Kennedy. Their history is unexceptional in the middle of this era, swinging with other Republican-leaning voters. And a large majority of them supported the Republicans in the Reagan era, but the industrial consolidation and the uncertainties about government retirement programs began to impact these older women late in the decade.[90]

The recession and the backlash against the conservative Republican attempt to achieve dominance wiped out the historical Republican majority among the older blue-collar and noncollege electorate. Every election of the 1990s was a dead heat among the Aging Female Blues: in 1992, Clinton received 44 percent of their votes, to 42 percent for Bush; in 1996, Clinton took 49 percent, 6 points ahead of Dole with 43 percent; and in 2000, Bush got 50 percent to Gore's 48 percent.[91]

Today, a line runs right down the middle of this space in the contested electorate, with 47 percent aligned with the Democrats on one side and 45 percent aligned with the Republicans on the other.

The Aging Female Blues do not love government, though more would regulate than leave things to corporations and individuals. Their responses are muted by being part of a working-class culture that resents elite limits on their lifestyles and choices. Nonetheless, they are essentially as divided on the role of government as they are on the political parties. The one thing they are not divided on is "big corporations." They view them very coolly (41.7 degrees), with twice as many negative as positive responses. They look out on corporate America and see companies that lack commitment to their employees, while CEOs are enriched. In this case, the values of the CEOs are contributing to the uncertainties facing the Aging Female Blues.

THE AGING MALE BLUES—AGAINST THE CONTROLLERS These men, comprising 10 percent of the presidential electorate, are very close to joining the F-You Boys in the Republican world. If anything, they are more proudly patriotic and give the Republicans a massive 40-point advantage on keeping America strong—more than any other group in the contested electorate. They say, bottom line, America should rely on its own military to make America secure and worry less about the support of other countries. They are almost as likely as the F-You Boys to own a gun.

When we asked the Aging Male Blues in Tampa Blue what they liked about George W. Bush, they responded with references to his military leadership. "He's aggressive with the military," said one man, explaining, "if something happens, it's being taken care of." Another man put it plainly, simply saying that Bush is "for America." In fact, they like the whole conservative package that he offers: "He is 'military minded' and believes in a strong military"; he "believes in consolidating and reducing spending and return[ing] taxes."[92]

There is broad support for "putting the money back in people's pockets."[93] One man explained his rationale: "I think that it would be important if we could cut taxes like the president wants to do and curtail spending as much as possible because just putting money in people's hands, you know, could help the economy greatly."[94] That reflects a deeper trust in President Bush. As one put it: "He's a man of his word. He's honest. And I think he's looking at our future and trying to preserve our way of life here."[95]

These do sound like voters who will rally to the Bush administration's approach on the war on terrorism and determination to cut taxes. When these aging noncollege men are asked which party is better on keeping America strong, the interviewer can barely get the question out before they rush to say Republican: 60 percent, to just 20 percent who choose the Democrats. The result is only a little better on taxes: 52 percent to 30 percent. This hardly seems like contested ground.

These aging men are not very fond of Bill Clinton, whom they associate with a weakened military and values and a president who personally tried to take away their guns. Many of these men share the generational experience of Bill Clinton and came to a very different view of their shared history.

These men are not very excited by the abortion-choice symbols, but they sure care about guns. They have very positive views of the NRA, giving it a 61.9-degree thermometer rating: 58 percent react warmly to the NRA. Indeed, while these voters are very open to most government regulation, they do a complete flip when it comes to the government telling people what to do with their guns and SUVs: 39 percent say "government protects,"

AGING MALE BLUES

GOVERNMENT REGULATION

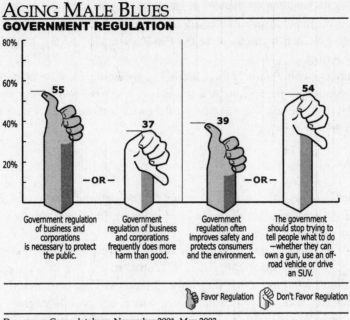

| Government regulation of business and corporations is necessary to protect the public. | Government regulation of business and corporations frequently does more harm than good. | Government regulation often improves safety and protects consumers and the environment. | The government should stop trying to tell people what to do —whether they can own a gun, use an off-road vehicle or drive an SUV. |

Favor Regulation   Don't Favor Regulation

Democracy Corps database, November 2001–May 2003.

while 54 percent say "back off." No other group of voters in the contested electorate feels so strongly about getting the government off their backs. They are obviously the torchbearers here for a working-class and rural culture under siege. No wonder a majority of 53 percent call themselves political conservatives.

In Tampa Blue, these mostly older blue-collar men could not have been more passionate and articulate on the question of Democrats and big government. It is inexplicable to them that the Democrats want a controlling government that tells people what they can do. These men have a lot of history under their belts and lived through the civil rights era, busing, affirmative action, welfare, the women's movement, gays in the military, and weapons bans, which have impacted their position in the workplace and family, even their time off. So they have a well-developed view about the basic philosophic orientation of the two parties. In general, they view the Democrats as interfering in their lives with excessive government and heavy taxes:

They want more government, more control.

They need more money to be able to do that.

That's the traditional Democrat-Republican. Democrats want bigger government. Republicans want smaller government, more localized government. I think it is the basis for the two parties. . . . [96]

I think it's a philosophy. I think letting the government keep your money,
they do a poor job with it. And if you believe it's the people are paying
out of our pockets, we make better decisions with our money than the
government does.

Amen.[97]

They are flabbergasted at how Democrats, through the cumbersome appa-
ratus of government, "think they can do a better job of controlling your life
than you can."[98]

But these older men, with nearly full work lives, are hardly naive when
it comes to the control and power of corporations, how they treat their
workers, and what influence they have in politics. That is reflected in their
thermometer rating for big corporations, which is a cool 44 degrees. These
voters are balancing which controller must be pushed back in any given
period.

The tax-cut debate sets off all sorts of alarms in their heads, because
here they think they know who is the controlling force and who has their
hands in the public treasury. They know the rules of the game, even without
reading the fine print.

Little rumors I've heard. Tax cuts aren't going to benefit anybody unless
you're up on the higher plateau. The low-level workers aren't going to
get a thing out of it. . . .

Tax cuts are going to benefit the ones that make money, not the ones
that actually work for it.

The tax cut was supposed to benefit everybody.[99]

They want to put money back in people's pockets, but which level of
pockets?[100]

They fully understand the rationale that the elites have for this exercise.
They "go into [the] theory of trickle-down theory: the rich will help the
poor; businessmen will pick up the economy." And, "you know, and maybe
that's the correct way to do it, but it hasn't worked so far."[101]

That leads them to want to see the corporations contribute something as well: "I think that [the president] needs to hit the corporate America and have them pay some taxes, you know, your big companies, like Wal-Mart and Tyco."[102] They see the end of job security and employer-provided retirement benefits as detrimental effects of a modern world that rewards employers at the cost of employees:

How many corporations ship jobs overseas just to save money?[103]

Now, the companies are taking away the private pensions where they were promised and they worked all their lives.[104]

With age, these noncollege men are aware that they "don't trust either one"—government or the corporations. One man looked for a solution to the dilemma that might resolve it against government: "But the companies are limited by competition to a certain extent, where the government is not limited. They're the only ones in town [who can] look out for themselves." The market puts limits on corporations but government can operate without bounds. But another man resolved the dilemma at a different level: "That's the good thing. We can vote for the government, but we can't vote for an insurance company or for a doctor." Another man shared this fear of unchecked corporations, observing; "The thing about the corporations is that, basically, they're enormous powers without any control. At least with the government, the people you've got something to say or do about it, as little as it might be. But when it is the corporations, you've got no idea what the power is doing. . . ."[105] Accordingly, this group is frustrated that democracy can limit the government, but people have no voice when it comes to companies.

Their struggle with such questions about which is more controlling and which is worse leaves these older men outside the loyalist world, where the answers seem more certain.

The Aging Blue Men do not vote like the F-You Boys. They align with the Republicans, but only by 13 points, about half of that for the F-You Boys. That gives the advantage to the Republicans, but these voters are on guard against the controllers who make their life difficult. In 1992, they voted for Clinton over Bush by 10 points (45 to 35 percent), but 20 percent also voted for Ross Perot. In 1996, they voted for Dole over Clinton by 7 points (46 to 39 percent), but 15 percent held out for Perot, well above the national norm.[106] In 2000, Al Gore was not their guy; indeed, he seemed hand in glove with a controlling government that wanted to tell them how to live. Bush beat him 58 to 39 percent among the Aging Blue Men.[107]

But the skepticism about markets and the private sector, and the need to balance the controllers out there, makes these voters alert to changing times and changing fortunes. It is possible that their F-You Boy proclivities will lead them to support leaders who stand up for America. But it is possible that other political instincts will compete—the need to keep in check corporations that seem to have little regard for their employees. These men are aging, and they understand the consequences of bankrupt pension funds or a bankrupt Social Security system.

These men, along with much of noncollege and blue-collar America, find themselves on the short end of history, as America becomes more diverse and more educated and globally engaged. The controllers have the power, they think, which is why their needs are rarely addressed in the public world. That is why they too are at the center of the contested world. The better-educated may be growing in numbers, but all these contested groups in the blue-collar world together make up 36 percent of the electorate. They may be in decline, but they matter.

For their own reasons, each of these groups—from the Well-Educated Women to the Aging Blue Men—are the odd ones out. Their priorities are different from those of the loyalists, they are conflicted and reluctant to close off choices, and they have their own issues or their own ways of thinking about things. They are annoying to the loyalist political world, which has worked hard, and with some success, to get them to vote on the issues and the principal divide of the Two Americas. But they still remain apart and as big as either party bloc, which is why any shift to new issues or new battle lines will have them in mind. They are the subject of the strategies to come.

PART V

Breaking the Deadlock: The Republicans

The setting is the Lincoln Study on the second floor of the White House residence, where a fictional Karl Rove, senior adviser to the president, is presenting his initial campaign plan for the elections ahead.[1] Rove has served as President Bush's principal political adviser since his first run for governor of Texas and now plays a larger-than-life role in the White House. "All politics is Rove," as Tip O'Neill might say, but as Nicholas Lemann observes, "Rove has a much bigger charter than his predecessors."[2] His job description ranges from recruiting Republican House candidates and networking with conservative support groups and corporate donors to shaping the president's economic and tax policies, domestic agenda, and foreign policy. What limits the president puts on the position are not at all clear in practice, though the one case we know about suggests not many. After the 9/11 attacks, Rove was barred from the war cabinet and National Security Council meetings. He was surprised and unhappy, according to Bob Woodward, but on October 7, when the president was to speak to the nation, he called Rove that morning to be with him in the White House Treaty Room where America's response was launched.[3]

Today, the agenda is "2004 and Beyond," though, as with Rove's job description, the words do not communicate obvious limits. Rove is seated in a chair with papers and binders piled on his lap, some notes spread out on the coffee table. Only a few feet from where Lincoln's desk sits in front of the double-paned window overlooking the South Lawn and the Washington Monument, the president sits on the couch across from Rove.

Chapter 9

STEP ONE:

Winning in Our America

**The Two Americas
2004 and Beyond**

Office of Strategic Initiatives

Mr. President, you are going to win. Trust me.

I've heard that one before.

Yes, sir, I did say that. This time, though, there won't be any Friday surprises. No DUIs. No special prosecutor indicting your defense secretary, like they did to your dad. We have a plan, which we'll review today, where

> ## Why It Exists
>
> ### The 49% Nation
>
> <u>First Time Since 1880's that:</u>
>
> • **3 consecutive Presidential elections where neither party gets 50% of the vote**
>
> • **3 consecutive congressional elections where neither party gets 50% of the vote**
>
> • **First election since 1876 where the popular vote winner loses the presidency**

Reprinted from "72 Hour Task Force," Republican National Committee.

tactics is strategy and strategy is tactics. If we are disciplined, keep our focus, execute and build on the work we've done so far, no problem.

And so we don't get to spend November with Jeb? So, what was it, six points we were supposed to win by? And whose idea was it to spend all that time in California? How badly did I get my ass kicked?

Sir, I . . .

Aw, shit. You know I'm just ribbin' ya. You're still the boy genius.

Mr. President, we will do everything we can and more, as you'll soon see. Somehow, some way, some shape, some form we'll make it happen, but there is no getting around the fact that Barone is right, this is a 49 percent nation. There are two Americas, one red and one blue.[1]

So what is tactics is strategy, and strategy is tactics shit?

Exactly!

NB: Pardon this interruption, but from time to time I will want to clarify and elaborate. In this case, I focus on the equating of tactics and strategy, which is very important to the Republican approach to the current impasse. Republican thinking begins by embracing, not fighting, the Two Americas. With their current hold on power, there are strong incentives for Republicans to keep the structure of the Two Americas but work all the levers to win within it. As we shall see, Republican strategists believe, probably accurately, that they moved the 49 percent nation to a 51 percent electorate in 2002 with intensity of effort and motivation.[2] Those are the tactics. But

Republican strategists also believe that the same Reaganesque vision that energizes their supporters can prove more broadly compelling, particularly in the shadow of 9/11, thereby expanding their side of the divide and changing the electoral balance for many years to come. Bill Keller was one of the first to write of George W. Bush as "Reagan's Son"—not a "Reagan poseur," by any means, but as "the fruition of Reagan . . . advancing a radical agenda that Reagan himself could only carry so far." He could take "the Reagan Presidency" to its "third term," and "at this rate we may well see the fourth."[3]

There are a lot of questions about their approach, but the Republicans' biggest advantage in this period may be their embrace of the Two Americas. Their plan to win under the current deadlock is the same as their plan to break the deadlock and create a sustainable majority. Democrats may have to choose between tactics and strategy.

> *Sir, our strategic plan is called the "Two Americas," because the Two Americas is our strategy. For years, the media and the liberals have been whining about "culture war." Well, damn it, we're at war, all right. We'll be at war for the rest of this year and in 2008 and the rest of the damn decade because we have the chance to create a historic and long-standing Republican majority with the "America" that respects faith, the entrepreneurial spirit, and freedom. In order to build our majority, we will try to make it easier, not harder, for the rest of America to give us another look. We're perceived as inclusive and open-minded. We'll embrace Hispanics, blacks and whites, the Evangelicals, but also the Catholics and Jews and Muslims. Our plan is not to knock down that big wall that was built up between the Two Americas but to build it higher. We have the chance to create an inclusive Republican majority, like McKinley did after 1896.*
>
> **I've heard plenty about McKinley, thanks. What are you getting at?**
>
> *Sorry, sir, but just picture it: two exhausted parties, like two dog-tired boxers, but one wins out with a new vision and a coalition to back it up and reigns for decades. We'll assemble a majority around our core beliefs and our convictions—the same values that are simply common sense in most living rooms around the country.*

NB: Karl Rove's fascination with 1896 is widely reported, and in Nicholas Lemann's detailed profile in *The New Yorker*, Rove talks of 1896 as an election followed by a "period of dominance."[4] Rove in fact does not specify the length of dominance, but he implies something fairly grand and enduring, certainly something worth achieving. The 1896 realignment school in political science described a three-decade Republican presidential ascendancy, up to the Depression of 1929, but in the new historical accounts, the period is much shorter. As it turns out, it is hard to dismiss a decade in which the Republicans were repudiated in the 1910 congressional elections, the party itself shattered in the face of progressive pressures, and lost twice to Woodrow Wilson, whose program was popular until the country turned against his internationalism.[5] Minimizing the Democratic resurgence and the progressive reaction against pro-corporate government policies, both at the beginning of the twentieth century and at the end, is important to conservative strategizing about the deadlock. While focused on winning the next election in a period of parity, it is easy to move to a framework where the Republicans are the natural party of government, perhaps hegemonic.

> Our starting point, however, is getting our tactics right so we win this election on our side of the Two Americas. First things first, Mr. President.
>
> We will take nothing for granted. Under your leadership, we hold the White House, every executive agency, every board and commission. We have our boys awaiting orders in the House and Senate. Your Rangers, Pioneers, and other top fund-raisers are already working furiously to hit up our biggest donors. You are well on your way to shattering the record set in 2000. And all our groups and associations are ready. We're at their meetings; they're at ours. They've invested a lot and they are not willing to let this investment go the way of the stock market bubble. We will work relentlessly to win any advantage anywhere. We now know that every vote counts and every state matters.
>
> I promise we will get our vote, and then some. But so will they. The Democrats will corral all their NOW and NAACP friends—knock on every door, talk to whoever will listen. Sir, they'll get out their vote, because they're mad as hell. They hate what you're doing. They hate that the people love you. They hate that you're stealing some issues right out of their pot. They'll have union organizers on people's backs for a year, telling them, "George Bush is out to bust the union." All those trial lawyers, public employees, and service workers, they'll scare them to death. Bottom line, the Democrats are not out of the game, not by any stretch of the imagination.
>
> We start with the 49 percent nation that Ronald Reagan passed down to us.

Four Keys to Winning in 2004

- The Republican 100 percent solution
- Moderating the consequences of the 100 percent solution
  - Diversity
  - Compassion
  - No Gingrich
  - Environment
- Back to the future—stopping history
  - Hispanics
  - Suburban women
- Stealing contested and dislodged groups

Mr. President, we're aiming for 100 percent of Republican support— 100 percent turnout and 100 percent of their votes for you. Now, we'll never get 100 percent in either case, but it's a goal. We've been moving toward it for a while now. We'll never get there, of course, but the payoff for trying is so great that success here makes the rest of our job much easier.

We begin, as always, with the Evangelicals. The white Evangelicals are 17 percent of the electorate—almost one in five voters—and they are becoming for us what African Americans have been to the Democrats. We're not there yet; about 72 percent align with us, at least 14 points below what blacks give Democrats, maybe more.[6] But we're on the right track. By our calculations, the proportion of religious conservatives in the 2000 electorate declined 3 points, while the number of union households went up. But in 2002, we reclaimed 4 points, and more gains are possible.[7]

NB: Faith is the first principle of the Bush White House, and identification with Evangelicals will shape the character of whatever strategic course the Republicans take. When conservative critic and would-be speechwriter David Frum walked into the White House for his first day of work, the first words he overheard were "missed you at Bible study." Each morning, the president reads some minisermons from *My Utmost for His Highest* and opens up every cabinet meeting with a prayer, and major policy deliberations at the White House, including the decision to attack Iraq, are informed by Scripture. "Modern Evangelism," David Frum makes clear, is the White House's "predominant creed."[8]

George W. Bush speaks of God as a powerful presence: "We do not claim to know all the ways of Providence, yet we can trust in them, placing our confidence in the loving God behind all of life, and all of history." His God is involved in our daily lives: "No matter what our background in prayer, we share something universal, a desire to speak and listen to our maker and to know His plan for our lives."[9] He invites individual expressions of faith and engagement with God through "the power of prayer," to which he bears witness. And more than that, "the miracle of recovery is possible" through faith, and "it could be you"—as it was him.[10] "When you turn your heart and your life over to Christ, when you accept Christ as the savior," Bush said back in his 2000 primary campaign, "it changes your heart. It changes your life. And that's what happened to me."[11]

The president of the National Religious Broadcasters introduced Bush to their convention as a man who "unapologetically proclaims his faith in the Lord Jesus Christ," producing what *The Washington Post* called "rock star adulation."[12]

Well, of course, we'll be faithful to the Evangelicals.

Mr. President, we must be faithful to a fault. Go after late-term abortions. Fight stem cell research. Prayer in school, we must keep preaching. Faith-based initiative, pass it. Cloning, ban it. Supreme Court nomination, do it. Even though the pro-choice army will make plenty of noise, you will hold the line on protecting human life.

The South is as close to being instinctively Republican and automatic as any place in the country. It's the face of the modern Republican Party, from Frist to DeLay, Gingrich and Lott, and, of course, there is you, Mr. President. Every time voters turn on their TVs, they know we are the Southern party, which is just fine by us. Our large majority is sometimes diminished by a big black turnout in Mississippi or North Carolina or by the growth of cosmopolitan centers, like Atlanta or Raleigh-Durham. But there are stronger countertrends, especially with the explosive growth of Exurbia—the outer metropolitan ring of counties, part suburban, part rural, where our people gravitate to newer houses, better schools, and bigger churches. We have a home field advantage in Williamson and Collin counties back in Texas. But we have these boom counties all across the Southwest and the South. Look at what's happened in Georgia. These are our folks.

Every day, to some degree, we give them what they want: faith, lower taxes, smaller government, and less regulation. We let them keep their guns, and our pro-business policies prove to them that we're the party that wants them to get rich.

When we win the South, we are halfway there. But Florida is a different matter.

Mr. President, everything we do increases our support with white men. They are a vital part of our base and we are working toward earning 100 percent of their support. The blue-collar guys liked Ross Perot because he wanted to clean up government and because he stood up for America. Well, we're the ones doing both. These guys are not looking for anything from us. All we have to do is cut their taxes, stand by their Second Amendment rights, let 'em keep their SUVs and Hummers, show a little chip on your shoulder when it's convenient, and kick the trial lawyers once in a while. They may not like your positions on trade, but you are their commander in chief. When you say in that determined voice "there will be a day of reckoning for the Iraqi regime" or "the people who knocked these buildings down will hear all of us soon," they are part of the crowd pumping their fists and chanting "U.S.A.! U.S.A.!" Just keep sticking it to the UN. No french fries. And keep Hillary in the news.

Our business base and upper-income supporters, the men, are very enthusiastic. Why wouldn't they be? In Texas, we did tort reform, capped jury awards, and took on the trial lawyers. They signed on and hit the jackpot.

Tax cuts. Tax cuts. Tax cuts. Every year, never let up. Abolish the estate tax. End the unfair double taxation of dividends. Coming soon: putting an end to the current tax system, radical tax reform, flat tax. Although you and I know it is never going to happen because we have too many supporters invested in this system, we can deliver some fabulous things. We will end corporate taxes.

The place we may have the biggest problem with our 100 percent solution is the countryside. Of course, it could also be our biggest victory. In 2000, we won over 60 percent of white rural voters because, more so than anyone else, they were voting to change the moral tone in Washington. Small-town and farming America did not like the spectacle in the White House. Will they vote now to reward us for setting an example for young people? Man, let's hope so, because there is a lot at stake.

The swing states—Oregon, Nevada, New Mexico, Arizona, Arkansas, Missouri, Iowa, Minnesota, Wisconsin, West Virginia, New Hampshire, and Maine—almost all of them have high proportions of rural voters. We have to remind them persistently of which America they live in. Faith. The president and the first lady, Laura Bush. A strong military. Teaching your son to hunt. Texas. The ranch. Our materials are already full of images of you, in your work shirt, behind the wheel of your pickup, driving down a long gravel road off into the Crawford countryside.

We have to make a big offer, a strong investment in the economy and the lifestyle of rural America. Keep upping the ante on the farm bill. Publicize the Europeans whining about our farm subsidies. Battle the French over biotech crops. Keep a tight grip on tobacco and sugar cane production to hold prices up. Fifteen states receive three-quarters of U.S.D.A. spend-

RED, BLUE & BATTLEGROUND STATES

ELECTORAL VOTES IN 2004

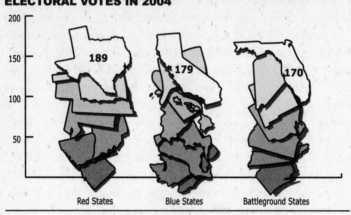

ing, and a dozen of those are ours.[13] I think it goes without saying that there is no more important investment than keeping these folks happy.

To get to 100 percent, our coalition partners have to do a much better job than they have done up until now. To be honest, the left's coalition partners have been more active and outperformed us in getting their loyalists to vote.

NB: Principal Republican strategists argue that the 2000 election became very close at the end, in significant measure because the Democrats did a better job of organizing and getting out their vote. A joint project of the White House and the Republican National Committee reports: "In both the 1998 and 2000 [elections], the Democrats turned a corner and did a better job of motivating and turning out their voters." This reflects an aspect of the reality acknowledged earlier: turnout was up among African Americans and very likely union families as well, and independents broke strongly for the Democrats in cosmopolitan states and metropolitan areas in the last few presidential elections. This was likely produced by the overall polarization of the electorate, but Republicans have focused on one aspect of the shift: Democrats making gains due to intensive and effective late organizing. With some drama, Republican strategists graphically display "the poll gap"— the gap between the last public poll in each state and the final result on Election Day. They show New Hampshire, a 10-point Republican poll advantage, reduced to only a single-point on Election Day, a 9-point drop or gap; in Maine, an even race was anticipated by the published preelection polls, but Bush lost by 5 points, a 5-point poll gap; in Ohio, the Republicans were supposedly 9 points ahead, but they won by only 4 points; in Wisconsin, a 4-point poll lead turned to a dead heat and a win for Gore; and worst of all, Florida, only a 2-point poll gap, but the difference between a predicted small win of 2 points and actual election disaster.[14]

That poll gap is not particularly convincing, as most national polls showed the race tightening in the final seven days, in advance of any get-out-the-vote effort.[15] The state-by-state shift was considerable in places with high minority and union populations, like Ohio, California, and New Jersey, but also high in New Hampshire and Maine, where no such explanation is possible.

Why do the Republican strategists focus on late organizing? The most likely reason is that they are using the poll gap to motivate their own supporters and, indeed, mobilize more support from their loyalist base. They want to empower their supporters by showing that individuals can shift the balance in this deadlocked system. In the 2002 congressional elections, the number of votes cast for the Republicans reached 51 percent, enough to tip the balance in the Senate and gain a few seats in the House. Republicans and conservatives did indeed vote in disproportionate numbers, according to the postelection polls, as did the pro-NRA and pro-life voters. Intensive organizing by the party and conservative support groups might well have contributed to the rise, but 9/11 and the president's campaigning on security issues, voters' top reasons for voting Republican, also may have had something to do with it.[16]

The focus on late organizing, however, elicits a Republican silence on further explanations for the poll gap. One possibility lies with Ralph Nader, who yielded half of his 5 percent bloc in the final week, though that cannot account for the scale of the change. The simplest explanation is that the election shifted toward the Democrats in the final weeks, reflecting the issues, choices, and dynamics that increasingly characterized the decade. Cultural war and polarization of loyalists on both sides likely shifted the electorate back to the default position, where the country really stands, evenly divided, the Two Americas. It is likely that the current Republican strategy of accepting the divide and furthering the polarization will preserve this dynamic in future elections.

This time, we'll have our 72-hour task forces talking to our grassroots. And our grass is taller and thicker this time around. There won't be any surprises. I hate to say I was there early, but it's something I've been saying all my life—that the value of communicating one-on-one is invaluable.

Goldwater's legacy is alive today. I didn't start organizing until after he ran for president. But he's the reason many of our conservative troops first got into politics. When Ronald Reagan spoke for him on TV, he lit up the lights at the campaign's switchboards with people pledging support. They didn't get the votes, but they created the army. When most of students on college campuses were joining the lefties, I organized those YAFers—Young Americans for Freedom—into our own counterculture. We knew the future was ours, and we were right. Those college Republicans are our ground troops now. With all the clutter of nonstop news and advertising, their retail politics and person-to-person contact are what cut through.[17]

Our troops will not be beaten again on the ground.

Mitigating the Effects of the 100 Percent Solution

Mr. President, the 100 percent solution does not work if the Democrats have a 100 percent solution. This is why Newt Gingrich failed. This is why the country is divided in two. If our focus on faith communities provokes an outcry from their pro-choice women and cosmopolitan communities, our gains are counterbalanced, maybe even erased. If our effort to reduce taxes, government spending, and regulation alarms social groups that depend on government, they too may turn against us—and offset our gains. Our defense of gun rights and a better business climate could lead to a negative reaction in suburban communities, particularly on the environment. Our Southern identity and our opposition to quotas could resonate against us in minority communities, but also among suburban and better-educated voters who want moderate government.

Our challenge is to raise the cultural armies in our America while not waking the sleeping giant in their America.

Many of our conservative allies hate to hear you say, "I'm a compassionate conservative." But as we both know, the term is less important than our unfailing effort to moderate the potential consequences of the 100 percent solution.

NB: The story of the last decade has been the growing intensity of sentiment and loyalties on both sides of the partisan divide, right through the 2000 election. But the Bush campaign did try in 2000, by focusing intently on education, to soften Bush's ideological image after religious conservatives helped him win a divisive primary over the independent-minded John McCain. Increasing loyalist turnout therefore requires a much greater effort to offset the polarizing consequences among independents who may be tilting toward the Democratic camp.

The conceptual tools used by Republicans include generosity and compassion, the safety net, diversity, religious pluralism, civility of tone, women's equality, and a wholesale scrubbing of conservative language.

The umbrella for the strategy is a compassionate conservatism that believes, according to Bush, that "everyone deserves a chance, that everyone has value, that no insignificant person was ever born." "We believe that all are diminished when any are hopeless." So while today's conservatives are for a less intrusive government and fostering a more entrepreneurial and productive private sector, they do not favor "an indifferent government." After all, "We are a generous and caring people." Modern conservatives reject the every-man-for-himself ethic that weighed down the movement in the past: "We don't believe in a sink-or-swim society." In fact, their view of government is deeply informed by the faith that conservatives bring to politics: "The policies of our government must heed the universal call of all faiths to love a neighbor as we would want to be loved ourselves."[18]

This recalls Bush's Inaugural Address when he pledged "our nation to a goal: When we see that wounded traveler on the road to Jericho, we will not pass to the other side."

It is unclear whether these vague and generous social goals and compassionate rhetoric have any real meaning when the federal budget must rely heavily on deficit spending just to meet the many other goals of the conservative project, not the least of which are year-on-year tax cuts, generous farm aid, and immense increases in defense spending. In principle, though, the Bush White House consciously avoids politically costly clashes and symbolic battles over spending cuts on programs for the most needy.[19] Unlike the Gingrich Congress, the Bush administration has not sought to sack school lunches and thus has not endured an army of protesting schoolchildren surrounding the U.S. Capitol. And when the Congress in the middle of the night dropped the refundable tax credit for low-income families, the president spoke out in favor of restoring it.

Such "generosity" may temporarily patch the fraying threads of the safety net, but the Bush team's skilled needlework may not be enough to save it from the weight of the conservative project, heaviest in the punitive aspects of the administration's proposed welfare reforms. Over the next five years, more than 100,000 welfare recipients will lose child care benefits, and those still getting welfare assistance will see their benefits cut by 30 percent.[20]

Welfare reform is not the only issue on which the administration walks a fine line. Bush's speeches emphasize opportunity for minorities, from increasing funding for historically black colleges like Howard University and Morehouse College, to praising Hispanic business owners for "the incredible impact the Hispanic small business person has on the country," to reassuring Muslims and Arabs that we "treasure our friendship." When addressing a large meeting of religious broadcasters, Bush interjected, without an apparent transition, "It's been said that 11:00 A.M. on Sunday is the most segregated hour in America." And then he added an admonition, as if ministering himself: "We all have a responsibility to break down the barriers that divide us. In Scripture, God commands us to reach out to those who are different, to reconcile with each other, to lay down our lives in service to others."[21]

Unlike his father, this President Bush seeks to make diversity a hallmark of his administration. And while the White House is overall quite homogenous—occupied largely by white Evangelical men—the president prides himself on his staffers' diversity and is often photographed surrounded by a sea of white, black, Hispanic, and female faces. The first hint that this Republican administration would show a different face to the world came at the 2000 convention where the likes of Pat Buchanan and Pat Robertson were nowhere to be found while Colin Powell, Condoleezza Rice, and Bush's Hispanic nephew, George P. Bush, took center stage.[22] In fact, Powell and Rice have played prominent roles in the Bush White House, illustrative of an administration comfortable with diversity.

However, Bush's public admonition to "reach out to those who are different" apparently does not apply to affirmative action. A matter of days after his comments to the broadcasters, the Bush Justice Department filed an *amicus* brief with the Supreme Court to overturn the admission practices of the University of Michigan Law School. The university, with the support of several dozen Fortune 500 companies, the American Bar Association, and the former superintendent of the U.S. Military Academy at West Point, was seeking to maintain a policy that facilitated racial and ethnic diversity as the proper setting to learn the skills necessary to operate in a diverse society and global economy. The administration, backed by Governor Jeb Bush of Florida, sided with the conservative public interest groups that are part of the Republicans' loyalist network. Only after the court ruled in favor of the law school and diversity did Alberto R. Gonzales, the Hispanic White House counsel, tell an assembly of Hispanic officials that President Bush "has consistently recognized the value of diversity on the nation's campuses."[23]

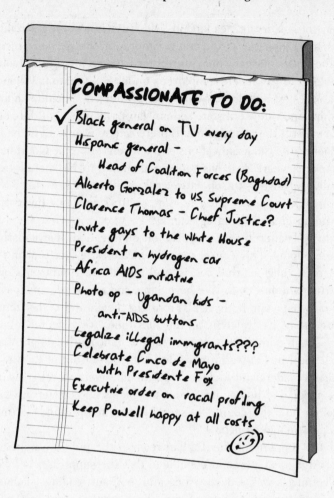

Diversity does not quite extend to gays and lesbians, though in light of George Bush's history on the issue, even White House meetings potentially trumpet a new area of tolerance. When Bush first ran for governor against Ann Richards, his east Texas chairman warned that prominent gay appointments conflicted with "their culture," reminding him that homosexuality "is not something we encourage, reward, or acknowledge as an acceptable situation."[24] When hate-crime legislation containing language that specifically protected gays was before the Texas legislature, Governor Bush declined to support it, telling reporters that all crimes were hate crimes. This came just months after Matthew Shepard's grisly murder reminded America how disturbing hate crimes are. In the 2000 campaign, before he obtained the nomination, Bush returned a donation from an organization of gay Republicans. But by the time Bush reached the White House, the president had bravely graduated to the realm of neutrality and went mute—the lowest common denominator for "moderate" leadership. "Bush's instincts on gay rights issues were clear and emphatic," Frum notes. Simply put, *"Do not touch them."* Bush avoided the explosion that would have come with a repeal of the spousal benefits extended to gay federal employees under Bill Clinton. When the Supreme Court extended the zone of privacy to include homosexual relationships and threw out state sodomy laws, the president did not rush to support a constitutional amendment, preferring to wait until he had "let the lawyers look at the full ramifications of the recent Supreme Court hearing."[25] This is one area where Bush has not figured out how to be "morally traditional and socially inclusive"—the operative goal in this strategy.[26]

The president speaks often of the country's religious diversity, which took on much greater meaning after 9/11. Americans view the attacks as an assault by Islamic fundamentalists on our freedom, particularly on our religious freedoms. This consensus underscored the fact that in America, we have many religions that coexist and tolerate each other. As one focus group participant observed, "We have a mix and nobody seems to care what you are or what your faith is."[27] From the beginning of his term, Bush emphasized that "we welcome all religions" and "we welcome all prayer."[28] While the Bush administration was crafting policies that might make relations with the Muslim world more difficult, it went out of its way to meet with Muslim leaders and include Muslims in America's religious diversity. This was a signal at home and abroad to liberals and conservatives that, as Frum points out, the country's "security was in the hands of moderate, unhysterical, unbigoted people."[29]

After the toppling of the Taliban regime, the public watched the unveiling of Afghan women and concluded that the suppression of women in Muslim countries was a deep wrong and, without reading Islamic scholar Bernard Lewis, a critical part of their backwardness and instability. Just months after the United States went into Afghanistan, more than 85 percent of voters supported targeting U.S. funding to promote programs to strengthen women's rights in Islamic nations.[30] From Radio Free Europe's home in Prague, Laura Bush assured Afghan women that "the isolation the Taliban regime forced on you is not normal," and that "before the Taliban, women were elected representatives . . . [and] a vital part of Afghanistan's life."[31] Now, when the president articulated his fuller vision of the war on terrorism, he affirmed that "brutality against women is always and everywhere wrong."[32] In Bob Woodward's account, *Bush at War,* the president viewed the Taliban's "oppressive treatment of women" as one of its worst offenses, and he hoped its overthrow would bring the liberation of women in Afghanistan and elsewhere in the Muslim world.[33] Bush has sought to place the U.S. role in ending terrorism into a larger context, telling a group of graduates, "We are the nation that liberated continents and concentration camps. We are the nation of the Marshall Plan, the Berlin Airlift and the Peace Corps. We are the nation that ended the oppression of Afghan women, and we are the nation that closed the torture chambers of Iraq."[34]

As Bush was raising his voice for women's equality abroad, he ordered his Department of State not to contribute to the United Nations Population Fund because he contended that the fraction of the $34 million donation that was earmarked for China—one of 142 participating countries—would apparently have been spent on "population-planning activities." As a result, an emergency obstetric care initiative set to begin in Burundi—where one in eight women dies giving birth and where only a quarter of women even have midwife assistance—was canceled, going the way of a midwife-training program in Algeria, an AIDS center in Haiti, and an initiative to reduce maternal childbirth deaths in India.

Back at home, the Bush administration led the effort to "reform" Title IX, the 1972 federal law that requires schools to provide equal opportunities to both sexes to play sports, before giving up under pressure.

To avoid offsetting polarization of the Democratic loyalists and possibly alienating independents as well, the Republicans have become acutely sensitive to language in the post-Gingrich era. In the Republican primaries, when McCain's reformist challenge threatened Bush's candidacy, Bush became the "reformer with results." He sought not power in Washington but "to change the tone" to one of "civility and respect"—as if national Republican Party leaders had little interest in that impeachment stuff. Incorporating a new kind of Republican doublespeak, "businesses" became "employers," "parents" were now "moms and dads" and, no longer seeking "tax cuts," Republicans wanted "tax relief."[35]

Mr. President, our environmental agenda is the area in greatest need of a linguistic overhaul. We have a clear policy direction that has been staked out over many years and pursued without apology. It is a policy that meshes well with who you are. You come from an oil family and oil region and from a state where the business and political culture says, "Let it rip." We want America producing more energy that is more affordable to consumers. That means less burdensome regulation. We have backed drilling in ANWR, when our Republican friends were wobbly. We are helping the power utilities get out from under these unrealistic regulations. We're opening up the national forests to more logging. And we've stopped precipitous and unnecessary government mandates intended to reverse so-called global warming.

And let's be clear. Our friends in the Americans for Balanced Energy

Choices, Competitive Enterprise Institute, Edison Electric Institute, and Alliance for Automobile Manufacturers are very appreciative.

But as Frank Luntz wrote in his manual for Republicans, "The environment is probably the single issue on which Republicans in general— and President Bush in particular—are most vulnerable." We paid a big price for the administration's decision to review Clinton's executive order on arsenic. We did not need Luntz to tell us that the " 'arsenic in our water' imbroglio" was the "biggest public relations misfire" in our first year in office. That was followed by the vice president's dismissal of conservation as "personal virtue."[36]

Language and good intentions matter, and that is why we are now so devoted to using our technology to develop a hydrogen car and being able to talk about your vision for "zero pollution."

NB: The Luntz manual for Republican officials on how to talk about the environment includes the following pointers, among others:

- "First, assure your audience that you are committed to 'preserving and protecting' the environment but that 'it can be done more wisely and effectively.' "

- "Provide specific examples of bureaucrats failing to meet their responsibilities to protect the environment."

- "The three words Americans are looking for in an environment policy are 'safer,' 'cleaner,' and 'healthier.' "

- "Emphasize common sense."

- On global warming, emphasize that the scientific debate remains open and "technology and innovation are the key." " 'Climate change' is less threatening than 'global warming.' "

Luntz concludes with a homily for Republican officeholders: "William Shakespeare wrote, 'One touch of nature makes the whole world kin.' I'm joining you today to share a little bit of my personal family history and why I think we all as Americans share a common interest in protecting our common legacy—the environment."[37]

In the State of the Union, the president set out a goal for the country: "to promote energy independence for our country, while dramatically improving the environment." He then proposed $1.2 billion to support research over ten years "so that America can lead the world in developing clean, hydrogen-power automobiles."[38]

For the record, under the Bush administration, the EPA formally cited only 15 percent of "significant non-compliers" between 1999 and 2001. Less than half of the offenders paid fines, which averaged between $5,000 and $6,500. A draft EPA report on the environment was edited by the White House to scrub discussion of risks presented by global warming. The proposed hydrogen fuel-cell research budget barely rises above symbolic, and even if it spurred development, General Motors cannot imagine selling a million such cars before 2015. For the intervening decade or decades, the administration vigorously opposes any action to raise fuel efficiency standards for cars or to mandate available new technology for power plants.

> *Mr. President, the public worries about your policies regarding the environment have dropped noticeably since you took up the issue. Overall, 41 percent now want to continue heading in your direction, while somewhat more, 50 percent, want to go in "a significantly different direction"—but that is only a 9-point disadvantage on the environment, an issue on which Republicans conventionally get slaughtered.*[39] *It is a long way from arsenic to hydrogen cars, but we're making progress.*
>
> *The bottom line is, we still have a lot of east Texas oil in our blood, and that's okay. We just need to show that we believe in American technology and in rolling up our sleeves to produce the coal, oil, and gas America needs. We'll do better this way than by filing a bunch of lawsuits and having government bureaucrats create one-size-fits-all regulations. I think they will appreciate this approach in West Virginia and Michigan.*

Back to the Future

Our strategy runs up against some trends that are pretty threatening, if we were simply to allow history to take its course. The first is the growth of the Hispanic population and its rising proportion of the voting electorate, particularly in Florida, Nevada, Arizona, and New Mexico, but even Colorado. They are also a major and growing part of the suburban diversity of Illinois and New Jersey, both of which are now almost out of reach, and we need to keep an eye on Virginia as well. On June 19, 2003, the U.S. Census officially declared Hispanics the largest minority group in America. And listen to this: in the two years since the census, Hispanic population growth and immigration have accounted for half of all population growth, something that was not supposed to happen until 2014. This process is accelerating.[40]

Right now, we may be losing Hispanics by almost 20 points.

To quote the flight controller in Apollo 13, "Failure is not an option." If we don't do better, we're dead. We have to get in front of this train! Whatever the polls say about our progress, we can't give up. We have to keep looking for an angle.[41]

There are clear signs of progress. You held Gore to only 62 percent, which is a hell of a lot better than Dole, 10 points better. Texas has something to do with it, but not everything. You are very popular with Hispanics—at least 60 percent express positive feelings about you. And while the office of president is different from that of governor, your brother carried one-half of the non-Cuban Hispanics in Florida and Rick Perry got a third of the Hispanic vote against the Hispanic Democratic candidate for governor in Texas.[42]

NB: To keep perspective, there is little evidence that Hispanic votes shifted to the Republicans after 9/11 and in the 2002 elections for federal offices. An analysis of ten state polls conducted for Fox News shows Democratic U.S. Senate candidates getting two-thirds of the Hispanic vote. In California, where there was exit polling, Gray Davis won 65 percent of the Hispanic vote, comparable to four years earlier.[43] And a national survey of Hispanic voters conducted in spring 2003 shows an unnamed, generic Democratic nominee received 48 percent of the vote, with 34 percent for Bush and the remaining 18 percent undecided. If one looked at only those respondents with a preference, the Democrat gets 58 percent, 4 points short of Gore in 2000. This offers some moderate hope for the assembled Republicans, but they would be wiser to discount the gains. The survey was conducted in the aftermath of the Iraq war, with the president's popularity at a high point. The large undecided bloc, disproportionately Democratic, will break heavily for the Democratic nominee once he is known, likely pushing the Democratic number back up to earlier levels. For Republicans, the task remains daunting.[44]

We have focused on the Hispanic middle class because research indicates that Hispanics become more independent as they move up the economic ladder, unlike African Americans. But who knows whether that mobility will be big enough and fast enough to offset the population growth at the base of the ladder? Our research is examining whether we can make headway with younger Hispanics, new citizens, and ex-soldiers where there are strong patriotic feelings. We will find an angle, you can count on that.

Given the stakes, there are no limits to our aspirations for Hispanic appointments and Hispanic public issues. Supreme Court nomination, of course. Top-brass military positions. New cabinet appointments. Antidiscrimination executive orders. Photo ops on top of photo ops with military units. Presidential trips to Spain and Mexico. And there is no single action that could have a greater impact than a new program to legalize the status of long-term illegal immigrants.[45]

The second historic trend is the growing education of the electorate, particularly women, and especially suburban women. This is Karen's overriding focus. And the press think it is quaint to inaugurate a new doll each election—"soccer moms" or "waitress moms." But again, this is deadly serious stuff. Whatever they're called, we have to get their attention and stall the shift toward the Democrats.

NB: Depending on the estimate, the college educated will form between 35 and 41 percent of the 2004 electorate. Because of the increase in attendance at four-year colleges as well as mortality patterns, the college proportion of the electorate grows by about 2 percentage points each presidential election.[46]

With the college-educated men, things are under control. We know what they want and how to give it to them. They earn a lot, want to earn a lot more, and are strong supporters of the tax cuts. We can't lose focus, though, as many of them are starting to hang out in cafés with the latte class. Also, we need to remember that their wives are not politically correct or dependable.

The college-educated women are the problem. They are growing in staggering numbers. Politically, they are split between the Two Americas, but culturally, they think they live in Boston. They certainly live in a different world from the noncollege women with young families who really are part of our family—those women vote for us over the Democrats by over 20 points. But the women with a college education, they just aren't family.

The program is not complicated, but as our military leaders tell us, it must be robust. Back to education. AIDS in Africa. Women's rights in the Muslim world. Concern for the environment. Don't forget that most of these women live in worldly suburban areas and want to know that you are a moderate, tolerant guy.

NB: Karl Rove has a long history of using the education issue to soften up suburban women voters, who are often turned off by conservative Republican candidates. Early in his career while advising former Texas Governor Bill Clements, Rove wrote a memo laying out the rationale for targeting these women in particular. "The purpose of saying you gave teachers a record pay increase is to reassure suburban voters with kids, not to win the votes of teachers," Rove told the governor. "Similarly," Rove explained, "emphasizing your appointments of women and minorities will not win you the support of feminists and the leaders of the minority community; but it will bolster your support among Republican primary voters and urban independents."[47]

Stealing Some Voters

Sounds good. Are we done? The Rangers are playing the Yanks tonight and ARod has a twenty-game hitting streak.

Sir, just a minute longer. We have a few more basic things to cover. I'm sure you won't miss anything.

All right . . . Where can we pick up some more votes?

Mr. President, the sky is the limit! We'll make it a lot easier on every other front if we can steal us some of these votes. This is where we have some fun. We can mess with their groups, co-opt some issues, put them on the defensive.

NB: The voters in play, Karl Rove appreciates, are largely members of the contested and dislodged groups discussed in this book. But as Rove appreciates, "There is no middle!" "*Middle* is the wrong word," Rove explained to Nicholas Lemann, instead suggesting that " 'the unattached' is a better way of putting it. Because to say 'middle' implies that they are philosophically centrist in outlook, and they aren't. Some of the people who are unaffiliated are on the left. Some of the people who are unattached are on the right. Some of the people who are unattached are hard to characterize philosophically at all on the traditionally left-right continuum."[48] Understanding that his search for playing fields is not constrained by so-called centrists or moderates gives the Republicans a playbook that is full of opportunities, some of which may trespass onto Democratic territory.

As a former direct-mail consultant, Rove is very comfortable targeting and narrowcasting to gain an unexpected and perhaps nearly invisible upper hand.

By all accounts, Karl Rove relishes these opportunities and is little constrained in the play by conservative ideology and cultural precepts—as long as the policy stance does not undermine their position with their loyalist supporters or key financial backers. Thus, while conservative Republicans had been pursuing tough immigration policies, Rove supported loosening restrictions and favored amnesty. Rove was responsible for forcing the navy to cancel the use of the bombing range on Vieques Island in Puerto Rico, subject to local protests. He favored imposing compensatory steel tariffs to protect the domestic steel industry and steelworkers from foreign imports.[49]

An Abundance of Opportunities

✓**Devout Catholics**

✓**Married Blue Women**

✓**Golden Girls**

✓**F-You Union Boys**

✓**Young and Restless**

Who is up for grabs? No details, just the basics.

Here it goes:

Devout Catholics. *We have the scorecard on this one. Mark it a success. We started early last time, saw the opportunity among the practicing Catholics, and met with the activists. The trends have been moving away from the Democrats for a long time, but with the Clinton scandal and abortion, you demolished Gore among Devout Catholics—the regular churchgoers.*[50] *We need to stay the course with your strong support of human life and our emphasis on compassionate conservatism.*

Married Blue Women. *Again, our scorecard is good. No group was more put off by Clinton's trashing of the White House and Starr's revelations than these blue-collar women with families who are trying to raise their children right. Right now, they look like loyalists. Your devotional style and commitment to family and the compassionate agenda, packaged together with the children's tax credit, should strengthen the bond between you and these women. We will figure out how to bring back the Clintons.*

Golden Girls. *Again, the scorecard is potentially very good. They wanted to vote for you on values and for the Democrats on Social Security. For two elections, we have battled with dueling prescription drug plans— the Democrats probably got a leg up in 2000 and we got a leg up in 2002. On the table now is the biggest new entitlement program in four decades: three hundred and fifty BILLION dollars and rising—a REPUBLICAN prescription drug plan! That's worth lighting up a cigar. Don't think we won't spend a lot letting those Golden Girls and those Aging Blue Women know about it. This is a big offer. It's worthy of a big advertising campaign. And they'll get it.*

F-You Union Boys. *We have checked that box big time. While Clinton and Gore stiffed the working people in the good ol' US of A—by refusing to protect the steel industry and the steelworkers—we said, first, your grievances are real, and then we delivered on our promise, all the while weathering the storm of elitist condemnation. The ongoing benefit is that we get to keep fighting with the E-UUUU, the W-T-OOO, and, bless us, the French—and to talk about it all the way across Pennsylvania, Ohio, West Virginia, Michigan, Wisconsin, Minnesota, and Iowa. The good news is that culture war allowed us in 2000 and 2002 to eat away the edges of the Democrats' support among white union workers in big industries, as well as some of those aging blue-collar men who don't like being controlled by anybody. These voters want their guns as well as their union cards. We can eat away a little more in 2004, even while we make life miserable for those public sector and service unions that don't drift into our America.*

The Young and the Restless. *We have an offer for young people that they can't refuse. Uncle Sam wants you. Young voters have been a tough sell for us in every election since 1992, but maybe 2004 will be different. These young people have not responded cynically to Iraq, like the liberal political class, and they understand that George W. Bush is speaking directly to them. They may come out of Iraq with a new sense of American purpose and idealism.*

NB: In the period since the 9/11 attacks, young white men and particularly young white women under thirty years of age have moved toward the Republicans.[51] This may be a result of Bush's efforts to characterize the terrorist attacks on America as a generational challenge: "Since September 11, an entire generation of young Americans has gained new understanding of the value of freedom, and its cost in duty and in sacrifice." Now "history has also issued its call to your generation," Bush told the West Point graduates, but widening the call. And when the president greeted the returning sailors off the coast of San Diego at the close of the Iraq war, he recalled "the character" of our forces at Normandy and Iwo Jima, and then noted, it "is fully present in this generation."[52]

> *And if none of this works, Mr. President, I want to show you our plan to topple the remaining pillars of the Democratic Party. First, Jewish supporters by your embrace of Sharon. Then trial lawyers by our relentless attack on reckless litigation. And then their union base by our privatizing the federal workforce. And THEN—*
>
> **Karl, we've run over.**
>
> *This is awesome stuff, sir. You can ask for a new resolution authorizing force—maybe this time for Iran—just like before the congressional elections, only this time in January, right before New Hampshire. The Democrats go nuts squabbling over it and—*
>
> **Karl, the Rangers are up first tonight . . .**
>
> *Yes sir, Mr. President. Well, at least the Yankees can't score while we're hitting, right? We'll save the rest for next week's meeting. Thank you for your time, sir.*

Chapter 10

STEP TWO:

Reagan's America

T he idea that tactics and strategy equate is predicated on a big assumption, a big bet about America's current period—that the core Republican coalition, inspired by the Reagan vision, can grow big enough to break the political deadlock in the country. That assumption allows for a warm embrace of the Two Americas and betrays a confidence that the values and beliefs, along with the philosophy of government and faith in the individual nurtured on one side of the division, are right for these times and will soon grow to dominate the thinking on the other side, which will then wither. The hope is that Reagan's America of 49 percent can grow into something much greater.

Mr. President, it is possible that we can do more than win the next election. We can make history. September 11th changed the country and, with all due respect, it changed you. You had already consolidated and rebuilt the Reagan coalition that faltered in the nineties and placed us in a position to regain the majority. September 11th did more than that: it gave you a chance to govern successfully and tackle the terrorist threat and big issues for the country. With the clear sense of direction that Ronald Reagan gave

BUSH JOB APPROVAL

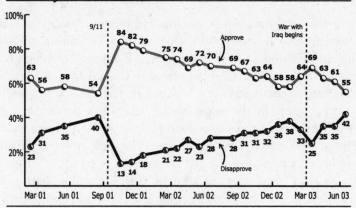

Democracy Corps database, March 2001–July 2003.

us and America, the Republican Party just might become the indispensable party for these times.

NB: The discussion begins with a conceit—the idea that Reaganism proved popular and successful and provides the infrastructure of ideas for a compelling perspective for our times. The Reagan coalition, we know, faltered early and crashed in 1992. Rebuilding the Reagan coalition, as illustrated by the 2000 election, got the Republicans at best back to parity, not to a new majority. Specifically, they regained Reagan's lost vote in the rural areas and among white blue-collar voters and married women without a college degree; they consolidated for the moment the Perot voters who remained suspicious of Clinton, Gore, and the Reformed Opportunity project.

The project itself was not so compelling before 9/11. While Bush's approval rating reached 63 percent after his inauguration and joint session address to the Congress, his ratings quickly began to fall, dropping to just 51 percent the day before the attacks.[1] His tax-cut budget gave him no boost when it passed, which contrasts with Clinton on the passage of his budget. Bush lost ground when Senator Jim Jeffords switched parties over the Republicans' extreme agenda and, again, when the energy plan was unveiled and seen as unbalanced, favoring production and oil over conservation and renewable energy sources. Then Bush's fortunes dipped sharply as the economy weakened. While voters usually give new presidents a honeymoon, this one failed to win over any converts, as 75 percent of Gore

voters continued to give Bush negative ratings nine months into his presidency.

Before the al Qaeda attack on the Twin Towers and the Pentagon
made "security and terrorism" top issues, Bush's Reaganism centered on
being the anti-Clinton on faith and tax cuts. Faith was important because
it affirmed every day that Republicans were headed in a different moral
direction. But tax cuts were not a high priority for the country in 2000 or
in the period since. In the midst of the president's tax debate, only 10
percent of voters cited taxes as a concern, instead highlighting issues like
the economy, education, and health care.[2] At best, the combination of
faith and tax cuts preserved the status quo, that is, parity; at worst, it was
proving less than compelling for a public that was pulling back from the
Bush presidency. The conservative critic and White House speechwriter
David Frum expressed great respect for Bush's personal qualities but concluded, "Despite these virtues, on September 10, 2001, George Bush was
not on his way to a very successful presidency." His early direction left
the Republicans short of a national majority in 2000, his tax-cut proposals
were pushed through the Congress without popular support, and his domestic vision was not big enough to move the country.[3] This would
change after 9/11, when America was recast in a new Cold War–like role
and the president stepped up as a leader willing to use America's military
power for a moral end.

> *Mr. President, we will have a chance at a bigger election margin if we get
> two things right. First, we have to govern successfully, which requires taking
> on the big issues and getting the job done. And second, our strongest sup-
> porters and the country need to know we have a sense of purpose, a direc-
> tion for the country. This is why Ronald Reagan was so important. Bill
> Clinton will seem even more like just a blip on the radar screen if we
> reclaim and revitalize Reaganism.*

NB: Conservatives are fully mobilized to elevate Reagan and Reaganism. Washington National Airport is now Ronald Reagan Washington National Airport. The sprawling new federal office building—for some, a
symbol of big government—is now christened the Ronald Reagan Building
and International Trade Center.

In March 2001, at the outset of the George W. Bush presidency, the
aircraft carrier *Ronald Reagan*, CVN 76, Nimitz class, was christened in
Newport News, Virginia. Former first lady Nancy Reagan did the honors
and was joined by a reunion of some 500 Reagan alumni. The ship's logo
had four stars, representing the "four pillars of freedom—liberty, oppor-

tunity, global democracy and national pride," according to the captain. Affixed beneath the stars was Reagan's oft-used motto, "Peace Through Strength." President Bush, when he took the microphone, underscored the point and the continuity: "As president, Ronald Reagan believed without question that tyranny is temporary, and the hope of freedom is universal and permanent; that our nation has unique goodness, and must remain uniquely strong."

Nancy Reagan, according to Peggy Noonan, unofficial keeper of the Reagan flame, said to Laura Bush, "Please tell me that all those modern sculptures are gone." She assured her, "They're gone." And from the "first lady's garden?" Reagan queried. "There too," Bush said. Noonan reports Nancy's smile and relief. The trespassers to the Reagan history are gone, along with all their trappings.[4]

The new Reagan historians compete with one another for the superlative that most powerfully communicates unqualified greatness. First was Dinesh D'Souza, a former senior domestic policy adviser in the Reagan White House, who writes, "Reagan did more than any other single man in the second half of the twentieth century to shape our world," equal to the role that Franklin Roosevelt played in the first half. But to keep perspective, he concludes, "Only the two nation builders, Washington and Lincoln, occupy a more elevated place in the presidential pantheon." Peter Wallison served as White House counsel during the Iran-contra scandal and writes most recently that Reagan was a "conviction politician," an "idealist," which makes him "unique among modern presidents" and unlike any of his predecessors, "with the possible exception of Lincoln." While the legacy of Roosevelt, Truman, Eisenhower, and the like left little behind, according to Wallison, Reagan still sets the parameters on the policy choices of all presidents, whether Clinton or George W. Bush.[5]

Peggy Noonan tries to ground all this in the public's acclaim, in the "growing national consensus that Ronald Reagan was great." She cites a 2001 CNN poll that asked Americans to choose the greatest president. Reagan topped the list, but only 18 percent chose him, somewhat short of an American consensus. She settles on the vast range of politicians who would emulate him, and concludes, "There is a kind of general agreement in America that he was the last great man."[6]

His greatness, according to the new histories, translated into two areas of policy success and transformation for America: the economy and American strength, including the defeat of the Soviet Union. The backdrops for Reagan's performance were the aimless economic policies of both Democrats and Republicans, which gave the country high inflation, unemployment, and interest rates, combined with collapsing regulatory structures for energy and prices. His economic policies of cutting taxes, deregulation, and promoting trade produced, in these histories, growth, low inflation, falling gas prices, 20 million new jobs—in sum, "a mighty economic expansion." All of these new histories grant Reagan the credit for the economic expansion of the 1990s as well, creating an even more remarkable record of growth.[7]

These hagiographers are not deflected in their narrative by the exploding deficits, the failure to control spending under Reagan, slow income growth and rising inequality, and the subsequent tax increases enacted by Reagan, Bush, and Clinton.

On America's position in the world, the starting point is the humiliation of the Iran hostage crisis and the military in decline—failed missions, low post-Vietnam morale, and the lack of spare parts that left ships in port and planes grounded. Reagan immediately raised military spending, confronted the Soviet Union with the truth of its "evil" nature, supported "freedom fighters" everywhere, and, most important of all for the new Reagan histories, doggedly pursued SDI, the Strategic Defense Initiative or Star Wars program, over the opposition of the whole arms control community, to convince the Soviet Union it could no longer compete with the West. Because Reagan was willing to go it alone, would not compromise on SDI, and would possibly abrogate the ABM treaty, the Soviet Union, according to these histories, "abolished itself"; it "finally fell, crushed by a hundred forces, but most immediately by its inability to keep up with the United States."[8]

Despite the popularity of this argument with conservatives, historical accounts of the period largely contest the claim. Soviet officials were more concerned about the new instability than the actual threat from SDI and had no plans to compete. A much more immediate cause of the collapse was the economic decline, accelerated by Gorbachev's reforms, and as Frances Fitzgerald observes, itself a product of "the failures of the system created by Lenin and Stalin—not from any effort on the part of the Reagan Administration."[9]

Nonetheless, SDI's role in the fall of the USSR is an important part of the new history and mythology, which includes a willingness to throw off international constraints and stand alone and steadfast in defense of freedom.

Mr. President, you were right on point with what you said at the USS Ronald Reagan ceremony: "So as we dedicate this ship, I want to rededicate American policy to Ronald Reagan's vision of optimism, modesty, and results."

NB: The elephant in the room is President George Bush, the 41st president of the United States who was at the helm when the Reagan majority collapsed. This is likely a difficult subject for George W. Bush and for Karl Rove, who worked for both of them and talks elliptically about how "in the aftermath of war, sometimes public attitudes change, and people who successfully prosecuted wars are no longer in office . . . I think that happened recently in our experience."[10]

But there is nothing elliptical about the conservative commentary on that period. Ronald Reagan handed his successor, George Bush, a successful economy that included two decades of sustained economic growth, so strong it carried Bill Clinton beyond his vices and big-government health-care proposals. But when Bush abandoned his no-new-taxes pledge, former Bush speechwriter John Podhoretz writes, he walked away not just from his promise but from the "Republicans' central unifying principle." He also walked away from a ninety-two-month economic boom that had made the Republicans the party of economic growth, according to conservative activist Grover Norquist. Had Bush "left on automatic pilot, the national and Republican coalition were poised to reach new heights."[11]

In fact, on every point on the Reagan checklist, Bush failed the Reagan revolution. After an inflammatory Republican convention in 1992, Bush downplayed abortion and proposed few new initiatives. While Ronald Reagan increased military spending and dared the Soviets to keep the Strategic Defense Initiative alive, "George Bush the Elder," Noonan writes, "didn't view SDI with the same hungry imagination" and joined the national current to cut defense spending. In Iraq, the elder Bush eschewed the moralistic impulses of Ronald Reagan, to the regret of some of today's leading neoconservatives. Lawrence Kaplan and William Kristol describe the Bush administration as true believers in the "realpolitik" of the foreign policy establishment, which accordingly left Saddam Hussein with his armies, ready to slaughter the Kurds and Shiites.[12]

At the christening of the USS *Ronald Reagan,* Peggy Noonan wondered maliciously to herself as Bush spoke, "Every time he praises Reagan, who was different in so many ways from his father, I bet he wonders if his listeners are thinking, 'Yes, Reagan was the man your old man wasn't.' "[13]

But the focus on the failings of the former president allows Reagan conservatives never to probe what went wrong, never to ask why the Reagan majority was lost so quickly. The Reagan greatness narrative includes no commentary on the Republican loss of the U.S. Senate in 1986, before the Iran-contra scandal, no discussion of the 1988 campaign that hung on to power by reducing Reaganism to an ugly culture war, no discussion of the 1992 election when Republican support dropped 16 points, and no discussion of the decade of the nineties when the Republican presidential vote averaged 39 percent.

The new Reagan history is silent on the minimal income growth for most Americans during the eighties, the increasing inequality and visible symbols of corporate greed, and the expanding middle-class grievances that brought the 1992 upheaval. Looking back from this vantage point, the majority of Americans thought the decade brought decline, growing financial pressure; boom and bust, unreliable economic policies, and greed over civic virtues.[14] A few brave conservative commentators raised cautionary flags about Reagan's impact on middle-class incomes and his failure to challenge social spending and thus really test popular support for the conservative project.[15] But for Bush the younger, the conservative inheritance is Reaganism triumphant.

Throughout his national political life, George W. Bush has never doubted the Reagan inheritance and has focused relentlessly on each of the planks that his father abandoned. This was the direction he took in his 2000 campaign but even more so while in the White House and looking forward. With Reagan's legacy obscured by more than a decade of political acrimony, Bush has sought to enliven each theme and renew the Reagan vision and coalition, to be tested with the voters in 2004 and beyond.

The Reagan Checklist

✓ **Importance of faith and protecting religious practice**

✓ **Cut taxes**

✓ **Entrepreneurship and business-led prosperity**

✓ **Strong military and America's commitment to freedom**

Mr. President, in 2000, the American people were fed up with Clinton's scandals. Two in three voters wanted a change in direction on moral issues. They knew the military did not respect its commander in chief. They hated the Washington bickering. And the Democrats opened the door and gave us an opportunity to clean house. After the Clintons energized conserva-

tives, Al Gore embraced every cultural liberal icon in the book—from abor-
tion and guns to gay unions. Buddhist temple fund-raising and "no
controlling legal authority" gave us trust and honesty as issues. We wanted
to change the tone, and they sure as hell gave us a chance to do that!

NB: But once in the White House, without Clinton to kick around
every day, George Bush's Reaganism was hardly shuffling the political deck.
He used the mantra of faith, tax cuts, and strength, but they did not prevent
his political slide before 9/11 on some issues, and afterward on others.

The first element of Bush's pre- and post-9/11 Reagan vision was faith.
After all, it was Ronald Reagan who first made the commitment to faith
that brought religious conservatives and Evangelical Christians into the Republican fold. But Reagan himself was quite secular in practice and raised
the subject of religion in a more distant, abstract, and historical form. Reagan spoke generally about rediscovering our values and supporting the family: "Of all the changes that have swept America the past four years, none
brings greater promise than our rediscovery of the values of faith, freedom,
family, work, and neighborhood." He reminded us that our nation could not
have been "conceived without divine help." "America was founded by people who believed that God was their rock of safety." As a result, we are
"one nation under God," with our freedom—the "universal right of all God's
children."[16] Of course, he spoke out often against abortion and for restoring
prayer in schools. God and prayer pervade the Reagan narrative on America.

The Bush commitment to faith is much deeper, more personal, and of
a different kind. As observed earlier, Bush's God is a powerful presence,
which shapes daily lives. Bush's invited expressions of faith and involvement
with God recognize the power of prayer and the miracle of recovery through
faith.

When he takes faith into public life, Bush is far from the ceremonial
president Reagan was. He opposes abortion with more eloquence; his televised speech on stem cell research put him squarely on the side of "human
life" as a "sacred gift from our creator," not to be devalued or compromised.
Bush speaks often of the need to restore prayer in school, but at the front
of his political agenda is his faith-based initiative to have "social services
provided by religious people." In a shift away from government, "I welcome
faith to help solve the nation's deepest problems."[17]

The second element of his pre-9/11 vision was tax cuts. On this point,
Reagan was often eloquent on the virtues of economic policies, centered
on lowering tax rates: "Send away the handwringers and the doubting Thom-
ases. Hope is reborn for couples dreaming of owning homes and for risk-
takers with vision to create tomorrow's opportunities." "Every dollar the

government gives to someone has to first be taken away from someone else. So, it's our moral duty to make sure that we can justify every one of your tax dollars." "The economy bloomed like a plant that had been cut back and could not grow quicker and stronger."[18] He spoke often of the liberation of the "spirit of enterprise," the private sector, and "small, independent businessmen."

George Bush's tax narrative reads like a series of underwhelming applause lines, with little elaboration:

> The best way to stimulate this economy is to have robust tax relief for the American people.

> Folks, we're not talking about the government's money in Washington, we're talking about your money.

> We should also strengthen the economy by treating investors equally in our tax laws. . . . To boost investor confidence, and to help the nearly 10 million senior [sic] who receive dividend income, I ask you to end the unfair double taxation of dividends.

> One of the central elements of this plan is to accelerate the tax reductions which Congress has already passed.

> We've got people looking for work today. We want to help people today. We want to expand the economy today.

> It is important for Congress to know, a robust relief plan helps the entrepreneur in this country.

> For the sake of long-term growth and to help Americans plan for the future, let's make these tax cuts permanent.[19]

In contrast to the elevated appeals of Reagan, Bush's justifications for tax cuts are usually material and practical, and focus on getting people to spend or providing them with relief as quickly and as permanently as possible. In any case, the underlying rationale has been a moving target.[20]

Also unlike Reagan, Bush has not elaborated on the benefits of a business-led prosperity, as his speechwriters have operated under orders that he speak not about "business" but "employers," which in practice has him talking almost exclusively of "small business."[21] Without Reagan's more intimate connections to working America, the Bush team has decided to be cautious about the tax cuts' full meaning. After all, as late as the end of July 2002, 60 percent of voters said Bush is too close to big business and 51 percent said he was "president for the oil companies."[22]

The result is a fairly flat case for his economic and tax-cut plan. Even in the spring of 2003, voters by a margin of two to one said it was more important for the government to "provide needed services" than to help Americans by "cutting taxes."[23]

The third element in the Reagan equation was a strong military and a willingness to be assertive about America's interests and defending freedom. George Bush before 9/11 championed some of the symbolic issues that communicated if not strength then at least bravado and cast the Republican fate with the social conservatives. He was governor of Texas, a state with a historically strong military tradition, but in modern times a state that has carried out 301 of the 845 executions conducted nationally since the death penalty was reinstated.[24] He stood with the gun owners and the NRA, even when it offered up TV advertising with Charlton Heston brandishing a Kentucky long rifle and warning Al Gore, "I'm coming after you with the rifle clutched in my cold hand."[25] Bush passed budgets with higher military spending and announced his intention, in good Reagan tradition, to pull out of the ABM treaty in order to accelerate America's program of anti-missile defense.

Bush was on script and reinforcing, perhaps too literally and narrowly, Reagan's vision. It gained the president little support and did not protect him once the economy tumbled or when he faltered on some issue, like arsenic in drinking water or energy conservation. He was weakening seriously.

Then the planes crashed into the Twin Towers and the Pentagon, and the world was turned upside down. The "country changed more in the past ten hours than it had in ten years," Frum observed from the reconstituted White House, "and the political language of the 1990s was now as dead as Hittite."[26]

September 11th changed everything. The country has awakened: 72 percent say rogue nations, armed with weapons of mass destruction, working with terrorists, pose an extremely or very serious problem. The country is listening, and I think you have a much larger voice now, and we have a chance to blow much more air into President Reagan's sails. We can't afford to waste this opportunity. We need to reclaim the themes that resonated with the public under Reagan: faith in family and God, more opportunity for small businesses, less government and fewer taxes, a strong

The Threat of Terrorism
How Serious?

Rogue nations, like Iran and North Korea, armed with weapons of mass destruction, and working together with global terrorist organizations.

Extremely serious problem	37%
Very serious problem	35%
Serious problem	21%
TOTAL SERIOUS PROBLEM	93%

military, and an exceptional America prepared to stand up, alone if necessary, for freedom.

More than ever, we must control the agenda, always addressing the next big problem.

Now is the time for us to implement our vision of America. The American people don't want us sitting on our hands; they want us to try new things, to dare to make big decisions, even if they aren't popular, because they are the right thing to do. That's the Reagan banner. When people hear "Ronald Reagan," they remember success, honesty, greatness, a robust economy, positive change, a progressing America, not one wallowing in "malaise." If we play our cards right, twenty years from now, you, sir, will be mentioned in the same breath as Ronald Reagan.

NB: Before 9/11, George W. Bush was faltering. The new Bush confronted the 9/11 challenge and breathed new life into the Reagan rhetoric on American strength, exceptionalism, and freedom. Bush's uninspired Reaganism of September 10th gave way, within days, to a much more integrated, coherent vision, powered by security, which the country remains ready to hear. Suddenly, a more godly Bush, now prepared to speak of right and wrong, may be relevant for each of the Two Americas. His economic message remains flat, but at least he has a clarity of purpose on the most immediate threat facing people.

In his speeches after 9/11, the president spoke as a wartime leader and laid out broad principles that unify the Two Americas. He established first that America will surely respond and defeat this assault on America's way of life. On this point, he did not have to be particularly eloquent, as he said at Ground Zero in New York City: "And the people who knocked these buildings down will hear all of us soon." Establishing in effect the "Bush doctrine," he drew a line in the sand and called on all countries to make their choice: "Every nation has a choice to make. In this conflict, there is no neutral ground. If any government sponsors the outlaws and killers of innocents, they have become outlaws and murderers themselves. And they will take that lonely path at their own peril."[27] He made clear that the outcome was not in doubt: "Whatever the duration of this struggle and whatever the difficulties, we will not permit the triumph of violence in the affairs of men—free people will set the course of history."[28]

Bush was determined to win the battles in Afghanistan and Iraq, but also to define the enemy more broadly—as any rogue nation with weapons of mass destruction and sponsored terrorists. "The gravest danger to freedom," Bush declared, "lies at the perilous crossroads of radicalism and technology. . . . [Even] weak states and small groups could attain a catastrophic power to strike great nations." This new menace requires an active, engaged American response: "For the war on terror will not be won on the defensive. We must take the battle to the enemy, disrupt his plans, and confront the worst threats before they emerge. In the world we have entered, the only path to safety is the path of action. And this nation will act."[29]

While this war would be fought for security and safety, the president defined the danger from the outset as an attack on our way of life by those who are "evil." He echoed Reagan's challenge in 1983 of the "evil empire," to the consternation of the "détente" consensus. Now Bush would reclaim a moralistic posture for America in the world.

> Yet, I am certain of this: Wherever we carry it, the American flag will stand not only for our power, but for freedom.

> Different circumstances require different methods, but not different moralities. Moral truth is the same in every culture, in every time, and every place. Targeting innocent civilians for murder is always and everywhere wrong. There can be no neutrality between justice and cruelty, between the innocent and the guilty. We are in a conflict between good and evil, and America will call evil by its name.[30]

This stance leaves America with exceptional obligations and a unique role to play—the one that has motivated it since its founding and that makes it a light to the rest of the world. "This threat is new; America's duty is familiar. Throughout the 20th century, small groups of men seized control of great nations, built armies and arsenals, and set out to dominate the weak and intimidate the world. In each case, their ambitions of cruelty and murder had no limit. In each case, the ambitions of Hitlerism, militarism, and communism were defeated by the will of free peoples, by the strength of great alliances, and by the might of the United States of America."[31]

The conservative glitterati, long invested in a robust, moralistic U.S. foreign policy and nursing their policy defeats under Bush the Elder and Clinton, have rushed to cheer the honorable victories in Afghanistan and Iraq and have dubbed this "the Bush era." At the same time, they insist on establishing two overarching points: the legitimacy of the new American unilateralism, grounded in morality, and the decades of weak American responses to terrorism, particularly under Clinton.

While it is difficult for the Bush administration to attack directly the Clinton administration, its conservative supporters are determined that Clinton's "failings" on terrorism should weigh as heavily on the American consciousness as Carter's failings on Iran. Lawrence Kaplan and William Kristol, who helped lead the neoconservative charge on Iraq, described the Clinton approach as "a brand of wishful liberalism" that "looks to the world community and its institutions as the ultimate source of international legitimacy" and "is profoundly uncomfortable with the unilateral assertion of American power." The Clinton administration puttered around worrying about globalization and global warming, while ignoring genocide in Rwanda and acting meekly in Bosnia. Worst of all, the pathetic, long-distance missile response to repeated al Qaeda attacks on American assets was weak and feckless and only emboldened their efforts.[32] Under Clinton, America was the "unipolar power" but so uncomfortable with the idea of dominance and the use of our power that it looked to be handcuffed by the United Nations Security Council and other international bodies that would give the United States permission to act when they deemed appropriate. Bush threw off those shackles and asserted principles that, Charles Krauthammer writes, "amount to an unprecedented assertion of American freedom of action and a definitive statement of a new American unilateralism."[33] In this context, *New York Times* columnist Maureen Dowd is certainly right that banishing "the wimpy Europeanist traditional balance of power" was important to the initiative: "The more America goes it alone, the more 'robust,' as the Pentagon likes to say, the win will be."[34] For the administration, dramatically going it alone in the face of UN and European opposition or indifference establishes the new principles for the use of American power and America's place in the world, and at the same time educates the American public about the new era.

The Bush Era

The Weekly Standard
February 11, 2002

Bush has charted the course of an expansive new American foreign policy, a paradigm shift equal to the inauguration of anti-Communist containment more than a half century ago. He has taken the war on terrorism beyond a police action to round up the perpetrators of the September 11th attack, and transformed it into a campaign to uproot dangerous tyrannies and encourage democracy, making the world much safer for free peoples.

Robert Kagan
William Kristol

Mr. President, we will remind the American people of your leadership and your calm, measured response to September 11th, just as we did in 2002. It is a completely legitimate issue and should be the basis by which the American people judge you. Before the midterm congressional elections, the Democrats accused us of playing politics with the blood of our soldiers. First Daschle attacked you and declared that you should apologize to Democratic senators who are also veterans for your "outrageous" comments in that speech in Trenton; then Gephardt actually accused you of "playing politics with the safety and security of the American people," in The New York Times, *no less! Whether they like it or not, homeland security and the war on terrorism are our issues. When voters were asked after the 2002 elections, the biggest reason people gave for voting Republican was "to support the war on terrorism and a strong military." Today the country trusts Republicans over the Democrats on security by 30 points. On homeland security, by 40 points. No wonder the Democrats want to take politics out of the issue.*[35]

The war on terrorism is like a new Cold War. You and Harry Truman responded in the same way to the threat, but the liberals and the left never got it quite right. They are floundering again.

Obviously, a lot depends on what the Democrats do on the war, the economy, and, God forbid, any further attacks. We can't assume that the American strength and exceptionalism theme can carry the whole Reagan project. This is why we need to stay the course on the compassionate agenda, jobs, and our optimistic vision of America. Is there a Bush era? Do we believe what we are saying? For sure, it has energized the whole project for now, but is it durable?

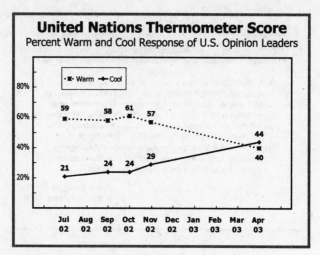

Reprinted from "The 2002 Challenge," Kenneth Mehlman.

The good news is that we have some indicators that show a deeper public understanding of our mission. The thermometer rating for the United Nations is falling—suggesting that internationalism is in retreat and the Bush foreign policy is on the rise. Down. Down she goes.

We've been going through your mail and pulling certain postcards from ordinary folk. Some support you and some have questions, and they all live in competitive counties in battleground states. Take a look at this first group. They are quite personal, and they give us a good sense that you are touching people, maybe like Ronald Reagan. In post–September 11th America, there is a heightened sense that you are the right moral leader for our country.[36]

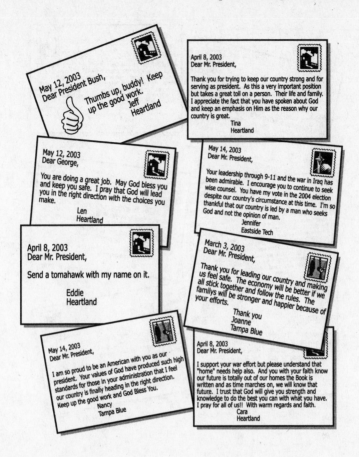

May 12, 2003
Dear President Bush,

Thumbs up, buddy! Keep up the good work.

Jeff
Heartland

April 8, 2003
Dear Mr. President,

Thank you for trying to keep our country strong and for serving as president. As this a very important position but takes a great toll on a person. Their life and family. I appreciate the fact that you have spoken about God and keep an emphasis on Him as the reason why our country is great.

Tina
Heartland

May 12, 2003
Dear George,

You are doing a great job. May God bless you and keep you safe. I pray that God will lead you in the right direction with the choices you make.

Len
Heartland

May 14, 2003
Dear Mr. President,

Your leadership through 9-11 and the war in Iraq has been admirable. I encourage you to continue to seek wise counsel. You have my vote in the 2004 election despite our country's circumstance at this time. I'm so thankful that our country is led by a man who seeks God and not the opinion of man.

Jennifer
Eastside Tech

April 8, 2003
Dear Mr. President,

Send a tomahawk with my name on it.

Eddie
Heartland

March 3, 2003
Dear Mr. President,

Thank you for leading our country and making us feel safe. The economy will be better if we all stick together and follow the rules. The familys will be stronger and happier because of your efforts.

Thank you
Joanne
Tampa Blue

May 14, 2003
Dear Mr. President,

I am so proud to be an American with you as our president. Your values of God have produced such high standards for those in your administration that I feel our country is finally heading in the right direction. Keep up the good work and God Bless You.

Nancy
Tampa Blue

April 8, 2003
Dear Mr. President,

I support your war effort but please understand that "home" needs help also. And you with your faith know our future is totally out of our homes the Book is written and as time marches on, we will know that future. I trust that God will give you strength and knowledge to do the best you can with what you have. I pray for all of us!! With warm regards and faith.

Cara
Heartland

Eddie, you'll get your Tomahawk all right.

Sir, I was struck by how much your personal faith and relationship with God obviously resonate with voters. They appreciate the strength you gain from prayer.

Now, in fairness, these postcards were sent during the buildup to the war in Iraq and after, but generally they praise your tough stand on terrorism. Some of them talk about the war on terrorism and problems at home, but usually start by thanking you or cheering America. "Go U.S.A.!" However, we must pay attention to the "but" or "warning" about "pressing issues" and domestic issues that they want you looking at. People have lives and a broader set of concerns, and I know you are aware of that. They think you are coming up with an economic revitalization plan and that you will be addressing domestic problems. They are sending us a message, as one lady put it, "Don't forget about us at home."

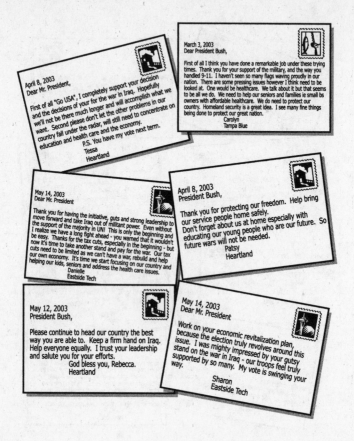

March 3, 2003
Dear President Bush,

First of all I think you have done a remarkable job under these trying times. Thank you for your support of the military, and the way you handled 9-11. I haven't seen so many flags waving proudly in our nation. There are some pressing issues however I think need to be looked at. One would be healthcare. We talk about it but that seems to be all we do. We need to help our seniors and families ie small bs owners with affordable healthcare. We do need to protect our country. Homeland security is a great idea. I see many fine things being done to protect our great nation.
Carolyn
Tampa Blue

April 8, 2003
Dear Mr. President,

First of all "Go USA", I completely support your decision and the decisions of your for the war in Iraq. Hopefully we'll not be there much longer and will accomplish what we want. Second please don't let the other problems in our country fall under the radar, will still need to concentrate on education and health care and the economy.
P.S. You have my vote next term.
Tessa
Heartland

May 14, 2003
Dear Mr. President

Thank you for having the initiative, guts and strong leadership to move forward and take Iraq out of militant power. Even without the support of the majority in UN! This is only the beginning and I realize we have a long fight ahead - you warned that it wouldn't be easy. Thanks for the tax cuts, especially in the beginning - but now it's time to take another stand and pay for the war. Our tax cuts need to be limited as we can't have a war, rebuild and help our own economy. It's time we start focusing on our country and helping our kids, seniors and address the health care issues.
Danielle
Eastside Tech

April 8, 2003
President Bush,

Thank you for protecting our freedom. Help bring our service people home safely. Don't forget about us at home especially with educating our young people who are our future. So future wars will not be needed.
Patsy
Heartland

May 12, 2003
President Bush,

Please continue to head our country the best way you are able to. Keep a firm hand on Iraq. Help everyone equally. I trust your leadership and salute you for your efforts.
God bless you, Rebecca.
Heartland

May 14, 2003
Dear Mr. President

Work on your economic revitalization plan, because the election truly revolves around this issue. I was mighty impressed by your gutsy stand on the war in Iraq - our troops feel truly supported by so many. My vote is swinging your way.
Sharon
Eastside Tech

NB: This recognition of an emerging domestic agenda follows a review of the postcards from voters in our contested communities. The selection was carefully made in consideration of the president's feelings. A fuller set of postcards, containing very strong worries and admonitions about the deferred domestic agenda, the weak economy, and the neglect of the middle class, will be presented in the chapters concerning the Democratic hopes for the future.

This is why we need to keep our compassionate agenda in the limelight, even while we showcase your leadership as commander in chief—while powerful, the war may not be enough to carry us. These notes are a warning: don't neglect the home front, get the economy moving, do something about health care! We don't want to be blindsided by Carville and "it's the economy, stupid!" again.

May 14, 2003
Dear Mr. President,

Thank you for the quick end to the war. Maybe now it's time to turn your focus on our homeland and put into motion the promises that were made during your campaign. Better healthcare, do not increase work hours - US, the most overworked nation to begin with, more educational funding, higher salaries for those who shape our future. Please get the economy back on track. We can't be the ones to help others all the time. It's time for our country to make improvements for our quality of life.
Beth
Tampa Blue

March 3, 2003
Dear President Bush,

I feel you are doing a great job with out nation. You support us and our way of life as Americans. The thought of war frightens not only me and your family but the entire nation. However, we know this is a necessary step that needs to be taken to ensure our freedoms. I would also like you to consider other major area as well including education and health insurance.
Keep up the good work!
Betsy Jean
Tampa Blue

April 7, 2003
Dear Mr. President,

Get Saddam - he's a Bad Seed! I'm proud of you for that decision!! Also, We as Americans are here for you - please go out & ask us! Get different opinions of all class levels. Working together we can make a better America! We need to reform America's assistance plans and get all able Americans working, and help those that truly can't.

Jenna
Tampa Blue

May 12, 2003
Dear Mr. Bush,

To date I think you have done a good job as President. I realize your first year of your term 9-11 happened and so many things have went downhill from there. I think it was a good decision to go into Iraq. We needed to take control of a out-of-control situation. I hope that when our troops return from Iraq and Afghanistan you can concentrate on our struggling economy. Many people are without work, health care, prices have spiraled upward and our education system needs revamping. Please try to aid our country now.
Thank you,
Kim
Heartland

May 14, 2003
Dear Mr. Bush,

I think you are doing a fairly good job running our country. I believe you are a strong moral man who truly wants the best for America. Please improve the quality of education for our children, work on the economy and improve our healthcare system. I will be watching what your platform will be for the election in 2004.
Paula
Tampa Blue

NB: There is some evidence that George W. Bush has created not a bridge to the twenty-first or twenty-second century, but to Ronald Reagan, the person and leader, whose legacy may give more life to the modern project. In 1985, I conducted focus groups in Macomb County, Michigan, the home of the Reagan Democrats. At that time, these blue-collar Democrats spoke of Reagan as someone who stood with the "small people." Today, in Tampa Blue, Heartland Iowa, and Eastside Tech, they talk of Bush as "just like everyone else," as one woman described it, "the way you see him at home in his blue jeans and his cowboy hat." One of the men said, "He's patriotic and he comes off as a regular type of guy, kind of like you could sit down and talk to him." One Eastside Tech man set him off from the local partisans: "He doesn't maintain that elitist attitude that I think is indicative of all our Republicans."

In Macomb County almost twenty years ago, they described Reagan as "honest," which was associated in part with having "high morals" but also with being "a straight shooter—tells you what he is going to do"; "I don't think that man will back down." The Macomb County discussion went full circle: "he has guts"; "Reagan is straight as an arrow—John Wayne"; "whatever he says he will try and stick by"; "right or wrong"; "he has high morals." This determined consistency, the Reagan Democrats thought, made them proud to be Americans, after the wavering of Jimmy Carter.

Today, the swing voters in Heartland say Bush is "up-front and honest with people. He doesn't beat around the bush. Tell them what he thinks, whether you like it or not." A better-educated compatriot in the Eastside says the same: "He does believe what he says. He's not saying something to just make you happy. He does say what he believes in." The men in the Eastside Tech describe him as a "straight shooter—he shoots from the hip. He tells you how he thinks it is"; "I don't think he backs down easily. He's a fighter when he needs to be"; "passionate"; "very-self-assured manner." The women in Tampa Blue admire this style of leadership; "won't be walked on," "decisive," "he's a no-nonsense kind of man." And like the voters in Macomb County, they make the connection to honesty: "He's sincere and honest, I think"; "honest, has values, sticks to what he believes."

This honesty is reinforced by Bush's religious faith, something that did not gain Reagan much attention, for obvious reasons in Macomb County. Today, across these swing areas, voters describe Bush in these ways: "He's Christian and a good parent"; "has the nerve and faith to do what has to be done"; "morally grounded"; "God-fearing."

"I don't know a lot about politics," one Heartland Iowa woman observed, "but I know he has a religious background, and I think that's very important, especially with the things that are going on." For a woman in Tampa Blue, this is what the country needs: "A religious man, a praying man; moral standards high; experienced with the military and the nation's defense."

Bush's "honest" leadership style is reinforced by the cultivated, indirect contrast with President Clinton and his administration, though this has no Reagan or, for that matter, Jimmy Carter parallel. Swing voters describe Bush as "morally responsible," someone who "knows right from wrong," "less scandalous." In addition, they very often describe him as a committed family man: "He's a father and a husband and he's got nice parents"; "he's got such a nice family"; "he's really family-oriented too."

In Macomb County, again almost twenty years ago, many talked about Reagan's leadership in personal and parental terms. "I think of it as a parent myself," one man said. "I make a decision, and I have to stick by that decision. . . . It is the same way with Reagan." Another man agreed: "That is the most important part of being a parent: they are looking at an overall picture just like we as parents do for our children." Today, in the face of the current threats to the country, an Eastside Tech woman saw Bush as providing "an incredible amount of strength. . . . He was calm when it could have been crazy." A woman in Tampa observed that he is a "good role model and all-American, someone that a kid could look up to"—something they think was lost during the Clinton presidency.

Clinical psychologist Renana Brooks, writing in *The Nation*, observes that Bush uniquely speaks of crisis, threats, and causes for fear, urging people to "hug your children," but then, speaking in the first person, tells the country, "I will not forget this wound" or "I will not relent." By that means, George W. Bush is creating a feeling of dependency on him, as if only he has the strength and resolve to deal with the threat.[37]

Voters in Macomb County thought Reagan "built us back as a nation" and made America stronger. Today, there is a strong sense that Bush is himself "patriotic" and, as a man in Tampa Blue points out, he "instilled a sense of patriotism in the country that was missing." Another man agreed: "He's a man of his word. He's honest. And I think he's looking at our future and trying to preserve our way of life here."[38]

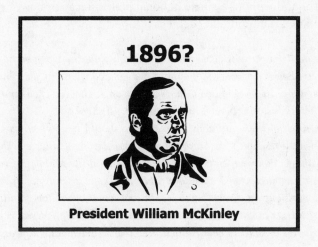

1896?

President William McKinley

Mr. President, your job approval reached an unprecedented level after September 11th. Your 90 percent mark was 10 points above that for your father just after the Persian Gulf War.[39] It has averaged 62 percent over 24 months. These are fabulous numbers. No president has done this since Eisenhower.

NB: The president's strength contrasts with the Democrats in this period who are viewed, at least among swing voters, as weak, divided, and without any clear direction—not a small problem if you want to be taken seriously in these strategic battles. That was likely exaggerated in the immediate aftermath of the Iraq war, when party divisions were evident. Nonetheless, the swing voters in the contested communities seemed to describe a weakened party. "I think they are a little disorganized right now," a Tampa Blue woman told us, adding, "I think they really floundered after the election." The men talked about the Democrats, variously: "not this year" said one man, while another agreed, "they had their day in the sun I guess." "I think they lost their focus" another man told us. "Yeah, they need to restructure themselves." In Heartland, the women spoke of the Democrats as "a little weak right now"; "fumbling"; "confused"; "haven't a clue where they are going." A man said, simply, "They are struggling." In Eastside Tech, the men described the Democrats as "fighting"; "confused right now"; "losing"; "scared"; "they need leadership"; they appear "on the sidelines."[40]

That leaves the Democrats viewed consistently less favorably than the Republicans, even though the two parties are at parity electorally. Using the thermometer reading for the two parties, the Republicans, who are likely credited for addressing the attack on the country and who act with uncommon political unity, get a reading of around 56.3 degrees. The Democrats, out of power and without a single national political leader, have a somewhat lower standing at around 52.8 degrees.

> *The Republican Party is viewed more favorably than the Democratic Party. We're consistently warmer, sometimes 5 degrees higher. In fact, over the last two years the Republican Party has been higher in each and every poll.[41] That's historic. Now, how do we make history?*
>
> *On some of the more divisive issues, we should ease off the gas pedal for a while. President Reagan did not speak a lot about the "evil empire" during an election year. Successful peacemaking in the Middle East would help. And we don't need sideshows like the damn arsenic controversy or our Congress cutting twelve million kids and scores of military families out of the child tax credit package in the middle of the night. We also have a steady stream of soldiers being killed over there, and morale appears to be waning. We can't have that.*
>
> *Having reached this point, how could we not use the election for something bigger? The Reagan legacy is what takes us beyond day-to-day political tactics. It gives us a larger agenda, and the American people will respect us for being bold, tackling the greatest problems, being successful, and moving forward.*

NB: The Bush administration has embarked on a bold agenda of large-scale tax cuts and rising deficits, creating a moment of decision for the country where it will be forced to either raise taxes or substantially curtail domestic social spending. It has unveiled plans to privatize about half of the federal government's civilian workforce. Its faith-based initiative is intended to shift some delivery of social services from government to the churches. They have greatly diminished the regulatory burden on business and the tax burden on corporations and top income earners. They have diminished the progressive nature of the tax system by lowering the top rates and pushing to abolish the estate tax. They have proposed block-granting to the states a whole range of programs, like welfare reform, that are bound to produce further cutbacks in aid for the poor. They have moved to reconstitute Medicare as a market-based, rather than government-administered, health program for seniors. They have introduced the idea of privatizing Social Security by creating individual investment accounts, though they have been very careful rhetorically and are careful not to endorse any specific reform proposal.

Reluctant to cross some invisible line, the administration has held back from some parts of the conservative agenda, such as school vouchers, really reducing spending for federal retirement programs, and privatizing Social Security. The administration, Bill Keller observes, is "debating the timing of the assault on Social Security," not whether to move forward or not. The president no longer views the subject as a "third rail" of American politics.[42]

As almost none of these specific proposals are popular on their face, the Republicans are relying either on their banked political capital from the war and the president's standing or on the reality of the revived Reagan perspective. As Keller points out, these actions add up to an ambitious vision for America: "markets unleashed, resources exploited. A progressive tax system leveled, a country unashamed of wealth. Government entitlements gradually replaced by thrift, self-reliance and private good will. The safety net strung closer to the ground . . . A global common market that hums to the tune of American productivity. In the world, America rampant—unfettered by international law, unflinching when challenged . . ."[43]

If they succeed in unraveling the social contract, diminishing government, and elevating the market, they also, Nicholas Lemann reminds us, remove the reason why people sometimes vote for the Democratic Party.[44] If they were to succeed, Keller imagines that the two terms of the Reagan presidency will be joined by two from Bush.[45]

This is why Karl Rove contemplates the election of 1896 and the Republican era that it ushered in. It is not hard to understand his fascination. After a period of economic tumult and a series of dead-heat elections, the two parties joined a titanic battle that left the Democrats marginalized and confined electorally in declining regions and the Republicans ascendant and entrenched in the growing and wealthier parts of America but also encompassing the artisans and working classes in the burgeoning industries. Nearly all of New England, and also New Jersey and Wisconsin, shifted

Republican by more than 12 points. Previously competitive states, like New York, Indiana, and California, shifted to the Republicans over the period of 1896 to 1928. Pennsylvania, Michigan, Illinois, Wisconsin, and Iowa became one-party Republican states.[46] The Republicans under President McKinley successfully identified themselves with America's emerging manufacturing might and industrial future, rather than its small landholding past, with the new over the old, the national over the local, and aspirations and hope over grievance and anger. They formed an activist and economically nationalist government, committed to promoting America's economic development and America's interests.[47]

The hope for the Republicans today is that they, like the McKinley Republicans, have "figured out a new governing scheme through which people could view things and could conceivably enjoy a similar period of dominance."[48] Rove is contemplating the hegemony that has proved so elusive over the past half century.

Or this might be a colossal misjudgment of the country's mood and aspirations and a gigantic overreach. Without any electoral mandate and scant evidence of popular support on the issues in the polls, there is good reason to question the reality of such aspirations for 2004. Keller allows for the possibility that Bush could succeed in his ambitious agenda and thus offer a remarkable tribute to Reagan, but he also imagines that Bush could "overreach"—"which means it will be a failure on a grand scale."[49]

Whether it will be one or the other depends also on the choices the Democrats make in this period.

PART VI

Breaking the Deadlock:
The Democrats

A t the time of this writing, the Democrats have not yet selected their presidential nominee for 2004, and much of the party's message
and identity has yet to be determined. But campaigns take place at historic
moments and within a framework of choices that bear heavily on what is
possible. Certainly Ronald Reagan's enduring impact on the Republicans
goes well beyond "The Speech" for Barry Goldwater that became his tem-
plate for the coming decades, as Bill Clinton's to the Democrats goes beyond his detailed plans and policies and the many drafts of his State of the
Union addresses.

In light of this, I asked a group of Democratic political advisers to sit
together to determine the strategic choices to be made and the plan to be
developed that will enable the Democrats to win in a very competitive
environment. I also asked them to think farther down the road. Given that
the Republicans' hold on the federal government provides them with so
many advantages, is it possible to break out of the current political framework that leaves the parties in battle at parity?

In the spring of 1992, a number of key advisers to Bill Clinton's presidential campaign pulled out of the day-to-day primary battle for what was
known as "the Manhattan Project." While Clinton had just won the New
York Democratic primary, his standing had been tarnished and a large majority of the country thought he did not have the integrity to serve as president. At the lowest point in the primaries, according to a *New York Times/*
CBS poll, just 15 percent offered a favorable view of him, with 40 percent
viewing him unfavorably. He trailed badly in the polls to President George
Bush. These advisers pondered the strategic choices before them and
crafted the plan that would enable Clinton to run effectively for president.[1]
"In the Presidential Election of 1992," notes Samuel Popkin, political scientist and long-standing observer of presidential campaigns, "a president
once acclaimed as unbeatable was defeated by a candidate initially declared
unelectable." After Bush set a record with an 89 percent approval rating in
a Gallup poll, columnists began to speculate about the scale of his electoral

prospects. Popkin flags Roland Evans and Robert Novak, who wrote at the time, "There is something intangible and mystical in the new relationship that now appears to bind the president and his country, affording him precious new strength." *Newsweek* offered the headline "Dream On, Democrats."[2]

Today, six fictional Democratic advisers, facing an equally daunting task, have assembled to think through their options.[3] They are working around a dining-room table, though occasionally adjourning to the kitchen and small living room of this summer home belonging to a strong supporter of the party. Around the table sit the general strategist, a media consultant, a campaign manager, and two seasoned political associates. The pollster is standing at an easel finishing the opening presentation to the team.

The Two Americas

Pollster. *You know what I know, the latest national polls on the presidential race. His numbers are more than respectable, but hardly intimidating. More important, I think we have broad buy-in on the essential parity of the two parties, the deadlock, and the deepening partisan polarization of the last decade. That is at least an important factor. We are all more than a little impressed with what they have accomplished with their loyalist supporters, and we see where we stand with ours, which is fine. You have this rich picture of the contested political landscape. It is very rich in opportunity, and some big strategic choices lie ahead.*

And finally, I think we agree, likely for the last time, on the Republicans' essential strategic direction. They want to maintain the structure of the Two Americas. That is their best shot to win. They want to show off this model, but they also think it's a pretty car and if they give it a good

push it could gain momentum and produce a big win. They basically believe in it. It is how they envision America. They think it is a politically
successful model, undermined from the inside by the pragmatists, like Bush
the Elder, and undermined from the outside by the infidels, like Bill Clinton. If they can get the model to really pick up speed, they think it just
might be possible to break through the political deadlock.

There are a lot of levers on that model, and they will pull back on a
few where there is some resistance and introduce some new ones, but mostly
they need to execute the plan.

Judge. I agree on the main point, they want the status quo. In the
context of this election coming up, I would not shake things up. Why would
they opt to change what got them here?

Libby. They are using a different model from the one we've used in
politics. Which is how to keep your base together and add people in. He
has 100 percent of his to 75 of ours. Do you settle for that, or do you go
for a different game?

Max. For sure it's intriguing, but I'm just not in awe of the strategy.
I see where they're going but, unless I read it wrong, the strategy has a
pretty low ceiling.

Wolf. What world are they in? Do you think there are a lot of voters
out there hungry for a new gilded age?

Max. A lot depends, a lot, on their tactics to win over Hispanics and
women. What if they just say, "Hey, we're more at home in the Democratic
world?" Then they are back to 50–50, at best.

Judge. I agree we are close to parity, but I don't think it's really 50–
50. I'd rather be in their shoes than our shoes.

Pollster. Why?

Judge. 9/11. The texture of the world has changed the way people talk
and think. This is real time. People walk around looking at the same picture differently now after 9/11. Bush is part of that picture and that changes
things.

Pollster. 9/11 tilts the scales, as does the White House's effectiveness
in managing political events. But society continues to unfold, culturally
and socially, and I'm not sure they can put up their hand like a traffic cop
and stop it. You cannot change the fact of the rising proportion of Hispanics. No matter how much hand-wringing, the number of college graduates
will go up 2 points from the last election, near 40 percent. There is the
accumulation of unaddressed issues, all of which tip the scale back.

Libby. When I look down the road, even six months, I actually see a
world with thousands of deficit stories, thousands of quagmire stories in
Iraq. You may have 3.5 percent growth, but no movement in wages, in

earning power. Hey, both the economy and the war on terrorism could be bogged down.

Biggs. *I have a singular view of this election. It has to be portrayed as a big and serious election. And there is a real tendency for the Democrats to make everything local and shy away from big issues and contrasts. They have a great fear of nationalizing things. This time, everything has to start, "This is a serious time in American history."*

Judge. *I think what it means is you've got to change the debate. I mean, in the 2000 election, basically their strategy was the smaller the election the better; the more this is about personality, the better. And that's how they won the election. Because it wasn't about anything real. It was just about who you want to hang out with for four years in your living room. I think we have to change the debate by raising the level of the debate.*

Pollster. *Well, we do not leave this room until we lay out how the Democrats do exactly that: win the election and break the deadlock.*

Chapter 11

THE "ELECTION PROJECT"

The Democrats also have an abundance of opportunities, as there are at least six strategic paths that plausibly allow them to run competitively and perhaps even trip up the Republicans and propel the Democrats into the lead. These options overlap and reinforce one another, but each model sets a distinct direction. The first is the Agenda Gap, the simplest of the six, which essentially shines a spotlight on the gap between public priorities and the president's. The second is the Two Americas. Under this framework, the Democrats basically accept the division that has been handed to them and make the most of it. Some have called it the "Gore plus" strategy. The third option is the Corporate Frame, and it centers the election around the core corporate, business identity of the Republicans, forcing a contrast between their allegiance to big business and the Democrats' popular commitment. This is the "populist" option, full of opportunities and risks. Fourth is 100 Percent Über Dem, for lack of a better term. This choice involves focusing efforts primarily on the traditional support groups of the Democratic Party. The fifth option is a strategy of Reassurance, emphasizing from the outset confidence-building positions on issues such as defense and values. This is where the DLC Democrats are most comfortable, but they will not likely want to be confined here. The

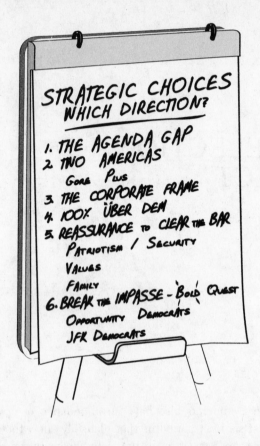

STRATEGIC CHOICES
WHICH DIRECTION?

1. THE AGENDA GAP
2. TWO AMERICAS
   Gore Plus
3. THE CORPORATE FRAME
4. 100% ÜBER DEM
5. REASSURANCE TO CLEAR THE BAR
   Patriotism / Security
   Values
   Family
6. BREAK THE IMPASSE - Bold Quest
   Opportunity Democrats
   JFK Democrats

final option is the only strategic choice that really makes a bold offer, not only to break the impasse but also to offer a compelling vision for the times. It puts back on the stage the vision of JFK and the Opportunity Democrats.

STRATEGIC CHOICE 1: THE AGENDA GAP

The genesis for the Democrats—and likely square one for all six strategies—is the big gap between the public's agenda and that of the Republicans in Congress and the White House. Ignoring the political consultants and the lobbyists for the moment, this is the key to the questions posed in this book by voters. There is precious little public support for the revitalized Reagan agenda, except for keeping the country strong and addressing terrorism. The gap and disjunction with the public are also what create possibilities, some tactical and some strategic, as Democrats try to change the probabilities ahead.

The postcards to the president presented in Chapter 10 are the best introduction to the priorities underlying the thinking of the public.[1] The notes from voters in Tampa Blue, Heartland Iowa, and Eastside Tech are a window into an America that remains thankful to the president for his leadership but is poised to engage a range of deferred issues. They also point the public narrative back to the middle class and reveal a yearning for a country that creates opportunity for everyone. This creates political possibilities, not just for the short term, but also for a much bolder attempt to achieve sustaining partisan hegemony.

These postcards were written to the president at the end of focus group discussions held in 2003, before, during, and after the Iraq war. Like the cards that the president read in the Republican meetings in Chapters 9 and 10, these show a public very anxious to get back to the other issues in their lives. That these concerns are so close to the surface is a measure of the power of the issues they reflect. These voters want the president to address more than the Middle East and to think about "the homeland"—health care, the economy, schools and education, Social Security and Medicare, and the environment.

Also in the postcards, beyond the specific issues, is a desire for the president to recognize the middle class and its struggles and not to favor the big corporations so much, revealing an emergent sense of middle-class grievance. "Please remember the 'little' people back in Iowa!" wrote one participant, while another urged the president to "treat everyone equal." Another pleaded that when Bush did his budget, he should "help find true tax cuts for low, middle, and above middle class families, so we'll not starve to death." Remember, they told him, "*we* are America!" Don't forget, they said, "you need to think more about middle America." The postcards warn against unfairly favoring corporate America, which these voters assume will get more than fair treatment from the president. A Seattle woman warned, "Don't just let the people with the deepest pockets speak the loudest and get heard!" A Tampa woman wrote, "Big corporations should be held accountable for their actions including layoffs, cutbacks and taking from the little people," and policies should not be pursued just "to line the pockets of the big people."

Finally, the postcards, particularly those from Eastside Tech, often add a sentence, sometimes a P.S., warning the president off on some of the cultural initiatives. One woman wrote about the job losses at her company and then about the "frivolous law suits," but then finished with this: "What

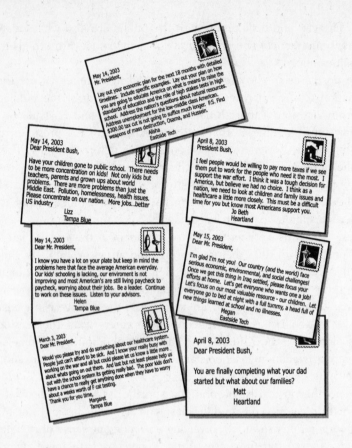

May 14, 2003
Mr. President,

Lay out your economic plan for the next 18 months with detailed timelines. Include specific examples. Lay out your plan on how you are going to educate America on what is means to raise the standards of education and the role of high stakes tests in high school. Address the nation's questions about natural resources. Address unemployment for the low-middle class American. $300.00 tax cut is not going to suffice much longer. P.S. Find weapons of mass destruction, Osama, and Hussein.

Alisha
Eastside Tech

May 14, 2003
Dear President Bush,

Have your children gone to public school. There needs to be more concentration on kids! Not only kids but teachers, parents and grown ups about world problems. There are more problems than just the Middle East. Pollution, homelessness, health issues. Please concentrate on our nation. More jobs...better US industry

Lizz
Tampa Blue

April 8, 2003
President Bush,

I feel people would be willing to pay more taxes if we see them put to work for the people who need it the most. I support the war effort. I think it was a tough decision for America, but believe we had no choice. I think as a nation, we need to look at children and family issues and healthcare a little more closely. This must be a difficult time for you but know most Americans support you.

Jo Beth
Heartland

May 14, 2003
Dear Mr. President,

I know you have a lot on your plate but keep in mind the problems here that face the average American everyday. Our kids' schooling is lacking, our enviroment is not improving and most American's are still living paycheck to paycheck, worrying about their jobs. Be a leader. Continue to work on these issues. Listen to your advisors.

Helen
Tampa Blue

May 15, 2003
Dear Mr. President,

I'm glad I'm not you! Our country (and the world) face serious economic, environmental, and social challenges! Once we get this thing in Iraq settled, please focus your efforts at home. Let's get everyone who wants one a job! Let's focus on our most valuable resource - our children. Let everyone go to bed at night with a full tummy, a head full of new things learned at school and no illnesses.

Megan
Eastside Tech

March 3, 2003
Dear Mr. President,

Would you please try and do something about our healthcare system. People just can't afford to be sick. And I know your really busy with working on the war and all but could please let us know a little more about whats going on out there. And last but not least please help us out with the school system its getting really bad. The poor kids don't have a chance to really get anything done when they have to worry about a weeks worth of F cat testing. Thank you for you time,

Margaret
Tampa Blue

April 8, 2003
Dear President Bush,

You are finally completing what your dad started but what about our families?

Matt
Heartland

are your thoughts on abortion—I believe that you need to be the first Republican candidate to come out of the dark ages and give a woman the right to choose." Another woman asked the president to "think about the long-term effects of industrialization on the environment" but concluded with a stand-alone sentence: "And leave *Roe vs. Wade* alone!"

> **Max.** *I read those postcards, and I have to ask, is there any evidence that the country yearns for what the Republicans are delivering? Is it enough to be brutally successful but away from the problems that people are most concerned about?*
>
> **Judge.** *Terrorism is not away from the ball.*
>
> **Max.** *They could kick a trip wire on the environment, abortion, Social Security, kids, taxes, something, and the lights start flashing, "overreach, overreach."*

The political battles that have created the Two Americas have encompassed a finite number of issues critical to the polarization but have down-

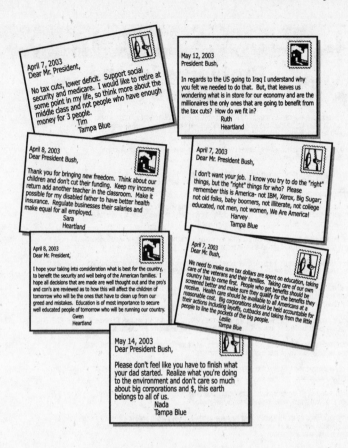

April 7, 2003
Dear Mr. President,

No tax cuts, lower deficit. Support social security and medicare. I would like to retire at some point in my life, so think more about the middle class and not people who have enough money for 3 people.
Tim
Tampa Blue

May 12, 2003
President Bush,

In regards to the US going to Iraq I understand why you felt we needed to do that. But, that leaves us wondering what is in store for our economy and are the millionaires the only ones that are going to benefit from the tax cuts? How do we fit in?
Ruth
Heartland

April 8, 2003
Dear President Bush,

Thank you for bringing new freedom. Think about our children and don't cut their funding. Keep my income return add another teacher in the classroom. Make it possible for my disabled father to have better health insurance. Regulate businesses their salaries and make equal for all employed.
Sara
Heartland

April 7, 2003
Dear Mr. President Bush,

I don't want your job. I know you try to do the "right" things, but the "right" things for who? Please remember this is America- not IBM, Xerox, Big Sugar; not old folks, baby boomers, not illiterate, not college educated, not men, not women, We Are America!
Harvey
Tampa Blue

April 8, 2003
Dear Mr. President,

I hope your taking into consideration what is best for the country, to benefit the security and well being of the American families. I hope all decisions that are made are well thought out and the pro's and con's are reviewed as to how this will affect the children of tomorrow who will be the ones that have to clean up from our greed and mistakes. Education is of most importance to secure well educated people of tomorrow who will be running our country.
Gwen
Heartland

April 7, 2003
Dear Mr. Bush,

We need to make sure tax dollars are spent on education, taking care of the veterans and their families. Taking care of our own country has to come first. People who get benefits should be screened better and make sure they qualify for the benefits they receive. Health care should be available to all Americans at a reasonable cost. Big corporations should be held accountable for their actions including layoffs, cutbacks and taking from the little people to line the pockets of the big people.
Leslie
Tampa Blue

May 14, 2003
Dear President Bush,

Please don't feel like you have to finish what your dad started. Realize what you're doing to the environment and don't care so much about big corporations and $, this earth belongs to all of us.
Nada
Tampa Blue

played or ignored many others that might redraw the political lines. To examine the gap between the public's issue priorities and the issues currently being advanced, we presented a list of problems to a nationally representative sample of voters, and they answered whether each problem was "extremely serious," "very serious," "serious," "not that serious a problem," or "not a problem at all." The percentage choosing the two most serious options, "extremely" and "very," were added together to indicate the total saying this is a major problem.[2]

September 11 has surely changed the political world: 72 percent of the electorate say the terrorist threat presented by rogue states like Iran or North Korea developing weapons of mass destruction and making them available to terrorist networks is a major problem facing the country, including 37 percent who say "extremely serious."[3] Threats that seemed almost beyond even a ghoulish imagination a decade ago are now horribly real for people and are reflected in the discourse of the country's leaders, increasingly dominated by the conservative political leaders. Of course,

Problems for the Country

	Extremely Serious	Major Problem (Extremely & Very Serious)
The state of health care in America, with rising prices for health insurance and prescription drugs, employers cutting coverage, cutbacks in money for Medicare and Medicaid, and over 40 million Americans with no insurance.	44	77
Rogue nations, like Iran and North Korea, armed with weapons of mass destruction and working together with global terrorist organizations.	37	72
The rapidly rising federal deficits, which will increase interest rates, lower investment, and leave the government without the resources to meet fundamental obligations such as Social Security, Medicare, and education.	30	59
The breakdown of the American family, with the divorce rate quadrupling since 1970 and even two-parent families spending 22 fewer hours with their children every week in order to work and earn enough.	30	59
The state of education in America, including shortages of quality teachers, declining standards, lack of funding, and the need for modern buildings and technology.	29	58
The middle class being squeezed, because their incomes are stagnant while prices are skyrocketing for housing, college tuition, and health care, with employers contributing less each year.	29	57
Big corporations having too much influence, as corporate lobbyists are able to get the lion's share of tax cuts for the wealthy, reduce environmental protections, and stop the government from acting on prescription drugs or health care.	28	54
The growing inequality in income in America, where middle-class income has grown just 10 percent over the last ten years, while the income of the top 1 percent increased nearly 250 percent.	26	52
Out-of-control federal government spending and programs, which can be reduced to provide tax relief and give greater responsibility to states and local communities.	21	44
America's dependency for our energy supplies on oil, most of it imported and most from unstable countries in the Middle East.	20	53
The outdated government regulations and bureaucracy that are stifling entrepreneurship, encouraging frivolous lawsuits, and driving small businesses into bankruptcy.	17	40
Global warming, caused by the buildup of heat-trapping gases, such as carbon pollution from cars and power plants, which will produce increased respiratory illnesses, longer heat waves, more intense storm systems, and natural disasters.	17	35
The high taxes on businesses and individuals, which deny them use of their own money to invest, save, and spend as they see fit, costing our economy more than $100 billion every year.	16	38
America globally engaged because of our economic and military leadership, but facing more terror threats, anti-Americanism, foreign competition undercutting U.S. employment, and less control over what happens in America.	15	44
The highest rate of immigration in a century, which is changing America's ethnic and religious composition. In fact, barely 80 percent of U.S. households now speak English at home.	15	30

leaders of both parties have urged action against such threats, but the disproportionate engagement after 9/11 has consequences. It is this central national task that gives the Bush presidency and the Reagan revolutionary project new life as they defend America's freedom and security.

The breakdown of the American family is also a top-tier issue resulting from a combination of weakening parental bonds and pressure from society and the labor market that has parents spending less time with their children. A sizable 59 percent of the country views this as a major problem (including 30 percent who say it is "extremely serious"), though that is well below the concern with terrorism. Nonetheless, the family is a serious issue, with both a material and values side, and no doubt both Democrats and Republicans will speak to the question. In focus group discussions, people worried about the ease of divorce, the "materialism" that allowed people to choose accumulating personal wealth over children, and the increased number of hours worked. People described it as a "huge" problem, and some, like a man from Tampa Blue, personalized it: "It's me, me, me." But the people surveyed struggled with what the government could do other than to insist that everyone, including parents, take "greater responsibility."

Terrorism is a fundamental issue for government. The family is a fundamental issue for society. These are the two legs that keep the Bush-Reagan project standing. If Democrats were to have a serious family agenda, that might change the parties' fortunes. In any case, what is striking is how marginal the entire Republican agenda is on big government, spending, regulation, and tax cuts. Just 44 percent describe out-of-control federal government spending and programs as a major problem for the country. Even fewer, 40 percent, focus on outdated government regulations and bureaucracy that are stifling entrepreneurship and encouraging frivolous lawsuits that hurt small business. And almost at the bottom of the public's long list of national problems are high taxes on businesses and individuals that deny them the use of their own money to invest and thereby harm the economy. Just 38 percent say this is a major problem facing the nation. Addressing terrorism and the family makes the Reagan project relevant to the country, but its frenetic work on the core agenda of reducing government and taxes gains little public interest. The contradiction is already apparent in the postcards that voters addressed to the president.

After a decade of incrementalism, the biggest issue for the country is health care. Topping all other problems, 77 percent say the rising prices for insurance and drugs, employers cutting back coverage, the government cutting back funding for Medicare and Medicaid, and the more than 40 million uninsured are a major problem, including 44 percent, almost half the country, who describe it as "extremely serious." This issue, it seems, has moved beyond small fixes and now leaves the country with a sense of health care in crisis and the need to think about a comprehensive response again.

The subject elicits a flood of anecdotes on absurd bills and stories of people going to Canada in search of cheaper drugs. It also brought a raft of anticorporate sentiment—"the big corporations, they are charging the big bucks"—as well as widespread calls for some kind of government intervention. A woman from Tampa Blue asked, "Can we get some regulation on the cost and the prices?" And half the group almost in unison responded, "yes," "yes," "definitely," "they should." The Heartland women were the same: "I think somebody needs to put control on how much things cost." The men were harder still: "This is one part where the government should get into, and say, 'Hey, listen, you guys can't do this. You can't charge this much.' You know, . . . this is where they're taking over our lives." Peppered throughout the groups were calls for universal health care: "everyone should have access to health care"; "a nationwide health care program works extremely effectively in many nations"; "we need some form of public insurance that everybody has." Even in the more upscale Eastside Tech, the men were on the edge: "I hate to say that anything should be socialized, but I'm coming to the point where I think health care should be a basic right and that everybody should have health care."

It is hard to imagine greater discordance between the public mood and the government's direction and philosophy on the number one problem for government action.

The other top-tier problem for the country is the rapidly rising deficits, potentially undermining future private investment and the government's financial capacity to address other problems, in particular to fund retirement programs: 59 percent call this a major problem, with 30 percent answering "extremely serious." Again, there is a marked discordance between the direction of current government policy, unconcerned with producing rising deficits, and the public's view of good governance.

Comprehensive problems with education—from shortages of quality teachers, declining standards, and a lack of funding to the need for modern buildings and technology—all scored very high: 58 percent major problem, with 29 percent "extremely serious." This is a much broader set of problems in the public schools than addressed by recent education initiatives passed by Congress and suggests a considerable federal role. It is interesting to note that almost all of the discussions in the focus groups centered on the teachers, from their poor quality, to the abuse they have to take, to their lack of accountability and, most frequently, to pay inadequate to attract quality people to the job and in accordance with their role in society.

Education was the issue that the Republicans set out to "steal" from the Democrats, and they were fairly successful during the 2000 election and in the first two years of Bush's presidency, particularly with the passage of bipartisan education legislation. But underfunding of the program and general cutbacks in domestic spending, along with education crises at the state level, have turned voters back to the Democrats on education. In a poll taken three months after Bush took office, Republicans enjoyed a 7-point advantage on education, but in the spring of 2003, Democrats had regained a 13-point lead on the education issue.[4]

That the excessive influence of corporations scores in the same range as the need to address education is a measure of the political temper of the times. Perhaps the Bush White House judges correctly when excising the word "business" from the president's speeches. When asked how important a problem for the country was corporate influence and its ability to get the lion's share of tax cuts for the wealthy, 54 percent said it was a major problem, including 28 percent saying "extremely serious."

When groups were asked why nothing had been done to address the various problems, the participants waxed eloquent about the tight bond between corporations and the wealthy on the one hand and the government and politicians on the other. A Tampa woman suggested that it was a simple equation: "Most of the people up there [getting the high incomes] are the people controlling the world." With a new wrinkle on the old song, a Heartland man said, "The rich get richer and the poor poorer and the guys have no real power." On the other hand, the big interests "buy the elections with their millions of dollars and take care of themselves."

Middle-class squeeze is also a top problem for the country and is defined by stagnant incomes and rising prices for housing, college tuition, and health care, combined with declining employer contributions: 57 percent call this a major problem, with 29 percent answering "extremely serious." Health care is a central element of middle-class grievances, and rising health-care costs are most vivid for middle-class people, leaving them feeling trapped. As a Heartland Iowa man put it, "If they don't get a grip on health care, you can piss away everything else you are talking about." This observation gains poignancy as voters talk about the middle class, the people who carry the heaviest burden for the country. This time, it is a Tampa Blue woman who tries her variation on the theme, "The rich are getting richer and the poor are getting poorer and us middle-class people are holding the fort down."

While about half the country describes growing inequality of income as a very "serious problem," it is a more vital issue for the squeezed middle class. The income gap has been growing rapidly through two and a half decades, accelerated in the Reagan era and likely in the Bush period, given the thrust of tax policies. But the last straw for the public is not wealth and high incomes as such. They do not favor policies that would punish people for being successful. But they cannot stomach the corporate tax loopholes that allow the privileged to use their lawyers, accountants, and lobbyists to shirk paying their fair share of taxes.[5] There is a special place reserved for CEOs, who have become cultural icons, even more than professional athletes, as "greedy" figures who sell out their employees. More than 60 percent of Americans say CEO wrongdoing is a "widespread problem" in a "system that is failing."[6] To a public judging the state of the country under Bush, this is an era of corporate excess very much at odds with the central instincts of the current Reagan project, which seeks to create greater latitude and lower taxes for business.

In 2004, while Democrats will present their views on terrorism and security, values and assisting the family, it is in health care, rising deficits, Social Security, education, middle-class squeeze, the economy, and corporate influence where the gaps are the greatest and where there is the most opportunity for gains. Without trying to sort out the main focus, one can see the health-care challenge earning Democrats an audience with Vulnerable Women (health care is one of their top three issues) and Aging Female Blues (top two issues). Education helps consolidate African Americans and Hispanics (top two issues) and particularly Super-Educated Women (their top issue), but it also reaches deep into the contested world, attracting the Well-Educated Women (top two issues) and the Young and the Restless (their top issue). While Social Security may seem an old horse, rising deficits elevate concerns and raise the importance of the issue in the contested world, not the Democratic loyalist world, where the middle has been mostly hollowed out. It is the top issue, not surprisingly, for the Golden Girls, but also for Vulnerable Women and the Aging Blues, Men and Women; importantly, it is the second most important issue for Country Folk, after the economy.[7] No wonder the Republicans are working so urgently on prescription drugs, lest the agenda gap become exposed here.

The strategy for Democrats is fairly simple: elevate the agenda gap.

STRATEGIC CHOICE 2: THE TWO AMERICAS

There is a strong case for Democrats sticking with the battle lines of the Two Americas and making the case for its America. While the existing framework has given the country our current parity, the underlying social trends, the opportunity for improvements in execution and message (vis-à-vis 2000), and the polarizing dynamic inherent in the Republican strategy all argue for Democratic gains within the status quo. If one really believes we are a "49 percent nation" and that those trends are favorable, then the Democrats should think long and hard before walking away from what they have built up. After all, the Democratic Party is in many respects the modern party, more relevant for addressing America's modern challenges.

That the parties remain evenly divided is hardly contestable. Over the past twenty months, 46 percent have aligned with each party, right up until the summer of 2003. The Democrats won the plurality of the vote in 2000, and even with the asymmetric off-year elections of 2002, featuring intense Republican organization, high conservative motivation, and Democratic demoralization, the centrality of security over economic issues, and a roughly Republican three-to-one financial advantage, the Republican vote for the House of Representatives still reached only 51 percent.

The social trends in the country continue to produce growing racial and immigrant diversity, a larger proportion of college-educated people, and larger cosmopolitan regions. Those same trends are producing a parallel, ongoing decline of white noncollege married as well as rural voters who have voted heavily Republican in recent years. Illustrative of the trend, nearly a third of the Generation Y voters are Hispanic, African American, or Asian, reflecting developing population and immigration patterns. And college admissions officers are worried about the shortfall of men, as women begin to dominate college ranks.

It is on these trends that John Judis and Ruy Teixeira have made their case for an emerging Democratic majority. Unfortunately, politics is never quite so linear, but it is hard to deny the reality—evidenced by the Republicans' frenetic efforts to erode Democratic support among Hispanics and the Well-Educated Women.

On the Republican side, there are counterbalancing social and cultural trends that include the growing Deep South and the Sun Belt states and, in particular, the budding exurban areas. The last development has clearly offset the impact of growing cosmopolitan areas and states and kept the South safely Republican, but the rise of minority and college-educated populations has threatened the Republican advantage in Florida and all of the Southwest, except Texas.

This second strategic path, the Two Americas, is premised on the idea that the Democratic worldview, its modern vision for America, is better suited to the challenges of these times than is the Reagan worldview. The Democrats in this option will run a presidential candidate who celebrates the country's diversity, both as a matter of individual rights and opportunity and as a matter of underlying strength for America in a global economy. The Democrats are the party of economic growth, fiscal stability, and full employment. They use government in a balanced way, above all to invest in education and skills that help people succeed in an Information Age. Despite the burst of the bubble and subsequent recession, Americans still believe in technology, the new economy, and progress.

Bill Clinton at the end of his term pointed the way into the twenty-first century and clearly associated the Democrats with the postmodern world and, to oversimplify, the coalition of loyalist groups that comprise "our America." He spoke of an America growing economically, paying down its debts, open, unafraid, and optimistic about the future; an America with a faith in the power of science and technology, investing in education; one that uplifts the poor, helps families with child care and health care, ensures safe communities, and extends and modernizes Social Security and Medicare; tackles the biggest environmental problems; and builds an America where diversity is a strength.[8]

The conservatives are made nearly giddy by the possibility that the American triumph in Iraq has put a stake in the heart of "postmodernism" and "multiculturalism"—the strange worldview that sees the world as "a series of competing stories," none more valid than the next. From this perspective, according to Joel Kotkin and Fred Siegel in *The Weekly Standard*, the cosmopolitan elites, from the mainline established churches to the media and Hollywood, opposed the war and are "the losers in the postwar era." Viewed as a redefining event for America, the war, they tell us, has "redistributed our ideals of honor for the coming generation."[9] Postmodernism will presumably retreat, but the same should have been true when Ronald Reagan raised the specter of the "evil empire" and "won" the Cold War. The gamble on postmodernism is not just one of demography, which is real enough, but also one of patterns of thinking related to the changing economy, competing lifestyles, technology, information needs, and global integration. William Bennett was one of the generals in the battle against the modern, but "to say that Mr. Bennett lost all his culture wars as decisively as he lost his $8 million would not be an overstatement," culture critic Frank Rich of *The New York Times* writes. Cataloging the winners and losers, much as *The Weekly Standard* might, Rich notes, "Hip-hop is the dominant youth culture of the land." Here, in modern America, Eminem and 50 Cent are entertainment giants, humanities and arts endowments are rising, and Senator Rick Santorum, after his Bennett-like comments on gays, has "disappeared into the Dr. Laura witness protection program." What is more, "Mr. Bennett's afternoon talk-show nemesis, Jerry Springer, is not only still on the air" but seriously considered running for the Senate and in London, there is now *Jerry Springer—The Opera*.[10]

Before the close of its session in June 2003, the Supreme Court overturned Texas statutes on sodomy and applied privacy protection to homosexual behavior. Speaking for the majority, Justice Anthony Kennedy stated, "The petitioners are entitled to respect for their private lives. The State cannot demean their existence or control their destiny by making their private sexual conduct a crime." Doing so, Justice Kennedy wrote, is "an invitation to subject homosexual persons to discrimination both in the public and in the private sphere." Given the symbolic centrality of homosexuality to the cultural divide, it is hard to imagine how the Court could have been more provocative. Perhaps in the closing paragraph it tried, when declaring, "As the Constitution endures, persons of every generation can invoke its principles in their own search for greater freedom"—affirming the malleability of the Constitution and the learned truths of each generation, rather than the absolute principles given to us for all times. Not surprising, then, is the reaction of Justice Antonin Scalia, who described the decision as "a massive disruption of the current social order" and, more provocative yet, as evidence that the Court is now "the product of a law-profession culture, that has largely signed on to the so-called homosexual agenda."[11] If we take Justice Scalia at his word, the right is losing the cultural battle.

The "Clinton Wars" and Al Gore's campaign began to weaken the Democrats in 1998 and continue to suppress support in rural areas, among noncollege voters, particularly married women, and among the religiously devout, particularly Catholics. But why should we presume that this is immutable? Why do we assume that a new candidate will continue to carry this burden to the same extent? Any kind of opening on values and trust should gain a larger audience for the Democrats' central message. Any gains on these attributes change the rural dynamic and the vast swath of states that could swing the election.

Democrats regaining their postmodernist voice are likely to continue the trends that have given them increased support among minorities and among the Super-Educated Women and Secular Warriors that dominate the Democratic loyalist world. With the exception of the Union Families, all the loyalist groups related positively to the Internet, immigrants, and NAFTA, placing them comfortably in the postmodernist camp. The Democrats built up their side of the Two Americas mostly without strong support among nonunion working-class voters. But their perspective has a reasonable chance to gain further support among a number of the contested groups, in particular the Postgraduate Men and Well-Educated Women, as well as the Young and the Restless. Together, these contested groups make up a quarter of the electorate. The discordant voices are the Nader voters who are fully part of the postmodernist world but reject the associated globalism and openness to business. That is no small disjunction, offsetting the seeming inevitability of postmodern focus.

With all the Clinton-Gore problems on trust and with Al Gore almost a textbook secular candidate—strong on gun control and abortion rights, and in favor of gay unions—he still split the country 50–50. If for no other reason, the Democrats are right to think long and hard about such a strategic break from the current model, especially as other dynamics specific to this election could move the Democrats up from where they were in 2000. Some of the political advisers liked the tactical simplicity of this.

> **Libby.** *So you're saying, if our nominee is neither a rogue nor a braggart, we do better with contested voters and build a larger bloc around our view of America?*
>
> **Biggs.** *Right. If I understand this second option, essentially he's saying we need to run the Gore campaign but with an added values or faith component. It's Gore plus. And it's entirely possible. Hell, given the Democratic primary process, our candidates may end up doing that by default.*

The Rove 100 percent strategy, centering on a commitment to faith and prolife, favoring business and low taxes, antigovernment, antiregulation, and aggressive military posturing, is polarizing and will likely increase the unity of Democrats and create pressure for Democrats to go for 100 percent support in their world, in effect to maximize support on their side of the Two Americas. In some sense, this is inescapable. Culture war is certain to beget greater Democratic unity and mobilization, unless the Republicans succeed in looking less threatening. But if Democrats blow up Republican efforts to look mainstream, the fruits could be an explosion equal in force producing greater Democratic support among the Secular Warriors and the Super-Educated Women, Union Families, and African Americans and Hispanics. Indeed, all of these groups have become marginally more Democratic over the eighteen-month period I have monitored the current battle, just as the loyalist Republican groups have become more supportive of the Republicans.[12]

This surely leaves many of the contested groups up for grabs, as the strategy essentially reinforces the polarizing dynamics that leave them alienated or ambivalent, but in any case without a firm partisan home. There will be a battle for the more culturally conservative Hispanics, as well as for the Well-Educated Women, Golden Girls, Devout Catholics, and the Young and the Restless. Nothing has changed, except perhaps the growth of the modernist forces, the reaction to the Republican culture war, and possibly a Democratic nominee who can attract votes beyond the secular world. But some of the advisers were not buying this approach.

> **Judge.** *It just doesn't work for me. We're fine-tuning an old model when a whole new line of cars is out. People are looking at things through new eyes after 9/11.*
>
> **Max.** *Three million people have lost jobs. And health-care costs are up 13 percent.*
>
> **Judge.** *Not all issues are equal.*

STRATEGIC CHOICE 3:
THE CORPORATE FRAME

In the general election of 2000, Al Gore introduced a populist formulation of the Reformed Opportunity mission, highlighting the need to ensure that all families share in our general prosperity as well as the need to check the power of big corporate interests, acknowledging the excesses of the pharmaceutical, tobacco, and insurance companies. He was down more than 10 points and quickly moved ahead, eventually leading by 5 to 8 points, before falling back during the presidential debates. Gore's general election campaign was actually a three-month interlude during a decade in which Democrats played down championing average people against the avarice of the privileged few and private interests. The last time the public heard a full-throated cry about disproportionate power and uneven opportunity was in 1992 when Clinton ran against the excesses of the 1980s, but also against CEOs, whom he described as the "jet-setters and feather bedders of corporate America." The Reformed Democrats walked away from an aggrieved middle class on material issues as well as values, leading many working-class voters to join the revolt against the Democrats in 1994, then pulled back after Monica Lewinsky and the Clinton impeachment and again from Al Gore when he could not win voters on the issue of trust. As a consequence, the Democrats suffered a marked decline in support among blue-collar voters and Americans without college degrees. This decline was evident by 1994 among the Aging Male Blues and by 1998 among the Married Blue Women, Aging Female Blues, and Country Folk, even producing weaker support among Vulnerable Women and Union Families.

The current political landscape reflects these patterns, with the lines starkly drawn. In the Democratic loyalist world, the only way noncollege groups qualify for membership is by belonging to a union or by coming from a minority community. The Super-Educated Women, the Secular Warriors, and Cosmopolitan State voters are disproportionately better educated. On the other hand, the Republican loyalist world is nearly defined by the Faithful, Country Folk, F-You Boys, and F-You Old Men, who are largely white married voters without college degrees. Indeed, the largest blocs in the contested world are the Married Blue Women and the Aging Male Blues who, in this period of war and worry, lean Republican by more than 12 percentage points. More exposed noncollege and blue-collar voters who should be Democratic loyalists—the Vulnerable Women and Aging Female Blues—lean toward Democrats by only a few points.

It may well be time to revisit the mood of 1992 and remember the election that the Republicans and pundits and elites and some Democrats describe dismissively as "class warfare." But while it is true that 9/11 created new political dynamics favorable to George W. Bush, it is hard to miss the other big change in the country. A whole variety of forces are coming together, including more than two decades of increasing income inequality, full-blown corporate scandals, complete with images of Enron and Tyco, Kenneth Lay and Dennis Kozlowski, Richard Grasso and his $140 million compensation package, laid-off workers and worthless pensions. The result is an economic downturn characterized by stagnant incomes and rising health-care costs. It is also a period when the wealthiest Americans and the biggest corporations had their taxes slashed.

There is good reason to believe that the new imbalances are producing a building voter reaction with the potential to stall or reverse some of the voter trends that produced the Two Americas, which have been drawn largely along cultural lines. Today, voters express particularly negative views of corporations and CEOs, more so than for the "wealthy," but still a heightened noncultural development. Big corporations received a cool 45.8-degree rating from voters during the period of this research.[13]

In addition, three-quarters of voters say they get "very angry" about "corporate CEOs receiving large salaries even while their companies are losing money and laying off workers," while two-thirds feel that way about "companies that keep accounts in countries like Bermuda to avoid paying taxes, but still receive government contracts." Both figures are well in excess of the percent getting "very angry" about the federal government spending the Social Security surplus, as a modest point of comparison.[14]

The intensity of the public reaction was replayed among the political advisers who spend their lives trying to elect candidates or working with elected officials to gain the public's support in this changing social context.

Wolf. The truth is that two years before the 2000 election, the fourteen largest corporate lobbyists in America got together and said, "We're going to make George Bush president of the United States." They made him president, and he's paid off like a slot machine.

The fact is that all the swing groups, without exception, share a deep sense of suspicion of corporate America. And I think all the scandals have exacerbated that. I think this is a fundamental theme: restoring balance and ending this sort of rampant corporatism. I think people feel they've gone too far.

Biggs. We can't let fourteen lobbyists get up and dictate what's in the national interest. We need a president who's strong enough to dictate what's in the national interest.

Max. *We want a system that's not rigged. We want a reward system where hard work is how you get ahead, not cheating.*

Libby. *Yeah, we should lead with that because we can rip their heart out.*

But understand that adopting the corporate framework is quite a break, albeit one with the potential to disrupt the political patterns that underlie the deadlock. If one ranks groups arrayed in the Democratic loyalist world by their feelings about big corporations, the most negative in the Democratic camp are the white Union Families (42.1 degrees) and Secular Warriors (42.2), followed by African Americans (43.8). But the anticorporate reaction is not the strongest among the Democratic loyalists; it is not a "base strategy" in conventional political terms. The anticorporate appeal reaches into the contested world and even the Republican loyalist world. The Country Folk in the Republican camp are almost as negative (44.6 degrees) as the Democratic groups. Indeed, in the contested world, we find the most anticorporate voters of all: the Golden Girls (43.0), Vulnerable Women (41.8), and Aging Female Blues (41.7). Challenging the country's current direction through the corporate framework, more than almost any single act, pushes back against the historic patterns.

The corporate frame for the election, then, offers the Democrats the chance to build greater unity in the Union Families that are under pressure from Republicans on guns and trade issues. More important, the strategy opens up the biggest segment of the contested electorate, the Aging Blues, both Men and Women, who are anticorporate but also most skeptical about the United States getting more deeply involved abroad, as in Iraq. In addition, the Democrats could tip the Vulnerable Women, mostly nonmarried and earning low wages, into the loyalist camp. The posture could potentially help Democrats with the Married Blue Women and Golden Girls, though serious values concerns about the Democrats put distance between them and may hold these groups back. It could help Democrats get back their support among the Country Folk, which is why Republicans are so quick to cry "class warfare."

While this seems simple enough, polarization and the big political battles of the last half century have rooted the parties in the Two Americas, in particular limiting the middle-class role in the Democratic world. The corporate frame might attract blue-collar and noncollege working-class voters at the expense of potential support among the Postgraduate Men, Well-Educated Women, and the Young and the Restless, who rate big corporations closer to 50 degrees. It may limit the ability to get an audience with the Privileged Men in the Republican camp, the one group that seems least comfortable there on cultural grounds.[15]

This is a reasonable caveat, and indeed, it made some of the Democratic political advisers uncomfortable, given the postmodernist gains in the last decade. But there is at least some reason to believe that Democrats, for now, can have their cake and eat it too. With the Republicans waging culture war, many of the postmodern voters have clung more strongly to their America, diminishing the likelihood of an unintended reaction against the corporate strategy. The more secular and cosmopolitan voters are getting a daily lesson on why the Republican world is not a very welcoming home for them. In fact, the 2000 election was something of a test run, as these loyalist groups—Super-Educated Women, Secular Warriors, and the Cosmopolitan States—gravitated even more strongly to the Democrats, as if they had never heard Gore's populist rhetoric.

Still, the political advisers react to a potential negativity of tone in the corporate framework that seems to clash with the postmodern style and vision of the Reformed Opportunity Democrats, including the Bill Clinton orientation to life, which is self-consciously hopeful about the future for the country. This was the mantra of the 1996 campaign and part of the criticism of Gore's effort in 2000.[16] It was on the minds of the political advisers, who were most divided on this point.

> **Libby.** *I think we might have to be a little more subtle with the populism than Al Gore was.*
>
> **Max.** *We have to do it in a more positive way. I mean, describing how we help corporations do the right thing, with a big view about the economy.*
>
> **Libby.** *Right, the pro-capitalist populist.*
>
> **Judge.** *It has to be a forward-thinking populism rooted in traditional values. There was an edge and anger to Gore that I think put people off.*
>
> **Libby.** *Don't go backward, go forward. I think it was a cursing the darkness kind of thing.*
>
> **Judge.** *Look at the most effective politicians in the last ten years, who went negative. Look at Mitchell and Clinton. Smile right through it. Smile and be positive first and then they pulled the trigger subtly. I don't think there's any appetite for the raw negative politics that may have worked ten years ago.*
>
> **Wolf.** *Yeah, but as imperfect as he was, Gore did reasonably well.*

But there are other reasons, besides the sensibilities of the postmodernists, that constrain the potential efficacy of the corporate framework. The Democrats' ability to redraw the current battle lines for the Two Americas is diminished by their lack of credibility on the core concept: championing the people and taking on the powerful special interests. First, their position is diminished by their "values problem." While this may seem like a wholly different realm, the party's inability easily to identify with the lives of Middle America blocks the passage, one that a Ronald Reagan was able to pass through in an earlier era. Politicians who want to "take away" people's guns show a lack of respect for the traditional family and military, in the eyes of Middle America. Likewise, politicians who seek middle-class tax hikes and are hostile or indifferent to people's faith are not likely to be embraced as the people's advocate.

As a sign of the barriers to passage, it is worth looking at the very warm and positive thermometer ratings given to the NRA among those open to the Corporate Framework—the Country Folk (61.3 degrees) among the Republican loyalists; the Young and the Restless (56.4), Married Blue Women (54.6), and Aging Male Blues (61.9) in the contested world; even the Union Families (52.3) in the Democratic world. Guns symbolize a way of life, and Democrats will emerge as the natural advocates only when they are not so distant across a broad range of values questions.

The political advisers tried to tackle the values problem in this framework, but it is unclear whether this is sufficient, absent more traditional expressions about faith and understanding regarding threats to the family.

> *Wolf. Values need to be addressed in many areas, but I'm tired of playing defense. I don't want to accept their terms on the values debate. We need to define our own values. They have a set of values, particularly economic values, that are fundamentally different from ours, but ours are much more in sync with the majority of people in this country. We've got to lift this thing to the level of a values debate. We run away from the word "values" because they've stolen it and redefined it to mean gay people and abortion.*
>
> *Biggs. And the values debate is also what's best for the country. It's "Oh, if it's good for GM, it's good for you." Our attitude is "If it's good for America, then, damn it, it's good for GM."*
>
> *Max. I agree with that. I think there's a further values element. Most Americans deeply believe you should get rewarded for doing the right thing. You do hard work, you get rewarded for it, not for cheating.*
>
> *Libby. And when your parents are old, you can afford to make sure they have a decent and dignified death.*
>
> *Wolf. What we're all saying is that in our America we get rewarded for the work we do and not for cheating. We take responsibility and we're accountable. All these values are being trampled on right now.*
>
> *Biggs. To beat George Bush, you've got to make him choke on the corporate piece of his economic pie.*

The Democrats' political strength in the corporate framework is also greatly diminished by the perception that the Democrats, just like the Republicans, are financed and controlled by the same corporate and special interests. For sure, the Republicans and George W. Bush are seen as too close to business, but when asked which party would do a better job "standing up to the special interests in Washington," the Democrats have only a 5-point advantage over the Republicans.[17] When asked in the context of the current battles which party would do a better job "closing tax loopholes and tax shelters," just 33 percent said the Democrats and an even smaller number, 25 percent, said the Republicans. Fully 41 percent of voters said "neither" or "don't know," exceeding the number that chose either party.[18]

The absence of a credible Democratic reformist agenda which, as Michael Waldman has made clear, was abandoned after 1992 and currently overshadowed by the Democrats' reluctance to give up on conventional campaign finance, has left the Democrats with limited credibility in taking up the corporate banner. Voters look around at the unaddressed problems and conclude that the same collection of powerful corporate interests get their way no matter which party is in power. For the ordinary citizen, the main reason the big problems are not getting addressed is not the political deadlock of our current parity, but is a result of the political deals that leave politicians "controlled." As one man in Heartland Iowa observed, "They buy the elections with their millions of dollars and take care of themselves." Politicians create the "tax loopholes" that allow the well-to-do and corporations (read, "the Enron people") to use their attorneys and tax people to further enrich themselves. A man in Tampa Blue observed that the "politicians were on the boards of all these artificial, inflated [in value] companies, like Enron." And when it comes to health care, one Eastside Tech women's group achieved unanimity: the big corporations have a "huge lobby" and "they throw so much money into government to protect themselves" that nothing is going to happen.[19]

This perception is reinforced by the large infusion of corporate political contributions to both parties over the last two decades. On the Democratic side, the surge came after the Democratic Congressional Campaign Committee began wooing business PACs with the message that business needs friends with power and the Democrats hold it. When the Republicans took power from them in 1994, Gingrich added the warning, for those who passed up the chance, "It's going to be the two coldest years in Washington." On the Republican side, they have perfected the art, as they gathered in 75 percent of the contributions from the pharmaceutical industry, more than $20 million in the 2002 election cycle alone. When it came to a key vote in the House of Representatives on reducing drug prices in the summer

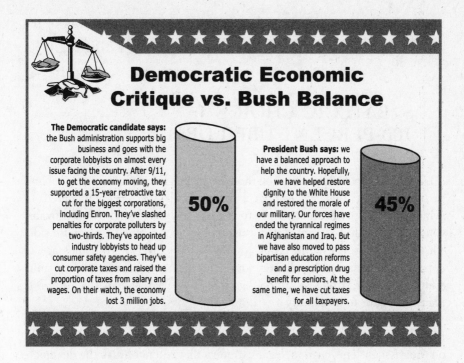

Democratic Economic Critique vs. Bush Balance

The Democratic candidate says: the Bush administration supports big business and goes with the corporate lobbyists on almost every issue facing the country. After 9/11, to get the economy moving, they supported a 15-year retroactive tax cut for the biggest corporations, including Enron. They've slashed penalties for corporate polluters by two-thirds. They've appointed industry lobbyists to head up consumer safety agencies. They've cut corporate taxes and raised the proportion of taxes from salary and wages. On their watch, the economy lost 3 million jobs.

50%

President Bush says: we have a balanced approach to help the country. Hopefully, we have helped restore dignity to the White House and restored the morale of our military. Our forces have ended the tyrannical regimes in Afghanistan and Iraq. But we have also moved to pass bipartisan education reforms and a prescription drug benefit for seniors. At the same time, we have cut taxes for all taxpayers.

45%

of 2003, those members who voted with the pharmaceutical industry received three times as much in campaign donations from drug companies as those who opposed it.[20]

Still, as complicit as Democrats are in the problem, George W. Bush has a special relationship to the corporate issue that makes it hard to set aside. The Eastside Tech women say that "he's geared toward the higher echelons and big business" and worry that "he's going too much toward industry." And on the environment, "He could care less," said one woman. For proof, just "look at Texas." Similarly, a Heartland woman mused, "Well, [Bush] is from big oil. Oil industry doesn't really care about the environment." Bush, it seems, has given a new power to the corporate framework that is difficult to ignore.

However diminished the Democrats are by lack of nuance or lack of values or by complicity in a corrupt campaign finance system, the corporate message framework today defeats the Bush framework, which is rooted in security, restoring trust, and tax cuts. Bush remains popular because of his wartime role and personal virtues, but even a negative, anticorporate formulation, as presented in the graph, stripped of values, is preferred by voters, 50 to 45 percent, over a robust description of Bush's form of Reaganism. It is likely that a better-developed, values-based, and more expansive, positive message could defeat the Reagan formulation, even in the current environment.

STRATEGIC CHOICE 4: 100 PERCENT ÜBER DEM

There is a popular school of thought in the Democratic camp, championed by labor, that suggests we have made all this too complicated. In some sense, Republican attempts to build a coalition with as many loyalist voters as possible has legitimized a parallel project on the Democratic side. All the energy you expend trying to take the edge off of your message to appeal to "centrist" or "moderate" voters detracts from efforts to build unity and excite your strongest support groups. Rove has shown that this is a plausible route to a majority.

The best strategy, then, is pretty simple: identify the groups that can form the core support in your majority coalition and speak directly to them on their issues. This is an inelegant strategy that will not break the deadlock, but it might win an election. African Americans are the number one group in the Democratic coalition, given that 86 percent align with the Democrats. The conservative war to bring down the Clinton presidency energized these voters, who felt further victimized by the illegitimate election of 2000. Hispanics align with the Democrats by 55 to 37 percent, an 18-point advantage. But given their economic vulnerability and the importance of civil rights, why not build to a larger majority, as happened in 1996 when Republicans were intensely anti-immigrant? Two of the strongest Democratic groups are the Super-Educated Women and the Secular Warriors, with Democratic support reaching 60 percent or more. But with the right to choose, expanded roles for women, and the structure of environmental protection all under threat, it is possible to imagine even higher levels of support. White Union Families are in the loyalist camp but are giving Democrats only a 53-to-40 percent majority. This is a respectable 13-point margin, but down in 2000 and in the 2002 off-year elections. It is possible, perhaps even likely, that the Democratic margin could be significantly larger among Union Families if Democrats were speaking more directly to them on employment, corporate abuse, and trade issues, as well as health care and Social Security.

With a greater focus on the issues that are key to the Democratic coalition, the Democrats might gain support among a range of contested groups, such as Vulnerable Women and Aging Male and Female Blues who are more populist and worried about their retirement security.

The 100 Percent Über Dem strategy also has the best chance of wooing the Ralph Nader voters back into the Democratic majority. After all, with those voters, Democrats would have had more than 50 percent of the vote in 2000 and been free of the debilitating parity that gave the country George W. Bush. The strong emphasis on loyalist issues, particularly abortion, the environment, and trade protection, can enlarge Democratic possibilities. The 2000 Nader voters are also among the most intensely anti-Republican comparable to African Americans, even though 65 percent call themselves independents.[21]

The political advisers were skeptical about the numbers and had reservations about a strategy that set goals so close to parity, where margins of error could put the whole effort at risk.

> **Judge.** *The underlying assumption in this worldview is that we've got the numbers, so let's turn them out. Enough of this Republican-lite shit. We should quit talking about faith-based initiatives with the White House and get back to our own issues.*
>
> **Biggs.** *Judge, we only have 53 percent with the Union Families. What the fuck are you talking about?*
>
> **Judge.** *That's circular thinking. The numbers are produced by the current fog. The folks on this track say, Take blacks, Hispanics, and downscale women. If you get all those numbers up, turn people out, we'll win. No contest. And the way we turn them out is to be for something that's more traditional.*
>
> **Libby.** *That's what they're saying on the other side too.*
>
> **Judge.** *Exactly. And like the other side, but for our people. If you take on Wall Street and show it's screwing the little guy, then you can pull in rural voters too.*
>
> **Biggs.** *I don't see the numbers. I don't think it's there. Add it all up. It is a big gamble.*

One of the extraordinary accomplishments of today's Republican Party is its suppression of historic internal splits and divisions that have proved unmanageable in the past. A party increasingly united in Reagan's vision, led by a Republican president defending a country under attack, has silenced for the moment any signs of conflict between libertarians and moralists, deficit hawks and tax cutters, or big business and small business, reflected in the near unanimity of Republican caucuses in Congress, particularly the House. That all of these groups are getting what they want most from public life no doubt makes this an easier task. Undoubtedly, though, if the Republican project began visibly to falter, some of these fissures might become more obvious again.

The tensions in the Democratic coalition have not been silenced, and it is possible that a 100 percent Democratic strategy might elevate tensions, absent the unifying dynamics operating on the Republican side. The priorities of the minority communities, the well-educated and cosmopolitan areas, and union and blue-collar groups that form the Democratic coalition do not automatically combine into a postmodern synthesis. As a starting point, how does one resolve the strong desire for fiscal balance and caution among the better-educated segments of the coalition with an equally strong desire of other groups for increased social spending? This tension is even more marked when one looks at potential support groups, like the Postgraduate Men and Well-Educated Women, who are drawn to the Democrats on cultural issues but uncertain on the economic ones. How can this strategy address the trade issue, central to the Union Families, while virtually all the other loyalist groups are indifferent or favorable to expanded trade and agreements? Again, in the contested world, how does one resolve the fact that some groups, like the Aging Male and Female Blues, are drawn to the Democrats on opposition to trade, while others, like the Well-Educated Women and the Young and the Restless, are drawn to support for trade? How does one resolve the relish of some secular support groups for culture war and some noncollege groups for class war?

STRATEGIC CHOICE 5: REASSURANCE TO CLEAR THE BAR

It is quite possible that the structure of thinking about issues and the state of the country and even the social currents favor the Democrats, but that large segments of the electorate simply cannot get to those choices because they are blocked by two fundamental areas of doubt: security and values. Until Democrats reassure voters that they share mainstream thinking on these two issues, they will not get an audience. This strategy for Democrats assumes that there is a sequence to the vote decision that no amount of victory laps on the economy or corporate malfeasance can short-circuit. Voters first have to see that you clear the bar on principles before you qualify for the meet.

For a powerful example, when asked which party would do a better job keeping America strong, all voters trust the Republicans by an overwhelming 30 points (53 to 23 percent). Across the contested landscape, the Republican advantage on security is 34 points, evident among the Well-Educated Women, the Young and the Restless, Devout Catholics, and the Aging Male Blues. That Democrats have 15- to 20-point advantages among these groups on health care may not matter if voters cannot get past what this model presumes is a primary and prior consideration.

For this strategy, the two historical events that have intervened to block the "emerging Democratic majority" are Clinton's impeachment and the 9/11 terrorist attacks on America. Setting aside the perversity of equating the two, together they diminished the Democrats on values and on making the country secure.

In the postcards written to the Democratic presidential candidate, the swing voters of Tampa Blue, Heartland Iowa, and Eastside Tech give a lot of credence to the idea of reassurance. They make a point of saying, have "high standards," please "stand for family," and don't be "too soft," and they think God should be important to someone in the White House.

One early postcard, written to President Bush rather than to the Democratic nominee, suggested some things for him to get right at the beginning: "Don't take the [White House] furniture ☹. Stay on high moral ground. Keep your pants zipped!!!!" The not very subtle implication is that Democrats have some values questions to address.

The Democratic Leadership Council, the organization representing more conservative Democrats, is similarly blunt in the area of national security. With the Democratic primary season heating up in the summer of 2003, they warned that the Republicans have "significant advantages when it comes to strength and even patriotism." They call on the emerging Democratic candidate to "actively communicate our patriotism to the public," show their admiration for the men and women in uniform, strengthen homeland defenses, and improve the military.[22]

The strategy to break the deadlock, then, is as simple as the Agenda Gap or Corporate Framework. Take up first things first, namely, the very real doubts that block the way.

> **Judge.** *We have to clear the bar on the requirements for the job, and right now, we're not clearing that bar. And in fact, every day I wake up, I think we're less likely to clear the bar.*
>
> **Max.** *How do you do it?*
>
> **Libby.** *The DLC feels you've got to do the cultural stuff first. They think there's such an erosion right now on that, that if we can't fix it then we'll never get anywhere. Defense first and foremost, then values and family. We need to take the heat out of the cultural issues, like guns.*
>
> **Judge.** *The DLC would say, "Look, there aren't any more black people to move to vote for us. We've hit our top end on that." The question is, do we go for the professionals? Do we go for these high-growth suburban areas? We have to go after these people in the middle and we have to give them confidence that they can trust us with their checkbook and at the same time show them that we're not strange, San Francisco–style freaks on cultural things. And we have to assuage their concerns on guns and do some quiet things on abortion. But we go third rail with these people on defense and family. We have to build a candidacy.*
>
> **Biggs.** *I think we may have to achieve a certain level of credibility on that. There's no doubt about it. But if we intentionally lead with that,*

instead of changing the debate to something that works for us, such as the economic values debate, then we're doomed. Values and America have to be integrated into any strategy, but we shouldn't lead with our chin.

It is worth recalling that the powerful "putting people first" economic message for the 1992 Clinton campaign was not at all powerful until it incorporated a preamble: the government has failed the average person.[23] Voters needed to hear first the reassurance that Clinton shared their skepticism about government before they would listen to a call to action on the economy and health care, a call that they were desperate to heed. While voters have grown much more trusting of Democrats on a broad range of issues, including government spending and deficits, this period has different requirements, given what has happened to our country.

The challenge of this strategy is even greater if you assume that the solution lies as much in the character of the candidate as in the issue positions.

Libby. *Here's one thing. I think we've got the corporate piece as a springboard. It puts them on the defensive on their weakest link in their argument. And we've got to define ourselves as respectful of both family and religion, as well as accepting of America's sense of its own goodness. This is okay with me. But they've got a guy that people instinctively like. Their guy, as much as anything, emanates the values that they're espousing. He gives light and truth to what you're saying. And that's the piece we don't have in our story line.*

    Max. *So where the hell do we go to get that?*

Chapter 12

TOWARD A BOLD POLITICS:

The JFK Democrats

The five strategic options, with the possible exception of the Corporate Frame, are likely to leave intact the established voting patterns and issues of the Two Americas. Their purpose is not to blow up these structures but to get the most out of the current battle lines. Therefore, to varying degrees, they are status quo options. They are pragmatic and opportunistic about the current parity and look for adjustments, add-ons, or other ways to confound the Republicans. However, they are not status quo on the hopes for winning with bigger margins or more consistently. Any of these could raise Democratic prospects within the Two Americas.

The starting point is the focus on the agenda gap. This gap, as we have seen, is largest where the Democrats are already relatively strong or competitive, and thus gains here will likely reinforce existing patterns. There were some groups that were left out, such as the Country Folk in the Republican world, who were very concerned about the economy and Social Security. But the bigger problem is a strategic one. This is a decision to fight issue by issue, without establishing a framework that competes with that of the Republicans. Given the Republicans' current adeptness, this is likely to end up a tactical duel, and they have much bigger weapons. The Two Americas strategy essentially bets on the power of the postmodern demographic and cultural forces, much as the Republicans are betting on the cultural reaction. This is by definition a status quo option, but one with a happier ending for the Democrats than the status quo strategy pursued by the Republicans: as America becomes more diverse, better educated, and cosmopolitan, the Democrats become increasingly aligned with a diverse, global, and modern America.

The 100 Percent Über Dem strategy proposes that Democrats target and energize the loyalist voting blocs in the Democratic coalition, as the Republicans have done successfully on their side, to achieve a higher Democratic vote and turnout and thus give the Democrats at least a momentary leg up in the parity battle. Presumably, legitimated by the Republican efforts, the Democratic campaign would use issues, symbols, and organizations more effectively and with more zest. While this strategy might garner a higher vote from Union Families, it would essentially build more support in the loyalist world and grow one side of the Two Americas.

The reassurance-first strategy is very different, as it aims to reestablish the Democrats' credibility on the war on terrorism and homeland security, and on values and the family, rebuilding the trust and comfort level that allows voters to listen to Democrats on a not inconsiderable list of powerful issues, not least of which is restoring the economy's growth. This might tilt some groups into the loyalist world, like Vulnerable Women, and ironically win more support among Union Families that do not share the DLC view of global trade and other issues. More likely, the reassurance route would allow Democrats to become more competitive again with Country Folk, Married Blue Women, and Aging Male and Female Blues who have been put off on values and security, and get back to pre-Iraq and pre-impeachment approval levels with these groups. Again, the strategy could be very effective, though mainly allowing Democrats to win within the current Two Americas. Even in 1996, when Bill Clinton won with 53 percent of the simulated vote without Perot, the Democrats had shed a good portion of their middle-class vote.

The Corporate Frame adds new dimension and responds to an important dynamic in current thinking, though its principal advantage, unless much more broadly framed, is to help Democrats systematically reclaim the Middle America groups lost since 1992. If the strategy did this alone, the electoral balance would significantly tilt, assuming no unintended offsetting losses elsewhere and assuming Democrats could present this positioning in an expansive way. The last chapter raised many doubts on this point, but the potential is great. Given the strength of anticorporate sentiment, both in the contested world and among Country Folk, one has to take seriously the opportunity to shake up the current patterns.

Each of the strategies is plausible, some even compelling, and no doubt when worked together through a single narrative could move the Democrats into a very competitive position for 2004 and beyond. When we eventually look back to 2004, it would be surprising if Democrats did not head down one or a combination of these roads, any of which would constitute a rational decision for Democrats intent on driving the Bush conservatives from the White House. The postmodern forces, anticorporate sentiment, upward pressure among loyalist voters, and reassurance on patriotism and values are powerful strategic concepts that can shift the balance.

In the short term, probably none of these strategies fundamentally challenge the status quo of the Two Americas, even as they point toward potential Democratic electoral victories. Over the longer term, it is possible that social and cultural trends, a deeper identification with modern forces, effective governance, and tough-minded ways to marginalize the conservatives can win growing numbers of voters to the Democratic side of the divide. Democrats might themselves grow comfortable with the Two Americas as a strategy for establishing Democratic hegemony. Whether the Corporate Framework breaks new ground, draws new lines, and produces net gains all depend on the execution, which is harder than it seems. To be effective, the corporate framework has to inculcate values concerns that frequently clash with the instincts of the Democrats' more secular support; its gains in new territory have to come without losing old territory or dividing the Democrats. As E. E. Schattschneider points out, when you draw different lines, you change the coalition of forces, and the gains are hardly automatic.[1]

Staying within the Two Americas framework has serious risks that could leave the Democrats on the outside looking in. Democratic commitment to waging the war on terrorism and maintaining a strong defense, and reassurances on values and the family may never really get heard if terrorism is ongoing and America moves from war theater to war theater. If this is the case, the Democrats' sound issue positions and the Republicans' unpopular agenda never end up mattering. It is possible that the public consciousness is so shaped by 9/11 and the administration's determination to carry the war to successive battlefields that the country settles for a "wartime" leader. It is also possible that the various Democratic strategies clash with each other and exacerbate fractures in the Democratic world. Pro-trade, fiscally cautious Cosmopolitan voters and antitrade, pro–social insurance Union Families may wonder what holds them in the same coalition. It is possible that Democratic voters, watching the confident rule of the social conservatives, are demoralized and just cannot match the aspiration for higher and higher unity and turnout on the Republican side. At the same time, it is possible that the Republicans' linguistic tactics and issue pilfering, including a new drug benefit for seniors, limit the reaction against the conservative agenda and diminish Democratic support with the Golden Girls and Well-Educated Women. Perhaps Democrats continue to fight group by group, issue by issue, tactically, and just get outbid on issues like education and retirement.

And in the realm of things beyond human control, there could be a strong but short-lived economic recovery, and voters could decide to give the Republicans the benefit of the doubt. Maybe the reaction against postmodernism proves stronger than postmodernism itself, at least for a few more years. And maybe the Democrats nominate a clueless candidate for president, as has happened in the past, who just does not engage the issues raised here. In short, there are many ways for Democrats to falter, even if they take up a sensible strategic course, because the parity of the parties does not leave a lot of room for error.

But 2004 or 2008 offers a potentially much bigger moment for a much bigger election if the Democrats respond in a bold way to the opportunities that have come together in this period. Indeed, reflecting back on this half century that no party has tamed, this may be the moment for another bold party initiative to reclaim the times, to pursue hegemony. This must seem very odd, as Democrats hold on by their fingernails as a minority party in all branches of government. But this was the situation for the Republicans in 1980, when Reagan Revolutionaries took control of the Senate and White House and established beachheads on the Supreme Court, and gave voice to a new conservatism, enhanced by being at the center of power. Today Democrats stand at a nexus of forces and developments that could become a powerful political moment if they act boldly to bring down the whole conservative edifice and construct a new edifice of their own.

First is the lack of legitimacy and lack of mandate. A majority of Democrats and 40 percent of the country say that George W. Bush was not legitimately elected.[2] While this remains a powerful motivator for party activists, there is a parallel reality: the absence of a mandate and the lack of support for the Bush agenda of dismantling government and the social contract. That Republican policies are radically out of sync with the priorities and direction of the country must be seen as an opportunity for a putsch, allowing Democrats to organize and overturn those who use power illegitimately. The gap on issue after issue between the public and the powerful is an accumulating case for dispossessing the Republicans of power. The evidence before 9/11, both to the right and left, was that this Reaganesque edifice was in trouble, unable to stand on the legs of tax cuts and faith alone. This structure remains shaky and could be further weakened by their radical tax-cut, deregulatory, and antienvironment agenda. But right at the fault line is the growing contradiction between the Republican effort to reduce government—both to help their base supporters and to undermine Democrats—and the public's desire to use the government to address problems facing the country. This will come to a head before or after 2004, when the Republicans advance a risky change in Social Security.

The absence of a mandate and the utter lack of public support for their policies become relevant and gain poignancy because of more than two decades of growing income inequality and growing dissatisfaction with middle-class living standards and shrinking opportunities. Both the 1980s and 1990s brought dramatic rises in inequality and, for perhaps five years in the late nineties, most families worked more hours for largely stagnant incomes. In the Bush period, incomes fell 2.2 percent in 2001, and continued to decline through to the fall of 2003, about which middle-class voters express an increasing sense of grievance, particularly with rising health-care costs.[3] At the same time, the richest Americans, the top 400 earning over $87 million a year, recently got a 20 percent tax cut, an average savings of $8 million each. Corporate CEOs are reviled and symbolize the greed that characterizes our current period. At this moment, the Republicans are intent on unraveling what social insurance exists for the economically vulnerable and retirees, even in the face of growing insecurity.

All of this could become quite immediate and inescapable if voters begin to doubt the Republican course in managing foreign affairs and ensuring the country's security.

The Bush strategy is no doubt bold, pursuing Reagan ends, acting as if Republicans had a mandate from the country. But their colossal gamble is the Democrats' colossal opportunity.

By highlighting the gap between public wants and government action, Democrats have the chance, in light of 2000, to challenge not just the specifics of their policies but also the legitimacy of their acting without a mandate.

But the whole edifice can collapse if the Democrats use the moment to mount an assault not just on specific policies but on the entire Reagan project—the idea that tax cuts for the wealthy and enriching the few and promarket and corporate policies are really the best way to bring prosperity to the country as a whole. In light of the corporate scandals and the public revulsion with the greed and bad values of CEOs, is this not the time for a Bill Clinton who says, paraphrasing from 1992, "These policies have ushered in a gilded age of greed, selfishness, irresponsibility, excess and neglect. For decades but harder now each year, the forgotten middle class watches their economic interests ignored and their values run into the ground."[4]

Today, when voters are presented with a simple economic contrast, they favor the Democrats' economic critique over Bush's broad tax-cut policy by 15 points (56 to 41 percent) when prefaced with the assertion, "President Bush's only economic policy is tax cuts, mostly for the wealthy, and they haven't helped the economy or the middle class." The elemental strength in this minimally developed message is in the unfair tax advantages and the focus on the middle class and whole economy.

By joining the battle here, at the heart of Reaganism, the Democrats make it very difficult for the Republicans to move tactically to some other issue or program. They will have to defend Reaganism.

Because of the forces coming together and the Republican overreach, Democrats have the opportunity to pose a series of stark choices, building to a full Democratic alternative. That is why this is a crucial moment, a turning point.

Because the Republicans have overreached on behalf of corporate interests in an age of public revulsion against it, Democrats have the opportunity not just to attack but to become champions of the whole, by defending the public interest and its values. While Republicans advance tactically and politically toward a goal of 100 percent of their most loyal, the Democrats can advance strategically toward a goal of a 100 percent America where all can share in the country's bounty. The Democrats' passion is not for the top 1 percent, the top 400 who earned at least $87 million a year and tripled their income in the past decade and now see their taxes cut on average by $8.3 million, but for the more than 140 million citizens who work hard for their families' betterment but are squeezed economically.[5] The Democrats identify with the values of the whole, including responsibility and community, rather than greed and superindividualism. In practical terms, this means the Democrats can aspire again to reclaim the middle-class voters lost in 1968 and 1994.

I came to the realization about the new possibility for "opportunity" while listening to people from Ohio and North Carolina in a wholly different project respond to this question: "The Declaration of Independence says, 'All men are created equal.' What does that mean?" These voters, some without college degrees and some with, but none very poor or very rich, quickly moved beyond any hypocrisy of the original signatories and established some principles for our times. People are "equal before God" but only for an instant in life. A noncollege woman from Cleveland imagined two babies, "those two infants were equal the second they were born, but do they have an equal chance in life?" She answered her own question: "Not at all, which is extremely unfair."

They moved in each of the four focus group discussions, without

prompting, from the words "all men are created equal" to the word "opportunity" and a fairly expansive concept of "equal opportunity." Another Cleveland woman said, "We should all be entitled to the same thing. Just the necessities. Just being able to have a home or a job, equal opportunities." Another woman included the "ability to vote, to live here, to have a chance to get a good job, with a good schooling." In Charlotte, the college-educated women began with the same translation of the words—"Equal to me means equal opportunities"—and almost the same expansive concepts: "Everybody should have a fair chance to make it, to get an education. Some people accept the opportunity . . . but everybody should have that opportunity." "A fair shake," another woman added, "like [she] was saying, an equal opportunity, it doesn't matter what race, sex, or religion you are, you have basically equal opportunity . . . for employment, education, life, living." And another woman added on to the sentence "to be successful, to make it on your own." One blue-collar man from Charlotte reflected on the Declaration and said it means in America "you don't have a ruling class," which means, "everybody has an opportunity to . . . be the best they can be," to recall the aspiration of U.S. Army advertising: "Be all that you can be."

Across the groups people lamented that NBA basketball stars and corporate CEOs are superrich, while teachers and cancer researchers struggle: "That's not equal opportunity for me. That is misplaced values," a Charlotte woman concluded. In the real world, people who are intrinsically equal are blocked: "Nowadays, I think too many people feel like the deck is stacked against them because of business practices, forces outside. The whole world situation makes people feel like thing[s] aren't equal anymore, but they're not sure of how or why and what they can do about it."

Across the groups, there was a consensus that in America everyone is "entitled" to equal opportunity. Many ask, "But are they attainable to everyone?" and conclude no. Many others felt that "everybody has a chance to advance. And it's up to them [if they] take responsibility." For a noncollege Cleveland man, there is sufficient opportunity to make the result acceptable: "We all have the same right to opportunity, and we all observe the same thing, and we have the opportunity to reach those goals."

What I found most striking was that this conversation never broke down into a gripe session on race, quotas, or affirmative action. To be sure, some people see special advantages for minorities, but their view of the meaning of equality could evolve into an extended discussion of opportunity involving their own lives without being cramped by race. Some discussed history through perceptual lenses that recognized race and gender. In both Charlotte discussions people noted that the right existed if you were "not slaves": "I mean, race is what it was all about back then." The circle encompassed initially "the property owners, it was the rich," but expanded. It was presumptively men but is progressively encompassing women: "We're better than we were," one woman said, but they didn't expect to be equal. Now, one of the blue-collar men could note, matter-of-factly, "Everyone is created equally, but the opportunities are not equal to everyone. There's racial divides, class divides." Still, others, including these blue-collar men in Charlotte, saw expanding opportunities as part of what makes America exceptional:

> Well, I think that we can never create a perfect society and I think that we've made huge strides in improving the situation as far as racism, equal opportunity, and all of that, and I don't think we should lose sight of that. I think that things are much better today than they ever were, and it's the nature of democracy to include all.

> I just think it's a basic for the United States, I mean we are a true melting pot. It means it's part of the reason why we're as successful of a country as we are at this point.

"It's the basis for our country, and I don't think we would be where we are today if it hadn't provided equal opportunity to everybody," one man concluded, and then he offered an expansive view of opportunity and America:

"People had the freedom to go and do things as they see fit and it's made our country stronger."

What this narrative says is that America has matured over this half century and now can be fully part of a new aspiration for opportunity that encompasses both our diversity and the broad desire of people to have a chance at a better life. It may have taken fifty years, but opportunity has reemerged full of possibility.

In the postcards from Tampa Blue, Heartland Iowa, and Eastside Tech, the people reflected the crisis and spirit of unity following 9/11, including an increased confidence in government's capacity to address the country's broad challenges. They wrote of community, where programs "benefit the entire population" and all citizens are equal and "given the same benefits." The country needs to come "together" and act for "the needs of the whole." This is an aspiration that will be important to Democratic thinking in this period.

The public's embrace of "opportunity" reminds us that the Democratic Party once claimed the concept for itself, before the battle for civil rights defined the parties in racial terms and narrowed most Americans' definition of opportunity to mean racial equality. When the Clinton administration walked away from the middle class after 1992, it too contributed to the contraction of the meaning of opportunity, at least as a party project. It was reflected partially but concretely in the 1994 congressional defeat, but also in 1998 and 2000, as the Democratic coalition lost many of its working-class and noncollege supporters while contested blue-collar voters, like the Married and Aging Blues and Country Folk, tilted Republican.

May 12, 2003
Dear Mr. President,

Please help all Americans to have a brighter future. Treat everyone equal. Think that everyone is the same and make sure we are all given the same benefits. You did a great thing when we went to war and after 9-11 you help hold our country together.
Rachele
Heartland

April 14, 2003
President Bush,

Being the loudest or strongest doesn't make you right. The needs of the whole - whether that means all nations of the world or the people of this country - are more important than the desires of the few - USA or the most wealthy Americans
Adam
Eastside Tech

May 14, 2003
Dear President Bush,

Think of the American people and develop real programs that benefit the entire population: i.e. universal healthcare, responsible foreign policy, energy independence, and economic stimulus. Act as a global partner with all other nations. Stop you imperialist and arrogant behavior to others.
Chas
Eastside Tech

But the Opportunity Democrats, starting with John Kennedy, advanced a vision of America where we have an obligation to ensure that all share in our country's great bounty, from the poorest to the middle class. The gap between reality and the ideal of opportunity creates an unending sense of purpose for Democrats, accepted by presidents from Johnson to Clinton. Kennedy expressed a confidence in—indeed, brimming optimism about— our capacity to face the new challenges, particularly our changing economy, using government as the instrument of our empowerment. Kennedy came to place equal rights at the center of his political project, an inspired move then but even more so today. An expansive commitment to equal rights is now congruent with an expansive view of opportunity, given the deepening norms about rights and tolerance and the growing importance of America as a diverse country. Finally, Kennedy insisted that America be militarily unassailable so that it could bring peace but also so that the countries of the world would look to America not as simply exceptional in arms but as exceptional in opportunity. The character of our country was essential to the character of our foreign policy.

This is a moment for JFK Democrats or Opportunity Democrats advocating a 100 percent America where all share in America's bounty. The project poses the choice between a country that works for the few and one that creates opportunity for all. That choice subsumes the populist critique of excessive corporate influence into a broader statement about special interests and the interests of the nation.

But JFK Democrats take on other big battles in the context of contending worldviews. These Opportunity Democrats have an instinctive faith in the ability of government to act as an instrument of community—to address inequality, raise education levels and income, and help families manage work, maintain their health, and gain a secure retirement. That means they will challenge directly the unrelenting conservative attack on government and its capacity to act for community.

As with Kennedy, citizenship brought opportunity but also the obligation to contribute to America keeping its promise. That was the call to Peace Corps and Vista, as volunteers allowed us to realize our ideals. That allows Democrats to reclaim responsibility, as a commonsense value for a country that works for all and an elemental critique of those who act irresponsibly and make it harder for America to succeed.

Finally, JFK Democrats, open and engaged in the world, will be progressive and idealistic about America itself, rather than simply idealistic about promoting free societies abroad. Conservative critic David Brooks, writing after the defeat of the Iraqi regime, wondered what lessons the nervous majority who rallied to the president would draw. To get at it, he constructed an imaginary twenty-year-old, "Joey Tabula-Rasa," who is attracted to the democratic interventionists because they speak of "good and evil," and while they might overreach, "he gives them credit for their idealism, their hope, their grand vision." Perhaps confounding old categories, it is the Republicans who now look "progressive."[6] But that is a worldview that invites and creates the potential for a powerful Democratic alternative where Democrats, progressives, and idealists join the battle for a 100 percent America. Like Kennedy, the United States seeks to lead the world, but its power is greatly multiplied by the admiration of people all across the world for our historic role in promoting freedom. In this context, it is the Democrats who are the progressive and idealistic force that can attract the young people to the project of our times.

The strategy is bold because it seeks an epic battle between the Reagan Revolutionary view of the world and the Democrats' Opportunity vision— and because it represents a radical break for the Democrats. The battle could easily just slide into the next round of fighting between two tired worldviews, battered by a half century of unfinished war. While the Republicans would prefer to battle Democrats group to group and issue by issue at places of their choosing, they will fight for Reaganism if challenged. In the end, they believe that it is a successful political model that can win over the country. It is a radical break for the Democrats because they have not challenged Reaganism directly and in principle since 1992, have never addressed the challenge of opportunity in an age of growing inequality, have rarely appealed so broadly outside the established loyalist walls, and have not had the confidence to return to the original Opportunity Democrats without being "reformed."

> **Max.** *So we are all JFK Democrats now.*
>
> **Biggs.** *I like it. I've done campaigns where you just keep adding good ideas to a list. The longer the list, the harder it is. I prefer to funnel everything through the one you're going to go with. It's just my overall preference. It's much easier to communicate with people with one big story line. Here, we're proposing a view of a 100 percent America, and everything fits into that view.*
>
> **Max.** *In our 100 percent America, where all have the opportunity to succeed, corporate interests do not take precedence over the interests of our children or over the interests of our country.*
>
> **Wolf.** *As opposed to being for the little people, we now become for the country.*
>
> **Biggs.** *We have to tell people we want to lead America into a new era and offer a new kind of patriotism. People before us created a great country where everybody contributed and everyone had the chance to suc-*

ceed, not a country that's overrun by corporate lobbyists, but a country with a special sense of destiny. The Republicans have an unthinking reflex to align with the 1 percent or with corporate power, but not with the country and what this country is about.

Wolf. I think we ought to give Bush a little credit because he's actually crystallized the debate. He lost by 500,000 votes, and he's governed like he had a huge mandate. And they have a fundamental philosophy, they think we ought to tax work and not wealth. They believe that unbridled corporatism is the best thing for the country. That's the choice.

Max. So why aren't we the patriotic party? I'll answer my own question. We are! That's what it means to stand up for a 100 percent America.

Biggs. And that is the answer to values. When you just talk about it, you run the risk of looking tactical and insincere. But here we elevate things by defining what it means to be patriotic. Patriotic is believing in a 100 percent America, taking things through that same funnel. There is absolutely nothing patriotic about succumbing to powerful interests at every juncture. I reject that definition of patriotism. Certainly we can all stand up, put our hands over our hearts, and sing the anthem, and we can do that as well as anybody, but in the real America, the real country that we want to build, it is not patriotic to run up $44 trillion in debt or leave 44 million people without health insurance.

Wolf. That's Biggs's fundamental point—if you allow private interests to overwhelm the public interest, that's not patriotism. Working to make America admired to the world, that's patriotism.

Strategy Over Tactics

Tactics favor the Republicans in this period since their strategy is to preserve and strengthen the coalitional possibilities in the Two Americas—first by pushing toward 100 percent among their loyalists, then winning more than their fair share of the contested groups, and finally disrupting some Democratic groups with provocative initiatives. If the Democrats want to wage a bold challenge, not just to bring down the Bush presidency in the context of parity but to get voters to turn to a compelling alternative for the times, then all steps are strategic. All political moves need to be evaluated by whether they contribute to the story line leading to Opportunity Democrats.

One could parry the Republican moves, and Democrats will certainly seek to solidify their support with groups under attack, such as Hispanics, seniors, suburban women, and members of industrial unions.

But to tarry would be a trap.

It will be hard not to battle for seniors, particularly the Golden Girls. While many of the Republican initiatives are symbolic, in the case of seniors, their guns are loaded with real money, in particular, prescription drug coverage. In this approach, the Republicans are acting much as Eisenhower and Nixon did in repeatedly raising Social Security benefits and, in the process, continuing to get around 60 percent of the senior vote. This follows the example of Christian Democratic and conservative parties in Europe that always kept the initiative and stayed ahead of the social democrats by raising state pensions particularly before elections.[7] And while the Republicans' long-standing majority with seniors gave way at the end of the Reagan era, pensioners have continued to vote conservative across Europe.

With the F-You Old Men already strongly Republican, the hope now is to win over the Golden Girls who gave Gore the edge in 2000 and supported the congressional Republicans in 2002. But perhaps these women, decidedly conservative on family and marriage issues, might now have other material reasons to vote Republican.

The Democrats will no doubt challenge the scale of the effort, which may soon look like a poor substitute for the kind of security Medicare traditionally gave, particularly if drug costs continue to rise. The Democrats will challenge the shift to private insurers and, more important, ask why the government explicitly rules out action to hold down prescription drug prices. In the end, Democrats will ask, "Whom do you really trust to fund fully such government insurance and to address prices?" It is possible that this tactic becomes too sour to the Republicans' conservative tastes over time.

But every minute the Democrats spend rejoining leaves them trapped in tactics, seeking to win a battle to interpret policy, when the Republican arguments will be magnified by tens of millions of dollars of corporate advertising money. In 2002, after the infusion of nearly $27 million from the pharmaceutical industry, 43 percent of voters concluded that "both the Republican and Democratic candidates supported a prescription drug benefit for seniors."[8]

The battle for seniors is illustrative of the need to trump tactics with strategy. The choice before the voters is not competing approaches on prescription drugs but competing views of America. Democrats must preach opportunity for all, starting with universal education but advancing a modern social contract, with social support appropriate to this new age. Republicans believe that the public interest is best served when government gets out of the way and leaves outcomes to the market.

The political advisers for the prospective Democratic nominee, though starting from diverse perspectives, addressed the prescription drug issue and raised it to the level of strategy in the context of 100 percent America.

> **Max.** *What we need to do, over and over again, is ask the question, Why won't they control the prices?*
>
> **Wolf.** *You know why. They think if they enrich the drug companies they enrich America.*
>
> **Judge.** *And by elevating the issue, we take it beyond seniors or any particular group or even any program. This is about their whole view of America. They can't address rising health-care costs, the biggest single factor undermining middle-class living standards, because they are always looking out for a few big interests instead of the country.*
>
> **Biggs.** *There is nothing patriotic about rolling over for pharmaceutical companies when the generation that fought to preserve our freedom now needs us to fight for them.*

Thus, the Democratic plan for 2004, 2006, and 2008 does not engage group by group, though the battles may take place there. This is the difference between tactics and strategy. It is also the difference between trying to amend the Two Americas and fundamentally changing it.

If the Democrats were to adopt the Corporate Frame, which is certainly a possibility in the shorter term, that effort would include a new set of targets: the Country Folk, Union Families, and Aging Blue Men and Women. The Democrats would use the anticorporate vehicle to close the cultural distance evident in the current battle for the Two Americas. The goal is to get access to groups now foreclosed by the dominant cultural division.

But in a battle to substitute the 100 percent America view of the world for the Reagan view of the world, you are drawing the line in a new way

STRATEGY
OVER TACTICS
TARGET GROUPS - TURN THE DIAL
VALUES AND PATRIOTISM
GREED VS. RESPONSIBILITY
SPECIAL INTERESTS VS. AMERICA
CEOS AND THE MIDDLE CLASS
EXPOSE THE REPUBLICAN LOYALIST
    STRATEGY - POLARIZATION
EXPOSE THE AGENDA GAP
EXPOSE BUSH
ELEVATE DOUBTS ON ECONOMY
ELEVATE DOUBTS ON FOREIGN AFFAIRS
REFORMIST -
    ANTIESTABLISHMENT POLITICS
ADDRESS BIG PROBLEMS -
    NOT PROTECTING OLD PROGRAMS

and not trying to add on groups to the existing coalition. If you are successful in creating a new big choice, the line moves, issues change, groups shift, some come into view that were not previously visible when the line traveled down the cultural divide. By making this strategic change, Democrats could find themselves reentering a dialogue with old Perot voters, who now seemed deeply ensconced in the Republican camp. The Opportunity Democrats may be turning the clock back to 1992 or even 1964. Country Folk and Aging Blues—indeed, Iowa and Missouri—could be the heart of 100 percent America instead of just tactical opportunities. But you get to those groups by drawing different lines, not by looking more intently at the current array of groups.

To draw a new line, Democrats need to focus on any issue or join any battle that makes it more likely that voters will listen to the story of the Opportunity Democrats.

VALUES AND PATRIOTISM Opportunity Democrats want a discussion about the values to be honored and which values are under siege. They want a discussion about America and what it means to advance the nation, to be patriotic. Values, rather than simply a reassurance tactic to get mileage out of the old story, are now a natural and important part of the narrative. Democrats want to talk about the choice between responsibility and greed, between working for special interests and working for the whole country. This choice allows Democrats to talk about their values and their love of country. There is no substitute for Democrats being comfortable with faith and the elemental idea that people want children to learn right from wrong and the family to be strong enough to protect and nurture them. But responsibility is closely linked to personal responsibility, which means being accountable, thinking of others and community, not just oneself. It includes self-restraint over excess. In the context of 100 percent America, the Democrats are aligned with responsibility and averse to the greed that threatens it. Responsibility is virtually a condition of citizenship in a 100 percent America.

CEOs AND MIDDLE-CLASS SYMBOLS   CEOs and the middle class are the powerful symbols that expose the choice and reveal the values underlying the alternative directions for the country.[9] Accordingly, Democrats will want to reinforce the sensibilities of the Country Folk in Heartland Iowa who blurted out, "money," "greed," and "Enron" when they heard the words "big corporations"—the companies that "try and run the little guy out." They will want to be attentive as well to the sensibilities of the Aging Male Blues in Tampa Blue who felt the president "needs to hit the corporate America" that ships jobs overseas and "takes away the private pensions." In that, the Democrats regret the "greed" that has offended the sensibilities of a financially squeezed middle class.

EXPOSING THE LOYALIST STRATEGY   Shining the spotlight brightly on the Republicans' 100 percent loyalist strategy—the issues, rhetoric, and buy-offs for the Republican coalition base groups—is critical if voters are to see the main choice between Reaganism and a 100 percent America. And getting past the rhetoric of compassion, diversity, and love of the environment is doubly important—not just to throw a monkey wrench into the Republican machine but to give greater clarity to the big choice. By exposing the base strategy in the Republicans' America, Democrats are likely to do better in their base in their own America, with higher turnout of cosmopolitan, minority, and union voters.

EXPOSING THE AGENDA GAP   Opportunity Democrats will also need to shine the spotlight on the immense gap between the big issues the citizenry wants to address and the expansive agenda of this revived Reagan

Revolution. This may be the lever that brings about the sudden collapse of Republican governance. Bush is held up by the war against terrorism and the need to provide security and also by faith and support of family, buttressed by seeming good intentions in surprising areas. But as we know from the earlier discussion, this Rovian-Reaganist strategy falters when security is not center stage. The public has no interest in its small government, antiregulation, high deficit, and high tax-cut regime. The public waits for its agenda on health care, the economy and middle-class incomes, family security, education, limiting corporate influence, and more. As the public begins to understand what is being addressed and what is not, the country may hit a tipping point.

There is a danger that a simplistic attack on the agenda gap could leave Democrats seemingly against trying any new solutions, while protecting old approaches, even in the face of new challenges. That diminishes as a potential problem if Democrats are advancing new ideas for the future, which JFK Democrats will certainly be doing.

EXPOSING BUSH   The spotlight on the 1 percent and neglect of the 100, on the Republican base strategy, on what Bush does and not just what he says, and on the agenda gap with the public may cumulatively also produce a pull-back from Bush himself—the Reaganesque leader, honest and straightforward, sharing the values of ordinary folks, passionate for America. Honesty was Reagan's formula to associate himself with the people and the country, but Bush could find support eroded on both ends.

EXPOSING THE ECONOMY   The public is much more likely to hit the tipping point when it grows more doubtful about the economic course of the country. In the summer of 2003, voters had a lot of causes for concern: three million had lost their jobs since the presidential election; median income had fallen through four successive quarters; business pessimism discouraged investment; 401(k)s had lost significant value and most corporate pension funds were underfunded.[10] A majority of the public (57 percent) was already indicating that it wanted to go in a "significantly different" economic direction, compared to just 38 percent who wanted to "continue" in the direction Bush was headed.[11] The public believed strongly that the deficits were hurting the economy and by a wide margin wanted to go in a significantly different direction here as well (53 to 36 percent).[12] While robust growth could change the course of things, the fundamental bet of the Opportunity Democrats is on low-income growth for the great majority of the country, increasing inequality, rising health-care and benefits costs, cuts in middle-class public services, and a deepening middle-class squeeze. This cluster of issues raises doubts about the current administration but concentrates the doubts in areas that lead voters to a vision of a 100 percent America.

In this, the Democrats may follow the lead of a voter in Eastside Tech who wrote on his postcard to the Democratic nominee: "It's the economy, stupid—Learn It, Live It, Love It." If he had actually worked in the "war room," he would also have noted the follow-up admonition, "Don't forget health care," which may end up the right combination for this period.

DOUBTS ON FOREIGN POLICY   Democrats will have to raise fundamental doubts not about the need to fight the war on terrorism but whether the Bush foreign policy makes that more difficult and costly. The unilateralist assertion of America's interests is rooted in the Reagan view of America and the world. Because of 9/11, the Republicans have been able to give renewed life to unilateralism, even if other key concepts were faltering politically. The administration has demonstrated its ability to manage international events to further its political ends at home, but sometimes reality has a way of breaking through. Within two months of the close of the Iraq war, 41 percent of the country was already saying, "The war in Iraq was not worth the cost of U.S. lives and dollars." Moreover, the public is growing quickly doubtful about the unilateralist, Reagan style. In midsummer, a majority of 52 percent emerged in the country saying, "America's security depends on building strong ties with other nations," with only 39 percent saying, "America's security depends on its own military strength." That represents a significant growth of internationalist sentiment in reaction to Iraq.[13]

The president's instincts, as well as his policy in the war on terrorism, are unilateralist. When first assessing the likelihood of other countries joining the war against Afghanistan, Bush said to Bob Woodward, "We may be the only ones left." And then Bush added, "That's okay with me. We are America." At the end of the conflict, he came to believe that international coalitions and international bodies were not sufficient for confronting rogue states. With the successful use of American power, you create a "slipstream into which reluctant nationals and leaders can get behind" our efforts.[14]

These instincts and policies, which are so central to the Reagan vision and coalition, are already producing dramatic results in the world. With the exception of Israel and Great Britain, positive views of America have dropped sharply almost everywhere. For close allies, like Canada, Spain, Italy, and South Korea, positive responses are down around 10 points since the summer of 2002, growing to a 20-point fall in France and Brazil and with the bottom falling out in Russia, Morocco, Indonesia, Turkey, and

Jordan. In most countries surveyed across the globe, less than half the public has a favorable view of America, dropping to 27 percent in Morocco, about 15 percent in Indonesia, Turkey, and Pakistan, and 1 percent in Jordan. Feelings about George W. Bush are much harsher—about two to one negative across all the countries surveyed.[15]

The crash of perceptions of America has consequences both for America as a leader and for America's ability to advance its interests. For example, the world is divided, 46 to 49 percent, on whether "America is a beacon of hope and opportunity." Large majorities in key countries, like Brazil, France, Indonesia, Jordan, South Korea, and Russia, say America is "not a force for good in the world."[16] When it comes to concrete relationships based on threats and common interests, amazingly, more people in the world say the United States is "a danger to world peace and stability" than say Iran is, by 49 to 36 percent—including Brazil and Indonesia, two of the most populous countries and dominant in their regions. Concretely, large majorities of the public and most of our traditional NATO allies want a more independent relationship with the United States rather than to remain close. This includes France (76 percent), Turkey (62 percent), Spain (62 percent), Italy (61 percent), and Germany (57 percent).[17] Without a perception of shared interests or goals or at least a grudging respect for America's intentions, there is little inducement to align with America—at least for the public. We now know that governments often go back and forth on how much they distance themselves from the United States, as evident in Germany and South Korea. Italy, Turkey, and India, close allies of the United States, could not provide key support before, during, and after the war because of overwhelming public opposition to U.S. policy.

In the United States, the public understands the global change. Just before the war in Iraq, 55 percent thought America was less respected by people in other countries, while a mere 8 percent said more respected. And they believe that has consequences, as 82 percent say such respect is very or somewhat important to our national security.[18] These views, dismissed by the new neoconservative thinking as part of the failed internationalist view of the world, gain support with many critical foreign policy analysts. They see America now acting in ways that set in motion "countervailing trends . . . contrary to our interests," that delegitimate "American power," and deny us the use of international institutions that have conventionally advanced our interests.[19] In this light, there is already evidence that the public is pulling back from Bush's strongest competence, foreign affairs. In July 2003, three months after Iraq, just 47 percent wanted to continue with Bush's foreign policy, while an equal number, 46 percent, wanted the country to go in a "significantly different direction."[20] Indeed, after the war, by almost two to one according to public polls, the public said the United States should bring in the United Nations to manage things rather than have the United States "manage things in Iraq on its own for the time being." By more than three to one, the public said the United Nations should "have the lead responsibility for setting up a new government in Iraq."[21] The declining standing of the UN is, for the revived Reagan Revolutionaries, a measure of their success, but is highlighted here simply to underscore the point that the public is in a more complicated state of mind.

Democrats will have to show a seriousness of purpose about waging the war on terrorism, even as they elevate existing doubts about the current course. But there is good reason to believe that Democrats will want this debate.

REFORMIST POLITICS   Opportunity Democrats will have to be reformist and antiestablishment if they are to be heard on the central choice, whether posed narrowly in the corporate framework or broadly: the 1 percent America versus the 100 percent opportunity America. Democrats, very much a part of the special interest politics of Washington, will not be heard or prove compelling or really be able to draw a new line unless they represent change and a genuine force against established ways of doing things.

ADDRESSING SERIOUS ISSUES   No party can dominate the times unless it is seen to be addressing the serious problems facing the country. While the Republican agenda may be out of sync with the public's, the same is not true of their seeming willingness to address big problems. This was first evident in the Gore-Bush election, when Gore actually trailed Bush, 41 to 43 percent, on which candidate would do a better job addressing the country's problems. While the public was not enamored of Bush's proposals to divert Social Security funds into private savings accounts, at least he was trying to fix something that was perceived to be in trouble in the future.[22] The same is true during his presidency. When voters were asked in 2002 whether the Democrats or Republicans are better on tackling the country's domestic problems, the public chose the Democrats by only three points. Some of this has to do with the big terrorist threat, but the Republicans at least look like they are willing to bring change and reform to education and even Medicare. Tackling problems diminishes the threat of the "third rail," even as Democrats run election after election on protecting Social Security or the "lock box," popular and important positions but not ones that put Democrats in the middle of the challenges central to this book.

The gap between the public's agenda and the Reagan agenda becomes

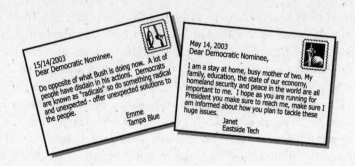

15/14/2003
Dear Democratic Nominee,

Do opposite of what Bush is doing now. A lot of people have disdain in his actions. Democrats are known as "radicals" so do something radical and unexpected - offer unexpected solutions to the people.

Emme
Tampa Blue

May 14, 2003
Dear Democratic Nominee,

I am a stay at home, busy mother of two. My family, education, the state of our economy, homeland security and peace in the world are all important to me. I hope as you are running for President you make sure to reach me, make sure I am informed about how you plan to tackle these huge issues.

Janet
Eastside Tech

explosive only if Democrats are tackling "huge issues" and, as indicated in the voter postcards to the nominees, only if they are offering "unexpected solutions." What is the point of being Opportunity Democrats in the John Kennedy mold if you are not optimistic about the capacity of the country to use government to address problems? And what is the point of being a JFK Democrat if the solutions are not new and inventive? Kennedy remains among the three most popular U.S. presidents because he brings to mind a youthful energy, optimism, and big aspirations for the country, from landing a man on the moon to making peace for the world.[23] The Democrats need a problem-solving agenda that makes them the indispensable party, given the challenges facing the country.

While this book cannot become a party platform, it is important to provide examples of policies consistent with the framework of the JFK Opportunity Democrats. To this end, we conducted an informal survey of progressive think tanks and policy analysts, looking for bold and innovative policy ideas.[24] Because the policy agenda is constructed to advance the idea of a 100 percent America, it cannot be fully congruent with the policy priorities of the Democrats' most important support groups. How could it be? This bold initiative is not a Rove strategy of rewarding the base and stealing some groups. If this agenda successfully advances the strategy, it should create some discomfort; otherwise it fails the test of discontinuity and boldness. This project will try to rebuild the social contract, but in light of the new, unaddressed challenges, not the old ones.

The political advisers joined the task of building an agenda.

Judge. *So our criteria are pretty clear by now. The election has to be about something real, policies that are serious and address real problems. There has to be a point to all this that people can see in their lives.*

Wolf. *Any policy on this list needs to be fresh, new, interesting, inventive. Enough defending the past, defending what's in place. These policies have to show a different future.*

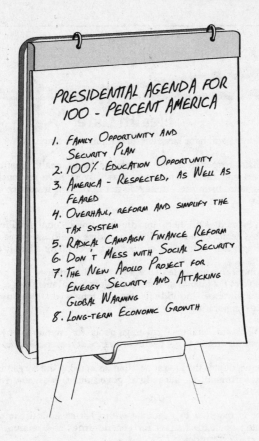

PRESIDENTIAL AGENDA FOR
100 - PERCENT AMERICA

1. FAMILY OPPORTUNITY AND
   SECURITY PLAN
2. 100% EDUCATION OPPORTUNITY
3. AMERICA - RESPECTED, AS WELL AS
   FEARED
4. OVERHAUL, REFORM AND SIMPLIFY THE
   TAX SYSTEM
5. RADICAL CAMPAIGN FINANCE REFORM
6. DON'T MESS WITH SOCIAL SECURITY
7. THE NEW APOLLO PROJECT FOR
   ENERGY SECURITY AND ATTACKING
   GLOBAL WARMING
8. LONG-TERM ECONOMIC GROWTH

Judge. *If these policies are real, they will show our values.*

Max. *If we are JFK Democrats, we need to show a government able to do new things.*

Libby. *And skepticism about government at the same time.*

Biggs. *At least some of them better be surprising, which means unpopular with some of our interest groups.*

Judge. *Every policy must underline the difference between our direction and theirs.*

1. FAMILY OPPORTUNITY AND SECURITY PLAN[25]

Wolf. *What I like about it is that it is absolutely huge, a break with the past, but really gets to the future. It is a new way to come at the problem.*

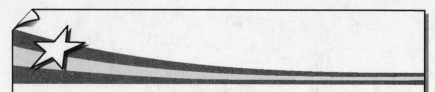

Health Care

- All Americans will have basic health insurance coverage.

- Individuals responsible for acquiring basic health insurance for themselves and their family—much as drivers have responsibility for acquiring auto insurance—if they do not have basic insurance from their employer.

- The government will help middle-and low-income families with a refundable health-care tax credit to subsidize health insurance coverage, on a sliding scale, for families earning up to $50,000 for a family of four.

- Every American guaranteed access to health insurance at a group rate, comparable to the guarantee federal employees and members of Congress have to insurance. Individuals are no longer on their own facing insurance companies.

- States will create "universal coverage pools" for anyone to buy coverage and allow individuals to get health insurance at reasonable rates.

- The state negotiates the lowest possible rates, using the bargaining power of the government, as the federal government does now for federal employees.

- The state is required to negotiate with pharmaceutical companies for lower rates, open the market for generic drugs and reimported brand drugs from G7 countries.

- Maintain the existing employer contribution for health care coverage and an added requirement for higher wages, if coverage is reduced.

- New federal insurance policy for long-term care.

- Maintain Medicare; also Medicaid as an option for the poor and lowest income.

Some of our people will hate it. It uses government to get universal support and expands the social insurance available to families. It is more but less. It centers on the family, supporting all families, but requires greater responsibility. It is flexible, fits the way people work, but is also good for employers, makes America more competitive. It is a big offer.

Libby. *The center of the Family Opportunity and Security Plan focuses benefits on individuals and families. That should be our philosophy, break the automatic link with employment.*

In the current period, it is impossible to imagine a vision of 100 percent America that does not put health care as the central task. In tackling this problem, the Democrats take on one of the biggest uncertainties for families, where corporate influence has left the individual exposed to the market on price and security. The Democrats' goal in this area is straightforward: universal coverage and constrained prices. By tackling this terrain, the entire battle is recast, with Democrats not having to outbid the Republicans on insuring children or on covering prescription drugs for seniors. And the Democrats are now competing for voters of all ages on health care, particularly middle-class families.

What is new is the individual mandate and the guaranteed access to negotiated affordable coverage, but it is built on the current system of employer-funded and private insurance. There is no "government-run health insurance" for the Republicans to kick around. Union employees can and will continue to negotiate coverage and burden sharing. But the plan greatly expands people's ability to get affordable coverage while expanding individual responsibility. The general direction of the proposal is informed by the debate about the provision of social insurance for families in the developed countries. The United States stands out not just in the lack of provision for families but also in the dependence on the employment contract. Looking ahead, Karen Kornbluh writes in *The Atlantic's* special issue on "The Real State of the Union," people are much more likely to achieve dependable insurance if you break the link to employment. This is particularly true today when so many are self-employed or work in small businesses, when employers are pushing down their own insurance contributions, and when parents are looking for ways to work more flexibly.[26]

The ideas reflect the public's desire to make major reforms but not to radically transform the health-care system. The public supports almost any government initiative that addresses some aspect of the health-care crisis and moves the country toward universality and 100 percent opportunity America. A nearly unanimous country (84 percent) would expand the current program for low-income children's health insurance "to provide coverage for people without health insurance"; three-quarters favor an employer mandate "requiring business to offer private health insurance for their employees"; and in line with the public's openness to action of some kind, three-quarters favor "offering uninsured Americans income tax deductions, tax credits, or other financial assistance to help them purchase private health insurance on their own."[27]

Family Policy

- Right of all parents to 12 weeks of family and medical leave to care for newborn.

- A new family-leave fund to cover 75 percent of wages or salary up to a maximum of $750 a week.

- A fully refundable child tax credit of $1,500 per child (declining after two) in recognition of the family's role in raising children successfully.

Max. The attraction is the social contract—parents trying to be responsible and society saying we value your contribution.

Wolf. But again we establish the social contract with the family and get the employer out of the way.

Judge. If we keep this up, business may be with us.

To get serious about supporting the family and parenting, the Democrats will have to revisit family and medical leave, but now it will have to be paid and readily available to all families. This is a big statement by JFK Democrats about the family and America.

The first act of the Democratic Congress under President Clinton was the passage of the Family and Medical Leave Act, and Bob Dole paid a big price for his opposition come the 1996 presidential election. But it was in reality a small step, mostly a symbolic right, an unaffordable leave for many who were eligible and not available for many low-wage employees working in smaller companies. A central plank in Theda Skocpol's thinking about building a partnership with American families is recognizing the central social contribution of parents. The starting point is family and medical leave, which is valuable support for new parents and perhaps a catalyst for broader efforts to fashion "a more family-friendly economy and society."[28]

On child care, Democrats will need to be as flexible as parents must be to maneuver the challenges of working and raising a family. The Democrats should be ready to recommend serious new federal standards and training, vouchers, and greater encouragement to use church facilities, where so many parents feel more comfortable leaving their children. It is hard not to forget those women in Tampa Blue who depend on the church day-care and after-school programs to get through their day. Why shouldn't this be a Democratic idea? The federal government already uses extensively the Catholic Charities, Salvation Army, and other faith-based institutions to deliver a diverse range of social services. Rather than viewing these as a grudging add-on to government programs, Democrats should embrace them as a way to relate to families in the real world.[29]

2. 100 PERCENT EDUCATION OPPORTUNITY

Max. The one thing we agree on, more than anything else, is that the Democrats never again give up on education and allow the country to think Republicans are more devoted to it. If our commitment is to 100 percent opportunity in education, then our job is never done, just as the parents' job is never done.

Libby. We can make progress, but we must be vigilant year after year, expanding opportunity so every kid has the best shot possible.

The plan starts with a bold new position on education: universal access to college and post–high school skill training. This is an area where the Republicans are reducing the federal role, but Democrats want to achieve a new relevance with the Young and the Restless and with middle-class families generally. Universal access to college is a big offer central to our vision of opportunity. It is also a big middle-class tax cut.

Rising college costs are a significant piece of the middle-class squeeze, as more and more families seek to provide their children with a college education. In 2002, for example, college costs rose 10 percent, while college assistance under the HOPE Scholarships did not rise. At the same time, the federal government is cutting funding to universities by reducing what is deductible for the purpose of calculating scholarship and loan eligibility. The consequence is a rising middle-class financial burden for a college education and a sense of opportunity blocked.[30]

The other area for potential social payoff and for innovation is in early childhood and school readiness where problems contribute fundamentally to the growing inequality and limiting of future opportunities. Middle- and upper-income children come to school with a vocabulary of 20,000 to 30,000 words, while lower-income kids come with 5,000 to 6,000.[31] At the

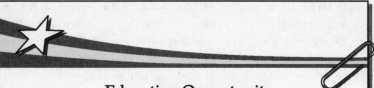

Education Opportunity

- The Universal Access to College Tax Credit. This is a refundable tax credit sufficient to cover the full cost of tuition and fees at public colleges and universities and can be used for all post-high school skill training.

- While the country agrees to this great expansion of opportunity, it also asks a great expansion of responsibility—requiring 40 hours of service a year for those taking the tax credit.

- Reduce the maximum class size in elementary schools across America to 20 students, with federal assistance to aid the schools with related increased costs. The goal is a more universal quality-teaching environment.

- 250,000 additional well-trained teachers, with special incentives for math and science teachers.

- 100 percent of students arrive at kindergarten ready for school success, including universal access of three-and four-year-olds to preschool, greatly expanded Head Start, particularly for early years, and greatly increased efforts on maternal health and early care for infants and toddlers.

same time, children arriving at school with learning and social development problems produce high long-term costs for the schools as well as society. Investments in getting children prepared for schools pay a return of $4 to $7 on every dollar spent.[32] Senior members and staff of the Minneapolis Federal Reserve argue that these investments should be considered "economic development," as they produce a greater return than the more traditional economic development projects, supported by cities and states.[33]

American Foreign Policy

- Support use of force and maintaining U.S. military power beyond challenge.

- Expand the numbers in the U.S. military to meet military and peacekeeping obligations and ~~and~~ ensure morale and readiness.

- Strong U.S. leadership in our many alliances and use of international organizations, including NATO and the United Nations, to fight the war on terrorism.

- Explicit recognition that the go-it-alone approach *is* costly and ineffective and hurts America's standing in the world and thus our security.

- Reprioritize nuclear nonproliferation.

- Full mobilization to upgrade America's homeland defenses—including securing borders and ports, aiding first responders, and funding city and state efforts. The Rudman plan would cost an estimated $25 billion a year.

- A JFK-inspired American foreign policy—an America respected and strong.

3. AMERICA RESPECTED AS WELL AS FEARED

Biggs. *I'm beginning to think that this big, big problem is going to turn out to be a big, big opportunity. We want this issue. Let's talk about America and the world.*

Wolf. *You're right. We win the security issue when people feel we* *want to talk about it. We're not shuffling and looking at our feet. Give me that pitch.*

Biggs. *We're forward looking, leading, not defending and protecting.*

Libby. *We look at the world self-confident and eager to talk about America's virtues. Opportunity Democrats. George Bush sees a world full of terror and threats and fears. To be honest, it's not very Reaganesque. Where's the optimism? We're the ones, confident of America, confident in working with the rest of the world.*[34]

Max. *We're JFK Democrats.*

4. OVERHAUL, REFORM, AND SIMPLIFY THE TAX SYSTEM

The public favors major reform of the tax system and most are determined to see corporate loopholes closed, which is where they see the tax as most unfair and most stacked against the ordinary citizen.[35] The public is not in so angry a mood that it would scrap the IRS and the current tax system; nor is it very supportive of any flat-tax proposal that has ever been specified. The public does, however, want major changes in the tax system that deal with the current inequities. The first is to lower the rising tax burden on the middle class, now the almost certain outcome of the Bush tax program. The second change is to close the loopholes that the most privileged use to shirk meeting their tax obligations.[36]

The public is lukewarm about the government intervening directly to reduce overall income inequalities, in fact, split 48 to 47 percent on the question. However, a 55 percent majority favors a larger government effort to reduce the differences between high- and middle-income people. The majority reaches 65 percent to aggressively shutdown corporate tax loopholes and shelters.[37]

Biggs. *I've never understood why tax reform and tax simplification are the unique passions of the right. It ought to be our passion.*

Judge. *We know the flat tax is too difficult to do and runs up against our philosophy of using the tax code to help the middle class.*

Biggs. *But we have to propose sweeping things that help the middle class and are also antielitist and antiestablishment. Let the Republicans squirm. And we should try to keep the corporate lobbyists locked outside the hearing room door. Get ordinary citizens there to sit in the gallery and watch to make sure Congress does the right thing.*

Tax Reform

- Major tax reform centered on eliminating corporate loopholes. The process begins with a loophole-closing citizen and economist commission, similar to the one used for the base closings, to recommend $75 billion a year in mandatory tax savings.

- Start with closing "Bermuda loophole" and other overseas tax shelters that allow corporations to avoid paying U.S. taxes; closing "janitors loophole" using insurance policies on all employees to collect when workers die; bar tax transactions with no business purpose.

- Bar corporate lobbyists from congressional deliberations on drafting legislation.

- Restore tax levels for corporations and on capital gains income to 2000 level restoring tax rates and eliminating new shelters.

- Ongoing agenda of middle-class tax relief, including the universal education tax credit, family leave, and child tax credit.

- Make the child tax credit fully refundable and provide tax relief for the families with low-wage jobs sacrificed in the Republican tax cut program.

- Eliminate Bush's tax cuts for the top tax rate and corporations; preserve child tax credit and abolition of the marriage penalty.

5. RADICAL CAMPAIGN FINANCE REFORM

"Patriot dollars" are the invention of Bruce Ackerman and Ian Ayres of Yale Law School. They have proposed a radically new approach to campaign finance reform involving two key elements, the "donation booth" and "patriot

Campaign Finance Reform

- Provide every registered voter with 50 "Patriot Dollars" to distribute to whatever political candidates he or she chooses. This is a plan for radical democratization, empowering people and giving them more choice—while swamping private money with public.

dollars"—a "massive democratization" of the system. The "donation booth" provides a public account for donations, which would be legally anonymous, thus theoretically breaking the chain of influence between donors and politicians. That proposal faces immense practical hurdles, while the "patriot dollars" proposal faces primarily a budgetary hurdle. Both ideas are inspired by frustration with conventional campaign finance reform, which is inevitably undermined by private contributors searching for some place to play.

The plan of the JFK Democrats includes only the proposal to create patriot dollars. Each registered voter would receive $50 to give to candidates and parties of his or her choice. Candidates would have to compete for their votes, as well as their patriot dollars, which would focus attention on the expanded world of small donors. They envision an army of new donors, many no doubt young, armed with their ATM cards and e-mail. Much more important from the point of view of campaign finance reform, the proposal swamps the current total of $3 billion of private campaign donations with an anticipated $5 billion in small publicly funded contributions. The current private donors would continue to do their thing under current law, but they would be less important to politicians now that small donors can play such a big role.[38]

It is easy to imagine in a 50–50 America, with the politics at parity, that the two presidential candidates would battle into the final weeks to a possible photo finish. Faced with the possibility of a Democratic win, every corner of corporate America will pour whatever it takes into Republican coffers, perhaps $200 million, to enable the Republicans to hold on to power and continue their probusiness policies. The Democratic candidate would then go on national television and appeal to the ordinary citizenry to save democracy from such a fate, and to everyone's amazement, 20 million of them would go online and each give $10, arming the Democratic campaign with $100 million in patriot dollars for the race to the finish line.

6. DON'T MESS WITH SOCIAL SECURITY

Max. This is the one area we have to stand up and protect.

This is one area where the social contract must be preserved and made dependably available in the future. This is a program that works and has at its heart universal contribution and universal benefits throughout working life and retirement. JFK Democrats will want to make the values case underlying our obligations—not just for seniors but as a commitment by the multiple generations who are part of this social contract. As Republicans seek to privatize Social Security, undermine its financial stability, and encourage generational war between young and old, Democrats should join this debate based on the principles of 100 percent America.

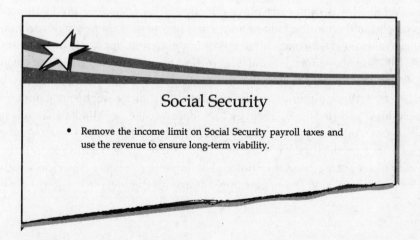

Social Security

- Remove the income limit on Social Security payroll taxes and use the revenue to ensure long-term viability.

7. THE NEW APOLLO PROJECT

The Apollo project provides an opportunity for America to take leadership in an area critical to the future, both for Americans and for the global community.[39] The goal is to achieve energy security, with a marked drop in the use of oil, by the rapid development of technologies and with incentives for changed consumer behavior. The further goal is for America to take the lead on an international issue deemed a major threat in most other parts of the world.

Near the close of his presidency, Bill Clinton spoke at a retreat of the Democratic Leadership Council at the FDR Presidential Library on the Democratic agenda for the twenty-first century. As America's most recent period of prosperity was coming to a close, Clinton posed a challenge not very different from the one John Kennedy made at the close of the 1950s: "What a country does with its prosperity is just as stern a test of its character and vision and wisdom as what it does when its back is against the wall." That challenge is in fact an eternal challenge for Opportunity Democrats who ask, "What is left to be done?" While Clinton was hardly short on answers, the one he gave the most time to was global warming, where he suggested a course consistent with the policy agenda set out here: "We will reverse the course of climate change while enhancing, rather than eroding, economic growth with new technologies and new sources of alternative energy." To close the deal, Clinton declared, "This is a huge, huge issue."[40]

While the Republicans press relentlessly for increased production of coal, gas, and oil in the United States and for opening up new fields around the world, the Democrats offer a radically different approach in the spirit of JFK and the effort to land a man on the moon. The Democrats will commit the country to develop America's vast energy resources in a way that strengthens America, fuels investment in energy technology and renewables, and drastically reduces U.S. dependence on Middle East oil. It also puts America in the lead in reducing the emission of heat-trapping gases that produce global warming. In all these areas, Democrats are the party of technology and the future. The hope is to inspire Americans with the possibilities and the opportunity to take on the biggest long-term challenges.

The New Apollo Project
for Achieving Energy Security and Reducing Global Warming

- A crash effort, comparable to Kennedy's initiative to land a man on the moon, though this time to achieve American energy independence and face up to global warming.

- Establish national goal of cutting U.S. oil consumption and carbon emissions by one-third in 25 years.

- Major investment in gasification of coal to make America's great supply of coal sustainable and clean (with carbon capture).

- Tax credits and incentives to achieve twenty percent of electric power from renewables, including solar and wind and development of bioenergy.

- Major new tax credits and incentives for companies and consumers to foster clean car technology to multiply sale of hybrid cars and make possible hydrogen fuel-cell cars.

- Create a global emissions trading system, with the U.S. introducing carbon limits and taking the lead on disseminating new technology.

Biggs. *No more bullshit on the environment. This is serious stuff, threatening the whole future, my kids. This is one area where I don't need to see poll numbers.*

Wolf. *Could not be a bigger contrast of philosophy, role of government, special interests versus the public interest.*

Judge. *And you had Gore devoted to it. Clinton spoke out on it on every possible occasion for the last three years of his presidency. Unlike the rest of the bullshit issues we deal with, this one is about something.*

Max. *Again, this is a moment to stake out big, inventive positions for* *the future, not just holding on to old programs. Go big and let them face their kids.*

Libby. *This is a twofer—global warming and energy security. Why would the president of the United States carry the water for these interests instead of standing up for America?*

The 2004 presidential election will likely be fought by two combatants, each armed with strategies and tactics, battling to close the half-century era that no party has tamed. The Democrats will be prepared for battle, likely employing one of the five alternative strategies that make the most of the current political contours. We should not underestimate the potential power of a Two Americas strategy that marshals the postmodernist forces or a reassurance strategy that allows them to be realized or a 100 percent base strategy that makes the most of the loyalist world or a Corporate Frame that opens up new territory for Democrats. Given the stakes involved in which party holds the White House and given the ability of the power holders to change political fortunes, it is hard to justify strategies that involve greater risk or that break with what has been built up over a half century.

But maybe the low-risk strategies involve greater risk. In any event, they leave America mired in the current polarized politics, divided. If it is right that postmodernist forces are winning out over the reaction, the heroic battle between the JFK Democrats and Reagan Revolutionaries takes place on favorable terrain.

After all, who are the modernizers? This is the key assessment that readers of this book and Democrats have to make. If people look at the prospects for prosperity and the growing marketization and globalization and ask, "Where do we fall short?" and "How can we make sure all are part of this community?" then "opportunity" will be the dominant theme in the narrative and Democrats the relevant party. If people ask, "How do we free the individual from all these constraints?" then a different narrative will dominate and the war of worldviews will not go well for the Democrats.

If Bush has greatly overreached, calling the Republicans' bluff offers the possibility of a major collapse. After all, are voters looking for a renewed Reaganism, or are they looking for a new opportunity agenda? The answer to this question has immense consequences for the outcome of this battle and how big a risk it is to join it. If the current policies of the Bush administration exacerbate the more than two decades of rising inequality, and throw up new symbols of excess and set off a new wave of middle-class grievance, it could yet be forced into an epic battle that brings down the infrastructure of the right.

The choice could hardly be starker: one party aspiring to use government to move society toward universal health care and universal post–high school education, address vast environmental challenges, rein in corporate power, and diminish the burdens on families caught in the middle; the other party proposing to empower entrepreneurs and the market, expand the role of faith-based institutions, and reduce the size of government. One party challenges the next generation to create an America respected for its opportunity and freedom and leading an interconnected world; the other heralds an America unequaled in its power and challenges the next generation to join America's quest to liberate individuals, wherever they are.

The battle elevated to that level could produce a big election with big consequences for the future position of both parties. But will it produce an 1896, as Karl Rove hopes? After a period of party parity and brutally close elections, 1896 was followed by a period of Republican electoral dominance. The Bryan Democrats ran again and again for the presidency but represented a losing reaction to America's industrialization and urbanization. For Rove, the lessons of 1896 were in the masterful campaign of Marcus Hanna that brought the voters by the hundreds of thousands to McKinley's home in Ohio, the new Republican coalition that brought the capitalists and the new urban workers together in support of the growing industrial order and against the rural reaction, and a Republican administration that used government, including rising tariffs and rising Civil War pensions, to make sure they held on to power.

Following McKinley's example, Rove has acted methodically to deliver on the agenda of the Republicans' most natural supporters in business and faith communities but also to win support of groups with targeted benefits—from trade protection for industrial workers to prescription drugs for seniors. Rove must have been inspired by the case of the Civil War pensioners, an expanding category of Union Army veterans, widows, and orphans, whose benefits grew not after the Civil War but during the political battles of 1880 to 1910, when the Republican administration devoted one-quarter of all federal spending to the pensioners. He must have admired the sleight of hand that allowed them to exclude veterans of the Confederate Army, almost all of whom were Democrats in the South.[41] But the focus on the patronage and benefits and favorable policies misses the hegemony that brought the support of industrial workers for the uncompromising party of America's burgeoning capitalism, the Republicans. For this, Rove might have learned more from reading Antonio Gramsci, the Italian Marxist theorist who wrote about worker support for nonsocialist parties, than from reading Robert Wiebe, historian for this period. Voters in the great wealth-producing regions and also many in the rural states identified with this new American economic order. Then, too, the country faced a choice: one party associated with the modernizing forces and the other seeking to hold them back; one party confident of the future and the other scared of it.

Today, the choice is really a judgment about which party, the Democrats or Republicans, is aligned with the modernizing forces and which will be given the chance to manage the future successfully. The JFK Democrats think they are battling for that honor.

Afterword: 2004
Toward Total War

2004 brought but glimmers of One America and all its possibilities.

It did bring George Bush's reelection as president, though no Reagan America.

It was momentous in many respects. 2004 was the country's first election since terrorists attacked the World Trade Center and Pentagon on 9/11. The campaign brought intense citizen engagement and an historic 5.9-point surge in voting that nearly swamped many polling places, the highest turnout since 1968. The major political parties and their allied groups spent a record $2.2 billion, including $600 million to fund waves of mostly negative campaign advertising, some almost a year before Election Day.[1]

2004 was nonetheless a status quo election. While many factors "explain" so close a result, Bush won by waging an all-out culture war that deepened and generalized the current cultural polarization of the country. In that, 2004 was simply the next phase of a spiraling cultural politics that began in earnest in 1984, accelerated in the 1990s, and was pushed to yet new, unimagined limits in 2000 and 2004.

The Republicans hammered three themes that together told people they should vote to defend their way of life. First, the country was attacked by a dark force that still threatens our safety, and this is no time to risk changing leaders. Bush's closing ad depicted a pack of wolves, while an announcer intoned, "In an increasingly dangerous world, even after the first terrorist attacks on America," John Kerry slashed America's defenses. As the wolves moved toward the camera, the announcer warned, "And weakness attracts those who are waiting to do America harm." For Bush, that evil gave his presidency a sense of purpose and provided the dominant backdrop for this drama, even before the first act began. For many voters, this was the whole story and all they needed to know to reelect Bush as president. Many voters said simply, "Let him finish the job."[2]

Second, George Bush, our president who retaliated for the country after 9/11, is a strong and resolute leader, while John Kerry, a politician who flip-flops on every issue, is weak and irresolute before the threat. The contrast had the added virtue of leaving Kerry wavering in the wind, political and inauthentic, and without certain principles. Kerry's statement at Marshall University, West Virginia, that, "I actually did vote for his eighty-seven billion dollars, before I voted against it," was quickly turned into a Bush attack ad and became a centerpiece of the attacks on Kerry. Other ads noted pointedly, "There's what Kerry says, and then there's what Kerry does," and "John Kerry. Whichever way the wind blows."[3] That characterization stuck, as the Bush campaign opened with these attacks with a vengeance just as Kerry emerged nationally and at every juncture in the campaign. These words were the ready association with John Kerry and a serious doubt for late deciders.

And third, George Bush is a man of good values, defending the family from the cultural pollution and permissiveness of the liberal establishment, while John Kerry is just too socially liberal. Bush was always presented with Laura Bush, expressing his "optimism, and belief in the American people," and in "our values that we depend upon—family, faith, the freedom we celebrate," underscoring what the public valued in his presidency, after the laxness of the nineties.[4] With increasing urgency, they warned about Kerry, "the most liberal member of the Senate," casual about abortion, gay marriage, and gun rights, a sixties antiwar activist contemptuous of our men in uniform who "dishonored his country, but more importantly the people he served with," an elitist out of touch with the values of mainstream America.[5]

Bush needed all three of these big choices to win, but the power was in their mutual reenforcement and their bottom line conclusion about the cultural threat. Together, they alerted people to wake up to the assault on their way of life and called on people to defend their values. In the end, the Republicans asked people not to judge Bush's performance in office but to vote their beliefs and worldview.

The power of these cultural forces are evident in every measure of change: who shifted to Bush since 2000, who moved to him in the final week and days, and who broke with their underlying Democratic Party identity to vote to reelect Bush. In every area, the spotlight goes to the most socially conservative groups. Bush's reelection was never assured by 9/11, as he was endangered until the end, but gained his majority on the force of deepening worries about Kerry's cultural elitism and extreme positions on abortion and gay marriage.

The campaign strengthened the essential structure of the Two Americas and widened the gulf between the religious and the secular, married and single, and the gun owners and the unarmed.[6] The socially conservative groups in the Republican loyalist world—The Faithful (white evangelicals), F-You Old Men (in fact, all older white blue-collar men), Country Folks (white rural), and the white Deep South—voted in even higher proportions for Bush. The socially liberal groups in the Democratic world—the Super-Educated Women (with graduate degrees) and particularly the Secular Warriors (no guns and no church)—voted even more strongly for Kerry than for Gore. African-Americans supported Kerry at nearly the extraordinary level of 2000 and raised their proportion in the electorate. In this respect, 2004 was polarizing: it intensified and widened the cultural divide. But the battle, the commitment and enthusiasm of the combatants, and the resulting polarization was hardly symmetrical. For Bush, this was the battle he wanted. For Kerry, these were a set of positions, some of which left him uncomfortable; he did not call on the country to rise up and defend post-modernist America, with its skepticism about absolutes and authority, its faith in diversity, equality, and new gender roles, rights and individual expression, change and social progress. Unlike many other Democrats, including Al Gore, this was not the battle he wanted.

Bush's determined cultural war was not limited to firing up Republican loyalist supporters, though it was certainly that. It energized and raised turnout disproportionately of Republican-aligned, socially conservative voters. By forcing people to choose sides in the culture war, they took their issues way beyond the base and into the contested and Democratic worlds. They turned the heads of many swing blue-collar voters, particularly white women and seniors, and seriously eroded Kerry's Catholic support. And they made inroads among socially conservative voters in union households and in some minority communities as well. They succeeded in driving the most conservative voters to Bush by keeping them focused on cultural worries and pushing aside other concerns, like Iraq or middle-class living standards, and other issues, like the economy and health care.

As must be evident by now, it is the Republicans who have the most to gain from status quo elections that keep deepening the cultural divisions, increasing the reality of the Two Americas. Social conservatives simply feel more threatened than the postmodernists by the social and cultural forces changing America. That is why the Republicans invested so heavily in the armaments of the culture war, even if it limits them to victories just beyond parity.

George Bush achieved a 2.5-point win over John Kerry and a 50.7 percent national majority, after the 2000 dead heat. But this election was very competitive, a virtual tie going into the last week, that could have broken either way. For Bush, it was half the margin achieved by Clinton in either of his elections and the smallest margin in the popular vote for any president winning reelection.[7] In the closely contested battleground states where nearly all the advertising and organizing was concentrated, Bush and Kerry fought to a draw and Bush gained less than 1 point (0.8) in percentage margin compared to 2000 in these same states.[8]

The election left the Republicans even more completely in control of all the institutions of the national government, but it did nothing to alter the essential parity of the parties that leaves us trapped in this hothouse politics. After all is said and done, the incumbent "wartime" president won 51 percent of the vote, and but for a 118,599-vote margin in Ohio, John Kerry would have taken the oath of office in January 2005. Kerry took 49 percent of the vote in Ohio, Iowa, and New Mexico. The Democrats enter the next campaign with perhaps 248 electoral votes in the bank from the 18 states and the District of Columbia that they have won in all four of the last four presidential elections—just 22 short of a national majority.[9]

The Republicans made real gains in the U.S. Senate, made possible by the simultaneous retirement of four Democrats from Southern states. The Republicans now hold 55 out of the 100 seats. On the other hand, in the House of Representatives, Democrats gained a net two seats nationally, excluding Texas, where a forced partisan reapportionment gave Republicans a 5–net seat gain to more than balance things out. Republicans hold a 30-seat majority in the 435-seat House. But in the battle for state legislatures across the country, the election brought no net Republican gains in seats, though the Democrats gained new majorities in seven legislative chambers, balanced by the four picked up by the Republicans, nearly all in the South.[10]

On Election Day, according to the exit polls, 37 percent of the voters identified with each of the major parties—an important Republican gain from 2000, when the Democrats held a 4-point advantage.[11] That may be all that matters, as it is the Republican managers who get to break out the champagne, but are they toasting a real partisan shift? As it turns out, Democrats had a 3 to 4–point advantage among registered voters in the year and month leading up to the election, as well as in the weeks and months afterward.[12] The Republican party gain on Election Day itself was more the result of the massive voter turnout and who was drawn into the electorate by the cultural battle than an actual shift in partisan loyalties. The same may be true for at least a portion of Bush's vote gain in the election: the 8 million voters who were newly mobilized to go to the polls for Kerry were surpassed by the 11.5 million new voters who went there to vote Bush.[13]

What we know for sure is that the Republicans went for the gains from cultural polarization, which is very different and more limited in ambition than setting out a vision of a new Reagan era. Despite all the eulogies at the Reagan funeral, the Bush campaign sought no mandate on tax cuts, small government, and probusiness policies. Its advertising was overwhelmingly negative, caricaturing Kerry as wishy-washy and indecisive, contrasting his failings with Bush's resolve, and focused on 9/11, the terrorist threat, and domestic security. Only a third of Bush's advertising was aimed at promoting the president, but even then, featured Laura Bush more than any allusion to Reagan.[14] Had the election centered on domestic issues and the administration's priorities, Bush certainly would have lost. Voters' biggest doubt about Bush after Iraq was his tax cuts for the wealthy.[15] Even on military and security issues, Bush sought support at a more elemental level, such as safety and not risking change, rather than support for an expansive and exceptional American role promoting freedom around the world. Here, too, voters were very doubtful that this approach brings greater security. By 51 to 40, voters on Election Day said that America's security depends more on strong ties with other nations than on the United States building up its own military strength.[16]

Fortunately for Bush, Ronald Reagan was not on the ballot, though it is hard for Republicans not to dream of a grander mandate.

The country was hungry for a different election centered on different issues and might have provided a mandate and, had the Democrats dreamed more grandly, perhaps a mandate of One America.

THE DEMOCRATS' UNEVEN TACTICAL BATTLE THAT ALMOST WON

After the fact, this all seems so obvious: with 9/11 and the specter of al Qaeda, abortion, and gay marriage, of course George Bush would win reelection. But Democrats came close to winning the election, despite the cultural dynamics. And the Democrats could have won a different election had they proved as determined to fight on their own issues and posed their own choices or advanced their own values and vision for America.

A majority of Americans went to the polls unhappy with the state of the country and wanting to go in a significantly different direction from the one steered by George Bush and his conservative administration.[17] Bush got relatively low marks for handling foreign policy, Iraq, the economy, and health care, which the public reaffirmed in polls in the weeks after the election.[18] The country was evenly divided on whether Bush's approach to the world makes America more secure, though not on Iraq, where a majority thought his policies make us less. A clear majority doubted his tax-cut economic policies would help them or the economy. And despite all the elite talk of an improved economy, a large majority thought good jobs are scarce and incomes stagnant, while health care costs skyrocket.[19] On Election Day, more voters wanted to vote on jobs, health care, and Iraq than on terrorism and moral values, but this was not their election.[20]

John Kerry, the Democrats, and their allied groups collectively accepted the apparent terms of the election—the historic parity that made this a close election from the start, the cultural polarization and dynamics of the Two Americas that was producing rising energy and support among loyalist groups, the anti-Iraq and anti-Bush sentiment that was opening up new ground, and the discontent with the economy and health care that fueled the desire for change. Like the Republicans, they had decided to wage a status quo election, that is, to wage this battle within the parameters permitted by the Two Americas. The cultural energies, combined with rising antiwar and anti-Bush feelings, and discontent on jobs and health care, seemed to be a powerful brew for change and indeed, brought a lot of new voters to the polls. From that perspective, there was little incentive to challenge the whole edifice, draw different lines, and offer a broad alternative to the modernist-values narrative shaping this election. That Democrats did not choose to shatter the mold was not an irrational choice.

It did produce a collective Democratic effort that was almost wholly tactical—a series of potentially powerful approaches to the election and the electorate that could undercut support for Bush and drive Democratic support beyond the parity. Indeed, most of these were advanced by our fictional Democratic advisers in chapter 11 on how to edge past parity. In the real-life campaign of 2004, this led the Democrats to engage on disparate fronts: underscoring the cultural trends to raise the passions of more secular and minority voters; focusing on powerful symbolic issues, above all, Iraq, but also black voter suppression, choice, and job outsourcing, which raise up the loyalist groups; highlighting the corporate excesses that upset many swing voters in the rural and blue-collar electorate; critiquing Bush's economic and health care policies that left middle-class voters squeezed; and reassuring many conflicted voters that you could trust John Kerry on security, taxes, and values. The Democrats engaged on all these important fronts, though in almost all cases unevenly, leaving John Kerry and the Democrats just short.

While Kerry did not rush to join the cultural combat, the Massachusetts Supreme Court decision on gay marriage, the controversy with the Catholic bishops on abortion and communion, and Kerry's advocacy of stem cell research effectively took the choice away from him. He was a cultural combatant. The spoils for elevating the cultural issues was keeping college graduates in place, despite Bush's strength with them on the war on terrorism and despite his probusiness economic policies. Indeed, postgraduates and the more Republican college-educated men shifted to Kerry.[21]

For John Kerry, his being a decorated Vietnam veteran and reassurance on security was the central rationale of his candidacy. That biography was the heart of his primary win, and Democratic voters rushed to his electability. When Kerry emerged with the nomination after Super Tuesday, he put his largest campaign investment yet on two sixty-second biographical ads including long footage of him in Vietnam. "When he pulled me out of the river," his crewmate exclaimed, "he risked his life to save mine." It noted that his bravery in combat earned him the Silver Star, the Bronze Star, and three Purple Hearts.[22] His convention was devoted wholly to presenting John Kerry as a soldier, ready to defend his country, "reporting for duty." In the debates, in a high proportion of his advertising and every rally speech, Kerry said firmly, "I will hunt down and kill the terrorists, wherever they are." And in the end, Kerry was successful on an issue that plagued Democrats and might have sunk his candidacy in the post-9/11 period. On Election Day, concerns about Kerry on security and being strong enough to defend the country were the lowest, dwarfed by concerns about values and his stands on abortion and gay marriage.[23]

Nearly all the loyalist Democratic groups, except union households, were intensely hostile to the Iraq war, and it became a powerful motivator of the Bush opponents. While Kerry struggled to find a clear point of contrast to confront Bush on Iraq, by the fall, the war became the principal pivot for challenging Bush's priorities. First, he challenged a go-it-alone policy that produced mounting U.S. casualties and bills for Iraq born solely by U.S. taxpayers. The nationalist impulse to "take care of America" was the main reason why rural and older voters, particularly the older blue-collar women and seniors, were most opposed to the war. Second, his pivot on

Iraq allowed Kerry to focus on the growing instability in Iraq and challenge whether Bush's approach to terrorism was really making the world more safe and secure.[24] While it was unimaginable that Kerry would best the president on security, he did cross a threshold on defending the country and being strong, narrowed the gap on who would do the best job on handling terrorism and, with the debates, closed it on foreign policy.[25]

The outside allied groups were the strongest advocates of an *Über Dem* strategy: focusing on the loyalist Democrats, attacking Bush on their issues, waving the bloody shirt to create an energized opposition that would rush the polls on Election Day. Indeed, their activities and focus helped create the voter surge, as ACT, The Media Fund, and MoveOn put the spotlight on a series of Bush vulnerabilities: prioritizing Iraq over America, WMDs, passing the national debt to our kids, job outsourcing and the elimination of overtime, Medicare and prescription drugs, no bid contracts for Halliburton, and Bush's ties to the Saudis. Other groups talked to unmarried women about rising health care costs, choice, and the need to make their voice heard. Still others targeted African-Americans, highlighting Bush's vast failings and indifference to their interests. The New Democrat Network targeted Hispanics, underscoring the minimum wage, health insurance, and the promise of a better life with the Democrats.[26]

Pervading the Democrats' approach was a critique of the powerful special interests that reign in George Bush's Washington. Earlier, I highlighted the hostility to big corporations that cut across the lines of the Two Americas and opened a window into the countryside and to older blue collar women in particular.[27] The outside groups attacked Enron, Halliburton, the drug companies, power companies, oil companies, and the Saudi Royal family, among others. In the primaries, John Kerry scolded those "Benedict Arnold" companies that "want to exploit the tax code and take jobs and money overseas at the expense of the American people."[28] And in his rally speeches in the final stretch, Kerry often declared, "Time and time again, this president has chosen the powerful and well connected over the hardworking middle-class families."

The entire Democratic effort focused on the Bush agenda that was most out of touch with the American public's priorities—tax incentives for jobs, outsourcing, tax cuts for the wealthy, the rising budget deficits, out-of-control health care costs, Social Security privatization, and a prescription drug plan more for the benefit of drug companies than seniors. In the final three weeks of the campaign, Kerry started to weave these together into a theme about middle-class living standards, an economy that fails to "lift up our families," and our determination to create a country "where the American Dream will once again become a reality for middle-class families."[29] It was the older blue-collar and rural voters who were most concerned with the economy that failed to generate good American jobs and with the corporate favoritism and excesses.[30] On Election Day, the biggest doubts about Bush among voters—including wavering Bush supporters—centered on the economy and jobs, tax breaks for the wealthy, and neglect of the middle class.[31]

This tactical approach to the election nearly worked, as mobilization efforts and the Democrats' issues raised the desire for change, energized Bush's opponents, and increased the motivation to vote. This approach helped send millions of new voters to the polls. If not for the larger group of Bush's new voters, we might be toasting these tactics. Kerry essentially matched Gore's support in all the Democratic loyalist groups, except Hispanics. Minority voters raised their percentage of the electorate from 19 to 23 percent, despite a general surge in voting across the electorate. The most secular and tolerant voters shifted to the Democrats. The most impressive were the nonchurch-going and nongun-toting voters, the Secular Warriors, but Kerry also raised his support level with young voters under thirty years

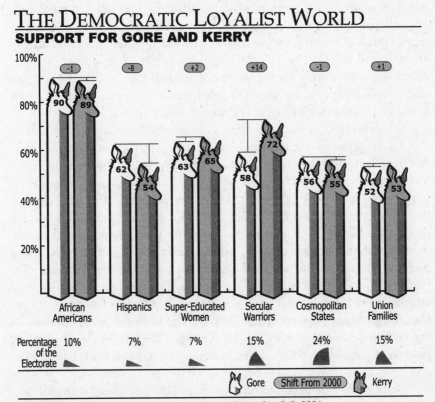

THE DEMOCRATIC LOYALIST WORLD
SUPPORT FOR GORE AND KERRY

2004 Democracy Corps postelection database, November 2–3, 2004.

(from 48 to 54 percent, compared to Gore). Unmarried women—single, divorced, and widowed—found no place in the Bush family circle, and they responded to progressive efforts to reach them: with increased turnout, they raised their vote share by 3 points to form 22 percent of the electorate and supported Kerry by 62 to 37 percent.[32] In the battleground states, the Democrats fought the election to a draw, but not enough to win, or give him Ohio, New Mexico, and Iowa.

But for all that was achieved, the Democrats pursued none of these tactics fully, with overwhelming intensity, pervasiveness, or consistency over the course of the campaign. Kerry successfully reassured on military and security issues, even on taxes, but not on values. Kerry was able to show he reported for duty but not to church. The Democrats apparently learned many lessons from 9/11 and the concern with Democrats on spending and deficits, but not the lessons of the Clinton impeachment and the concern with Democrats on trust and values that helped disfigure Gore in 2000. The "Swift Boat Veterans" group backing Bush successfully turned Kerry's Vietnam antiwar activism into an example of liberal excess. His tense dealings with the Catholic hierarchy made his faith unsettled and unaffirmed. That allowed the Republicans to paint Kerry as too socially liberal for America. That is where voters' biggest doubts centered, not on Iraq or security, and even less so on big government and taxes.[33] That left the Republicans free to build their pervasive cultural case and choice for the election. It is hard to succeed as an *Über Dem* when socially conservative union members and their family members or minority voters are being picked off by worries about the family.

The collective Democratic effort consistently hit Bush on his policies that favored the big corporations, but that was in the battleground states where, in fact, Bush barely slipped in. Nationally, where Bush accomplished a much bigger shift, voters barely heard the anticorporate soundings. Kerry never mentioned those "Benedict Arnold corporations" after he locked up the Democratic nomination. Indeed, while CEOs had emerged as symbols of the greed and CEOs making five hundred times more than their employees was the strongest line of attack, Kerry would not mention them, preferring to talk about powerful special interests.[34] In the postdebate period, as he staked out his claim for the middle class, he swung between attacks on "those at the top" and "the powerful and well-connected." In any case, his personal style and frequently recounted stories on his life among the rich and famous diminished him as an authentic battler against the powerful. Bottom line: the culture war was not pushed back by the class war.

While Kerry took positions on a woman's right to choose, tolerance, and science—the elements of a cultural positioning—he never articulated the

DOUBTS ABOUT KERRY

TOP THREE REASONS NOT TO VOTE FOR JOHN KERRY

2004 Democracy Corps postelection database, November 2–3, 2004.

underlying beliefs and worldview that shaped his thinking. There were good reasons not to get drawn into these issues, but the result was Kerry being neither fish nor fowl, as Bush proceeded to define him in the most extreme way.

Kerry ultimately won the "Iraq voters," but they did not come automatically, as he struggled all through August and September to develop a clear position and take the case to Bush. In the end, he focused on the deteriorating situation on the ground and the rising terrorist threat. On the other hand, Kerry raised and then walked away from the other line of attack: a go-it-alone foreign and Iraq policy that left Americans to bear the full burden of lives lost and the rising costs, which was shortchanging America at home. The original $87 billion Bush request had symbolized the deception and hidden costs, which lost the president support earlier and was the centerpiece of the broad Democratic attack from the spring; the increase to $200 billion in costs emerged as the biggest voter doubt about Bush's Iraq policy. These numbers were at the heart of an elemental impulse, take care of America, which is why this argument was at the heart of the strongest framing for the election—both defend America and fight for the middle class.

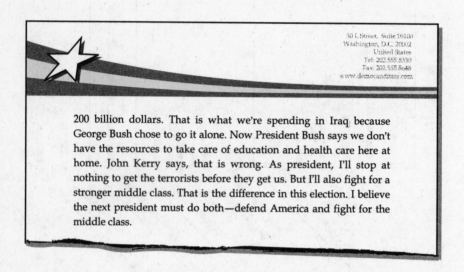

30 L Street, Suite 1010
Washington, D.C. 20002
United States
Tel: 202.555.8330
Fax: 202.555.8648
www.democanditate.com

200 billion dollars. That is what we're spending in Iraq because George Bush chose to go it alone. Now President Bush says we don't have the resources to take care of education and health care here at home. John Kerry says, that is wrong. As president, I'll stop at nothing to get the terrorists before they get us. But I'll also fight for a stronger middle class. That is the difference in this election. I believe the next president must do both—defend America and fight for the middle class.

This argument got the attention of the more nationalistic voters, mostly in downscale America.[35] The theme was advanced by the outside progressive groups at various times and Kerry affirmed it in campaign ads and in speeches in September. Then, worried that the position would be interpreted as a lack of resolve in the war on terrorism, the campaign dropped the theme before the debates.[36] That changed the character of Kerry's Iraq opposition, now more internationalist and antiwar and consequently, more culturally liberal.

While Kerry had plans on many issues, few had a scale large enough to be memorable in the way Bush had highlighted his plans for Social Security privatization or to make the tax cuts permanent. For sure, Kerry presented serious plans on health care, as well as energy, though there is no evidence that the public understood his general direction or principles on health care, and no point in which the country watched Kerry and Bush in a defining exchange on the issue.

On no issue was the lack of scale or vision, big idea, or defining exchange more evident than on the economy. The public had no idea what Kerry would do to create jobs or raise incomes, though he repeatedly said

DOUBTS ABOUT BUSH

TOP THREE REASONS NOT TO VOTE FOR GEORGE BUSH

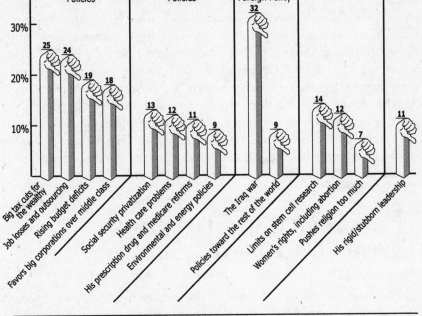

2004 Democracy Corps postelection database, November 2–3, 2004.

he would repeal tax breaks and create incentives for companies to create jobs in America. For a large proportion of the electorate, particularly the swing voters, the economy and jobs was issue number one and the biggest doubt about Bush. On Election Day, more voters said they wanted to vote on the economy and jobs than on security and safety and that was particularly true for the socially conservative voters who shifted to Bush at the end. Yet Kerry only addressed the economy intermittently after his convention and before the third debate. With about two and a half weeks left, he began to speak directly to the need to address middle-class living standards and create good jobs. While Kerry began to focus on the issue, the economy was already giving way to Iraq for anti-Bush voters and Kerry was losing ground to Bush on who could best handle the issue.[37]

When voters were asked on Election Day which candidate had clear ideas on what they wanted to achieve, Bush had an 11-point advantage (49 to 38 percent)—almost as large as his advantage over Kerry on the war on terrorism.[38]

Kerry would have run a stronger race had he and the Democrats fully embraced their tactics or relentlessly focused on a more integrated subset of these broad options. It is hard to imagine that Kerry would have failed to carry Ohio and the Electoral College. But it is easy to imagine that he would have failed to carry the country, even if he had gotten the tactics right. The tactics just did not add up to anything consequential when the Republicans were offering such a total worldview and total choice. To win a national majority, the Democrats would have had to engage or counter the cultural choice being advanced by the Republicans, which would mean drawing on the values at the heart of their worldview and building a narrative around a central aspiration for America, ideas like unity and strength, opportunity and responsibility, 100 percent or even One America, ideas that create a nation both strong and admired. The country was hungry for an alternative to the choice they acceded to in the end.

CULTURE WAR SHAPES THE 2004 ELECTORATE

The combination of the Republicans' culture war and the Democrats' uneven tactics shaped the 2004 electorate, with the end result: small Republican gains and consolidation of their power; the Two Americas, very much intact and strengthened, fully set in place, it seems, to define our politics for elections to come. But while this was a status quo election in the context of the Two Americas, a lot happened to produce the end result.

The Bush effort drove up support and the turnout of loyalist Republicans; at least as consequential, it raised the commitment of conservative voters to participate, changing the partisan character of the electorate. By generalizing the culture war beyond the base, they eroded the support of some of the more socially conservative loyalist Democrats, capping the ambitions of any Democratic base strategy. It shook many of the key groups in the contested electorate, particularly Catholics and seniors; it pulled back at the end a good portion of downscale and rural America that was unhappy with the country's direction.

The Democratic and Kerry efforts also consolidated support among Democratic loyalists and raised turnout, almost matching the motivational forces on the Republican side. With cultural forces dominating the material, Kerry made gains with college-educated men and postgraduate women, young voters, unmarried women, and the most secular in the Democratic base.

1. FIRST THINGS FIRST: MAXIMIZING THE REPUBLICAN LOYAL-ISTS. The Bush administration has been consumed, from its first inauguration, with increasing the support and commitment of its loyalist groups. That is about their whole purpose and direction but also, more crudely, about tax cuts for the top earners and business, and for families with children, as well as support for churches and their network of organizations. Bush's three-part theme—remember the terrorist attacks and don't risk change; strong leader or weak, flip-flopping Kerry; and man of good values or the extreme liberal for abortion and gay marriage—was red meat for the base. The Faithful, Country Folk, Deep South, F-You Boys, and F-You Old Men not only matched Bush's 2000 performance but increased his vote by 2 to 6 points. In every case but one, Bush overperformed, that is, his victory margin over Kerry was greater than the party margin for the group.[39] That is base politics at its best.

THE REPUBLICAN LOYALIST WORLD
SUPPORT FOR BUSH 2000 AND BUSH 2004

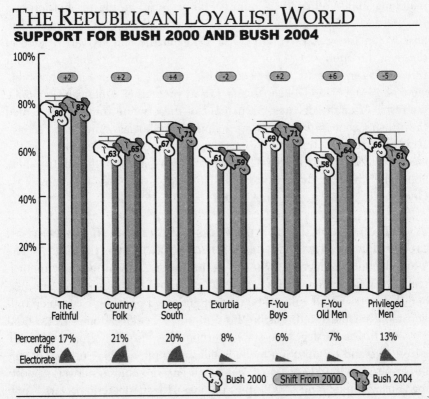

2004 Democracy Corps postelection database, November 2–3, 2004.

But to underscore the centrality of the values contrast in their overall message strategy, one needs to understand the Privileged Men—white, college-educated, married and, for most of them, incomes over $75,000, forming 13 percent of the electorate. They are on the privileged side of nearly all our divides, and Bush, therefore, showered them with a largesse of top-rate tax cuts, family tax credits, and probusiness policies, including less regulation and fewer lawsuits. Yet this group, less socially conservative and more internationalist, was the only loyalist group that fell short of 2000, indeed significantly short (61 versus 66 percent). Kerry increased his margin 10 points over what Gore achieved among the Privileged Men.

The Country Folk (white rural voters) are the other group that was out of sync with other loyalists and that tells us something about the dynamics of this election. In the end, they more than broke for Bush, but that did not happen until very late in the campaign. Bush was getting only 55 percent of the vote at key points until mid-October, 8 points below 2000, rising to 57 percent, then jumping to 63 percent a week before the election, matching 2000. While the Country Folk were as hostile to abortion and gay marriage as any group, except the Faithful, they were not typical loyalists.[40] On Election Day, only 52 percent felt the country was headed in the right direction; only 42 percent thought Bush's military approach to our threats was making us more secure; and only 21 percent had a favorable view of NAFTA, and likely Bush's job in protecting American economic interests. After the debates, 55 percent of these white rural voters denied that Bush's economic policies are helping middle-class Americans or creating jobs. But in the end, they accepted the cultural definition of the election, though reluctantly. Their vote margin for Bush surged 10 points above their basic party identity, and that swept away Kerry and many other Democratic candidates in rural states.

2. DARING TO CHANGE WHO VOTES—AND CHANGING THE PARTISAN CHARACTER OF THE ELECTORATE, THOUGH NOT THE COUNTRY. The 2004 election produced a historic rise in turnout, driven by many motivators—9/11, Iraq, George Bush, the 2000 tie and the prospect of another, and the partisan and cultural battle that enflamed passions. Seventeen million more people voted, raising the turnout percentage from 54.2 to 60.0 percent. In the battleground states, turnout was also driven up by massive advertising and organization by both sides, and intense get-out-the-vote efforts: the "72-Hour Task Force" campaign and the church networks boosting Bush voters, and ACT, the unions, "Election Action Days," and MoveOn's "Leave No Voter Behind" helping Kerry. Yet the voter surge was national, not disproportionately in the battleground states, suggesting that the stakes, the news, and the national thematic battle were the main forces drawing people into the electorate.

As we noted earlier, the Democrats had a 3 to 4–point advantage in party identification going into the election and afterward, but no advantage in the closing week and on Election Day, when the parties stood at parity. In addition, the average of the public polls of *all registered voters,* based on five surveys, showed Kerry with an edge, 47 to 46 percent in the final week, with Bush losing ground, but the public surveys of *likely voters,* reflecting the growing determination to vote, showed Bush moving up and with a lead of 48 to 46 percent.[41] The passions produced by tactics were apparently not as powerful as those from strategy. The passions of the postmodernists and antiwar voters were apparently not as great as those who thought their values were at risk from abortion, gay marriage, and John Kerry.

One-half of Bush's total vote gain nationally came from the "Red States"—the solid Republican states—and half of those from just Texas, Tennessee, Alabama, and Georgia.[42] Indeed, because of disproportionately high turnout in Republican and conservative areas, the Red States increased their proportion of the electorate from 32 to 33 percent. The Cosmopolitan States from the Two Americas dropped 2 points to 22 percent; the Blue, strong Democratic states dropped 3 points to 29 percent. Conservatives were disproportionately energized and increased their share of the electorate by 4 points and their margin for Bush by 8 points, giving him 84 percent of their votes. The moderate share of the electorate dropped by 5 points.

The impact of increased turnout of conservatives and voters in the Red States was multiplied by an increase in Bush's vote margin there, rising by 11 points in Alabama, 10 in Tennessee, 9 in Oklahoma, 7 in Louisiana, and 7 in West Virginia. In the Red States, the surge in Bush voting gave him a margin of 20 points (60 to 40 percent)—9 points above the underlying party alignment of these voters. Nothing like that happened in the battleground and Blue States, where the vote and party identification margins were virtually identical.

It is not at all clear that the differences in passions and uneven rush to the polls decided the battleground states and the Electoral College, but what happened in the Red States was a significant factor in Bush achieving a national majority and 3-point gain over 2000.

3. TAKING THE CULTURE WAR TO THE DEMOCRATIC LOYALISTS AND STEALING VOTES. In this cultural election, Kerry overtook Gore's performance with the Super-Educated Women and Secular Warriors. But there are many socially conservative voters to be found in the Democratic loyalist world, some of whom responded to a campaign that was dominated by cultural forces, battles, and issues. Union households and Hispanic voters were the center of the problem, who seemed particularly bothered by gay marriage, the new frontier in cultural politics in 2004.[43]

Kerry's margin among all union households dropped 3 points, and among white households, supposedly a loyalist group, Kerry won by a barely acceptable 53 to 46 percent. His vote margin was 7 points below the partisan leanings of these voters. In 2000, the gun issue held down the Democratic vote, but in 2004 that was joined by gay marriage and abortion. In union households, hostility to gay marriage was strong: 56 percent negative, setting them off from all the secular groups in the Democratic loyalist world.

The Hispanic vote rose as a proportion of the electorate to 8 percent, but Bush made important inroads, likely because of concerns about abortion and gay marriage, underscored by the Catholic Church's opposition. According to the exit polls, Bush got about 41 percent of the Hispanic vote, a gain of up to 5 points, clearly helping him in key battleground states.[44] In the postelection survey, Hispanic voters cited gay marriage as the second most important reason to oppose Kerry, just behind Kerry being a flip-flopper; overall, some 63 percent mentioned cultural worries.

By successfully extending the culture war to the Democratic loyalist world, Bush increased his national margin but made the biggest difference in Southwest battleground states and, of course, Ohio, where 34 percent of the voters were union households.

4. WAGING GENERAL CULTURE WAR AND WINNING CONTESTED VOTERS: SENIORS AND CATHOLICS. The book imagined a Karl Rove strategy for the election, which used "base issues," particularly the cultural ones, to raise the passions of the loyalists, while reaching out to contested groups with a material and policy offer: prescription drug benefits for seniors, school accountability for suburban women, and appointments and immigration reform for Hispanics. None of that was particularly successful, as the prescription drug plan was complicated and unpopular, school testing and bureaucracy clouded education reforms, and congressional conservatives killed the idea of legalizing illegal immigration. Without a material offer, the Bush campaign turned to the "base issues," abortion and gay marriage, in effect, extending the culture war to the contested electorate. Their success was most evident with Catholics, seniors, and noncollege-educated women.

Seniors were one of the greatest Bush victories in the 2004 culture war. Democrats had made gains in recent elections and President Bush's pre-

THE CONTESTED POLITICAL WORLD

SUPPORT FOR BUSH 2000 AND BUSH 2004

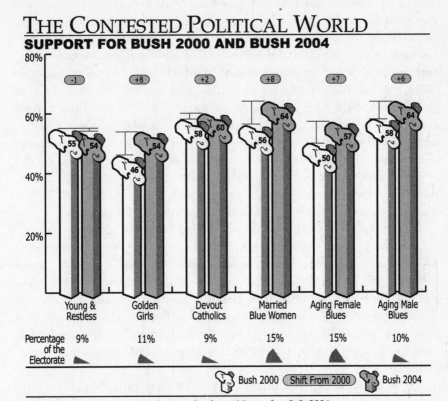

2004 Democracy Corps postelection database, November 2–3, 2004.

scription plan was deeply unpopular. Until very late in the election, despite Bush's standing on terrorism, Kerry was running respectably here. But unlike 1996 and 2000, the Democrats did not focus on "seniors' issues" at the end, even though seniors were strongly opposed to Social Security privatization; Kerry no longer criticized the spending in Iraq and neglect of America, the main grievance for seniors.[45] Absent those issues, seniors gave in to their social conservatism, which was deeply felt: no group was more opposed to gay marriage or worried about moral decline and Kerry's liberalism. And no group in the contested world shifted more against the Democrats. Overall, whites over sixty voted 58 to 41 percent for Bush, a 17-point margin and 11-point swing from 2000. Among the Golden Girls, the white women over sixty-five in my book, Bush moved his vote up from 46 to 54 percent. In the aged electorate, values ruled on November 2.

Tactically, the Bush White House had cultivated the Catholic bishops and clergy and worked closely with conservative lay organizations, championing their issues, particularly on stem cell research, abortion, and gay marriage. At the same time, John Kerry was a candidate uncomfortable in his own church, which would not embrace and affirm him, despite a lifetime of faith. These relationships and symbolic issues came to matter in 2004 because they were integral to the total conflict Republicans were waging. Catholics were over a quarter of the electorate and Bush carried them by 5 points (52 to 47 percent). He carried white Catholics by 13, according to our postelection survey (56 to 43 percent) and, according to our postelection survey, won practicing Catholics, the Devout, by 21 (60 to 39 percent). Overall, Bush gained 7 points in margin among Catholics, twice the size of Bush's national gains, which were a big part of Kerry's crash in support in the heavily Catholic eastern (and Blue) states.

Catholics were a swing group to the end because they were very uncomfortable in Bush's conservative political house. They were hostile to the Iraq war and go-it-alone foreign policy, opposed to Bush's plans on Social Security, and very doubtful of his progress on the economy.[46] In this election, all Catholics identified with Democrats by 5 points but gave Bush a 5-point margin in the vote—a 10-point gap. For the Devout, practicing white Catholics, the gap is 11 points, underscoring Catholics' discomfort with where they ended up politically in 2004, produced by the culture war.[47]

5. WAGING GENERAL CULTURE WAR AND WINNING CONTESTED VOTERS: FLIPPING DOWNSCALE AMERICA. College graduates, little concerned about the cultural turmoil, blithely went ahead and cast their votes equally for Bush and Kerry, just as they had for Bush and Gore four years earlier. But downscale America, concerned with the turmoil in the economy as well as security and values, was much more conflicted and volatile. The sharp Democratic losses, particularly at the end of the campaign among rural voters, seniors, and even Catholics, were part of a bigger story—the flip of downscale America gave this election to Bush.

Noncollege and blue-collar voters came to this election and even to the closing week with many doubts about Bush's tenure and direction. Overwhelmingly, they thought this economy's bounty was not for the middle class, which faces bleak prospects on jobs, income gains, and health care costs. They resented the foreign spending and neglect of America. They deeply resented the corporate excesses and the corporate influence in Bush's Washington. So for these voters, among the most socially conservative in the electorate, this was an election of crosscurrents and competing wars, had Democrats sought to wage one. To the very end, they were open to an alternative. In the postelection survey, 49 percent said they had wanted to hear how the candidates would make the economy and health care better, while just 43 percent wanted to know how the candidates would make us safe; among the Bush voters who might have shifted to Kerry, the margin for the economy was even greater, 55 to 42 percent. Among the white noncollege voters who broke overwhelmingly for Bush, the men leaned toward an economic exchange (49 to 44 percent), while the women to one on safety (49 to 43 percent). For sure, downscale Americans wanted a strong president before the dangers but also something more.

At some very late point in the campaign, they decided to accept Bush's big choices and the cultural election. When they did, the plates moved. Bush won very big, taking 64 percent of the Married Blue Women (white married noncollege), as well as 57 percent of the Aging Female Blues (white noncollege over fifty years) and 64 percent of the Aging Male Blues. Bush increased his margin by 12 points across them; he increased his vote by about 7 points.

That this was an unsettled and ultimately unfinished story is evident in the gap between this vote and these voters' party sensibilities. Among the Aging Female Blues, Bush's vote margin was 13 points stronger than the Republicans' advantage in party identification. It was 12 points for the Married Blue Women and 10 points for the Aging Male Blues. The culture war took these voters far beyond the political territory that they wanted to occupy.

6. CRASH IN THE EAST.   Bush's national majority was produced, not just by the turnout surge and Republican consolidation in the Red States, but also by a crash in the eastern states, little noted in the media. That crash happened when downscale America decided to vote the cultural line on the ballot. As these were largely safe states for Kerry, the outside groups did not mount pointed attacks on Bush there and the Kerry campaign did not advertize its biography, reassurance, or plans. The East was also economically stronger and not as troubled by job losses. That all left the national cultural dynamic to work its way, perhaps with even greater force. Kerry's margin compared to 2000 dropped sharply in New Jersey (down 10 points), Rhode Island (8 points), New York (7 points), Connecticut (7 points), and Delaware (6 points). According to the exit polls, Kerry's margin dropped 7 points among whites in the East, bigger than the drop for Southern whites.

The Democratic crash in the East was led by ethnic Catholics and noncollege voters, particularly the women.

The drop-off in Catholic support in the East is breathtaking, exceeding the general state drop for Kerry in all eight of the eastern states, where

Kerry's vote declined from Gore's. In most, the drop was more than double the rate for all voters. Among New York Catholics, for example, Kerry lost 19 points in margin compared with Gore—double the Kerry drop for the state. With Catholics comprising over 42 percent of the state's electorate, that probably overaccounts for the Kerry decline in the state.

The rest of the state decline in the East was led by the noncollege voters and white women, likely the noncollege white women at the heart of Downscale America that pulled down John Kerry nationally. But here, the late crash was exacerbated by the absence of a campaign. In New York, Democrats' support dropped 17 points among white women and 14 points among the noncollege educated; in New Jersey, Kerry fell 22 points among white women and 10 points among noncollege voters; in Connecticut, support among white women fell 17 points.

To track the Democrats' losses in the East, one goes and walks the blue-collar and ethnic Catholic precincts and talks to the women. They will no doubt tell you about George Bush, the family man who did the right thing on 9/11 and John Kerry, with all the uncertainties and his odd views about the family.

REPUBLICAN FUTURE

The Republicans have invested heavily in the Two Americas and now have an overwhelming interest in continuing to deepen and generalize its lines and choices. For them, the status quo is a strategy, which makes it a home game, with all the home field advantages. It allows them to comfortably pose a total choice that sucks up all the oxygen, leaves other choices and world views struggling for air. The Republicans are the party to keep the country safe before the global terrorists and the party to keep your family safe from the moral pollution.

Since the 2000 dead-even election, this approach produced significant shifts of Catholics, Hispanics, seniors, and blue-collar women at least to Bush, who seem to be receptive to cultural cues. The approach has driven some voters away, too, but not as many. The approach in 2002 and 2004 produced a surge of conservative and Republican voters to the polls.

In electoral terms, it is risky to invest everything in a strategy that leaves the country so close to parity. What if the Democrats nominated somebody not at war with his or her own church who could reassure on both security and values? Or a candidate with a passion and vision to raise up all Americans? Or a candidate from middle America, a populist advocate ready to advocate for those outside Washington? What if the Iraq war and the economy falter? What if there is a public revolt against Social Security privatization? What if Red America is topped out? What if the Republican Hispanic gains were for Bush, not the party, and what if anti-immigrant sentiment among conservatives drives Hispanics back to the Democrats? What if Catholics' instincts for social justice and ties to the more cosmopolitan states send them back to the Democrats, too? When all is said and done, the Republicans are still one state away from losing.

This is not so whimsical because the 2004 election was no political earthquake. The surge in interest and turnout was historic, but mostly contained within the bounds of the Two Americas. The two parties still own mostly the same set of states and electoral votes; no party's political fortunes have been changed in any fundamental or sustainable way. More importantly, large majorities in the country did not rush to any new set of principles around which one could build a new era and new common sense.

If this were to center on Reagan's ideas, the project would start with cutting taxes and small government, yet the biggest doubts about the president centered on his budget deficits, tax cuts for the wealthy, and failure to use government to address health care. Reagan's America puts business first, yet voter regard for corporations is not very high, with voters thinking Bush puts corporate wants ahead of the public interest. And a Reagan America would be assertive militarily, with America on its own promoting freedom in the world, yet the public is not supportive of a global Reaganism, preferring strong international ties to achieve security in this period. While Bush won respect for his faith and protection of values, he won little public support for Reagan's other principles.

Thus, the Republicans will have to be restless, even with their victories and control over the federal government. They will be tactical, trying to consolidate their gains and push to make them trends. They will promote Hispanics into high-profile positions and try again to legalize undocumented aliens; they will advance new tax credits for families with children; they will pour even more money into the seniors' prescription drug plan; and they will relish the battle for Supreme Court justices that would overturn federal protections for abortion. If Iraq does not stabilize, they will find an exit strategy, just as Reagan did in Lebanon, to take on easier battles for principle.

The 2004 election gave the administration the space to act more boldly, even if they got no mandate for Bush's domestic policies. Tax reforms, combined with a growing economy, could give new life to Republican top-down economic principles. Social Security privatization, if benefits are maintained and achieved through painless budget policies, could give new life to conservative principles on ownership and choice. The Republicans will be tempted to make this a Reagan moment.

If these plans, small and big, do not pan out politically, as has happened with much of Bush's first-term agenda, they have the option of returning to cultural politics. That is the default politics for the loyalists of both parties, and voters, too, are learning these habits through repeated elections centered on this cultural divide. Moving to a different politics requires unlearning a lot, discontinuities, and uncertainty. Both parties remain tantalizingly close to victory, which is what Republicans count on in the end. Cultural politics is still a home game for them.

DEMOCRATIC FUTURE

For the Democrats, the path to the future begins with a reckoning: there is no alternative to total war, indeed to a total campaign as well. That means they must pose an encompassing, holistic choice that elevates a few issues and that makes a few leadership qualities matter more than all others. It must be centered on people's worries and hopes, and be so clear about what is wrong and what must be fixed that all other agendas are crowded out. The narrative must be so compelling that the public loses interest in the story that Republicans are trying to tell about America.

That contrasts with 2004 when the Democrats posed no clear choice and the Republican narrative was dominant. Instead, this election was fought under the established rules of the Two Americas. For the Republicans, the Two Americas has become a powerful statement about defending America and defending people's way of life from the external terrorists and internal liberals. The cultural issues have crowded out other issues and even Republican politicians who would speak with a different voice. As a result, people have no difficulty telling you what Republicans believe and what they will do. That has allowed the Republicans to generalize the culture war on their terms into both contested and Democratic territory. Unless the Democrats join this fight in a new way, these convictions and the accompanying voting patterns risk becoming permanent.

There is no reason to believe the citizenry wants this future. A lot of voters, open to an alternative narrative, settled reluctantly for the cultural choice. Even as they went to the polls, white Country Folks, Catholics, Union Families, noncollege married women, and older noncollege men and women voters (the Aging Blues), each gave Bush a vote margin of 10 points or greater than their support for Republicans in general. These voters gave in to Bush because the Democrats did not pose a compelling choice that revealed their issues, beliefs, and plans for the future.

Democrats can no longer put off the debate about what they believe, the starting point for narrative and a choice in the election.

The instinctive starting point is the culture war itself, but recast in terms much more favorable to the Democrats. Kerry chose not to battle on this terrain, but a candidate coming from a different place and tradition, and perhaps at a different moment, might decide to champion central tenets of the postmodernist alternative—tolerance and diversity, individual and expanding rights, particularly for women, respect for the environment, learning, and social progress—while challenging Republican intolerance and use of government to impose their truths, limit rights, and despoil the public space.

Some critics believe that is just what the Democrats should do: emulate the Republicans and turn this great divide into a strategy for winning elections and consolidating power. The Democrats, John Sperling writes, "must become the party of Metro-America," proudly modern, moderate, and tolerant of differences of class, ethnicity, tastes, and sexual orientation." The party's "brand" is a "commitment to equality for women, gays, immigrants, labor, and other groups, and to progressive taxation." It is the party of inclusion, economic security, and science. Above all, it must challenge the Republicans who are deeply grounded in a traditional, backward-looking "Retro-America." They are committed to the "religious and cultural agenda" of the evangelical Christians, and to the "crony capitalists"—oil, mining, logging, energy, corporate farming, and defense industries—that live off massive government subsidies. The Democrats should become the voice of the aggrieved majority in Metro-America that is the engine of growth and that foots the bill for this retro politics.[48]

The problem with making the Two Americas a Democratic strategy is the limited ambition of running for only half of America. And will that half feel sufficiently threatened and aggrieved when they may be winning economically and culturally? Will the postmodernists' culture war have the same ferocity as that of the Christian social conservatives? And in light of the 2004 defection of blue-collar women and Catholics in the Cosmopolitan states, one has to ask, how sure are you of the loyalties in the Metro base? Even if it held, one has to win elections in America, governed by the U.S. Constitution, which gives disproportionate representation to rural areas and small states. Let us at least agree that any successful strategy for Democrats should begin by not conceding the U.S. Senate and the presidency.

George Lakoff, author of *Moral Politics,* also accepts these inherited sets of beliefs and values as a basis for Democratic strategy, though he has much more faith that Democratic ideals could win broad support in the country. In an updated essay for progressives, he describes a conservative worldview that sees grave dangers all around the family and nation, requiring a "strong, strict father" who insists on discipline and self-reliance—the path to morality, security, and prosperity. It stands alongside a progressive worldview whose family metaphor includes nurturing parents, accepting that children are essentially good and that they and the world can be made better. "The progressive vision is of community," Lakoff writes, an "America as family, a caring, responsible family . . . an America where people care about each other, not just themselves." Since Lakoff believes people have both family metaphors in their heads, the Democrats' strategic course need not be polarizing: "The goal is to activate *your* model in the people in the 'middle.'" Democrats, in effect, need to make the case for community, which can win broad support.[49]

Sperling and Lakoff offer very different prescriptions but, like most Democratic theorists, do not challenge the inherited patterns and structures that gave us the Two Americas. But in my book, I suggest the lower-risk course might be a bolder strategy that denies the inheritance—posing a choice and advancing a vision that cuts across the "Great Divide," turning a lot of the past into rubble. The country should be asked to choose between a vision of an America that works for the most fortunate 1 percent and a vision of a 100 percent America where we search restlessly for the areas where we fall short and for the answers to how America expands opportunity. These are special times, where twenty-five years of accumulating inequality, now years of stagnant incomes, and new insecurities in education, health care, and retirement demand a bold politics. Before the election, I proposed unleashing a "100 percent America, JFK Democrat," and the aspiration for one America.[50]

In the test of that big choice before the election, with the full backdrop of 9/11, the 100 percent America narrative dominated Bush's security and values narrative. Voters strongly preferred the JFK Democrat to George Bush's portrayal as "Reagan's Son." Opportunity was the more powerful value.[51] This holistic choice broke down the barriers and allowed the Democrats to win voters in contested, even surprising places. This is the America voters wanted to take to the world in the post-9/11 era.

This may or may not be the narrative of choice, but it suggests strongly that voters are hungry for an alternative to the culture war.

While tactics are no longer sufficient for Democrats, a powerful strategic course will need powerful tactics to prevail.

John Kerry was never able to make himself whole on values, even as he reassured on defending the country and on taxes. But for Democrats today, there is no room for silence on that question. Republicans made Clinton's impeachment a pivotal battle in America's culture wars or, as Sidney Blumenthal aptly writes, "The Clinton Wars." The years 1998 and 2000 began an exodus of many rural, blue-collar married and union voters, and for them, George Bush's rise to the presidency became a kind of restoration. To lower the din of the cultural clashes and to get heard on their choice, Democrats will have to reassure on values. Democrats will not emerge the champions of One America unless they are champions of its values, too.

And Democrats will never be able to storm the gates of the Two Americas unless they are outsiders, out of power, anti-Washington, antiestablishment, and populist. Democrats are out of power, but they sound and look like the establishment, parsing their words, cautious, in fact, tied down by special interests. To be truthful, voters did not really believe Kerry would take on the powerful special interests to bring change, which likely contributed to some voters giving up on him at the end.[52] Today, Democrats, confidently out of power, must be reformers to take down the Republicans.

The president will choose the first battles for a 100 percent America, but those are tactical opportunities of the first order. He does not have popular mandate for Social Security privatization, a major tax overhaul favorable to the wealthiest, or an open-ended war in Iraq. Bush's political overreach on his conservative agenda sets the stage for political battles that give reality and meaning to the Democrats' choice.

So, if One America—or even some alternative—is such a compelling narrative and if the supportive tactics are so necessary, why is it so hard for the Democrats to take up the flag? Why don't they just do it? Why does this seem so easy for the Republicans?

It is easy for the Republicans because they are invested in the status quo. Their strongest voting blocs and interest groups are almost all fully aligned with the Republicans' focus on security, values, and taxes. But the Democrats' loyalist groups, mostly secular and well educated, cosmopolitan, and suburban, and many of the party's leaders and biggest donors are not at all comfortable with a strategy that reaches deep into the countryside, becomes expressive about faith and family, critical of corporate excess and government waste, skeptical about the bounty in our current growth, and ready to think anew about America in the world.

In the end, the Democrats have not taken up One America because they are trapped in the Two Americas, which leaves them wary of change. But that timidity will leave them short. To achieve power and bring change, Democrats will have to break free of those constraints and go to war for their ideals.

Appendix A

RESEARCH FOR THE TWO AMERICAS

The primary research for this book includes the national surveys and focus group discussions for Democracy Corps, conducted by Greenberg Quinlan Rosner Research (GQR). The primary research period extended over eighteen months, from November 2001 until May 2003, though additional survey experiments were conducted after this period, in June and July. The surveys were conducted nearly monthly, each with 1,000 likely voters. In this period, GQR conducted 58 focus groups for Democracy Corps in three contested communities—blue-collar areas outside of Tampa, rural and small towns in central Iowa, and higher socio-economic areas outside Seattle.

DEMOCRACY CORPS SURVEY DATABASE

Greenberg Quinlan Rosner Research conducted fifteen national surveys, representative of the likely presidential year voting population. To achieve that, respondents were screened to include only those who were registered, had voted in the 2000 presidential election or were not eligible, and indicated that they were "almost certain" or "probably" would vote in the next national election. (Those who said there was only "a 50–50 chance" or would not vote were excluded.) The database in the end included 15,045 respondents, each of whom completed a 25-minute survey.

The survey included a standard set of questions, though Democracy Corps explored other topics not used in this book. Thus, when the book reports, for example, that white Evangelicals align with the Republicans rather than the Democrats by 72 to 23 percent, that is the result for the 2,612 white Evangelicals who answered that question over the 15 surveys. Since each survey included the same number of interviews and was conducted nearly monthly, one can also think of this as the average result for this eighteen-month period.

The Democracy Corps dataset used throughout this study was weighted to reflect the anticipated composition of the national electorate in the November 2004 general election. For this purpose, GQR examined the findings of the National Election Studies (NES), Bureau of the Census Current Population Survey (CPS), the Voter News Service (VNS) exit polls, and the national elections surveys of GQR, which have been tested and refined in relation to the observed results, the actual election outcomes. The demographic guidelines include the following:

Geography. During the research period, geographic quotas were established for interviewing in each of the 50 states based on turnout trends over the last 4 elections (1996, 1998, 2000, and 2002) and current registration, though the database was weighted to be representative of the likely 2004 presidential electorate.

Gender. The results were weighted so women formed 52 percent of each survey and the database. This is consistent with the VNS and Census for the 1996 and 2000 elections, but not with NES, which shows women at 55 percent.

Race. The surveys were weighted to the following distribution: 80 percent white, non-Hispanic; 10 percent African-American, non-Hispanic; 7 percent Hispanic or Spanish-speaking; and 3 percent for other responses. This distribution reflects the distribution and trends of the VNS data, which shows a 2-point per election increase in the Hispanic proportion over the last three presidential elections, conservatively reduced to a 1-point increase for 2004. The CPS data did not separate non-Hispanic white and African-American voters from the Hispanic respondents prior to 2000, ruling out trend analysis. The NES survey employs a different definition and shows a decrease in Latino voting in 2000, contradicting population patterns and other election research.

Age. Daniel Merkle and Murray Edelman, of the VNS team, acknowledge that their exit-poll methodology underestimates the proportion of seniors in the electorate. In a research experiment, they tracked people who declined to be interviewed at the polls (those who refused to participate or were simply missed by the interviewer): fully 29 percent were 60 years of age or older, compared to only 19 percent of those who responded at the polls. Similarly, the young were overrepresented in the exit polls (Merkle and Edelman, "A Review of the 1996 Voter News Service Exit Polls from a Total Survey Error Perspective," in Lavrakas and Traugott (eds.), *Election Polls, the News Media, and Democracy,* 2000). NES, on the other hand, had age problems as well: it showed both seniors and voters under 30 increasing as a percentage of the electorate (contrary to both VNS and the Census Bureau), while showing baby-boom voters, ages 40–49, decreasing as a percentage of the electorate. As a result, the distribution for the GQR surveys uses the Census Bureau (CPS) age distribution, modified by Census population projections for 2004 and to reflect turnout trends for each age group since 1996. Accordingly, the survey database was weighted to the following distribution: under 30 years (13.5 percent), 30 to 39 years (16.8 percent), 40 to 49 years (22.4 percent), 50 to 64 years (26.2 percent), and 65 years and older (21.1 percent).

Education. Education is the most difficult to estimate because of very different results and methodology for the NES/CPS estimates and the VNS exit polls. With the NES survey weighted to the CPS—that is, distributed identically for all education levels—these are treated as a single estimate. On the other hand, it is difficult to compare directly on college education, as the CPS has a separate category for associate's degree, while VNS does not prior to 2000. Even after adjustments, a large and unexplained gap remains between the exit poll methodology and the CPS post-election survey.

The academic literature on this gap is conflicting. Samuel Popkin and Michael McDonald argue for the methodology of the exit polls, which capture individual voters (rather than households) who definitively voted (rather than self-reporting a week or more later). Further, they argue that noncollege household members were more likely to respond to Census questionnaires after the 1996 election than college-educated members of the same household, which they argue produces a bias toward noncollege voters in the CPS and NES surveys (Popkin and McDonald, *Who Votes?* Blueprint, 1998). In further support of that position, Merkle and Edelman report that the proportion of college educated among exit-poll responders is comparable to the proportion among the non-responders. That would suggest that exit polls are representative of the voting population on education (though not on age).

Ruy Teixeira and John Judis argue that the VNS results are "mathematically impossible" based on overall population statistics (requiring an "implausible" turnout rate of 99 percent among college-educated voters). They highlight the inherent education bias created by the acknowledged VNS age bias—e.g., the underreporting of seniors who are less likely to hold a college degree (Judis and Teixeira, *The Emerging Democratic Majority*, Simon and Schuster, 2002).

Because of this debate, GQR has always used education targets that were a rough midpoint between VNS and CPS estimates, with repeated validation in comparison with the actual election outcome. In 2000, the GQR surveys, both those conducted for the Gore campaign and those conducted for Democracy Corps, accurately estimated the dead-even result.

For this project, the VNS and CPS results were projected to 2004, reflecting the past pattern of a near 2-point rise in the proportion of college graduates in each presidential election, and the results averaged to form the education weights. Thus, college graduates are projected to make up 41 percent of the 2004 presidential electorate.

SURVEY INDICATORS

The key measure of party support in this study is what we call "party alignment," which is party identification with the undecided allocated to the party they lean toward. Respondents were asked: "Generally speaking, do you think of yourself as a Democrat, a Republican, or what?" Republican support is composed of people who say they are Republicans, plus those independents who answer, "Republican," when asked, "Do you think of yourself as closer to the Democratic or Republican Party?" The parallel exercise defines the Democrats. Interestingly, all but 8 percent of the voters can be allocated to a party. (The trend in party-identification responses is discussed in Donald Green, Bradley Palmquist, and Eric Schickler, *Partisan Hearts and Minds. Political Parties and the Social Identities of Voters* [New Haven: Yale University Press, 2003, pp. 14–20].)

Party alignment was a more useful measure than party identification, without allocating the independents, because it left a lot of uncertainty on likely voter tendency. In fact, for nearly every group, party alignment (with independents allocated) produced a vote margin within a point or two of the generic congressional vote, a standard question for tracking vote tendency. This analysis suggests that generic vote is really a measure of party identification rather than a real expression of vote preference.

Party alignment was remarkably stable over this period, despite extraordinary public events. Across all the surveys, an identical proportion of the electorate aligned with each party, 46 to 46 percent. At the beginning of the period, after 9/11 and before Christmas, 2001, the Republicans had a minor 2-point advantage (47 to 45 percent); in the new year 2002, up until the election, the two parties were in a dead heat, 46 to 46 percent; and after the midterm elections well into the spring 2003, not much had changed, Democrats were ahead with 47 percent and Republicans had 46 percent, setting the stage at parity on the eve of the presidential elections.

The results for party alignment are also very stable for nearly all of the specific groups in the Republican, Democratic, and Contested Worlds over the period, even when one looks at the periods before and after the 2002 election. There are three exceptions to that pattern that are important to note. White voters under 30 years aligned more with the Republicans in the 2003 surveys (by a 18-point margin), compared to 12 points in 2002 and 7 points in 2001 (after 9/11). The more recent period involved much more intense coverage of military and security issues. On the other hand, white senior men and white senior women became less Republican. White senior men aligned with the Republicans by only 7 points in 2003 but by 10 points in 2002 and by 27 points in 2001; white senior women aligned with Democrats by 9 points in 2003, but were even in 2002.

Thermometer ratings were used to measure feelings toward individuals and groups. The rating is on a 100-degree scale, with 100 meaning very warm and favorable and zero very cold and unfavorable; 50 degrees is the midpoint, neither warm nor cool. Any rating above 50 degrees means a warm or favorable response; any below 50 means a cool, unfavorable one.

OTHER SURVEY DATABASES

In order to understand voting trends over this whole 50-year period, the study uses the University of Michigan's National Election Studies, which made it possible to look at not only demographic trends but also trends in attitudes and voting. For this book, I examined only presidential-year data, where surveys were conducted both before and after the election.

The study also relies on exit poll data for the elections from 1980 to the present. For the period 1980 to 1988, it uses the exit polls of CBS and *The New York Times* (CBS/ *New York Times* 1980–1988). For the period 1992–2000, the study employs the exit polls of the now-defunct Voter News Service, a research service for CNN, ABC, CBS, NBC, FOX, and the Associated Press.

FOCUS GROUPS

In the period between August 2001 and July 2003, Democracy Corps conducted ongoing focus groups among independent and weak partisan voters in these three communities. The Eastside Tech participants were college educated and with a household income in excess of $50,000 a year. The women participants were 27–42 years of age and the males slightly older, 32–49 years, to reflect the differing distribution of college degrees among men and women. The participants resided in select suburban areas outside Seattle, themselves above average in income and education.

The Tampa Blue and Heartland Iowa participants were non-college-educated (no four-year or graduate degrees) and had a household income below $50,000 a year. The women participants in these areas were 30–49 years old with at least one child under 18 and the male participants 45–60 years of age. The goal was to get married women with children, a swing group over the past decade, and to get somewhat older men who are more contested and independent. The Heartland participants resided on farms and in small towns in central Iowa, and Tampa Blue participants resided in the blue-collar suburbs surrounding Tampa.

Each of the participants completed a personal interview on their personal, employment, and social lives. The 2-hour focus groups were professionally moderated, with the discussion recorded and transcribed for analysis.

In addition, the research team, including myself, observed these areas, traveling town to town, exploring neighborhoods and commercial areas, visiting churches, libraries, co-ops, community centers and sports fields.

Appendix B

REPUBLICAN WORLD

Republican World (part 1)[1]

	ALL VOTERS	THE FAITHFUL	COUNTRY FOLK
Percent of All Voters[2]	100	17	21
Party Alignment[3]			
Democratic	46	23	39
Republican	46	72	53
Margin[4]	0	R+49	R+14
Independent[5]	25	20	26
Thermometer[6]	Degrees		
NRA	51.3	64.5	61.3
Warm[7]	42	58	54
Cool[8]	36	20	25
Net	+6	+38	+29
Pro-Life Groups	49.8	66.8	54.3
Warm	38	61	43
Cool	38	21	33
Net	0	+40	+10
Clinton	43.1	24.6	36.0
Warm	38	17	29
Cool	49	72	57
Net	−11	−55	−28
Big Corporations	45.8	50.0	44.6
Warm	31	36	28
Cool	38	31	39
Net	−7	+5	−11
Internet	67.9	64.1	63.3
Warm	61	55	53
Cool	12	14	15
Net	+49	+41	+38
Immigrants	53.3	49.4	47.8
Warm	39	32	29
Cool	26	30	31
Net	+13	+2	−2
NAFTA	47.9	44.7	44.9
Warm	29	26	25
Cool	28	31	31
Net	+1	−5	−6

1. *The Republican World.* The Faithful: white Protestants who are Fundamentalist/Evangelical/charismatic/Pentecostal. Country Folk: whites who live in counties outside metropolitan areas. Deep South: live in Alabama, Arkansas, Florida, Georgia, Louisiana, Mississippi, North Carolina, South Carolina, Texas, Virginia. Exurbia: high-growth counties in suburban and rural areas within 100 miles of a city greater than 100,000 population; excluding counties with high Hispanic, African-American, or senior growth. F-You Boys: white married men under 50 years of age, without a 4-year college degree. F-You Old Men: white male seniors, 65 years of age and older. Privileged Men: white married men with a college education (4-year or advanced degree).
2. These are likely presidential-year voters.
3. The percentage of presidential-year voters who align with each party. That includes the percentage who identify with a party, as well as the independents who lean toward the party.

Deep South	Exurbia	F-You Boys	F-You Old Men	Privileged Men
20	8	6	7	13
35	35	30	38	32
59	56	63	56	61
R+24	R+21	R+33	R+18	R+29
25	26	27	24	29
58.6	57.0	73.5	52.6	49.4
50	50	72	48	44
27	29	13	36	40
+23	+21	+59	+12	+4
53.3	53.0	56.8	49.2	49.5
43	42	47	36	41
34	34	30	37	40
+9	+8	+17	−1	+1
33.5	35.1	34.4	35.9	33.4
27	29	28	32	27
61	59	59	57	61
−34	−30	−31	−25	−34
47.9	48.1	48.2	47.4	51.7
34	36	34	35	43
34	36	35	36	31
0	0	−1	−1	+12
67.1	67.6	68.0	58.1	72.8
59	60	66	40	72
13	13	12	17	7
+46	+47	+54	+23	+65
52.0	51.1	48.1	47.2	56.0
35	36	33	32	44
27	30	31	36	21
+8	+6	+2	−4	+23
47.1	45.8	41.1	44.8	50.9
29	25	21	30	38
28	29	38	35	28
+1	−4	−17	−5	+10

4. The margin is the net advantage for the leading party (leading party percentage minus the trailing party). Where the Democrats lead in the group, there is a "D" before the margin; where the Republicans do, there is an "R."

5. The independent number reflects respondents who say they are independent even though many lean Democratic or Republican. The Democratic and Republican numbers reflect party identification that includes independent respondents who indicated that they lean Democratic or Republican.

6. "Rate your feelings toward some people and organizations, with 100 meaning a very warm, favorable feeling; zero meaning a very cold, unfavorable feeling; and 50 meaning not particularly warm or cold. You can use any number from zero to 100, the higher the number the more favorable your feelings are toward that person or organization. If you have no opinion or never heard of that person or organization, please say so."

7. *Warm* is the percent giving a thermometer rating above 50 degrees.

8. *Cool* is the percent giving a thermometer rating below 50 degrees.

Republican World (part 2)

	ALL VOTERS	THE FAITHFUL	COUNTRY FOLK
Percent of All Voters	100	17	21
Government regulation of business[1]			
Necessary	58	49	55
Harm	35	42	36
Net	+23	+7	+19
Government regulation for social ends[2]			
Protects	49	39	40
Stop telling people what to do	44	55	53
Net	+5	−16	−13
To achieve national security[3]			
Strong alliances	48	36	44
Strong military	41	50	44
Net	+7	−14	0

Tell me whether the first statement or the second statement comes closer to your own views, even if neither is exactly right:

1. "Government regulation of business and corporations is necessary to protect the public." OR "Government regulation of business and corporations frequently does more harm than good."
2. "Government regulation often improves safety and protects consumers and the environment." OR "The government should stop trying to tell people what to do—whether they can own a gun, use an off-road vehicle, or drive an SUV."
3. "America's security depends on building strong ties with other nations." OR "Bottom line, America's security depends on its own military strength."

Deep South	Exurbia	F-You Boys	F-You Old Men	Privileged Men
20	8	6	7	13
55	53	54	56	56
37	41	42	33	38
+18	+12	+12	+23	+18
44	44	29	46	49
49	50	64	48	45
−5	−6	−35	−2	+4
41	42	37	42	44
47	47	54	47	47
−6	−5	−17	−5	−3

Republican World (part 3)

	ALL VOTERS	THE FAITHFUL	COUNTRY FOLK
Percent of All Voters	100	17	21
Which Party Is Better on the Issues[1]			
Keep America Strong			
Democrats	23	11	20
Republicans	53	71	56
Net	R+30	R+60	R+36
Health Care			
Democrats	50	32	43
Republicans	28	44	31
Net	D+22	R+12	D+12
Retirement/Social Security			
Democrats	47	28	40
Republicans	32	49	35
Net	D+15	R+21	D+5
On Your Side			
Democrats	40	21	33
Republicans	35	57	42
Net	D+5	R+36	R+9
The Economy			
Democrats	40	22	34
Republicans	43	61	47
Net	R+3	R+39	R+13
Taxes			
Democrats	35	19	30
Republicans	47	65	49
Net	R+12	R+46	R+19
Education			
Democrats	43	23	36
Republicans	35	55	38
Net	D+8	R+32	R+2

1. "Tell me whether, overall, you think the Democrats or the Republicans would do a better job with this issue. If you do not know, just tell me and we will move on to the next item: keeping America strong, health care, retirement and Social Security, being on your side, the economy, taxes, and education."

DEEP SOUTH	EXURBIA	F-YOU BOYS	F-YOU OLD MEN	PRIVILEGED MEN
20	8	6	7	13
15	17	17	19	12
64	66	67	61	71
R+49	R+49	R+50	R+42	R+59
39	44	43	44	49
38	34	37	34	33
D+1	D+10	D+6	D+10	D+16
37	38	35	42	43
41	42	44	38	41
R+4	R+4	R+9	D+4	D+2
29	32	28	31	30
47	44	48	44	46
R+18	R+12	R+20	R+13	R+16
31	33	29	34	28
52	52	57	50	59
R+21	R+19	R+28	R+16	R+31
27	28	24	31	25
57	57	62	54	65
R+30	R+29	R+38	R+23	R+40
32	33	31	34	39
46	46	44	40	43
R+14	R+13	R+13	R+6	R+4

DEMOCRATIC WORLD

Democratic World (part 1)[1]

	ALL VOTERS	AFRICAN AMERICANS	HISPANICS
Percent of All Voters	100	10	7
Party Alignment			
Democratic	46	86	55
Republican	46	8	37
Margin	0	D+78	D+18
Independent	25	16	22
Thermometer	Degrees		
NRA	51.3	41.8	53.0
Warm	42	27	43
Cool	36	44	34
Net	+6	−17	+9
Pro-Life Groups	49.8	50.0	52.0
Warm	38	35	39
Cool	38	33	35
Net	0	+2	+4
Clinton	43.1	78.7	54.7
Warm	38	79	53
Cool	49	9	36
Net	−11	+70	+17
Big Corporations	45.8	43.8	47.0
Warm	31	28	31
Cool	38	39	36
Net	−7	−11	−5
The Internet	67.9	68.4	71.8
Warm	61	62	66
Cool	12	16	12
Net	+49	+46	+54
Immigrants	53.3	52.1	61.4
Warm	39	39	51
Cool	26	29	19
Net	+13	+10	+32
NAFTA	47.9	49.9	52.1
Warm	29	29	36
Cool	28	26	29
Net	+1	+3	+7

1. *The Democratic World*. African Americans: African Americans who do not consider themselves Hispanic or Latino. Hispanics: Hispanic or consider themselves Latino or Spanish-speaking American. Super-Educated Women: postgraduate women. Secular Warriors: never or hardly ever attend church and do not own a gun. Cosmopolitan States: New England, New York, New Jersey, and California. Union Families: white union members and those with a union member in their immediate family.

SUPER-EDUCATED WOMEN	SECULAR WARRIORS	COSMOPOLITAN STATES	UNION FAMILIES
7	15	24	15
58	63	52	53
36	30	40	40
D+22	D+33	D+12	D+13
26	30	28	26
31.9	35.0	42.2	52.3
20	24	32	45
61	55	46	35
−41	−31	−14	+10
38.7	31.0	42.9	48.4
29	19	32	37
55	60	46	40
−26	−41	−14	−3
46.0	54.0	48.1	45.2
40	53	45	42
44	35	42	45
−4	+18	+3	−3
44.2	42.2	45.0	42.1
30	27	29	25
43	42	40	44
−13	−15	−11	−19
73.0	73.3	70.0	65.9
72	69	65	58
6	9	10	13
+66	+60	+55	+45
64.9	58.0	57.8	52.4
58	45	46	38
13	19	21	27
+45	+26	+25	+11
51.5	49.0	48.5	42.2
33	30	30	25
20	26	28	37
+13	+4	+2	−12

Democratic World (part 2)

	ALL VOTERS	AFRICAN AMERICANS	HISPANICS
Percent of All Voters	100	10	7
Government regulation of business			
Necessary	58	60	60
Harm	35	32	38
Net	+23	+28	+22
Government regulation for social ends			
Protects	49	58	56
Stop telling people what to do	44	36	37
Net	+5	+22	+19
To achieve national security			
Strong alliances	48	51	53
Strong military	41	39	39
Net	+7	+12	+14

Super-Educated Women	Secular Warriors	Cosmopolitan States	Union Families
7	15	24	15
66	65	62	61
28	29	32	33
+38	+36	+30	+28
68	58	57	49
26	37	37	46
+42	+21	+20	+3
60	58	51	51
26	33	39	38
+34	+25	+12	+13

Democratic World (part 3)

	ALL VOTERS	AFRICAN AMERICANS	HISPANICS
Percent of All Voters	100	10	7
Which Party Is Better on the Issues			
Keep America Strong			
Democrats	23	53	25
Republicans	53	23	50
Net	R+30	D+30	R+25
Health Care			
Democrats	50	77	59
Republicans	28	8	22
Net	D+22	D+69	D+37
Retirement/Social Security			
Democrats	47	77	51
Republicans	32	10	31
Net	D+15	D+67	D+20
On Your Side			
Democrats	40	76	51
Republicans	35	8	30
Net	D+5	D+68	D+21
The Economy			
Democrats	40	72	45
Republicans	43	15	38
Net	R+3	D+57	D+7
Taxes			
Democrats	35	64	42
Republicans	47	19	43
Net	R+12	D+45	R+1
Education			
Democrats	43	74	50
Republicans	35	12	34
Net	D+8	D+62	D+16

Super-Educated Women	Secular Warriors	Cosmopolitan States	Union Families
7	15	24	15
26	27	23	27
40	41	50	50
R+14	R+14	R+27	R+23
61	62	56	56
19	16	24	23
D+42	D+46	D+32	D+33
56	59	52	54
25	19	29	27
D+31	D+40	D+23	D+27
48	55	45	46
26	20	31	30
D+22	D+35	D+14	D+16
45	55	43	46
38	27	40	37
D+7	D+28	D+3	D+9
44	48	38	41
40	33	45	42
D+4	D+15	R+7	R+1
56	55	47	48
25	20	32	31
D+31	D+35	D+15	D+17

Appendix D

CONTESTED POLITICAL WORLD

The Contested Political World (part 1)

	All Voters	Winning[1]	
		Post-graduate Men	Well-Educated Women
Percent of All Voters	100	6	11
Party Alignment			
Democratic	**46**	**41**	**45**
Republican	**46**	**52**	**49**
Margin	0	R+11	R+4
Independent	25	31	23
Thermometer	Degrees		
NRA	**51.3**	**41.6**	**41.2**
Warm	42	35	30
Cool	36	51	49
Net	+6	−16	−19
Pro-Life Groups	**49.8**	**43.4**	**47.1**
Warm	38	34	38
Cool	38	49	44
Net	0	−15	−6
Clinton	**43.1**	**37.8**	**38.1**
Warm	38	33	32
Cool	49	57	55
Net	−11	−24	−23
Big Corporations	**45.8**	**49.1**	**47.4**
Warm	31	41	32
Cool	38	36	34
Net	−7	+5	−2
The Internet	**67.9**	**74.4**	**71.6**
Warm	61	75	69
Cool	12	6	8
Net	+49	+69	+61
Immigrants	**53.3**	**58.7**	**57.6**
Warm	39	49	43
Cool	26	21	20
Net	+13	+28	+23
NAFTA	**47.9**	**53.2**	**50.6**
Warm	29	39	30
Cool	28	25	22
Net	+1	+14	+8

1. *Winning.* Postgraduate Men: white men who have a postgraduate degree. Well-Educated Women: white women with a 4-year college degree, but no postgraduate degree.
2. *Swinging.* Young and Restless: whites under 30 years of age. Golden Girls: white women 65 years of age or older. Devout Catholics: white non-Hispanic Catholics who attend church weekly.
3. *The Blues:* Vulnerable Women: white, low-wage working women with a total family income last year, before taxes, less than $30,000. Also includes white single/separated/divorced or widowed and noncollege graduates. Married Blue Women: white married women without a 4-year or postgraduate college degree. Aging Female Blues: white women, 50 years or older without college degrees. Aging Male Blues: white men, 50 years or older without college or postgraduate degrees.

	Swinging[2]			The Blues[3]			
	YOUNG AND RESTLESS	GOLDEN GIRLS	DEVOUT CATHOLICS	VULNERABLE WOMEN	MARRIED BLUE WOMEN	AGING FEMALE BLUES	AGING MALE BLUES
	9	11	9	14	15	15	10
	41	47	46	50	40	47	39
	53	45	48	42	53	45	52
	R+12	D+2	R+2	D+8	R+13	D+2	R+13
	29	21	25	24	23	22	29
	56.4	45.6	47.6	49.6	54.6	49.0	61.9
	47	33	37	36	43	36	58
	30	39	37	34	29	35	26
	+17	−6	0	+2	+14	+1	+32
	51.5	51.8	65.4	51.2	55.8	54.3	51.1
	42	39	58	39	45	42	37
	39	34	20	36	32	31	34
	+3	+5	+38	+3	+13	+11	+3
	43.4	40.7	38.7	42.3	35.0	39.4	36.4
	37	35	33	35	29	34	32
	49	50	55	48	58	52	57
	−12	−15	−22	−13	−29	−18	−25
	50.1	43.0	46.9	41.8	44.2	41.7	43.6
	38	23	33	23	25	22	30
	34	39	37	42	39	42	43
	+4	−16	−4	−19	−14	−20	−13
	75.4	54.3	66.3	63.9	64.1	57.8	57.3
	77	32	57	50	54	40	41
	7	19	13	14	15	18	19
	+70	+13	+44	+36	+39	+22	+22
	56.4	47.6	55.2	50.3	48.9	48.1	46.8
	46	32	42	34	31	32	30
	22	34	26	31	32	34	35
	+24	−2	+16	+3	−1	−2	−5
	52.7	46.9	51.6	47.4	46.9	44.5	38.1
	37	21	34	23	23	20	21
	21	22	23	24	24	27	44
	+16	−1	+11	−1	−1	−7	−23

The Contested Political World (part 2)

		Winning	
	ALL VOTERS	POST-GRADUATE MEN	WELL-EDUCATED WOMEN
Percent of All Voters	100	6	11
Government regulation of business			
Necessary	58	65	63
Harm	35	31	30
Net	+23	+34	+33
Government regulation for social ends			
Protects	49	60	57
Stop telling people what to do	44	36	37
Net	+5	+24	+20
To achieve national security			
Strong alliances	48	52	55
Strong military	41	41	33
Net	+7	+11	+22

Swinging			The Blues			
YOUNG AND RESTLESS	**GOLDEN GIRLS**	**DEVOUT CATHOLICS**	**VULNERABLE WOMEN**	**MARRIED BLUE WOMEN**	**AGING FEMALE BLUES**	**AGING MALE BLUES**
9	11	9	14	15	15	10
64	51	59	56	54	52	55
31	35	36	33	35	36	37
+33	+16	+23	+23	+19	+16	+18
53	50	58	49	46	49	39
42	41	36	43	48	44	54
+11	+9	+22	+6	−2	+5	−15
57	48	48	50	46	44	40
35	37	41	37	40	41	50
+22	+11	+7	+13	+6	+3	−10

The Contested Political World (part 3)

		Winning	
	ALL VOTERS	POST-GRADUATE MEN	WELL-EDUCATED WOMEN
Percent of All Voters	100	6	11
Which Party Is Better on the Issues			
Keep America Strong			
Democrats	23	18	18
Republicans	53	62	54
Net	R+30	R+44	R+36
Health Care			
Democrats	50	54	46
Republicans	28	29	30
Net	D+22	D+25	D+16
Retirement/Social Security			
Democrats	47	49	45
Republicans	32	37	34
Net	D+15	D+12	D+11
On Your Side			
Democrats	40	35	39
Republicans	35	39	38
Net	D+15	R+4	D+1
The Economy			
Democrats	40	34	37
Republicans	43	53	46
Net	R+3	R+19	R+9
Taxes			
Democrats	35	30	32
Republicans	47	60	48
Net	R+12	R+30	R+16
Education			
Democrats	43	48	44
Republicans	35	35	36
Net	D+8	D+13	D+8

Swinging			The Blues			
YOUNG AND RESTLESS	GOLDEN GIRLS	DEVOUT CATHOLICS	VULNERABLE WOMEN	MARRIED BLUE WOMEN	AGING FEMALE BLUES	AGING MALE BLUES
9	11	9	14	15	15	10
18	27	22	26	21	26	20
58	42	54	46	54	45	60
R+40	R+15	R+32	R+20	R+33	R+19	R+40
48	43	48	49	39	45	42
31	29	29	25	33	28	32
D+17	D+14	D+19	D+24	D+6	D+17	D+10
39	46	47	45	38	44	44
38	31	33	29	36	31	34
D+1	D+15	D+14	D+16	D+2	D+13	D+10
35	39	38	41	34	39	33
41	35	38	31	41	33	41
R+6	D+4	0	D+10	R+7	D+6	R+8
36	41	38	42	34	41	36
46	36	46	35	46	37	47
R+10	D+5	R+8	D+7	R+12	D+4	R+11
32	38	36	38	30	37	30
53	37	47	38	46	39	52
R+21	D+1	R+11	0	R+16	R+2	R+22
45	34	38	38	32	34	33
37	35	38	33	42	36	40
D+8	R+1	0	D+5	R+10	R+2	R+7

Notes

PART I: THE POLITICS OF PARITY

1. *The Washington Post* political staff, *Deadlock: The Inside Story of America's Closest Election* (New York: Perseus Books, 2001), p. 21.
2. See the discussion of party alignment in Appendix A. This is a measure of party support based on the standard question asking whether people identify with the parties. If independents or unaffiliated voters lean to one of the parties, they are allocated accordingly.
3. Even in 2003, just focusing on the period of the Iraq war and aftermath, 47 percent aligned with the Democrats and 45 percent with the Republicans.
4. Diana West, "Quiet Giggling in a Gloat-Free Zone; It's Difficult Not to Smirk at Democrats' Mourning in America," *Washington Times*, November 8, 2002.
5. John B. Judis and Ruy Teixeira, *The Emerging Democratic Majority* (New York: Scribner, 2002). Later I advance arguments consistent with Judis and Teixeira's general observations about emerging social currents.
6. The same divide ran through the 1,971 state senators. After the 2000 election, 50.7 percent of the state senators were Democrats and 46.9 percent Republicans. After 2002, the Republicans had the edge, but by an even tighter margin, 48.8 percent to 48.4 percent.

7. As Jeffrey Toobin argues convincingly, the election would have been won by Al Gore had there been a statewide recount or had the butterfly ballots not produced 3,407 Patrick Buchanan voters in Palm Beach County or had the African-American votes in Duval County been fully counted or had the overseas absentee ballots been properly handled (Toobin, *Too Close to Call: The Thirty-Six-Day Battle to Decide the 2000 Election* [New York: Random House, 2001], pp. 280–81).

8. Martin Schram et al., "Reagan, GOP Wins May Signal Major New Political Alignment," *The Washington Post,* November 5, 1980, p. A18.

9. Richard M. Scammon et al., *America Votes 22: A Handbook of Contemporary American Election Statistics* (Washington, DC: Congressional Quarterly, 1996).

1. TOWARD HEGEMONY

1. See David R. Mayhew, *Electoral Realignments: A Critique of an American Genre* (New Haven: Yale University Press, 2002), pp. 7–33.

2. John H. Aldrich, *Why Parties? The Origin and Transformation of Party Politics in America* (Chicago: University of Chicago Press, 1995), pp. 81, 93, 98–99; Joel H. Silbey, *The American Political Nation, 1838–1893* (Stanford: Stanford University Press, 1991), pp. 7, 14–15; Paul Goodman, "The First American Party System," in *The American Party Systems: Stages of Political Development,* edited by William Nisbet Chambers and Walter Dean Burnham (New York: Oxford University Press, 1967), pp. 86, 95; Richard P. McCormick, *The Second American Party System: Party Formation in the Jacksonian Era* (Chapel Hill: University of North Carolina Press, 1966), p. 3.

3. John Gerring, *Party Ideologies in America, 1828–1996* (Cambridge: Cambridge University Press, 2001), pp. 15, 161–63; Goodman, "The First American Party System," pp. 68, 75; James A. Morone, *The Democratic Wish: Popular Participation and the Limits of American Government* (New York: Basic Books, 1990), pp. 2–5, 66, 69–72.

4. Richard P. McCormick, "Political Development and the Second Party System," in Chambers and Burnham, *American Party Systems,* pp. 95–96; Louis Hartz, *The Liberal Tradition in America* (New York: Harcourt, Brace, 1955).

5. Arthur M. Schlesinger, Jr., *The Age of Jackson* (Boston: Little, Brown, 1945), pp. 6–8, 91–93, 346–47; Aldrich, *Why Parties?* pp. 104, 109; Morone, *The Democratic Wish,* pp. 75–76, 82; Silbey, *The American Political Nation,* pp. 78–79, 81–82; Gerring, *Party Ideologies in America,* pp. 170–71, 175.

6. McCormick, *The Second American Party System,* pp. 13–15; Silbey, *The American Political Nation,* pp. 8–9; Aldrich, *Why Parties?* pp. 130–35, 139, 143.

7. Silbey, *The American Political Nation,* pp. 138–39; Larry M. Bartels, "Electoral Continuity and Change, 1868–1996," *Electoral Studies* 17, no. 3 (1998): 291; Mayhew, *Electoral Realignments,* p. 57.

8. Gerring, *Party Ideologies in America*, pp. 111–14.

9. Theda Skocpol, *Protecting Soldiers and Mothers: The Political Origins of Social Policy in the United States* (Cambridge, MA: Harvard University Press, 1992), pp. 64–65, 109–12, 124–29, 149–51.

10. Charles Hoffman, *The Depression of the Nineties: An Economic History* (Westport, CT: Greenwood Publishing Group, 1970), pp. 271, 279–81; W. Elliot Brownlee, *Dynamics of Ascent: A History of the American Economy,* 2nd ed. (Chicago: Dorsey Press, 1988), pp. 274–86, 305–37; Frederick Lewis Allen, *The Big Change: America Transforms Itself, 1900–1960* (New Brunswick, NJ: Transaction, 1993), pp. 7–14, 22–26.

11. Allen, *The Big Change*, p. 88; William Jennings Bryan, *The First Battle: A Story of the Campaign of 1896* (Chicago: W. B. Conkey, 1989), pp. 123, 203, 205, 206; James L. Sundquist, *Dynamics of the Party System: Alignment and Realignment of Political Parties in the United States,* rev. ed. (Washington, DC: Brookings Institution, 1983), pp. 106–66; also see Donald K. Springen, *William Jennings Bryan: Orator of Small-Town America* (Westport, CT: Greenwood Press, 1991), pp. 15–23.

12. Gerring, *Party Ideologies in America*, pp. 65, 67, 69, 79, 82; H. Wayne Morgan, *William McKinley and His America* (Syracuse: Syracuse University Press, 1963), p. 131.

13. Morgan, *William McKinley and His America*, pp. 61–62.

14. Gerring, *Party Ideologies in America*, pp. 60–62, 116; Sundquist, *Dynamics of the Party System*, pp. 156–57; Morgan, *William McKinley and His America*, pp. 228, 233, 235; Matthew Josephson, *The Politicos, 1850–1896* (New York: Harcourt, 1938), pp. 647–57; R. Hal Williams, *Years of Decision: American Politics in the 1890s* (New York: John Wiley, 1978), pp. 122–23; Jerome M. Clubb, William H. Flanigan, and Nancy H. Zingale, *Partisan Realignment: Voters, Parties, and Government in American History* (Boulder, CO: Westview Press, 1990), p. 157.

15. Brownlee, *Dynamics of Ascent*, pp. 384–88; Allen, *The Big Change*, pp. 124–25, 140; Allan A. Lichtman, "They Endured: Democrats Between World War I and the Depression," in *Democrats and the American Idea: A Bicentennial Appraisal,* edited by Peter B. Kovler (Washington, DC: Center for National Policy Press, 1992), pp. 229–34; William Allen White, *A Puritan in Babylon: The Story of Calvin Coolidge* (New York: Macmillan, 1938), p. 342; Andrew Mellon quoted in Harvey O'Connor, *Mellon's Millions: The Biography of a Fortune—The Life and Times of Andrew Mellon* (New York: John Day, 1933), pp. 127–28, 132–33, 142, 310.

16. Bartels, "Electoral Continuity and Change," p. 289; Sundquist, *Dynamics of the Party System*, pp. 200–202; Arthur M. Schlesinger, Jr., *The Age of Roosevelt: The Crisis of the Old Order* (Boston: Houghton Mifflin, 1956), p. 242; Jordan A. Schwarz, *The New Dealers: Power Politics in the Age of Roosevelt* (New York: Alfred A. Knopf, 1993), pp. 45–51; Gerring, *Party Ideologies in America*, pp. 125–26.

17. Franklin D. Roosevelt, "The Forgotten Man" speech, in *The Public Papers and Ad-*

dresses: The Genesis of the New Deal, 1928–1932 (New York: Random House, 1938), vol. I, pp. 624–27.

18. Roosevelt quoted in Gerring, *Party Ideologies in America,* p. 208.

19. This list is from Stanley B. Greenberg, *Middle Class Dreams: The Politics and Power of the New American Majority* (New Haven: Yale University Press, 1996), p. 81.

20. Ann Shola Orloff, "The Political Origins of America's Belated Welfare State" in *The Politics of Social Policy in the United States,* edited by Margaret Weir, Ann Shola Orloff, and Theda Skocpol (Princeton: Princeton University Press, 1988), pp. 70–78; Theodore R. Marmor, Jerry L. Mashaw, and Phillip L. Harvey, *America's Misunderstood Welfare State: Persistent Myths, Enduring Realities* (New York: Basic Books, 1990), pp. 33–35; Franklin Roosevelt, "The Election: An Interpretation," *Liberty,* December 10, 1932, p. 8.

21. Schlesinger, *The Age of Roosevelt,* pp. 503, 584, 631–32. Also see Alonzo L. Hamby, "The Democratic Moment: FDR to LBJ," in Kovler, *Democrats and the American Idea,* p. 256.

22. John F. Kennedy, quoted in Richard Goodwin, *Remembering America* (Boston: Little, Brown, 1998), p. 129.

23. David Leege, "The Catholic Voter," paper presented at the Commonweal Foundation and Faith and Reason Institute, June 2–4, 2000, p. 3.

24. See Chapter 4, note 1, for a description of the formula for allocating the Perot vote between Dole and Clinton, which is based on the exit polls in 1996.

25. Greenberg, *Middle Class Dreams,* pp. 1–22.

26. Martin Wattenberg, *The Decline of American Political Parties, 1952–1996* (Cambridge, MA: Harvard University Press, 1998), pp. 142–43.

27. Mark D. Brewer, "A Divided Public? Party Images and Mass Polarization in the United States," paper presented to the American Political Science Association, August 28–September 1, 2002, pp. 11–13.

28. Larry M. Bartels, "Partisanship and Voting Behavior, 1952–1996," *American Journal of Political Science* 44, no. 1 (January 2000): 39–41.

29. Brewer, "A Divided Public?" pp. 6–7.

30. Ibid., pp. 13–20.

31. During the post–9/11 period, the Republican Party emerged with higher ratings than the Democrats: 56.3 degrees, compared to 52.8. For the Democrats that is in range with their position from 1992 to 1998, though their position rose to 55.0 degrees before the 2000 election, still well short of their historic position. While the Republican position rose in the 18-month period of the study, its thermometer rating dropped to 51.6 degrees in the summer of 2003, back in the range of the last decade of this era. See Greenberg, *Middle Class Dreams,* Figure A.4; Democracy Corps and Greenberg Quinlan Rosner Research time series on thermometer ratings, 1996 to 2003.

32. Author's analysis of National Election Studies (NES) data.

33. The literature shows the number of independents growing marginally, but a decline in the number of "pure" independents with no party leaning at all, after follow-up questions. That is completely consistent with the idea that the two parties are contesting the independents, who, in fact, may increasingly lean toward these well-defined parties. That does not change the fact that these voters identify as "independents" and might respond to a different politics if given the opportunity. See Bartels, "Partisanship and Voting Behavior," pp. 36–37.

34. Larry Bartels, "Electoral Continuity and Change, 1868–1996," *Electoral Studies* 17, no. 3 (1998): 295–96.

35. Red states were won by the Republican George W. Bush, blue states were won by the Democrat Al Gore. Battleground states are those decided by fewer than 6 points, except for West Virginia (Bush won by 6 points in 2000, but it is deemed "battleground" because it was Democratic in every other presidential election since 1988) and Washington (Gore won by 5 points, but it is not battleground because Democrats have won it in every other presidential election since 1988). Also, the percentage aligning with each party in the battleground states are based on the Democracy Corps database for 2001–2003.

36. Michael Barone, "Introduction: the 49 Percent Nation," *Almanac of American Politics, 2002* (Washington, DC: National Journal, 2001), pp. 21–45.

37. Judis and Teixeira, *The Emerging Democratic Majority,* p. 9.

38. Daniel Bell, *The Coming of Post-Industrial Society* (New York: Basic Books, 1999), pp. xv–xxiv, xxxv–xxxviii, lii–lx, lxxi, 112–19. Also see Bruce Arai, "From Post-Industrial to Post-Modern Society: New Theories of the Contemporary World," *Canadian Journal of Sociology,* vol. 23, issue 1 (January 1998); J. Tomas Gomez Arias and Laurentino Bello Acebron, "Postmodern Approaches in Business-to-Business Marketing and Marketing Research," *Journal of Business and Industrial Marketing* 16, no. 1 (2001): 7–20; David Harvey, *The Condition of Postmodernity: An Enquiry into the Origins of Cultural Change* (Cambridge, MA: Blackwell, 1990), pp. 8–9, 42–45, 54–60. By contrast, Nicholas Tompson describes the treatment of science and scientists in the Bush administration in "Science Friction: The growing—and dangerous—divide between scientists and the GOP," *The Washington Monthly,* July/August 2003; David Brooks, *Bobos in Paradise* (New York: Simon and Schuster, 2000) pp. 45, 256–57.

39. E. E. Schattschneider, *A Realist's View of Democracy in America* (Fort Worth: Harcourt, 1975), pp. 47–48, 62–66, 71–74. I am aware of Mayhew's convincing critique in *Electoral Realignments* of Schattschneider's case for realigning elections in general and the election of 1896, in particular. Mayhew's critique does not rule out the concept emphasized in this book, that the dominant conflict lines impact what issues are central and what groups get drawn into the electorate.

PART II: HALF CENTURY UNTAMED: 1952–2002

1. Gerring, *Party Ideologies in America*, p. 233.
2. Zachary Karabell, *The Last Campaign: How Harry Truman Won the 1948 Election* (New York: Alfred A. Knopf, 2000), pp. 210–11. Also, see David McCullough, *Truman* (New York: Simon and Schuster, 1992), pp. 658–59.
3. Sundquist, *Dynamics of the Party System*, pp. 271–77, 281–83; Kevin Phillips, *The Emerging Republican Majority* (Garden City, NY: Anchor Books, 1970), p. 199.
4. David Halberstam, *The Fifties* (New York: Ballantine Books, 1993), p. 205. Many of my general observations about the fifties are informed by this work.
5. Gerring, *Party Ideologies in America*, pp. 128, 134, 138, 152.
6. Adlai Stevenson quoted in ibid., pp. 248–49.
7. Adlai Stevenson quoted in Edward G. Carmines and James A. Stimson, *Issue Evolution* (Princeton: Princeton University Press, 1989), pp. 35–40; Sundquist, *Dynamics of the Party System*, pp. 355–56.
8. David R. Mayhew, *Divided We Govern: Party Control, Lawmaking, and Investigations 1946–1990* (New Haven: Yale University Press, 1991), Table 4.1.
9. Greenberg, *Middle Class Dreams*, p. 315.
10. Brewer, "A Divided Public?", p. 12.
11. NES data. Excluding the South and allocating the independent leaners to their respective parties, the country was fairly evenly divided in this period. In 1952, the Democrats had a 7-point edge (50.5 to 43.1 percent), but in 1956 and 1960, the Republicans had a 1-point advantage (45.1 to 44.3 percent and 46.4 to 45.5 percent, respectively).
12. Arthur H. Miller, "Political Issues and Trust in Government: 1964–1970," *American Political Science Review* 68 (September 1974), p. 953.
13. Lawrence Mishel, Jared Bernstein, and Heather Boushey, *The State of Working America 2002/2003* (Ithaca: Cornell University Press, 2003), pp. 36–37, 53–54.
14. Halberstam, *The Fifties*, p. 587.
15. Roger Kahn, *The Boys of Summer* (New York: Harper, 1987), pp. xviii–xx.
16. Halberstam, *The Fifties*, pp. 478–79, 508–09.
17. Robert Dallek, *An Unfinished Life: John Kennedy 1917–1963* (Boston: Little, Brown, 2003), pp. 294–95.
18. Richard N. Goodwin, *Remembering America: A Voice from the Sixties* (Boston: Little, Brown, 1988), p. 103.

2. THE OPPORTUNITY DEMOCRATS: REDEFINED BY RACE

1. Sorensen, *Kennedy*, pp. 198–99.
2. Ibid., p. 217.

3. Goodwin, *Remembering America,* p. 129.

4. Ibid.

5. John F. Kennedy, Inaugural Address, January 20, 1961, in Sorensen, *Kennedy,* pp. 245–48.

6. Gerring, *Party Ideologies in America,* p. 241.

7. Dallek, *An Unfinished Life,* p. 640.

8. Ibid.

9. Ibid., pp. 690–91.

10. Lawrence R. Jacobs, *The Health of Nations: Public Opinion and the Making of American and British Health Policy* (Ithaca: Cornell University Press, 1993), pp. 138–43.

11. John F. Kennedy, Inaugural Address, January 20, 1961, in Sorensen, *Kennedy,* p. 248.

12. Sorensen, *Kennedy,* p. 199.

13. Alan Brinkley, *The End of Reform: New Deal Liberalism in Recession and War* (New York: Vintage Books, 1996), pp. 126–36, 140–43.

14. Dallek, *An Unfinished Life,* pp. 311, 334.

15. Arthur M. Schlesinger, Jr., *A Thousand Days: John F. Kennedy in the White House* (Boston: Houghton Mifflin, 1965), pp. 74–75.

16. Richard Reeves, *President Kennedy: Profile of Power* (New York: Simon and Schuster, 1993), pp. 39, 126–33, 353–57.

17. Dallek, *An Unfinished Life,* pp. 580, 583.

18. Ibid., p. 589.

19. Ibid., p. 604.

20. Ibid., pp. 578–86.

21. Sorensen, *Kennedy,* p. 754.

22. Dallek, *An Unfinished Life,* p. 708.

23. Goodwin, *Remembering America,* pp. 272–78.

24. Ibid., pp. 278–81.

25. See Thomas Byrne Edsall with Mary Edsall, *Chain Reaction: The Impact of Race, Rights, and Taxes on American Politics* (New York: W. W. Norton, 1991), pp. 47–48, 51–52; George C. Edwards, *Presidential Approval* (Baltimore: Johns Hopkins Press, 1990); National Advisory Commission on Civil Disorders, *The Kerner Report,* New York: Bantam Books, 1968, pp. 114–15; U.S. Department of Justice, Federal Bureau of Investigation, *Uniform Crime Reports for the United States,* 1970, pp. 2–14; Gallup Surveys, August–October 1968.

26. Edsall and Edsall, *Chain Reaction,* pp. 57, 87–88.

27. Lyndon B. Johnson, "To Fulfill These Rights," commencement address at Howard University, June 4, 1965, in *Public Papers of the Presidents of the United States: Lyndon Baines Johnson, 1965,* vol. 2 (Washington, DC: GPO, 1966), p. 636.

28. Ibid., pp. 637–39; Robert X. Browning, *Politics and Social Welfare Policy in the United States* (Knoxville: University of Tennessee Press, 1986), pp. 105–08; Margaret

Weir, *Politics and Jobs: The Boundaries of Employment Policy in the United States* (Princeton: Princeton University Press, 1992), pp. 74–78, 84–88.

29. Theda Skocpol, *The Missing Middle: Working Families and the Future of American Social Policy* (New York: W. W. Norton, 2000), pp. 7–9.

30. Gary Orfield, "Race and the Liberal Agenda," in Weir et al., *The Politics of Social Policy,* p. 336; Sundquist, *Dynamics of the Party System,* p. 291; William A. Rusher, *The Making of the New Majority Party* (New York: Sheed and Ward, 1975), pp. 57–58; Edsall and Edsall, *Chain Reaction,* pp. 60–61.

31. See Weir, *Politics and Jobs,* p. 83.

32. Lewis Chester, Godfrey Hodgson, and Bruce Page, *An American Melodrama: The Presidential Campaign of 1968* (New York: Viking, 1969), pp. 280–81; Theodore H. White, *The Making of the President 1968: A Narrative History of American Politics in Action* (New York: Atheneum, 1969), pp. 344–49.

33. Spiro Agnew quoted in Sundquist, *Dynamics of the Party System,* pp. 386–87; Nixon quoted in A. James Reichley, *Conservatives in an Age of Change: The Presidential Campaign of 1968* (New York: Viking, 1969), pp. 174–202.

34. Phillips, *The Emerging Republican Majority,* pp. 37–38, 205–06, 291–92, 464, 470.

35. This accounting of the 1968 results is from Greenberg, *Middle Class Dreams,* pp. 114–17.

36. Phillips, *The Emerging Republican Majority,* pp. 1, 30, 206–07.

37. Carmines and Stimson, *Issue Evolution,* pp. 50–52.

38. Benjamin I. Page and Robert Y. Shapiro, *The Rational Public: Fifty Years of Trends in Americans' Policy Preferences* (Chicago: University of Chicago Press, 1992), pp. 63, 70, 74.

39. Ibid., pp. 156, 159.

3. THE REAGAN REVOLUTIONARIES: REDUCED TO CULTURE WAR

1. Rick Perlstein, *Before the Storm: Barry Goldwater and the Unmaking of the American Consensus* (New York: Hill and Wang, 2001), pp. 513–14.

2. Barry Goldwater from *The Conscience of a Conservative,* quoted ibid., pp. 64–67, 422.

3. Perlstein, *Before the Storm,* pp. 148–49, 166, 206.

4. Barry Goldwater, *The Conscience of a Conservative* (Washington, DC: Regnery Gateway, 1990), pp. 6–7, 18–19, 28, 32–35, 39, 56, 64; Phillips, *The Emerging Republican Majority,* p. 236.

5. H. R. Haldeman, *The Haldeman Diaries: Inside the Nixon White House* (New York: Putnam, 1994), pp. 117–19, 132, 183–86, 208.

6. For a discussion of the Philadelphia Plan and Richard Nixon, see Hugh Davis Gra-

ham, *Civil Rights and the Presidency: Race and Gender in American Politics 1960–1972* (New York: Oxford University Press, 1992), pp. 150–69; also see Hugh Davis Graham, *Collision Course: The Strange Convergence of Affirmative Action and Immigration Policy in America* (New York: Oxford University Press, 2002), pp. 67–74.

7. Reichley, *Conservatives in an Age of Change*, pp. 172, 206–26; Stephen E. Ambrose, *Nixon: The Triumph of a Politician, 1962–1972* (New York: Simon and Schuster, 1989), vol. 2, pp. 572–73.

8. Reichley, *Conservatives in an Age of Change*, pp. 137–44, 155–58; Richard G. Niemi, John Mueller, and Tom W. Smith, *Trends in Public Opinion: A Compendium of Survey Data* (New York: Greenwood Press, 1989), p. 76.

9. Norbert Goldfield, "The Nixon Years: Failed National Health Reform from Both Parties," *Physician Executive*, May 1992; Carole Gentry, "National Health Care: The Long Fight," *St. Petersburg Times*, July 24, 1989.

10. This litany of regulations was presented in Greenberg, *Middle Class Dreams*, p. 127, drawing on Mayhew, *Divided We Govern*, pp. 82–88.

11. Michael R. Beschloss, "A Question of Anti-Semitism," *Newsweek*, October 18, 1999.

12. This section draws on and excerpts part of my account in *Middle Class Dreams* on top-down prosperity, tax cuts, and Reagan's accessibility to working- and middle-class families (pp. 130–37, 143–48). There is a raft of new books about Reagan and the aftermath of his presidency, which I address in Chapters 9 and 10. Rather than revise this account, I have chosen to address the historical issues as part of the current political debate.

13. Gerring, *Party Ideologies in America*, pp. 125–58.

14. Haynes Johnson, *Sleepwalking Through History: America in the Reagan Years* (New York: Doubleday, 1992), p. 94; O'Connor, *Mellon's Millions,* p. 316; Ronald Reagan quoted in Kevin Phillips, *Post-Conservative America: People, Politics, and Ideology in a Time of Crisis* (New York: Random House, 1982), p. 9, also see pp. 133–39.

15. Garry Wills, *Reagan's America: Innocents at Home* (New York: Penguin Books, 1988), pp. 332–34.

16. George Gilder, *Wealth and Poverty* (New York: Basic Books, 1981), pp. 5–6, 8, 20, 27–28, 35.

17. David Stockman quoted in William Greider, "The Education of David Stockman," *The Atlantic,* December 1981, p. 47; Gilder, *Wealth and Poverty*, pp. 28, 63.

18. Benjamin M. Friedman, *Day of Reckoning: The Consequences of American Economic Policy Under Reagan and After* (New York: Vintage Books, 1989), pp. 135–39, 149; Bureau of Labor Statistics, "Employment and Earnings," January 1994, p. 182.

19. Peggy Noonan, *What I Saw at the Revolution: A Political Life in the Reagan Era* (New York: Random House, 1990), p. 270; Walter Dean Burnham, *The Current Crisis in American Politics* (New York: Oxford University Press, 1982), pp. 236–39, 282–89, 301.

20. Lou Cannon, *President Reagan: The Role of a Lifetime* (New York: Simon and

Schuster, 1991), pp. 40–41. Also see Noonan, *What I Saw at the Revolution*, pp. 149–51, 267, and Wills, *Reagan's America*.

21. Cannon, quoted in *President Reagan*, p. 90.

22. Noonan, *What I Saw at the Revolution*, pp. 124–26; Cannon, *President Reagan*, pp. 518–19.

23. Noonan, *What I Saw at the Revolution*, pp. 87–94; Cannon, *President Reagan*, pp. 90–94.

24. Cannon, *President Reagan*, pp. 108, 243–44; Greider, "The Education of David Stockman," pp. 44–45.

25. Cannon, *President Reagan*, p. 812.

26. Jane J. Mansbridge, *Why We Lost the ERA* (Chicago: University of Chicago Press, 1986), pp. 1, 13, 24–25; Kristin Luker, *Abortion & the Politics of Motherhood* (Berkeley: University of California Press, 1985), pp. 126–27.

27. Mansbridge, *Why We Lost the ERA*, p. 5.

28. Luker, *Abortion & the Politics of Motherhood*, pp. 138, 161, 186–91, 193–94, 207.

29. James Davison Hunter, *Culture Wars: The Struggle to Define America* (New York: Basic Books, 1991), p. 275.

30. Thomas Byrne Edsall, "The Reagan Legacy," in *The Reagan Legacy*, edited by Sidney Blumenthal and Thomas Byrne Edsall (New York: Pantheon Books, 1988), pp. 25–27; Reagan quoted in Edsall and Edsall, *Chain Reaction*, p. 141; Phillips, *Post-Conservative America*, pp. 5–22; Sundquist, *Dynamics of the Party System*, p. 422.

31. Mansbridge, *Why We Lost the ERA*, pp. 19, 215.

32. Theodore J. Lowi, *The End of the Republican Era* (Norman: University of Oklahoma Press, 1995), pp. 158–59.

33. Walter Mondale quoted in "The Religious Issue, With Gusto," *New York Times*, Week in Review editorial desk, September 16, 1984; Ronald Reagan, remarks at Reagan-Bush rally in Hammontown, NJ, September 19, 1984.

34. Cannon, *President Reagan*, pp. 93, 314–16, 510, 516–17.

35. David Ignatius, "Reagan's Foreign Policy and the Rejection of Diplomacy," in Blumenthal and Edsall, *The Reagan Legacy*, p. 174.

36. Cannon, *President Reagan*, pp. 483–86.

37. Roper Center, University of Connecticut, Public Opinion Online, CBS News/*New York Times* polls taken from survey of more than 1,000 American adults, June 1981 and February 1985.

38. Harris Poll, January 6, 2002, survey of more than 1,000 American adults via telephone and compared with results from polls taken in past years.

39. Cannon, *President Reagan*, p. 495; Ignatius, "Reagan's Foreign Policy and the Rejection of Diplomacy," p. 175.

40. Greenberg, *Middle Class Dreams*, pp. 312–14.

41. Reagan quoted in Sidney Blumenthal, *The Rise of the Counter-Establishment: From Conservative Ideology to Political Power* (New York: Times Books, 1981), p. 282.

42. Barbara G. Farah and Helmut Norpoth, "Trends in Partisan Realignment, 1976–1986: A Decade of Waiting," paper presented to the American Political Science Association, Washington, DC, August 29, 1986, table 1; Kathleen Knight, "Partisan Differences in the Understanding of Partisan Differences," paper presented at the annual meeting of the Midwest Political Science Association, 1987, table 1; Warren Miller, "Party Identification Re-examined" (Washington, DC: Center for National Policy, 1987), p. 27.

43. This section on the economy depends heavily on the recent results in Mishel et al., *The State of Working America, 2002/2003*. The economic state of the decade is best measured by using business cycle peaks, 1979 to 1989, which does not perfectly match the decade of the eighties and the Reagan era but is very close.

44. Mishel et al., *The State of Working America, 2002/2003*, pp. 36–37.

45. Ibid., pp. 55–56.

46. Ibid., pp. 160–61.

47. Ibid., pp. 125–26.

48. Ibid., p. 100.

49. Celinda Lake and Stanley B. Greenberg, "Liberalism Reconstructed: Survey on Liberalism in the 1988 Election," February 1989; Greenberg, *Middle Class Dreams*, p. 145.

50. Confidence is based on the percentage saying "very high" or "high," in surveys conducted by Gallup, reported by CNN, July 19–21, 1993. Also see Lake and Greenberg, "Liberalism Reconstructed."

51. Gallup surveys, 1983, 1985; Opinion Research Corporation national surveys, 1981, 1983, 1985, 1987.

52. This account of the Bush campaign and the diminishing of the Reagan vision includes material from Greenberg, *Middle Class Dreams* (pp. 11–14), which has been revised.

53. Lee Atwater quoted in Bill Greider, "The Power of Negative Thinking," *Rolling Stone*, January 12, 1989, pp. 51–53.

54. Hunter, *Culture Wars*, p. 279.

55. Bureau of the Census, *Money Income of Households, Families, and Persons in the United States: 1992*, Current Population Reports, Series P60-184, 1993, Table B-6; Lawrence Mishel and Jared Bernstein, *The State of Working America, 1992/1993* (Armonk, NY: M. E. Sharpe, 1993), p. 48.

56. George H. W. Bush, State of the Union, January 28, 1992.

57. Greenberg, *Middle Class Dreams*, pp. 312–14.

58. Walter Dean Burnham, "The Politics of Repudiation, 1992: Edging Toward Upheaval," *American Prospect* 21 (Winter 1993): 24–27.

59. These results are based on an analysis of the exit polls conducted by Voter Research and Surveys (VRS), the exit polls for the national television networks.

60. This report is based on the largest national survey of Perot voters, 1,200 interviews conducted across the country in proportion to the Perot vote in 1992. The survey

was supplemented by a national sampling of Bush and Clinton voters (800 interviews) and by a series of six focus groups with key segments of the Perot bloc: under-30 voters in San Bernardino, California; older, non-college-educated Perot voters in Bangor, Maine; under-50 non-college-educated voters in Akron, Ohio (one group consisted of only union workers). The national survey was conducted between May 13 and May 18. (Democratic Leadership Council, "The Road to Realignment: The Democrats and the Perot Voters," 1993.)

61. Perot voters split fairly evenly between Clinton (36 percent) and Bush (39 percent) in a race without Perot. But given the Perot voters' predominant Republican past, an even split represents a major gain for Democrats. Had Perot voters split evenly nationally, as the exit polls indicated they would, Clinton would have won with 53 percent of the vote.

62. Democratic Leadership Council, "The Road to Realignment."

63. Greenberg, *Middle Class Dreams,* pp. 163–65.

64. David C. Leege, Kenneth D. Wald, Brian S. Krueger, and Paul D. Mueller, *The Politics of Cultural Differences: Social Change and Voter Mobilization Strategies in the Post–New Deal Period* (Princeton: Princeton University Press, 2002), pp. 5–6, 253–54.

4. THE REFORMED OPPORTUNITY DEMOCRATS: THE LOST MIDDLE

1. The estimate of the Clinton and Gore votes is based on exit polls that asked the supporters of the third-party candidates how they would have voted if their candidate had not been on the ballot. In 1992, Perot voters broke evenly: 40 percent for Clinton and 39 percent for Bush, though 6 percent would have voted for other candidates and 15 percent would not have voted. In 1996, the Perot voters again would have split, though with many more opting out: 30 percent for Clinton, 30 percent for Dole, and 36 percent not voting. In 2000, the Nader voters would have broken two to one for Gore (47 to 22 percent), though many said they would not have voted (30 percent). Author's analysis of Voter News Service data.

   The cruder estimate would be simply to drop out the third party voters and calculate the Democratic percentage of the two-party vote. In that case, Clinton won with 53.4 percent in 1992 and 54.7 percent in 1996, and Gore won with 50.3 percent in 2000.

2. *The New York Times,* October 31, 1988; Lake and Greenberg, "Liberalism Reconstructed"; ABC News, *The '88 Vote* (New York: ABC News, 1988), pp. 18–20.

3. Bill Clinton, keynote address to the DLC's Cleveland Convention, May 6, 1991.

4. Ibid.

5. Bill Clinton, "A New Covenant: Responsibility and Rebuilding the American Community," Georgetown University, October 23, 1991.

6. Bill Clinton, address to Tri-State Democrats Unity Dinner, Sioux City, Iowa, September 6, 1991.

7. Bill Clinton, "A New Covenant," October 23, 1991.

8. Bill Clinton, keynote address, Democratic Leadership Council (DLC), Cleveland Convention.

9. Bill Clinton, announcement speech, Old State House, Little Rock, Arkansas, October 3, 1991.

10. Bill Clinton, address to the DLC, New Orleans, March 24, 1990; Democratic Leadership Council, "The New Orleans Declaration: A Democratic Agenda for the 1990s," National Conference, March 22–25, 1990.

11. Bill Clinton, "A New Covenant," October 23, 1991.

12. See Greenberg, *Middle Class Dreams,* pp. 225–27.

13. Bill Clinton, keynote address to Cleveland Convention.

14. Bill Clinton, "A New Covenant," October, 23, 1991.

15. Bill Clinton, address to Democratic National Committee, Los Angeles, September 20, 1991.

16. Greenberg, *Middle Class Dreams,* pp. 219–22.

17. Bill Clinton, victory speech, Little Rock, Arkansas, November 4, 1992.

18. See note 1 above for a description of these calculations and estimate of the Clinton vote.

19. Elizabeth Drew, *On the Edge: The Clinton Presidency* (New York: Simon and Schuster, 1994), p. 421; Elizabeth Drew, *Showdown: The Struggle Between the Gingrich Congress and the Clinton White House* (New York: Simon and Schuster, 1996), p. 11.

20. Gerald M. Pomper, "The Presidential Election," in *The Election of 1996: Reports and Interpretations,* edited by Gerald M. Pomper et al. (Chatham, NJ: Chatham House Publishers, 1997), p. 173.

21. Peter Goldman, "Afterword: The Small Deal," in *Back from the Dead: How Clinton Survived the Republican Revolution,* edited by Evan Thomas et al. (New York: Atlantic Monthly Press, 1997), p. 209.

22. Mishel et al., *The State of Working America, 2002/2003,* pp. 37, 41, 315.

23. Ibid., pp. 55–56, 125–26, 160–61.

24. Elizabeth Drew, *On the Edge: The Clinton Presidency* (New York: Simon and Schuster, 1994), pp. 48–50, 57–73, 83.

25. Joe Klein, *The Natural: The Misunderstood Presidency of Bill Clinton* (New York: Doubleday, 2002) p. 12.

26. Ibid., p. 160.

27. Department of Commerce, *Current Population Reports, 2000.*

28. See Larry M. Bartels and John Zaller, "Al Gore and George Bush's Not-So-Excellent Adventure," *Political Science and Politics,* March 2001.

29. The Gore Campaign, national survey of 1000 likely voters, November 2–3, 2000; Democratic Leadership Council, national survey of 1,200 voters, November 8–9, 2000, conducted by Penn, Schoen, and Berland.

30. Senator John F. Kennedy and Vice President Richard M. Nixon, debate, Chicago, September 26, 1960.

31. Al Gore, announcement speech, Carthage, Tennessee, June 16, 1999.

32. Al Gore, acceptance speech, Democratic Convention, Los Angeles, August 17, 2000.

33. Al Gore, "Broken Promises and Political Deception," *The New York Times*, August 4, 2002, section 4, p. 13.

34. Democracy Corps, national survey, August 3, 2000; national survey of 1,003 likely voters, September 4–6, 2000; national survey of 1,014 likely voters, September 27–30, 2000.

35. Democracy Corps national survey of 1,098 likely voters, September 20–23, 2000.

36. Stan Greenberg and Bob Shrum, "Strategic Framework: The Final Weeks," memo for Gore campaign, October 20, 2000; television commercial for Gore/Lieberman, GL-2023–30 "Super," first aired October 12, 2000.

37. Michael Waldman, *Potus Speaks: Finding the Words That Defined the Clinton Presidency* (New York: Simon and Schuster, 2000), p. 271.

38. Author's analysis of NES data.

39. Greenberg, *Middle Class Dreams*, pp. 34–38.

40. By 43 to 40 percent, voters thought Gore was the more likely to be fiscally responsible. See Mark Penn, "Turning a Win into a Draw," *Blueprint*, Winter 2001 (Why Gore Lost).

41. Mishel et al., *The State of Working America, 2002/2003*, pp. 64–65.

42. Klein, *The Natural*, pp. 148–49.

43. Drew, *Showdown*, pp. 93–106.

44. See Waldman, *Potus Speaks*, pp. 168–69.

45. George Stephanopoulos, *All Too Human: A Political Education* (Boston: Little, Brown, 1999), pp. 371–75.

46. Waldman, *Potus Speaks*, p. 154.

47. Bill Clinton, remarks at the DLC Retreat, Franklin Delano Roosevelt Presidential Library, Hyde Park, New York, May 21, 2000.

48. This is largely consistent with Sidney Blumenthal's characterization of the Clinton impact in *The Clinton Wars: An Insider's Account of the White House Years* (New York: Farrar, Straus and Giroux, 2003), pp. 59–64.

49. Drew, *On the Edge*, pp. 59–64.

50. Bob Woodward, *The Agenda: Inside the Clinton White House* (New York: Simon and Schuster, 1994), pp. 325–26.

51. Gary C. Jacobson "The 1994 House Elections in Perspective," paper presented to the Midwest Political Science Association, April 1995.

52. Mishel et al., *The State of Working America, 2002/2003*, pp. 100, 124–26, 160–61.

53. Greenberg Quinlan Rosner national survey for the Democratic Leadership Council, November 8–9, 1994.

54. Skocpol, *Missing Middle*, pp. 4–5.

55. Democracy Corps combined datase.

56. Democracy Corps national survey of 1,038 likely voters, September 13–17, 1998.

57. Klein, *The Natural,* p. 182.

58. Results for the congressional elections based on Voter's News Service (VNS) data, 1996–98.

59. Thomas et al., *Back from the Dead,* pp. 87–88.

60. Greenberg Quinlan Rosner Research, "The Progressive Majority and the 2000 Elections: A Report on Post-Election National Surveys," Campaign for America's Future, December 15, 2000.

61. Theda Skocpol, *Boomerang: Clinton's Health Security Effort and the Turn Against Government in U.S. Politics* (New York: W. W. Norton, 1996), p. xi.

62. Dan Balz and Ronald Brownstein, *Storming the Gates: Protest Politics and the Republican Revival* (Boston: Little, Brown, 1996), pp. 195–98.

63. Ibid., p. 14.

64. Scott Keeter, "Public Opinion and the Election," in Pomper et al., *The Election of 1996,* p. 117.

65. Waldman, *Potus Speaks,* pp. 90–91.

66. Thomas et al., *Back from the Dead,* pp. 177–78.

67. According to a postelection national study conducted by Greenberg Quinlan Rosner Research, 59 percent cited Clinton's support for domestic programs (education, Medicare, the environment) as the prime reason for their vote (Campaign for America's Future, national survey of 1,000 voters, November 12, 1996).

68. Waldman, *Potus Speaks,* pp. 215–16.

69. Skocpol, *The Missing Middle,* pp. 6–7.

70. Stephanopoulos, *All Too Human,* p. 360.

71. Democracy Corps, national survey of 1,016 likely voters, October 30–31, 2000.

72. Nearly two-thirds of 1996 Perot voters (64 percent) cast a ballot for Bush in 2000.

PART III: THE LOYALISTS

1. I owe this characterization to a conversation with David Halberstam, who has written more fully about Michael Jordan.

2. See the description of the survey methodology in Appendix A.

3. See Appendix A for a discussion on party alignment.

4. The mean thermometer score is displayed for each group in Appendixes B, C, and D.

5. See the discussion in Appendix A.

6. The specifications for the focus groups are discussed in Appendix A.

5. THE WORLD OF REPUBLICAN PARTISANS

1. These are self-identified Republicans, not independents, and well over 90 percent now normally vote for their own party in presidential elections. The self-identified Republicans together with the independents constitute a larger partisan group that we call Republican "aligned." In the period of this research, 46 percent of the likely voters were aligned with the Republicans.

2. David Brooks, "One Nation, Slightly Divisible," *The Atlantic,* December 2001, p. 53.

3. Alan Wolfe offers important insights into the "quiet faith," the religious tolerance of many middle-class Christians. I found it a useful guide as I began my own direct interviewing in this area, which is reflected in the community research in Chapter 7. See Wolfe's *One Nation After All: What Middle-Class Americans Really Think About* (New York: Viking, 1998), pp. 39–61, 67–72.

4. See Christian Smith, *Christian America? What Evangelicals Really Want* (Berkeley: University of California Press, 2000), pp. 15–17, 37, 162–63, 200, 202, 204, 206.

5. Hunter, *Culture Wars,* pp. 112–13.

6. Ibid., p. 130.

7. Smith, *Christian America?* pp. 212–15.

8. Jerome L. Himmelstein, "The Social Basis of Antifeminism: Religious Networks and Culture," *Journal for the Scientific Study of Religion* 25, no. 1 (1986): 7–9, 12.

9. The results for the partisan groups appear in Appendixes B and C, along with the specifications of each group. Unless otherwise stated, the results in this chapter are from the Democracy Corps combined data set of national surveys.

10. The results for the 2000 election are based on postelection surveys conducted for VNS. While there were no usable exit polls in 2002, those were approximated by the postelection surveys conducted by GQR.

11. The reported voting patterns for the presidential elections, 1952 to 2000, were based on NES postelection surveys of people who actually voted. NES is a national research center funded by the National Science Foundation (NSF) and located at the University of Michigan.

    The NES postelection surveys and the VNS exit polls are sometimes at odds. The differences are noted where appropriate.

12. The numbers are 48 to 41 percent in 1972, 46 to 40 percent in 1976, and 48 to 43 percent in 1980 (NES).

13. Author's analysis of NES data.

14. The 1984 results are based on the New York Times/CBS exit polls. The stable pattern for white Evangelicals is evident for both party identification and the presidential vote. On party identification, little has changed: 36 to 56 percent in 1988, 37 to 56 percent in 1992, 33 to 65 percent in 1996, and 37 to 58 percent in 2000. On presidential vote, the same pattern of stability holds: 28 to 55 percent in 1988, 29 to 55 percent in 1992, 31 to 58 percent in 1996, and 32 to 68 percent in 2000 (NES). (The NES study gives

the Democrats somewhat greater support in the 2000 election.) In 1988, they voted for Bush, 81 to 17 percent. The exit polls also show Clinton closing the gap a little in 1996, but still getting only 31 percent of the white Evangelical vote, to 61 percent for Dole. Results reported in Robert Booth Fowler, Allen D. Hertzke, and Laura R. Olson, *Religion and Politics in America* (Boulder, CO: Westview Press, 1999), p. 94.

15. Michael Lind, *Made in Texas: George W. Bush and the Southern Takeover of American Politics* (New York: Basic Books, 2003), p. 127, a mostly polemical account of George W. Bush.

16. Our primary measure for affect and feeling about organizations, leaders, and groups is the thermometer score developed by NES. The results and question wording appear in Appendix B. The thermometer score is a mean temperature on a scale from zero (extremely cold and unfavorable) to 100 (extremely hot and favorable). A 50-degree rating is the midpoint, where the respondent reacts neither hot nor cold.

17. Paul M. Weyrich, Free Congress Foundation newsletter, February 19, 1999.

18. James C. Dobson, Focus on Family newsletter, February 2001.

19. Author's analysis using the national surveys of the National Opinion Research Center (NORC) for 1972–2000. The surveys for NES show a similar pattern, but changes in question wording disrupt the time series.

20. Earl Black and Merle Black, *The Rise of Southern Republicans* (Cambridge, MA: Harvard University Press, 2002), p. 5.

21. Lind, *Made in Texas,* argues that Bush represents the plantation and Old South tradition in Texas, in contrast to Lyndon Johnson, who hailed from counties with smaller farms and more progressive traditions. That is interesting and likely true, but it misses the suburban South, with which Bush and other Republican leaders actively identify.

22. Lind, *Made in Texas*, pp. 108–127.

23. Author's analysis of NES data.

24. Balz and Brownstein, *Storming the Gates*, p. 203; author's analysis of NES data. In 1984, according to the NES postelection survey, the Republicans had a 47 to 39 percent advantage in party identification. In 1996, the Republican advantage had grown to 56 to 39, and to 57 to 32 percent in 2000.

25. Author's analysis of VNS data.

26. Ibid.

27. See Green et al., *Partisan Hearts and Minds*, pp. 141, 149.

28. In the Democracy Corps combined data set, 44 percent of those living in rural counties say they live in a rural area, while 40 percent say small town. Rural counties are those counties outside a Metropolitan Statistical Area (MSA).

29. VNS for 2000 and GQR postelection surveys for 2002. The VNS and NES data have a larger estimate of the white rural population, 18 percent (2000) and 19 percent (2002), as they take into account many small-town areas. The Democracy Corps surveys incorporate only those respondents who live in non-MSA counties.

30. Public Opinion Strategies and Greenberg Quinlan Rosner Research, "Election 2002: Rural Voters and Rural Issues," report for the W. K. Kellogg Foundation, December 2, 2002, p. 5.

31. Author's analysis of *New York Times*/CBS exit polls.

32. Richard Alm, "In Capital After Capital, the Word Is Out: Cut Spending, Don't Boost Taxes; States, Too, Sing the Budget Blues," *U.S. News & World Report,* March 10, 1986, p. 25; Curtis Hartman, "On the Road: Johnson County, Iowa; An American Tragedy," *Inc.*, May 1986, p. 110; Monroe W. Karmin, Cindy Skrzycki, and Pamela Sherrid, "The Skidding Economy; Big Bankruptcies and Weak Numbers Have Forecasters Worried," *U.S. News & World Report,* July 28, 1986, p. 16.

33. VNS exit polls in 1992, with a large sample, give Clinton 36 percent, to 44 percent for Bush, with Perot taking 22 percent. The NES postelection poll, with a much smaller sample of white rural voters, had the vote evenly divided: 37 percent for Clinton and 39 percent for Bush. A similar pattern holds in 1996. VNS, again with the much larger sample, gives Clinton 40 percent and Bush 49 percent, with 10 percent for Perot. NES shows 48 percent for Clinton and 42 percent for Bush, with 10 percent for Perot.

   White rural voters outside the South were evenly divided during both elections of the 1990s. In 1992, Clinton and Bush both got 38 percent, and in 1996, Dole edged out Clinton, 47 to 42 percent (VNS).

34. Even white rural voters outside the South voted heavily for Bush over Gore, 58 to 38 percent (VNS).

35. Susan Page, "Bush Policies Follow Politics of States Needed in 2004," *USA Today,* June 17, 2002, p. 1A.

36. See Appendix B for the results and question wording.

37. According to the Democracy Corps combined data set, 55 percent of white rural voters own guns; indeed, 36 percent have three or more guns. On changing attitudes toward the NRA, see Public Opinion Strategies and Greenberg Quinlan Rosner Research, "Election 2002: Rural Voters and Rural Issues," p. 27.

38. This section on Country Folk draws on focus groups conducted by Democracy Corps approximately every second month. In each wave, two groups were conducted in counties in central Iowa. All the participants were likely voters and identified themselves as independents or weak partisans. Each group was composed of roughly half Bush and half Gore 2000 voters. All the participants in Iowa lacked college degrees and the family income was below $50,000. The women were mothers between the ages of 30 and 49, with their children under 18 living at home. The men were between 45 and 60 and held blue-collar jobs. Each focus group included approximately ten people, lasted two hours, and was professionally moderated with the results taped and transcribed for later analysis. See Appendix A for methodology.

39. Noncollege rural women group, Des Moines, Iowa, May 1, 2002.

40. Noncollege rural women group, Des Moines, Iowa, February 12, 2002.

41. Noncollege rural women group, Des Moines, Iowa, May 1, 2002.

42. Noncollege rural men group, Des Moines, Iowa, January 7, 2003.

43. Noncollege rural women group, Des Moines, Iowa, January 7, 2003.

44. Noncollege rural men group, Des Moines, Iowa, January 7, 2003.

45. Noncollege rural men group, Des Moines, Iowa, April 8, 2003.

46. Noncollege rural men group, Des Moines, Iowa, February 12, 2002.

47. Noncollege rural men group, Des Moines, Iowa, August 28, 2002.

48. Noncollege rural men group, Des Moines, Iowa, January 7, 2003.

49. Republicans hold a 13-point advantage on the economy, leading Democrats 47 percent to 34 percent, Democracy Corps database.

50. Noncollege rural men group, Des Moines, Iowa, August 28, 2002.

51. Noncollege rural women group, Des Moines, Iowa, August 28, 2002.

52. Noncollege rural men group, Des Moines, Iowa, February 12, 2002.

53. Noncollege rural women group, Des Moines, Iowa, February 12, 2002.

54. Noncollege rural men group, Des Moines, Iowa, January 7, 2003.

55. Noncollege rural women group, Des Moines, Iowa, February 12, May 1, August 28, 2002.

56. Noncollege rural men group, Des Moines, Iowa, January 7, 2003.

57. Noncollege rural women group, Des Moines, Iowa, February 12, 2002.

58. Author's analysis of NES data.

59. I have defined exurban counties by considering population and housing growth as well as proximity to a city and by excluding cities and counties characterized by other social developments, such as those with predominant Hispanic in-migration, explosive growth of retirement communities, and those older, close-in suburbs with predominant African-American in-migration. This definition includes just over 250 counties and together these counties account for 8 percent of likely presidential voters.

    The specifications of exurban counties for this project include the following: counties with modestly high population growth for the period 1990–2000, that is, 26.4 percent or greater, twice the national average; counties where at least 20 percent of the 2000 housing stock was built in the previous decade; suburban or rural counties defined as nonurban, and excluding respondents who say they live in a small or large city. Excluded from exurban are counties where Hispanics account for 40 percent or more of the county's overall growth; counties within 20 miles of a city where African Americans account for 40 percent of the overall growth; and counties where the senior proportion is twice the national average and where the rate of senior growth is twice the national average.

60. William H. Frey, "Escaping the City and the Suburbs," *American Demographics,* June 2002.

61. Barone, "The 49 Percent Nation," p. 21.

62. Democracy Corps database.

63. See note 59.

64. These themes are evident in Lind, *Made in Texas*.

65. Susan Faludi, *Stiffed: The Betrayal of the American Man* (New York: Harper, 1999), pp. 16–24.

66. Ibid., p. 17.

67. Author's analysis of NES data.

68. Bureau of the Census, *America's Families and Living Arrangements,* Current Population Reports, pp. 20–537, June 2001, p. 3.

69. Center on Urban & Metropolitan Policy, *City Families and Suburban Singles: An Emerging Household Story From Census 2000* (Washington, DC: Brookings Institution, February 2002).

70. Greenberg, *Middle Class Dreams,* pp. 106–09.

71. Author's analysis of NES data.

72. Greenberg, *Middle Class Dreams,* pp. 34–48.

73. Author's analysis of *New York Times*/CBS exit polls.

74. Quoted in Michèle Lamont, *The Dignity of Working Men: Morality and the Boundaries of Race, Class and Immigration* (Cambridge, MA: Harvard University Press, 2000), p. 38.

75. Ibid., pp. 2–3, 10–11, 19–40.

76. Faludi, *Stiffed,* pp. 51–54, 84–89.

77. Ibid., pp. 114–21, 209–56.

78. Author's analysis of VNS data.

79. Debbie Howlett, " 'Body' Bulldozes into Politics, a New Arena for Ex-Wrestler," *USA Today,* November 5, 1998, p. 17A.

80. The single white men, as it turns out, are too libertarian and too pro-choice to join with the F-You Boys. As we shall see in Chapter 8, the older noncollege men (over 50) are too skeptical of corporate America to be part of the loyalist world.

81. In the four surveys conducted in 2003, the white senior men gave the Republicans a 7-point advantage, suggesting some unease with President Bush's direction. Are these *really* loyalists? With a sample size of 282 respondents for this period, I am reluctant to push them out of the loyalist camp, but Republicans should not take them for granted.

82. College men group, Seattle, Washington, February 19, 2002.

83. College men group, Seattle, Washington, January 8, 2003.

84. *New York Times*/CBS and VNS exit polls.

85. Author's analysis of VNS data.

6. THE WORLD OF DEMOCRATIC PARTISANS

1. Author's analysis of VNS data.

2. Bureau of the Census, *Voting and Registration in the Election of November 2000: Population Characteristics,* February 2002, p. 4.

3. Ibid.

4. George Will, "African American Inroads for the GOP," *The Washington Post,* April 27, 2003, p. 7B.

5. Mishel et al., *The State of Working America, 2002/2003,* p. 41.

6. Bureau of the Census, *Current Population Survey,* March 1994, 2000, 2001.

7. Department of Labor, Bureau of Labor Statistics, *News,* "The Unemployment Situation: May 2003," p. 2; Bureau of the Census, *Current Population Survey,* March 2002, prepared by Racial Statistics branch in cooperation with Population Division.

8. Author's analysis of VNS data. See Appendix A for a discussion of the competing estimates on Hispanic voters.

9. Bureau of the Census, *The Foreign-Born Population in the United States. Population Characteristics,* March 2000, pp. 5–6; John R. Logan, "The New Latinos: Who They Are, What They Are," report by Lewis Mumford Center for Comparative Urban and Regional Research, University of Albany, September 10, 2001, pp. 1–6.

10. Lisa Garcia Bedolla, University of California, Irvine (Department of Chicano/Latino Studies) and R. Michael Alvarez, California Institute of Technology (Division of Humanities and Social Sciences), "Similar Yet Different? Latino and Anglo Party Identification," February 4, 2002, p. 26.

11. Bureau of the Census, Population Division, *Hispanics in the U.S.,* 2000.

12. George Neumayr "A GOP Hispanic Heroine, To Everyone, That Is, Except the Republican Party," *American Spectator,* September–October 2002.

13. Bedolla and Alvarez, "Similar Yet Different?" pp. 12, 21, 26–27.

14. Congressional Hispanic Caucus Institute, membership list, 2003.

15. Department of Labor, Bureau of Labor Statistics, *Household Data and Annual Averages for 2001: Employed Persons by Detailed Occupations, Sex, Race and Hispanic Origin,* Table 11.

16. Bureau of the Census, *1997 US Economic Census, Survey of Minority-Owned Businesses,* Current Population Survey.

17. Bureau of the Census, *Health Insurance Coverage, 1999–2001.*

18. Melissa Therrien and Roberto R. Ramirez, *The Hispanic Population in the United States: March 2000,* Current Population Reports, U.S. Census Bureau, Washington, D.C., pp. 20–535.

19. Pew Hispanic Center and Kaiser Family Foundation, "National Survey of Latinos: The Latino Electorate," October 2002, p. 62.

20. Ibid., pp. 54–55.

21. Pew Hispanic Center, "March 2003 Report."

22. Thomas Hargrove, "War Casualties Include Many Minorities," Scripps Howard News Service, April 12, 2003.

23. Bedolla and Alvarez, "Similar Yet Different?" pp. 29–30, 32.

24. Pew Hispanic Center and Kaiser Family Foundation, "National Survey of Latinos," pp. 1–3.

25. Ibid., p. 4.

26. According to the VNS exit polls, in 1992, Clinton won women postgraduates 55 to 30 percent, and in 1996, 60 to 33 percent; in 2000, Gore won 63 to 34 percent.

27. College women group, Seattle, Washington, January 8, 2003.

28. Ibid.

29. College women group, Seattle, Washington, March 10, 2003.

30. College women group, Seattle, Washington, May 7, 2002.

31. College women group, Seattle, Washington, August 29, 2002.

32. Ibid.

33. College women group, Seattle, Washington, January 8, 2003.

34. Author's analysis of NORC data for 1972–2000.

35. Michael Korda, "Loaded Words," *Brill's Content*, February 2001.

36. Author's analysis of NORC data for 1972–2000.

37. Hunter, *Culture Wars*, pp. 44, 75–76, 114.

38. Ibid., pp. 188–89; also see Kenneth D. Wald, *Religion and Politics in the United States*, 4th ed. (Lanham, MD: Rowman and Littlefield, 2003).

39. NES and Democracy Corps combined data set.

40. Author's analysis of *New York Times*/CBS exit polls.

41. Author's analysis of VNS data.

42. Judis and Teixeira, *The Emerging Democratic Majority*, pp. 6–9.

43. Ibid., pp. 72–76.

44. These include the counties identified by Judis and Teixeira that included the top 50 high-tech counties, "tech poles." See Ross C. DeVol, *America's High-Technology Economy: Growth, Development, and Risks for Metropolitan Areas* (Santa Monica, CA: Milken Institute, July 13, 1999, p. 6, Figure 3), as well as the counties with one of the top 50 national universities (*U.S. News & World Report*), which obviously overlapped.

45. Author's analysis of NES data.

46. Author's analysis of *New York Times*/CBS exit polls.

47. Author's analysis of VNS data.

48. Author's analysis of NES data.

49. *New York Times*/CBS exit polls.

50. Author's analysis of NES and VNS data.

PART IV: CONTESTED AMERICA

1. All of the voters in the contested world are white, which follows from the character of the partisans. African Americans and Hispanics are among the two strongest par-

tisan Democrats and are very important to Democratic strategies for gaining the edge (see Chapter 6). The contested groups are defined by the close margin, big changes in party support, volatility, or disengagement and protest politics.

2. Green et al., *Partisan Hearts and Minds*, pp. 24–51.

7. THREE CONTESTED COMMUNITIES

1. See Appendix A for a description of the focus groups in the three communities.
2. *The Cook Political Report,* May 28, 2002, p. 32.
3. Federal Election Commission, *Campaign Finance Reports and Data,* Files H4IA05102 and H6IA03144, www.fec.gov, July 15, 2003.
4. The research and observation were conducted in towns in Hillsborough County, Florida, that had incomes close to the national median, reflecting the importance of this voter stratum in the contested world. That brought in the following towns in Hillsborough: Brandon ($51,639 median income), Citrus Park ($54,732), Egypt Lake-Leto ($35,403). In order to have large enough groups, we sometimes recruited people from similar towns in neighboring Pasco County, like Crystal Springs ($42,578), and Pinellas County, including Clearwater City ($36,494) and Palm Harbor ($45,404). These families hover around the national average and are middle-class for Florida (1999 national median, $41,994; 1999 Florida median, $38,819).

   In all cases, the focus group discussions included people who were white and without college degrees. The women were under 50 and the men were over 50, reflecting the character of the contested groups in Chapter 8.
5. The respondents in the focus groups were each asked to fill out an activity sheet. In Tampa, 65 women and 66 men responded to questions. Just over half the men and almost two-thirds of the women volunteered in some activity.
6. Hillsborough County Government Management and Budget Department Analysis of U.S. Census Bureau's Annual Household Vacancy Survey Data. Published in the online Community Statistics Resource.
7. George W. Bush speech at MacDill Air Force Base, March 26, 2003.
8. *Community News,* March 28–April 10, 2003.
9. Noncollege men group, Tampa, Florida, August 27, 2002.
10. See *Christian Voice,* vol. IV, no. 3 (March 2003).
11. The men's favorite show is *The West Wing* (20 percent), followed by *CSI* (18 percent), sports programs (15 percent), *ER* (11 percent), *Everybody Loves Raymond* (11 percent), *NYPD Blue* (9 percent), *24* (9 percent), *Law and Order* (9 percent), *JAG* (8 percent), *Boston Public* (8 percent), and *M*A*S*H* (6 percent).
12. Emily Nelson, "In Pursuit of a Hit Sitcom" *The Wall Street Journal,* May 12, 2003, p. B1. On TV viewership, 32 percent of the women say *Friends* is their favorite show, double that for their next favorite show.

13. Dallas Center Centennial Committee, "The First 100 Years 1869–1969," Dallas Center, Iowa, 1969, pp. 2–9.

14. Newton newsletter; "Santiago News," *Herald-Index,* provided by Newton Library, 2003.

15. See note 21 for a discussion of Heartland Liturgy.

16. Bureau of the Census, *State and County QuickFacts,* 2000. Prepared by Population Division in cooperation with the Housing Division.

17. "Agricultural Data for Decision Makers," Iowa State University. University Extension, June 2000. Reports for Jasper, Polk, Dallas, Boone, Guthrie, and Warren counties.

18. *Newton Daily News,* May 9, 2003.

19. Noncollege rural men group, Des Moines, Iowa, March 4, 2003.

20. Noncollege rural women group, Des Moines, Iowa, May 1, 2002; noncollege rural men group, May 1, 2002, February 12, 2002.

21. In addition to first-person observations in all three communities, this characterization was aided by analyzing local church listings. A more robust discussion of mainline Protestant denominations can be found in Roger Finke and Rodney Stark, *The Churching of America* (New Brunswick, NJ: Rutgers University Press, 1994), pp. 237–275.

22. Mark Silk, "Old Alliance, New Ground Rules," *The Washington Post,* February 18, 2001; Peter K. Johnson, "Forty Years on the Streets," *Charisma* magazine, from the Teen Challenge International Web site.

23. Pastor Mark Holmes, "On a Mission from God!" *Northeast Dallas County Record,* May 8, 2003.

24. David Swenson and Liesl Eathington, "Multiple Measures of the Role of Agriculture in Iowa's Economy," Department of Economics, College of Agriculture, Iowa State University, December 2002, pp. 7–9.

25. Jerry Perkins, "80's Farm Crisis Shook Iowa to Its Roots," *Des Moines Register,* October 26, 1999.

26. The area officially called Eastside in Seattle does not exactly match the area for this study, though there is a great deal of overlap. The research was conducted in the Eastside core cities of Bellevue, Kirkland, Redmond, and Renton and reaching to Issaquah, Duvall, Sammamish, and Woodinville. We also spoke with college-educated voters living in Auburn, to the south of Eastside and to the north of Lake Washington, as well as in Bothell, Edmonds, Lynnwood, and Mill Creek.

27. Sherry Grindeland, "Renton's Factory Past," *The Seattle Times,* January 10, 2003, p. B3.

28. The focus group discussions also recruited college-educated voters from the more northern suburbs in Snohomish County. This included towns with slightly lower median incomes but still well above the national average and with a disproportionate number of college graduates.

Renton, which includes Boeing facilities, has a somewhat lower median

($45,820) and proportion of college graduates (27.8 percent), but this did not figure centrally in this study of Eastside. We did recruit college graduates meeting our other criteria.

29. College men group, Seattle, Washington, August 29, 2002.

30. The participants in the focus groups were all college graduates. The women were age 27 to 42 and the men 32 to 49. The groups excluded strong partisans and were split between Gore and Bush voters.

31. The proportion of Hispanics is highest in Kent, with 8.1 percent, but Bellevue is at 5.3 percent and Redmond is at 5.6 percent.

32. Chris Soloman, "Eastside Immigrants," *The Seattle Times*, December 13, 2002; Chris Solomon, "A Good Place to Call Home. Eastside has bloomed from pioneer roots to today's high-tech powerhouse," *The Seattle Times*, January 24, 2003.

33. The focus groups included interviews with 99 women.

34. The focus groups included interviews with 98 men.

35. College men group, Seattle, Washington, August 29, 2003.

36. Survey by Redmond Parks and Recreation Department, presented in *Focus on Redmond*, Spring 2003.

37. J. Martin McOmber, "Creating an Ideal City—The Early Planners' Vision: Bellevue Would Be Everything Seattle Wasn't," *Seattle Times*, "A Hidden Past," October 22, 1998, p. B3.

38. Warren Cornwall, "A City Comes of Age," *The Seattle Times*, March 26, 2003, p. 10.

39. "Living East," *Greater Seattle Info Guide*.

40. Letter, *Focus on Redmond*, Spring 2003.

8. THE CONTESTED POLITICAL WORLD

1. All of the contested groups are composed of whites, primarily because African Americans and Hispanics are so strongly Democratic and discussed fully in "The World of Democratic Partisans." Indeed, that chapter discusses the imperative for Democrats to build greater unity and turnout among African Americans. Hispanics, a Democratic loyalist group, are, at the same time, very much contested between the parties.

2. Our window into the contested world, as for the partisans, is 15,045 interviews conducted with American voters in the 18-month period after 9/11. That large database of surveys conducted for Democracy Corps allowed us to look closely into the political thinking of refined segments of the American presidential electorate. In this case, it evaluates the contested political world where both parties struggle to get heard. See Appendix A.

3. Author's analysis of NES data.

4. Author's analysis of NES data.

5. Author's analysis of VNS data. Based on a study of the competing methodologies,

Democracy Corps uses a college estimate falling in between the two figures. Taking into account census projections to 2004, the Democracy Corps surveys estimate a college proportion of 41 percent in the next presidential election. See discussion in Appendix A on the appropriate education proportion.

6. Author's analysis of NES data. At the same time, VNS exit polls show the proportion as 17 percent over the last two elections.

7. Census results reported in Robert A. Rosenblatt, "College Gap Between Sexes Narrows, But Pay's Uneven," *Los Angeles Times*, March 15, 2001, p. A16.

8. Brooks, *Bobos in Paradise*, pp. 10–11, 34, 46–47, 233–35, 256–58. See Clem Brooks and Jeff Manza, "The Social and Ideological Bases of Middle-Class Political Realignment in the United States 1972 to 1996," *American Sociological Review*, vol. 62, issue 2 (April 1997).

9. Author's analysis of NES and VNS data. NES also has the two parties at parity, though showing Clinton winning by 3 points in 1992, Dole winning by 1 point in 1996, and Gore and Bush dead even in 2000.

10. Author's analysis of VNS data.

11. Author's analysis of Democracy Corps combined database.

12. Author's analysis of VNS data.

13. College women group, Seattle, Washington, March 10, 2003.

14. College men group, Seattle, Washington, March 10, 2003.

15. College women group, Seattle, Washington, March 10, 2003.

16. College men group, Seattle, Washington, March 10, 2003.

17. The women with four-year college degrees respond very similarly on choice questions about regulation. They think government regulation of corporations is necessary, not harmful (61 to 30 percent); they support government regulation for social protection rather than worrying about government intrusion on an individual's right to have guns and SUVs (59 to 35 percent).

18. College men group, Seattle, Washington, March 10, 2003.

19. Ibid.

20. College men group, Seattle, Washington, May 7, 2002.

21. College women group, Seattle, Washington, May 7 and August 29, 2002, January 8, 2003.

22. Ibid.

23. College women group, Seattle, Washington, May 7, 2002.

24. College women group, Seattle, Washington, August 29, 2002.

25. College women group, Seattle, Washington, March 10, 2003.

26. College men group, Seattle, Washington, August 29, 2002.

27. College women group, Seattle, Washington, March 10, 2003.

28. College men group, Seattle, Washington, August 29, 2002.

29. College women group, Seattle, Washington, February 19, 2002.

30. College men group, Seattle, Washington, August 29, 2002.

31. College women group, Seattle, Washington. May 7, 2002.

32. College men group, Seattle, Washington, August 29, 2002.

33. College men group, Seattle, Washington, May 7, 2002.

34. College men group, Seattle, Washington, March 10, 2003.

35. Ibid.

36. College women group, Seattle, Washington, March 10, 2003.

37. College women group, Seattle, Washington, May 7, 2002; college men group, March 10, 2003.

38. College men group, Seattle, Washington, March 10, 2003.

39. College women group, Seattle, Washington, May 7, 2002.

40. Ibid.

41. College women group, Seattle, Washington, March 10, 2003.

42. College men group, Seattle, Washington, January 8, 2003.

43. College men group, Seattle, Washington, March 10, 2003.

44. College women group, Seattle, Washington, August 29, 2002.

45. This section was greatly influenced by Anna Greenberg's thinking on young voters, ("New Generation, New Politics," *The American Prospect*, October 1, 2003).

46. Estimates based on the combined database of Democracy Corps surveys.

47. Author's analysis of VNS; Greenberg Quinlan Rosner Research postelection database.

48. Author's analysis of VNS data.

49. This may be artificially high, as these surveys all occurred in the post-9/11 period, when support for the president was very high, as well as for the Republicans on national security.

50. Mark Hugo Lopez, "Fact Sheet," *Circle*, March 2003.

51. Author's analysis of VNS data. Based on NES estimates, the youth proportion dropped from 12 percent in 1992 to 10 percent in 1996 to 9 percent in 2000. Both show a similar trend, a comparably low proportion in the most recent election.

52. *The Washington Post*/Kaiser Family Foundation/Harvard University, *A Generational Look at the Public: Politics and Policy,* October 2002, p. 12.

53. Author's analysis of NES data for 1952–76; *New York Times*/CBS exit polls for 1980–88.

54. Author's analysis of VNS data.

55. Leege, "The Catholic Voter," p. 3.

56. Ibid., p. 7.

57. Author's analysis of *New York Times*/CBS exit polls.

58. Leege, "The Catholic Voter," pp. 5–6.

59. Leege reports 45 to 45 percent in party identification (ibid., p. 5); also, author's analysis of NES.

60. NES, 2000, gives the total as 26 percent, but it has been as low as 20 percent in

the last couple of decades. According to VNS, it was 22 percent in 2000 but about a quarter in 1992 and 1996.

61. Author's analysis of VNS data.

62. Author's analysis of NES data.

63. Author's analysis of NES data.

64. Author's analysis of Democracy Corps combined data set.

65. Author's analysis of VNS data.

66. Tamar Lewin, "Catholics Adopt More Liberal Attitudes During Their Years in College, A Survey Finds," *The New York Times,* March 5, 2003, p. B8.

67. Leege, "The Catholic Voter," p. 7.

68. Theda Skocpol, "A Partnership with American Families" in Stanley B. Greenberg and Theda Skocpol, eds., *The New Majority* (New Haven: Yale University Press, 1997), pp. 104–32.

69. Author's analysis of VNS data.

70. Author's analysis of VNS data.

71. Author's analysis of VNS data. NES data report a similar trend, but has them at a lower proportion of the electorate: 14 percent in 1992, dropping to 10 percent in 1996 and 11 percent in 2000.

72. Author's analysis of NES data.

73. Author's analysis of NES data and *New York Times*/CBS exit polls for 1984 and 1988.

74. Mishel et al., *The State of Working America 2002/2003,* p. 161.

75. Noncollege women group, Des Moines, Iowa, May 1, 2002.

76. Author's analysis of VNS data. While college-educated voters increased support for the congressional Democrats in 1998, the noncollege women pulled back sharply. Democratic support among high school graduates dropped 4 points (52 to 48 percent) and those with some post–high school education dropped 5 points (46 to 41 percent).

77. Author's analysis of VNS data.

78. Author's analysis of VNS data.

79. Noncollege women group, Tampa, Florida, March 3, 2003; noncollege women group, Des Moines, Iowa, April 3, 2003.

80. Noncollege women group, Des Moines, Iowa, April 8, 2003.

81. Noncollege women group, Des Moines, Iowa, April 4, 2003.

82. Noncollege women group, Tampa, Florida, March 3, 2003.

83. Noncollege women group, Tampa, Florida, April 7, 2003.

84. Noncollege women group, Tampa, Florida, April 30, 2002.

85. Noncollege women group, Des Moines, Iowa, December 2, 2002.

86. Noncollege women group, Tampa, Florida, March 3, 2003.

87. Noncollege women group, Des Moines, Iowa, January 7, 2003.

88. Ibid.

89. Ibid.

90. Author's analysis of NES data and *New York Times*/CBS exit polls for 1984 and 1988.
91. Author's analysis of VNS data.
92. Noncollege men group, Tampa, Florida, February 11, April 30, August 27, 2002.
93. Noncollege men group, Tampa, Florida, April 30, 2002.
94. Noncollege men group, Tampa, Florida, August 27, 2002.
95. Ibid.
96. Noncollege men group, Tampa, Florida, April 30, 2002.
97. Noncollege men group, Tampa, Florida, August 27, 2002.
98. Noncollege men group, Tampa, Florida, April 30, 2002.
99. Noncollege men group, Tampa, Florida, February 11, 2002.
100. Noncollege men group, Tampa, Florida, April 30, 2002.
101. Noncollege men group, Tampa, Florida, January 6, 2003.
102. Ibid.
103. Noncollege men group, Tampa, Florida, June 3, 2002.
104. Noncollege men group, Tampa, Florida, April 30, 2002.
105. Noncollege men group, Tampa, Florida, August 27, 2002.
106. Author's analysis of VNS data.
107. Author's analysis of VNS data.

PART V: BREAKING THE DEADLOCK: THE REPUBLICANS

1. This account is fictional, which allows me to introduce the strategic discussion on the Republican side. I have never met George W. Bush, and I have met Karl Rove only once, so I do not even pretend any stylistic similarity. This account was aided by Bill Keller, "Reagan's Son," *New York Times*, January 26, 2003; Nicholas Lemann, "The Controller," *The New Yorker*, May 12, 2003; James Moore and Wayne Slater, *Bush's Brain* (New York: Wiley, 2003); Lou Dubose, Jan Reid, and Carl Cannon, *Boy Genius* (New York: Public Affairs, 2003).
2. Lemann, "The Controller," p. 71.
3. Bob Woodward, *Bush at War* (New York: Simon and Schuster, 2002), pp. 207–08.

9. STEP ONE: WINNING IN *OUR* AMERICA

1. The "49 Percent Nation" presentation is reported verbatim in the graphic on page 196. This is slide 5 of the Republican National Committee, "72 Hour Task Force." See Lemann, "The Controller," pp. 79–81.

   The graph is produced in its original form. The ever-alert David Mayhew notes that the 1876 should be 1888, when Grover Cleveland won a plurality of the votes but lost in the Electoral College to Benjamin Harrison.

2. Republicans won 50.7 percent of the total votes cast in the 2002 elections. Democrats won 46.3 percent. This is a raw tally of 70 million votes cast in all 50 states.

3. Keller, "Reagan's Son," p. 28.

4. Lemann, "The Controller," p. 75.

5. Mayhew, *Electoral Realignments,* pp. 79–81. I owe this intervention to David Mayhew, who remains vigilant about the correct reporting of this period.

6. Democracy Corps combined data set.

7. Republican National Committee, "72 Hour Task Force."

8. David Frum, *The Right Man: The Surprise Presidency of George W. Bush* (New York: Random House, 2003), pp. 3, 17; Howard Fineman, "Bush and God," *Newsweek,* March 10, 2003.

9. George W. Bush, State of the Union, January 28, 2003; George W. Bush, remarks at National Prayer Breakfast, February 1, 2001.

10. George W. Bush, remarks at National Prayer Breakfast, 2001; Bush, State of the Union, January 28, 2003.

11. George W. Bush quoted in Dubose et al., *Boy Genius,* pp. 155–56.

12. Dana Milbank, "Bush Links Faith and Agenda in Speech to Broadcast Groups," *Washington Post,* February 2003, p. A2.

13. Bob Dart, "Lawmakers Want to Fight Sprawl by Helping Farmers," Cox News Service, August 15, 2001.

14. Republican National Committee, "72 Hour Task Force." There are other explanations for the failure of the state polls, the simplest that many of them, sponsored by state media, were completed too early.

15. Based on the average of national media polls for each day, excluding Internet and advocacy polls.

16. 2002 postelection results reported in a memorandum for Democracy Corps and Campaign for America's Future, "The Price of Silence," November 13, 2002.

17. For interesting discussions of the college Republicans and that period for the right, see Lemann, "The Controller," pp. 68–70, and Moore and Slater, *Bush's Brain,* pp. 111–36; see also Peggy Noonan, *When Character Was King,* p. 86. The discussion on the new relevance of person-to-person contact is also derived from Republican National Committee, "72 Hour Task Force."

18. George W. Bush, "President Promotes Compassionate Conservatism," San Jose, California, April 30, 2002.

19. Lemann, "The Controller," pp. 81–82.

20. Children's Defense Fund, "President Bush's Welfare Reform Plan Leaves Millions of Children Behind," http://www.childrensdefense.org/fs_bushwelfplan.php.

21. George W. Bush, "President Bush Discusses Faith-Based Initiative in Tennessee," Nashville, February 10, 2003.

22. Dubose et al., *Boy Genius,* pp. 159–60.
23. Charles Lane, "U-Michigan Gets Broad Support on Using Race," *The Washington Post,* February 11, 2003, p. A1.; John M. Broder, "Administration Lawyer Lauds Affirmative Action Ruling," *New York Times,* June 28, 2003, p. A1.
24. Moore and Slater, *Bush's Brain,* pp. 208–10.
25. David Von Drehle, "Bush Unsure Ban on Gay Unions Is Needed; Backing Standard Marriage, President Sidesteps Question," *The Washington Post,* July 3, 2003, p. A2.
26. Frum, *The Right Man,* pp. 103–04.
27. Democracy Corps, "Politics After the Attack," November 13, 2001, pp. 7–8.
28. George W. Bush, remarks at National Prayer Breakfast, February 1, 2001.
29. Frum, *The Right Man,* p. 167.
30. Vietnam Veterans of America Foundation, Global Engagement, national survey, December 4–6, 2001, survey conducted by Greenberg Quinlan Rosner Research and Public Opinion Strategies.
31. Ann Gerhart, "Laura Bush's Signal to Afghanistan; First Lady Urges Women to Help Rebuild Nation," *The Washington Post,* May 22, 2002, p. C1.
32. George W. Bush, graduation speech at West Point, June 1, 2002.
33. Woodward, *Bush at War,* p. 217.
34. Dana Milbank, "Bush Lashes Out at Europe; President Says Aversion to Biotech Perpetuates African Hunger," *The Washington Post,* May 22, 2003, p. A1.
35. Dubose et al., *Boy Genius,* pp. 149, 158, 163; Frum, *The Right Man,* pp. 38, 204.
36. Luntz Research Companies, *Straight Talk,* pp. 132–33.
37. Ibid., pp. 131, 137, 146.
38. George W. Bush, State of the Union, January 28, 2003.
39. Democracy Corps national survey of 1,011 likely voters, June 17–23, 2003.
40. US Census Bureau, "Hispanic Population in the US," Current Population Survey, March 2003.
41. All the books on the White House report the obsession with making progress on the Hispanic vote. See, for example, Frum, *The Right Man,* p. 38, and Dubose et al., *Boy Genius,* p. 167.
42. 1996 and 2000 results based on VNS data; Bush popularity based on Bendixen and Associates national survey of 800 Hispanic voters, May 27–June 3, 2003; Fred Barnes, "The Emerging 9/11 Majority: The war on terror has created a new political climate in America," *The Weekly Standard,* November 18, 2002.
43. James Cimpel cited in Ruy Teixeira, "Hispanic Population Continues to Grow and So Do Democratic Chances," *Public Opinion Watch,* June 16–22, 2003.
44. New Democrat Network national poll conducted by Bendixen and Associates, 800 Hispanic voters, May 27–June 3, 2003.
45. Rove also was a strong supporter of legalizing the status of illegal immigrants (Frum, *The Right Man,* pp. 36, 38).
46. See Appendix A.

47. Moore and Slater, *Bush's Brain*, pp. 145–46.

48. Lemann, "The Controller," p. 81.

49. Frum, *The Right Man*, p. 36; Dubose et al., *Boy Genius*, pp. 213–14.

50. On the early Catholic contacts, see Lemann, "The Controller," p. 80, and Dubose et al., *Boy Genius*, p. 167.

51. Democracy Corps combined database for post–9/11 period compared to the 2003 period.

52. George W. Bush, "Presidential Address to the Nation," Washington, DC, October 7, 2001; Bush, graduation address at West Point, 2000; George W. Bush, "President Bush Announces Combat Operations in Iraq Have Ended," USS *Abraham Lincoln*, May 1, 2003.

10. STEP TWO: REAGAN'S AMERICA

1. Gallup, National Survey of 1,004 adults, September 7–10, 2001.

2. Democracy Corps national survey of 1,014 likely voters, July 15–20, 2003.

3. Frum, *The Right Man*, pp. 272–73.

4. Noonan, *When Character Was King*, pp. 5, 8–10.

5. Dinesh D'Souza, *Ronald Reagan: How an Ordinary Man Became an Extraordinary Leader* (New York: Free Press, 1997), pp. 7, 23; Peter J. Wallison, *Ronald Reagan: The Power of Conviction and the Success of His Presidency* (Boulder, CO: Westview Press, 2003), pp. xi, 3, 42–43.

6. Noonan, *When Character Was King*, pp. 12, 299.

7. D'Souza, *Ronald Reagan*, pp. 25–27; Noonan, *When Character Was King*, pp. 197–99; Wallison, *Ronald Reagan*, pp. 42–43.

8. D'Souza, *Ronald Reagan*, pp. 17, 27, 147–48; Noonan, *When Character Was King*, pp. 281, 297; see also Sidney Blumenthal, *Our Long National Daydream* (New York: Harper and Row, 1988), pp. 241–49.

9. See Frances Fitzgerald, *Way Out There in the Blue: Regan, Star Wars, and the End of the Cold War* (New York: Simon and Schuster, 2000); p. 475; Matthew Evangelista, *Unarmed Forces: The Transnational Movement to End the Cold War* (Ithaca, NY: Cornell University Press, 1999); Richard Ned Lebow and Janice Gross Stein, "Reagan and the Russians," *The Atlantic Monthly*, vol. 273, no. 2 (February 1994), pp. 35–37; Richard Ned Lebow and Janice Gross Stein, *We All Lost the Cold War* (Princeton, NJ: Princeton University Press, 1994); Nikolai Sokov, *Russian Strategic Modernization: The Past and Future* (Lanham, MD: Rowman and Littlefield, 2000).

10. Susan Page, "Bush's Year 3 Like 'First 100 Days on Steroids.'" *USA Today*, January 29, 2003, p. 6A.

11. John Podhoretz, *Hell of a Ride* (New York: Simon and Schuster, 1993), p. 172; Grover G. Norquist, "The Unmaking of the President: Why George Bush Lost,"

Policy Review, no. 63 (Winter 1993): 12–14; Grover G. Norquist, *Rock the House* (Ft. Lauderdale: VYTIS Publishing, 1995), p. 37.

12. Noonan, *When Character Was King*, pp. 297–98, Lawrence F. Kaplan and William Kristol, *The War Over Iraq: Saddam's Tyranny and America's Mission* (San Francisco: Encounter Books, 2003), pp. 43–44.

13. Noonan, *When Character Was King*, p. 11.

14. Center for National Policy, "The Real Story of the U.S. Economy 1950–1990" (Washington, DC: Center for National Policy, 1992).

15. David Frum, *Dead Right* (New York: Basic Books, 1995), pp. 36–41, 204; Fred Barnes, "Squeeze Play," *The Weekly Standard*, October 2, 1995, p. 12.

16. Ronald Reagan, State of the Union, February 6, 1985; State of the Union, January 24, 1984.

17. George W. Bush, Speech to National Religious Broadcasters' Annual Convention, Opryland Hotel, Nashville, TN, February 10, 2003; remarks by the President on stem cell research, August 9, 2001.

18. Ronald Reagan, State of the Union, January 25, 1984; "Address to the Nation on the Federal Budget and Deficit Reduction," April 24, 1985; Farewell Address to the Nation, January 11, 1989.

19. George W. Bush, "President Bush Pushes for Tax Relief in New Mexico," May 12, 2003; State of the Union, January 28, 2003; "Taking Action to Strengthen America's Economy," January 7, 2003; State of the Union, January 29, 2002.

20. Dubose et al., *Boy Genius*, pp. 192–93.

21. Frum, *The Right Man*, p. 38.

22. Democracy Corps national survey of 1,000 likely voters, July 22–24, 2002.

23. National Public Radio/Kaiser Family Foundation/Kennedy School of Government, "National Survey of Americans' Views on Taxes," April 2003, p. 1.

24. The Innocence Project, Benjamin N. Cardozo School of Law, Yeshiva University, April 21, 2003.

25. Leege et al., *The Politics of Cultural Differences*, p. 95.

26. Frum, *The Right Man*, p. 126.

27. George W. Bush, "Presidential Address to the Nation," October 7, 2001.

28. George W. Bush, State of the Union, January 28, 2003.

29. George W. Bush, graduation speech at West Point.

30. Ibid.

31. George W. Bush, State of the Union, January 28, 2003.

32. Kaplan and Kristol, *The War Over Iraq*, pp. 56, 60–61.

33. Charles Krauthammer, "The Unipolar Moment Revisited," *The National Interest*, Winter 2002/3, pp. 9–12.

34. Maureen Dowd, "I Vant to Be Alone," *The New York Times*, March 12, 2003.

35. Democracy Corps national survey of 1,002 likely voters, May 12–15, 2003.

36. These postcards were written by the participants in focus groups conducted by De-

mocracy Corps. The participants addressed one postcard to the president and one to the Democratic candidate for president. The salutation, text, and dates are un-edited, though names have been changed to ensure confidentiality.

37. Renana Brooks, "A Nation of Victims," *The Nation,* June 30, 2003.

38. The quotes about Reagan are from Greenberg, *Middle Class Dreams,* pp. 42–49. The contemporary discussion about Bush is from Democracy Corps focus groups conducted in the three target areas.

39. Woodward, *Bush at War,* pp. 205–06.

40. Karl Agne, "Democracy Corps Focus Groups May 2003," Democracy Corps, May 27, 2003.

41. Democracy Corps national survey of 15,045 likely voters, November 1, 2001–May 15, 2003.

42. Keller, "Reagan's Son," pp. 31, 43.

43. Ibid., p. 62.

44. Lemann, "The Controller," p. 83.

45. Keller, "Reagan's Son," p. 28.

46. V. O. Key, Jr. "A Theory of Critical Elections," in *Electoral Change and Stability in American Political History,* edited by Jerome M. Clubb and Howard W. Allen (New York: Free Press, 1971), p. 43; Sundquist, *Dynamics of the Party System,* p. 161.

47. See Robert H. Wiebe, *Self-Rule: A Cultural History of American Democracy* (Chicago: University of Chicago Press, 1995), pp. 117–80, and Wiebe, *The Search for Order, 1877–1920* (New York: Hill and Wang, 1967), both of which Rove cites as part of his understanding of the period.

48. Lemann, "The Controller," p. 75.

49. Keller, "Reagan's Son," p. 62.

PART VI: BREAKING THE DEADLOCK: THE DEMOCRATS

1. The fullest account of this effort is the *Newsweek* presidential project: Peter Goldman, Thomas M. DeFrank, Mark Miller, Andrew Murr, and Tom Mathews, *Quest for the Presidency 1992* (College Station: Texas A & M Press, 1994), pp. 245–68.

2. Samuel L. Popkin, *The Reasoning Voter: Communication and Persuasion in Presidential Campaigns,* 2nd ed. (Chicago: University of Chicago Press, 1994), pp. 237–38.

3. This discussion among the political advisers and consultants for a Democratic presidential campaign is fictional, as are the names. However, a number of experienced professionals and politicians participated in a two-hour discussion, which was recorded and transcribed. Each had read the core chapters of *The Two Americas* as introduction to the discussion. The participants included David Axelrod, James Carville, Rosa DeLauro, Rahm Emanuel, Douglas Sosnik, and myself. Bob Shrum and John Podesta also provided insights for this discussion.

11. THE "ELECTION PROJECT"

1. As indicated earlier, this is a selection of postcards written after a focus group discussion. They are unedited, exactly as people wrote them.

2. Democracy Corps national surveys conducted between May and June 2003. Due to the length of these items, a subset was asked in each of the two national surveys. In addition, to give the public a chance to talk more thoroughly about the problems, we presented focus group participants in Tampa Blue, Heartland Iowa, and Eastside Tech with longer descriptions of the major challenges facing the country.

3. The actual calculation: 37 percent "extremely serious" and 35 percent "very serious," for a total of 72 percent who say a major problem.

4. All Democracy Corps surveys asked which party would do a better job on a list of issues. The responses are from national surveys of 1,000 likely voters, April 7–10, 2001, and 1,002 likely voters, May 12–15, 2003.

5. Public Interest Project, 1,000-sample national survey of registered voters conducted June 17–22, 2003.

6. Author's analysis of Harris poll 1966–2002.

7. These are the average results over the eighteen-month period for the combined national surveys of Democracy Corps.

8. Clinton, remarks at the DLC Retreat, Hyde Park, May 21, 2000.

9. Joel Kotkin and Fred Siegel, "The Redistribution of Honor," *The Weekly Standard*, vol. 008, issue 32 (Winners and Losers in the Postwar Era, April 28, 2003), pp. 25–27.

10. Frank Rich, "Tupac's Revenge on Bennett," *The New York Times,* May 18, 2003.

11. *Lawrence* v. *Texas,* 156 L. Ed. 2d 508, 123 S. Ct. 2472, 2003 U.S. LEXIS 5013, 71 U.S.L.W. 4574, 16 Fla. L. Weekly Fed. S 427, 2003 D.A.R. 7036 (U.S. 2003).

12. Comparing the surveys in 2003 to those conducted before 2003, nearly all the loyalist groups in each camp became slightly more supportive of their respective parties. The contested groups in the middle remained stable, not moving in either direction.

13. Democracy Corps combined database.

14. Public Interest Project, national survey of 1,000 registered voters, June 17–22, 2003.

15. Mark Penn for the Democratic Leadership Council has labeled these voters "Office Park Dads." It is true that they are uncomfortable in the Republican loyalist world on cultural grounds, but they strongly like the Republicans on taxes and the economy and show no inclination to shift electorally.

16. Thomas et al., *Back from the Dead*, p. 17.

17. Democracy Corps, national survey of 1,017 likely voters, June 17–22, 2003, January 14–19, 2003.

18. Public Interest Project, national survey of 1,000 registered voters, June 17–22, 2003.

19. Noncollege men group, Des Moines, Iowa, April 8, 2003; noncollege women group, Tampa, Florida, April 7, 2003; noncollege men group, Tampa, Florida, April 7, 2003; college women group, Seattle, Washington, April 15, 2003; college women group,

Seattle, Washington, January 8, 2003; college men group, Seattle, Washington, January 8, 2003; college men group, Seattle, Washington, January 8, 2003; noncollege women group, Des Moines, Iowa, January 7, 2003.

20. Balz and Brownstein, *Storming the Gates*, p. 49; Sheryl Gay Stolberg, "House Passes Drug Bill; Battle Is Likely in Senate," *New York Times*, July 26, 2003, p. A11.

21. According to polls conducted for the Gore campaign, those were the issues that Nader voters responded to most strongly. These results for 2000 Nader voters were derived from the Democracy Corps combined data set.

22. Mark Penn and Pete Brodnitz, *The Door Is Open: Identifying Opportunities for Democrats*, New Democrat Network, August 7, 2003.

23. Greenberg, *Middle Class Dreams*, pp. 1–22.

12. TOWARD A BOLD POLITICS

1. Schattschneider, *A Realist's View*, pp. 47–48, 62–66, 71–74.

2. TNS Intersearch, Horsham, PA, survey of 1,513 adults, January 11–15, 2001.

3. Bureau of the Census, *Historical Income Inequality: Selected Measures of Household Dispersion*, Table 1E-1, 2000; Steven Greenhouse, "US Workers' Fears Rise As Jobs Are Lost and Pay Lags," *International Herald Tribune*, September 2, 2003, p. 12.

4. An adaptation of Clinton's "New Covenant" speech. For a discussion, see Chapter 4.

5. David Cay Johnston, "Very Richest's Share of Income Grew Even Bigger, Data Show," *The New York Times*, June 26, 2003.

6. David Brooks, "The Collapse of the Dream Palaces," *The Weekly Standard*, April 28, 2003, pp. 29–31.

7. Tim Burt, "Sweden's Budget Raises Tension in Coalition," *Financial Times*, October 14, 1998, p. 02; Ian Traynor, "Kohl Bungles Bungalow Summit," *The Guardian*, April 25, 1996, p. 20; Alison Smith and Ivor Owen, "Tories Revive Tax Message," *Financial Times*, April 7, 1992, p. 9.

8. Campaign for America's Future national survey of 1,992 voters, November 5–6, 2002.

9. Public Interest Project, national survey of 1,017 voters, June 17–22, 2003.

10. Harold Meyerson, "Squandering Prosperity," *American Prospect*, June 1, 2003.

11. Democracy Corps national survey of 1,014 likely voters, July 15–20, 2003.

12. Democracy Corps national survey of 1,011 likely voters, June 17–23, 2003.

13. Democracy Corps national survey of 1,014 likely voters, July 15–20, 2003.

14. Woodward, *Bush at War*, pp. 81, 341.

15. The Pew Research Center for the People and the Press, *Views of a Changing World, June 2003*, Pew Global Attitudes Project, pp. 19, 22.

16. ICM Research, "What the World Thinks of America," national survey prepared for the BBC, released June 16, 2003, pp. 8, 10.

17. Ibid., pp. 8, 10, 39; Pew Research Center, *Views of a Changing World,* p. 29.
18. Vietnam Veterans of America Foundation national survey of 1,005 likely voters, March 3–8, 2003.
19. David C. Hendrickson, "Toward Universal Empire: The Dangerous Quest for Absolute Security," *World Policy Journal* 19, no. 3 (Fall 2002): 2.
20. Democracy Corps national survey of 1,014 likely voters, July 15–20, 2003.
21. CBS News/ *The New York Times,* "Bush, Taxes and Foreign Affairs," national survey of 910 adults, May 9–12, 2003.
22. The Gore campaign, national survey of 1,003 likely voters, October 18–20, 2000.
23. Also see Michael Tomasky, "Get Happy!" *The American Prospect,* June 1, 2003, p. 24.
24. A number of institutes, organizations, and publications informed this write-up, including *The Atlantic Monthly* (special issue on the State of the Union), Coalition for the Advancement of Medical Research, Economic Policy Institute, Harvesting Clean Energy, Institute for America's Future, National Education Association, Progressive Policy Institute, Sierra Club, as well as the health-care platforms of Dick Gephardt, John Edwards, John Kerry, Howard Dean, and Joe Lieberman.
25. The health-care plan here is derived in large part from the one developed by Senator John Breaux, "The Breaux Plan: A Radically Centrist Approach to a New Health Care System," January 23, 2003.
26. Karen Kornbluh, "The Parent Trap," *The Atlantic,* January/February 2003, p. 114.
27. National survey conducted March 28–May 1, 2002, sponsored by National Public Radio, the Kaiser Family Foundation, and the Kennedy School of Government.
28. Theda Skocpol, "Unraveling from Above," *The American Prospect,* March-April 1996, p. 20.
29. Theda Skocpol, "Associations Without Members," *The American Prospect,* July–August, 1999, p. 66.
30. Paul Weinstein, Jr., *Universal Access to College Through Tax Reform* (Washington, DC: Progressive Policy Institute, May 20, 2003), p. 1.
31. Janice M. Gruendel, Margaret Oliveira, and Shelly Geballe, "All Children Ready for School: The Case for Early Care and Education," (Connecticut Voices for Children, February 2003), pp. 4–5.
32. See E. Zigler, M. Finn-Stevenson, and N. W. Hall, *The First Three Years and Beyond* (New Haven, CT: Yale University Press, 2002); L. Masse and S. A. Barnett, "Benefit-Cost Analysis of the Abecedarian Early Childhood Intervention" (National Institute for Early Education Research, Fall 2002), online at //nieer.org/docs/index.php?DocID=57; C. Bruner, "A Stitch in Time: Calculating the Cost of School Unreadiness," published electronically by the Finance Project, September 2002, online at www.financeproject.org/stitchintime.pdf.
33. Art Rolnick, "Early Childhood Development: Economic Development with High Public Return," *Fed Gazette,* March 2003.
34. See Brooks, "A Nation of Victims."
35. Many of the ideas on tax reform came from proposals prepared by Senator John

Edwards's presidential campaign, "A Worker and Shareholder Bill of Rights: John Edwards' Plan for Corporate Responsibility."

36. Public Interest Project, national survey of 1000 adults, June 17–22, 2003.

37. National Public Radio/Kaiser Family Foundation/Kennedy School of Government, national survey, February 5–March 17, 2003.

38. Bruce Ackerman and Ian Ayres, *Voting with Dollars: A New Paradigm for Campaign Finance* (New Haven: Yale University Press, 2002).

39. This agenda in the energy and environmental area benefited immensely from ideas advanced in Timothy E. Wirth, C. Boyden Gray, and John D. Podesta, "The Future of Energy Policy," *Foreign Affairs* vol. 82, no. 4, July/August 2003, pp. 132–55; by David G. Hawkins, director of NRDC Climate Center, testimony before House Committee on Energy and Commerce, "Hearing on Future Options for Generation of Electricity from Coal"; and in the energy agenda developed by Congressman Jay Inslee, who also used "Apollo" to capture the spirit of his proposals.

40. Bill Clinton, remarks at DLC Retreat, Hyde Park.

41. Skocpol, *Protecting Soldiers and Mothers*, pp. 65, 141.

AFTERWORD: 2004—TOWARD TOTAL WAR

1. Michael P. McDonald, "Up, Up, and Away! Voter Participation in the 2004 Presidential Election," *The Forum*, Volume 2, Issue 4, 2004, Article 4, page 1; Thomas B. Edsall and James V. Grimaldi, "On Nov. 2, GOP Got More Bang for Its Billion, Analysis Shows," *The Washington Post*, Thursday, December 30, 2004; Liz Sidoti, "$600 Million Spent on Presidential Ads," Associated Press, October 31, 2004.

2. Bush-Cheney '04 Campaign ad: "Wolves." In post-September 11 Democracy Corps polling, the percentage of voters supporting Bush for President never dropped below 44 percent (Democracy Corps polling of likely voters conducted July 24, 2002, to October 31, 2004). That was a frequent observation in focus groups conducted for Democracy Corps and, according to Diane Feldman, the Kerry campaign.

3. Bush-Cheney '04 Campaign ads: "Troops—Update"; "Intel"; "Windsurfing."

4. Bush-Cheney '04 Campaign ads: "21st Century;" "Changing World."

5. Swift Boat Veterans for Truth ad: "Sellout."

6. Among white Evangelicals and Catholics, there was a strong relation between church attendance and the vote. For example, white Catholics who attended church weekly supported Bush by a 23-point margin (61 to 38 percent), but among white Catholics who were not regular church attendees Bush won by just 8 points (54 to 46 percent). But offsetting religious trends obscures the overall relationship. White mainline Protestants, including the regular church attendees, shifted away from Bush, reflecting perhaps a reaction against the Evangelical tide. African Americans supported Kerry at a high level, regardless of church attendance. Thus, overall indicators of church

attendance are not a good guide to how religion impacted the 2004 vote (reported findings based on the 2004 exit polls and post-election polls of 3000 voters conducted by Greenberg Quinlan Rosner Research for Democracy Corps and the Institute for America's Future, November 2–3, 2004).

7. Federal Election Commission, "2004 Official Presidential General Election Results," (updated February 11, 2005). Bush: 62,028,285 (50.73%), Kerry: 59,028,109 (48.26%); Ronald Brownstein, "GOP's Future Sits Precariously on Small Cushion of Victory," *Los Angeles Times,* November 15, 2004; Eric Black, "2004 Election Was a Squeaker, in Historical Sense," *Star Tribune,* December 13, 2004.

8. The battleground calculations were based on a comparison of the results from 2000 and 2004 in the following states: Colorado, Florida, Michigan, Minnesota, Nevada, New Hampshire, New Mexico, Ohio, Oregon, Pennsylvania, Washington, West Virginia, and Wisconsin.

9. Ronald Brownstein, "Democrats Need a Red-Blooded Candidate to Staunch Losses," *Los Angeles Times,* November 8, 2004.

10. Democratic Legislative Campaign Committee press release, "Democrats at the State Legislative Level Buck National Trends and Make Gains," November 23, 2004.

11. That represents a gain for the Republicans, as in 2000, 39 percent identified with the Democrats and 35 percent with the Republicans, according to the exit polls.

12. Among the nearly 70,000 registered voters interviewed in the year leading up to the election as part of the National Annenberg Election Survey, 34.6 percent identified with the Democrats and 31.8 percent with the Republicans—a 2.8-point Democratic advantage. In the two weeks before the election, the average Democratic advantage among registered voters was 1.5 percent, for all the public surveys that reported party identification. In a national survey of 885 adults conducted by CBS/*The New York Times,* November 18–21, 2004, the Democrats had a 7-point advantage, 36 to 29 percent.

13. In the 2000 election, Al Gore received the votes of 51.0 million Americans. In 2004, 59.0 million Americans voted for John Kerry, an increase of 8 million voting for the Democratic candidate. In 2000, 50.5 million Americans voted for George Bush. In 2004 that number was 62.0 million, an increase of 11.5 million.

14. Matthew Ericson and Hugh K. Truslow/*The New York Times,* "The Great Ad Wars of 2004," *The New York Times,* November 1, 2004. Data from Nilesen Monitor-Plus and The University of Wisconsin Advertising Project. Sixty percent of Bush's ads overall were attack ads, topped up by an additional 10 percent of negative contrasts.

15. When voters were given a list of doubts about Bush and asked to choose their three biggest doubts about him, 25 percent cited his tax cuts for the wealthy, the second-highest doubt behind the war in Iraq (Democracy Corps/Institute for America's Future postelection survey of 2,000 voters, conducted November 2–3, 2004).

16. Democracy Corps/Institute for America's Future postelection survey of 2,000 voters, conducted November 2–3, 2004.

17. When asked "Generally speaking, *before* (today's/yesterday's) election, did you think that things in this country are going in the right direction, or did you feel things have gotten pretty seriously off on the wrong track?" 51 percent of voters said wrong track, while just 41 percent thought the country was headed in the right direction (Democracy Corps/Institute for America's Future post-election survey of 2,000 voters, conducted November 2–3, 2004). Similarly, 51 percent indicated that they wanted to go in a significantly different direction from Bush, and only 45 percent wanted to continue in Bush's direction (Democracy Corps national survey of 1,018 likely voters, conducted October 29–31, 2004).

18. A CBS/*The New York Times* poll of 885 adults conducted November 18–21, 2004, showed just 42 percent approving of Bush's job on the economy, only 40 percent approving of his handling of the situation in Iraq, and 44 percent approving of his foreign policy. An Associated Press/IPSOS Public Affairs survey of 1,000 adults conducted December 6–8, 2004, found Bush's approval rating for handling domestic issues such as health care, education, and the environment at 48 percent.

19. When voters were asked whether America's security depends more on building strong ties with other nations or more on our military strength, 51 percent chose strong ties while just 40 percent cited America's military strength. A plurality of these same voters felt that the war in Iraq had made us less rather than more secure (Democracy Corps/Institute for America's Future postelection survey of 2,000 voters, November 2–3, 2004). A CNN/Gallup/*USA Today* poll of 1,015 adults conducted October 9–10, 2004, showed that only 39 percent believed that Bush's tax cuts had helped the economy, and just 34 percent believed it had helped their family. On the economy in general, our postelection survey posed this choice: "They say the economy is doing well, but that's not true for middle-class and working people. Jobs are scarce, incomes stagnant, benefits are being cut, even while health care costs skyrocket." OR "The economy is showing real signs of success—record growth, highest home ownership ever, new jobs and rising stock values and our economy is moving in the right direction." By 60 to 38 percent, voters chose the first statement on middle-class squeeze over the statement on an improving economy (Democracy Corps Survey of 1,003 likely voters conducted September 12–14, 2004).

20. When asked what was the most important issue in their vote, 44 percent cited Iraq, the economy, or health care, compared to 38 percent who chose terrorism or moral values (Democracy Corps/Institute for America's Future postelection survey of 2,000 voters, conducted November 2–3, 2004).

21. In 2000, Gore lost college-educated men by 18 points, but Kerry made a net 8-point gain with these voters, losing them by just 10 points (44 to 54 percent for Bush). Kerry also made a net 3-point gain with postgraduate voters, winning 55 percent of these voters, compared to 44 percent for Bush (2000 Voter News Service exit poll and 2004 National Election Pool exit poll conducted by Edison/Mitofsky).

22. John Kerry campaign ads: "Heart"; "Lifetime."

23. When asked to choose their three biggest doubts about Kerry from a list, 92 percent selected an issue pertaining to values and social issues while just 50 percent cited an issue pertaining to national security (Democracy Corps/Institute for America's Future postelection survey of 2,000 voters, conducted November 2–3, 2004). In a list of negative attributes about Kerry, "Not strong enough on security and defense issues" was the lowest scoring of any of the other doubts about him, with less than a majority (48 percent) of voters believing that it described him well (Democracy Corps national survey of 1,503 likely voters, conducted October 26–28, 2004).

24. John Kerry, Speech at New York University, NY, September 20, 2004.

25. Kerry was viewed as a strong leader by 53 percent of voters, and 54 percent believed the phrase "will keep America safe" describes him well (Democracy Corps national survey of 1,503 likely voters, conducted October 26–28, 2004). On foreign policy, the candidates scored evenly over a three-week period in mid-October, but in the final days, voters gave Bush a 4-point edge on the issue (48 to 44 percent). On the war on terrorism, Kerry managed to cut Bush's 20-point September edge down to 12 points, 52 percent to 40 (Democracy Corps national survey of 1,018 voters, conducted October 29–31, 2004).

26. The Media Fund (America Coming Together's advertising arm), along with MoveOn.org, bore the brunt of early spending on the Democratic side. In the end, the Media Fund spent $48 million on a wide range of issue ads including jobs and outsourcing, attacks on Bush's priorities, the cost of health care, prescription drugs, and Bush and Cheney's ties to big corporations, including big oil, Halliburton, and the Saudis. The Media Fund also ran defensive ads on Kerry's plans for middle-class tax cuts to rebut an initial Bush salvo on taxes, and toward the end of the campaign ran a range of Ohio-specific ads to buttress campaign spending in that important battleground state. A subsidiary of The Media Fund, Break Off Bush, targeted African Americans.

    MoveOn.org was the next biggest spender among the outside organizations, with $21.4 million on a barrage of ads, often overlapping with The Media Fund. MoveOn's ads hit Bush on priorities and misleading on Iraq and WMD; on the economy, job outsourcing and cuts to overtime pay, and on Social Security and the deficit; on Medicare and the cost of health care; on Bush and Cheney's ties to big corporations and Halliburton; even on the expiration of the assault weapons ban. When Kerry came under fire from the Swift Boat Veterans for Truth, MoveOn ran ads comparing the military service records of Kerry and Bush.

    The other groups on the Democratic side included, but were not limited to: the AFL-CIO ($9.4 million on jobs, outsourcing, and priorities), Communities for Quality Education ($5.9 million on a range of state targeted ads criticizing Bush on education), The New Democrat Network ($2.5 million in advertising mainly targeted toward Hispanic voters on Bush's broken promises, the minimum wage, health insurance, Hispanic ties to the Democratic party, and the promise of a better life with Democrats), The League of Conservation Voters ($2.9 million on ads mainly focused on Bush and Cheney's ties to Big Oil and no-bid contracts for Halliburton), TruthandHope.org ($2 million of anti-Bush ads on Bush's wrong choices), the SEIU ($1.2 million on a range of ads including half a million dollars on Spanish language ads), The Sierra Club ($0.5 million on state-specific environmental issues), AFSCME ($0.35 million on advertising on Bush/Cheney ties to Big Oil, gas prices, and an emergency buy in Hawaii in the last week of the campaign), Save Our Environment ($0.3 million dollars on ads accusing the Bush administration of auctioning off the environment to big contributors), The Human Rights Campaign ($0.2 million on tolerance and "The Cheneys"), and The Environmental Accountability Fund ($0.1 million on pollution and mercury poisoning).

27. Among rural voters, 39 percent offer negative views of big corporations, compared to just 28 who view them positively; older blue-collar women are even more critical: 42 percent unfavorable and just 22 percent favorable (See Appendix B and D).

28. John Kerry, Seattle, Washington, February 3, 2004.

29. John Kerry, Milwaukee Area Technical College, WI, October 15, 2004.

30. Based on the following statement pair: "They say the economy is doing well, but that's not true for middle-class and working people. Jobs are scarce, incomes stagnant, benefits are being cut, even while health care costs skyrocket." OR "The economy is showing real signs of success—record growth, highest home ownership ever, new jobs, rising stock values, and our economy is moving in the right direction." Nearly two-thirds (64 percent) of older noncollege voters and 57 percent of rural voters sided with the first statement (Democracy Corps national survey of 1,003 likely voters, conducted September 12–14, 2004).

31. When voters were given a list of doubts about Bush and asked to choose their three biggest doubts about him, 86 percent chose ones relating to his economic policies, a significantly higher percentage than any other category. His tax cuts for the wealthy and job losses constituted the biggest economic doubts, cited by 25 percent and 24 percent of voters, respectively. Among wavering Bush voters, the concern over Bush's economic policies was even greater, as 96 percent cited economic concerns when asked their biggest doubts about Bush (Democracy Corps/Institute for America's Future postelection survey of 2,000 voters, conducted November 2–3, 2004).

32. The African-American vote was essentially unchanged from 2000, as Kerry won 88 percent of their vote, just 2 points below Gore's share in 2000 (2000 Voter News Service exit poll and 2004 National Election Pool exit poll conducted by Edison/Mitofsky); data about unmarried women from National Election Pool exit poll conducted by Edison/Mitofsky cited by Anna Greenberg and Jennifer Berktold, "Election 2004 Updated, Unmarried Women: unmarried women vote for change and strongly supported John Kerry," November 22, 2004.

33. When asked to choose their three biggest doubts about Kerry from a list, 92 percent

selected an issue pertaining to values and social issues while just 50 percent cited an issue pertaining to national security and only 28 percent chose fears about him raising taxes or expanding the size of government (Democracy Corps/Institute for America's Future postelection survey of 2,000 voters, conducted November 2–3, 2004).

34. A striking 62 percent of voters in the fall said they were more likely to vote for John Kerry after hearing this statement: "John Kerry says, we need a new approach to the economy that works for the middle class, not just the most privileged. In George Bush's Washington, the lion's share of tax cuts go to the biggest corporations and the wealthiest. CEOs now make 500 times more than their employees. Most people have seen no income increase in the last three years, while health care costs are up 40 percent. I have a different approach to the economy, centered on the middle class. We will end tax cuts for companies that outsource jobs, and provide incentives for companies that create jobs in America. We will repeal tax cuts for those earning over $200,000 to help families and small businesses with health care costs, and will cut middle-class taxes. We need to make our economy work for everyone." (Democracy Corps national survey of 1,004 likely voters, conducted September 26–28, 2004.)

35. Among voters overall, 40 percent said the message made them "much more likely" to support Kerry, but among voters with a high school degree or less, the percentage rose to 47 percent. The message resonated even more powerfully with downscale women, with 52 percent of older noncollege-educated women and 53 percent of unmarried women indicating that the message made them much more likely to support Kerry (Democracy Corps national survey of 1,017 likely voters, conducted September 19–21, 2004).

36. In fact, the campaign had a number of worries that were legitimate. First, that the position would be interpreted as opposition to staying in Iraq, and second, that Kerry supported increased troops and funding if necessary and the position implied Kerry would spend less.

37. At the end, Kerry spoke directly to voters in a campaign and set out the choice: "Our economy needs a kick start. Beginning with jobs for America's middle class, jobs that pay more with secure and affordable health care. New manufacturing jobs by giving tax breaks for companies that create jobs here. And good, high-tech jobs by growing new industries to be independent of Middle East oil. The President is satisfied with an economy of lower-paying jobs. I'm not. I believe America can do better." But that was just one of many issues raised in the closing phase of the campaign; John Kerry campaign ad: "Economy Kick Start."

38. Democracy Corps national survey of 1,018 likely voters, conducted October 29–31, 2004.

39. Democracy Corps postelection database of 3,000 voters from polls conducted November 2–3, 2004. Party margin refers to the difference in party alignment, which

is party identification with the undecided allocated to the party they lean toward. Initially respondents were asked, "Generally speaking, do you think of yourself as a Democrat, a Republican, or what?" Republican support is composed of people who say they are Republicans, plus those independents who answer "Republican" when asked, "Do you think of yourself as closer to the Democratic or Republican Party?" The parallel exercise defines the Democrats.

40. Over two-thirds of these voters (69 percent) had negative views of gay marriage, but just 48 percent had a favorable view of the Iraq war, 20 points below the favorability rating among voters who aligned with the Republican party (Democracy Corps/Institute for America's Future postelection survey of 2,000 voters, conducted November 2–3, 2004).

41. The average of the last five public polls of registered voters conducted before the election had Kerry getting 47 percent of the vote and Bush receiving 46 percent. However, the last seven polls of likely voters over the same period had Bush with a 2-point edge, 48 to 46 percent.

42. Ruy Teixeira, "Where Did Bush's Gains Come From?" *Public Opinion Watch,* November 17, 2004, http://www.emergingdemocraticmajority.com/pow/pownovember_17_2004.cfm.

43. When asked to choose a list of doubts about John Kerry, Democratic loyalist voters focused on gay marriage more than abortion. Among the contested and Republican loyalists, abortion and gay marriage were equally important (Democracy Corps/Institute for America's Future postelection survey of 2,000 voters, conducted November 2–3, 2004).

44. Ruy Teixeira, "Did Bush Really Get 44 Percent of the Hispanic Vote?" *Emerging Democratic Majority Weblog—Donkey Rising,* November 18, 2004, http://www. emergingdemocraticmajorityweblog.com/donkeyrising/archives/000951.php; Charles Kamasaki, Clarissa Martinez, and Jessica Muñoz, National Council of La Raza, "How Did Latinos Really Vote in 2004?" November 16, 2004; James W. Brosnan, "Hispanic Vote Less for Bush Than Exit Polls Showed," Scripps Howard News Service, December 2, 2004; Mark Mellman, "The Dems' Hispanic Problem," *The Hill,* February 23, 2005.

45. In 1996, the presidential election focused heavily on the $270 billion in Medicare cuts; in 2000, both campaigns advertised heavily on prescription drug benefits. Early on in 2004, the outside groups spent a lot of resources attacking the prescription drug plan, but late in the campaign, it did not figure centrally; nor did Social Security privatization. Just three weeks before the election, voters were asked, "Do you think the policies of the Bush administration have increased the cost of prescription drugs for the elderly, decreased the cost, or have the policies of the Bush administration not affected the cost of prescription drugs for the elderly?" A near majority (47 percent) indicated the Bush administration's policies had increased prescription drug costs, while just 11 percent said that the administration's policies had caused them

to decrease (CBS/*The New York Times* survey of 931 registered voters conducted October 14–17, 2004).

46. Just 35 percent of Catholics had a favorable view of the war in Iraq, with 52 percent responding negatively. By 54 to 39 percent they believe strong alliances are more important to America's security than military strength. On domestic issues, just 35 percent supported Bush's plan to allow individuals to invest a portion of their Social Security funds in private retirement accounts (Democracy Corps/Institute for America's Future postelection survey of 2,000 voters, conducted November 2–3, 2004) and only 38 percent believed Bush's case that the economy was making progress (Democracy Corps survey of 1,022 likely voters, conducted October 3–5, 2004).

47. Democracy Corps postelection database of 3,000 voters from polls conducted November 2–3, 2004, and data from National Election Pool exit poll conducted by Edison/Mitofsky, 12,219 respondents, November 2–3, 2004.

48. John Sperling, *The Great Divide: Retro vs. Metro America* (PoliPoint Press, 2004), pp. xvii–xxiii, 30–31, 122–23, 136–38, 151–55.

49. George Lakoff, *Don't Think of an Elephant! Know Your Values and Frame the Debate*, (White River Junction, VT: Chelsea Green, 2004), pp. 7–13, 21–22, 89–91.

50. Stanley B. Greenberg, *The Two Americas: Our Current Political Deadlock and How to Break It* (New York: St. Martin's Press, 2004, 1st ed.), pp. 274–318.

51. When voters were presented with the "100 Percent America, JFK Democrat" message and the "Reagan's Son" message and asked to pick between the two, the "100 Percent America, JFK Democrat" message was favored by a 12-point margin, 53 to 41 percent (Democracy Corps national survey of 1,014 likely voters, conducted July 15–20, 2003).

52. Kerry held a 3 to 4–point advantage over Bush on "being on your side" through seven Democracy Corps surveys over the course of October, but in the final days before the election, Bush took a one-point lead, 45 to 44 percent (Democracy Corps national survey of 1,018 likely voters, conducted October 29–31, 2004).

Index